THE TIES
THAT BIND

SOCIAL INSTITUTIONS AND SOCIAL CHANGE
An Aldine de Gruyter Series of Texts and Monographs
EDITED BY James D. Wright, *Tulane University*

V. L. Bengtson and W. A. Achenbaum, **The Changing Contract Across Generations**

Thomas G. Blomberg and Stanley Cohen (eds.), **Punishment and Social Control: Essays in Honor of Sheldon L. Messinger**

M. E. Colten and S. Gore (eds.), **Adolescent Stress: Causes and Consequences**

Rand D. Conger and Glen H. Elder, Jr., **Families in Troubled Times: Adapting to Change in Rural America**

Joel A. Devine and James D. Wright, **The Greatest of Evils: Urban Poverty and the American Underclass**

G. William Domhoff, **The Power Elite and the State: How Policy is Made in America**

G. William Domhoff, **State Autonomy or Class Dominance: Case Studies on Policy Making in America**

Paula S. England, **Comparable Worth: Theories and Evidence**

Paula S. England, **Theory on Gender/Feminism on Theory**

R. G. Evans, M. L. Barer, and T. R. Marmor, **Why Are Some People Healthy and Others Not? The Determinants of Health of Population**

George Farkas, **Human Capital or Cultural Capitol? Ethnicity and Poverty Groups in an Urban School District**

Joseph Galaskiewicz and Wolfgang Bielefeld, **Nonprofit Organizations in an Age of Uncertainty: A Study in Organizational Change**

Davita Silfen Glasberg and Dan Skidmore, **Corporate Welfare Policy and the Welfare State: Bank Deregulation and the Savings and Loan Bailout**

Ronald F. Inglehart, Neil Nevitte, Miguel Basañez, **The North American Trajectory: Cultural, Economic, and Political Ties among the United States, Canada, and Mexico**

Gary Kleck, **Point Blank: Guns and Violence in America**

Gary Kleck, **Targeting Guns: Firearms and Their Control**

James R. Kluegel, David S. Mason, and Bernd Wegener (eds.), **Social Justice and Political Change: Public Opinion in Capitalist and Post-Communist States**

Theodore R. Marmor, **The Politics of Medicare** (Second Edition)

Thomas S. Moore, **The Disposable Work Force: Worker Displacement and Employment Instability in America**

Clark McPhail, **The Myth of a Madding Crowd**

James T. Richardson, Joel Best, and David G. Bromley (eds.), **The Satanism Scare**

Alice S. Rossi and Peter H. Rossi, **Of Human Bonding: Parent-Child Relations Across the Life Course**

Peter H. Rossi and Richard A. Berk, **Just Punishments: Federal Guidelines and Public Views Compared**

Joseph F. Sheley and James D. Wright, **In the Line of Fire: Youths, Guns, and Violence in Urban America**

David G. Smith, **Paying for Medicare: The Politics of Reform**

Linda J. Waite et al.(eds.) **The Ties That Bind: Perspectives on Marriage and Cohabitation**

Les G. Whitbeck and Dan R. Hoyt, **Nowhere to Grow: Homeless and Runaway Adolescents and Their Families**

James D. Wright, **Address Unknown: The Homeless in America**

James D. Wright and Peter H. Rossi, **Armed and Considered Dangerous: A Survey of Felons and Their Firearms** (Expanded Edition)

James D. Wright, Peter H. Rossi, and Kathleen Daly, **Under the Gun: Weapons, Crime, and Violence in America**

Mary Zey, **Banking on Fraud: Drexel, Junk Bonds, and Buyouts**

THE TIES
THAT BIND
Perspectives on Marriage and Cohabitation

Linda J. Waite

Editor

Coeditors
Christine Bachrach, Michelle Hindin,
Elizabeth Thomson, Arland Thornton

Aldine de Gruyter
New York

About the Editors

Linda J. Waite is Professor of Sociology and Co-Director, Center on Parents, Children and Work, an Alfred P. Sloan Working Families Center, University of Chicago

Christine Bachrach is Chief, Demographic and Behavioral Sciences Branch, National Institute of Child Health and Human Development

Michelle J. Hindin is a Post-Doctoral Fellow, Carolina Population Center, University of North Carolina at Chapel Hill

Elizabeth Thomson is Professor of Sociology and Director, Center for Demography and Ecology, University of Wisconsin-Madison

Arland Thornton is Professor of Sociology and Senior Research Scientist, Survey Research Center and Population Studies Center, University of Michigan

ALDINE DE GRUYTER
A division of Walter de Gruyter, Inc.
200 Saw Mill River Road
Hawthorne, New York 10532

This publication is printed on acid free paper ∞

Library of Congress Cataloging-in-Publication Data

The ties that bind : perspectives on marriage and cohabitation / edited by Linda J. Waite; co-edited by Christine Bachrach . . . [et al.].
        p. cm. — (Social institutions and social change)
        Includes bibliographical references and index.
        ISBN 0-202-30635-6 (cloth) — ISBN 0-202-30636-4 (pbk.)
        1. Marriage. 2. Unmarried couples. 3. Domestic relations. I. Waite, Linda J. II. Bachrach, Christine. III. Series.

HQ734.T53 2000
306.81—dc21

                                                                                        99-059683

Manufactured in the United States of America

10 9 8 7 6 5 4 3 2

Contents

Acknowledgments   ix

Introduction   *1*

1   The Changing Shape of Ties That Bind:
An Overview and Synthesis
Christine Bachrach, Michelle J. Hindin, and Elizabeth Thomson   *3*

I.   Trends in Marriage and Cohabitation

2   Recent Trends and Differentials in Marriage and Cohabitation:
The United States
R. Kelly Raley   *19*

3   European Perspectives on Union Formation
Kathleen Kiernan   *40*

4   Historical Trends in Marriage Formation:
The United States 1850–1990
Catherine A. Fitch and Steven Ruggles   *59*

II.   Perspectives on How Unions Are Formed

5   The Evolutionary Psychology of Marriage and Divorce
Martin Daly and Margo I. Wilson   *91*

6   Theorizing Marriage
     Robert A. Pollak   *111*

7   Toward a New Home Socioeconomics of Union Formation
     Andrew J. Cherlin   *126*

III.   Values, Attitudes, and Norms about Marriage

8   The Transformation in the Meaning of Marriage
     William G. Axinn and Arland Thornton   *147*

9   Marital Values and Expectations in Context:
     Results from a 21-City Survey
     M. Belinda Tucker   *166*

10   Ethnicity, Immigration, and Beliefs about Marriage as a
     "Tie That Binds"
     R. S. Oropesa and Bridget K. Gorman   *188*

11   Values and Living Arrangements: A Recursive Relationship
     Guy Moors   *212*

12   Religion as a Determinant of Entry into Cohabitation and
     Marriage
     Evelyn L. Lehrer   *227*

13   A Typology of Processes of Commitment to Marriage: Why Do
     Partners Commit to Problematic Relationships?
     Catherine A. Surra and Christine R. Gray   *253*

IV. Economics, Role Specialization, and the Returns to Marriage

14 The Continuing Importance of Men's Economic
Position in Marriage Formation
Valerie Kincade Oppenheimer 283

15 Female Wages, Male Wages, and the Economic Model of Marriage:
The Basic Evidence
Robert A. Moffitt 302

16 Marriage, the Costs of Children, and Gender Inequality
Paula England 320

17 Understanding the Distribution of Housework between
Husbands and Wives
Beth Anne Shelton 343

18 On the Determination of Wages:
Does Marriage Matter?
Jeffrey S. Gray and Michel J. Vanderhart 356

19 Trends in Men's and Women's Well-Being in Marriage
Linda J. Waite 368

Index 393

Acknowledgments

This volume emerged from a conference by the same title held June 29–30, 1998, at the National Institutes of Health in Bethesda, Maryland. The conference was initiated and sponsored by the National Institute of Child Health and Human Development, with cosponsorship from the Family Impact Seminar and Child Trends. Linda Waite served as chair of the conference and the coeditors of the volume participated in planning it. The editors are deeply grateful to Theodora Ooms and Kristin Moore for their support of the conference, to Tracy Springer for coordinating conference logistics, to the two anonymous reviewers of each paper for their careful critiques of the draft papers, to Nicholas Dempsey for compiling the manuscript, and to Richard Koffler and Mai Shaikhanuar-Cota at Aldine de Gruyter.

INTRODUCTION

1

The Changing Shape of Ties That Bind: An Overview and Synthesis

CHRISTINE BACHRACH, MICHELLE J. HINDIN,
and ELIZABETH THOMSON

INTRODUCTION

Intimate sexual unions in the western world used to follow a clearly defined normative sequence: a couple fell in love, married, and had children. Today, that picture has become vastly more complicated: couples cohabit before or instead of marrying and they have children in circumstances ranging from marriage to casual sexual partnerships. Those who do marry are doing so at historically late ages, often after having become parents.

In the United States, premarital cohabitation has become the norm: 56% of women who first married in the early 1990s cohabited before marriage. In 1995, nearly one-fifth of single women ages 19–44 were cohabiting with a partner (Bumpass and Lu, 1999). In many Western industrialized countries, similar scenarios are playing out, although variations from one country to another can be dramatic: in the early 1990s, all but 8% of first unions in Sweden were cohabitations or marriages preceded by cohabitation; in Italy, only 12% of first unions began as cohabitations (Kiernan, this volume).

At the same time, marriage is occurring later and less frequently than in the relatively recent past (Saluter and Lugaila, 1998). In the United States, age at marriage was at an historic low in 1950: half of all women married by age 20 and half of all men by about age 23. By 1996, the median age at marriage had increased to 24.8 years among women and 27.1 years among men, both historic highs. Declines in marriage have been most dramatic among African-American men and women (Fitch and Ruggles, this volume). Currently 61% of white women and 31% of black women marry by age 25; 80% and 45%, respectively, marry by age 30 (Raley, this volume, Figure 2.3). To some extent, cohabitation has become a substitute for marriage; that is, the formation of an intimate coresident union has been delayed to a much lesser extent than the timing of marriage.

A third feature of changes in the ties that bind is the increasing separation of childbearing and marriage. In the United States, 95% of babies born in 1960 were born to married mothers. By the 1990s, only about two-thirds of births were occurring within marriage (Department of Health and Human Services, 1995; Ventura et al., 1999). This rapid increase in nonmarital childbearing resulted from two developments. First, birth rates to unmarried women increased dramatically, from 25 per 1000 women in 1975 to 45 per 1000 women in 1995 (Ventura et al., 1999). Second, the proportion of childbearing-age women who were unmarried (and thus at risk of having a nonmarital birth) also increased substantially, because women were waiting longer to marry and in some cases foregoing marriage altogether. Increased cohabitation has also been linked to the increasing separation of childbearing and marriage: births to cohabiting couples accounted for a substantial proportion of the increase in births to unmarried women during the late 1980s and early 1990s (Bumpass and Lu, 1999).

WHAT IS MARRIAGE AND WHY DOES IT EXIST?

In this volume, we define marriage as a legally and socially recognized union, ideally life-long, that entails sexual, economic, and social rights and obligations for the partners. Cohabitation, by contrast, refers to an intimate sexual union between two unmarried partners who share the same living quarters for a sustained period of time. Cohabitation differs from marriage along many dimensions: it does not normally invoke specific legal rights and obligations and it is generally less permanent than marriage (Waite and Gallagher, 2000). Compared to married couples, cohabiters are less likely to pool financial resources (Blumstein and Schwartz, 1983), are less sexually exclusive (Forste and Tanfer, 1996), and are more dependent on families of orientation (Rindfuss and VanDenHeuval, 1990). Several chapters in this volume also consider forms of intimate relationships in which partners see each other regularly but do not coreside. Such unions encompass a broad range of involvement and commitment, shading into casual dating relationships at one end and perhaps leading to cohabitation or engagement to marry at the other.

Marriage and marriage-like relationships exhibit strong universalities across time and cultures, but also vary in significant ways. The universalities may emerge from "human nature"—those features of the human makeup that predispose us biologically to behave in particular ways, and even to create cultures and social systems that reinforce or modify our predispositions. Variations in marriage may arise from what we might loosely call "environmental" conditions, including political and social institutions, cultural norms, and economic systems.

What all humans have in common is their evolutionary history. A species evolves when certain traits are more successful than others in contributing to "fitness" or the production of young that survive to reproduce themselves. Humans have evolved to possess traits (e.g., sexuality, nurturance) that foster conception and the care of young children. In virtually all human societies, they have also generated social systems that regulate these functions. Unlike many other mammals, humans are oriented toward biparental care: both the mother and father participate in the rearing of young and both gain status through childbearing. Not coincidentally, humans tend to establish enduring intimate relationships with their sexual partners, cemented by love, companionship, and economic cooperation or exchange. Humans are "fairly" but not completely monogamous; even in Western societies where polygamy is outlawed, the serial monogamy of many individuals is a reminder that we are not completely "programmed" to remain faithful to one life-long mate. Evolutionary psychologists have noted apparent universalities in mate selection, such that females are more responsive to status and males to youth and attractiveness. They suggest that such criteria enable males to maximize the number of children they sire and females to ensure the presence of a reliable mate to help their offspring survive to adulthood (Daly and Wilson, this volume).

Of course, human nature did most of its evolving under conditions very different from those we experience today—in hunter–gatherer societies with relatively simple means of providing for the necessities of life. Luckily, evolution provided humans with the ability to adapt to environmental change. In recent centuries, the pace of environmental change has been accelerating. This is particularly true with respect to the means of production: technological advances have greatly transformed what it takes to provide for basic needs, expanding in the process the educational requirements for producing a successfully functioning adult and transforming as well the relations between the sexes. In the process our cultures have changed: in Western cultures individualism and materialism have gained ground while control of the group over individual behavior has diminished (Inglehart, 1997). Social institutions have become large and complex, and technology has brought virtually all the world's cultures into potential contact with each other.

Variation in marriage behavior is strongly associated with the varying environmental conditions within which sexuality and reproduction occur. No grand theory to fully account for such environmental variations has emerged, but most theories contain some common themes. One is the importance of "rational choice" in decisions individuals make about partnership formation and dissolution. This theme is perhaps most evident in economic models (see Weiss, 1997; Pollak, this volume; Moffitt, this volume), but is also central to models in psychology (e.g., the theory of reasoned action, see Fishbein and Ajzen, 1975) and sociology (exchange theory, see Homans, 1961). The basic idea is that in making any kind of choice or decision, individuals weigh the costs and benefits of alternative courses of action given a set of external opportunities and constraints. They choose the course that is most beneficial and least costly to them.

Another common theme arises from the fact that marriage or the formation of any union requires the agreement of at least two people, each of whom has alternatives to consider. That is, the ccndition of the "marriage market," including the availability and characteristics of potential mates and the costs of searching (England and Farkas, 1986), may determine whether, when, and whom an individual marries. Matching and search theories indicate the processes by which each individual evaluates the attractiveness of a potential match and decides whether to make the match or to continue searching. Bargaining theory indicates the process by which individuals negotiate an agreement to marry or not marry, using their resources (e.g., attractiveness, social status, and alternative matches) as bargaining chips (Pollak, this volume; Cherlin, this volume). These same resources influence which partner has more power in bargaining after a marriage occurs (Blood and Wolfe, 1960).

A third theme in theories of marriage focuses on the fact that individual choices and dyadic interactions unfold in specific social and cultural contexts (see chapters by Axinn, Lehrer, Oropesa, Moors, and others, this volume). These contexts may vary dramatically along a variety of dimensions: the extent to which social, religious, and legal institutions promote or support marriage or define the characteristics of desirable mates, the norms concerning acceptable behavior for men and women inside and outside of marriage, and the economic and social conditions that structure opportunities and barriers to supporting a family. The selection of a particular mate and the maintenance of relationships may depend on structural factors such as propinquity, similarity, and social supports (Surra and Gray, this volume).

Shared cultural norms, meanings, and values evolve as a result of a constant interplay between individual behaviors and social responses. When a husband and wife strike a bargain over the division of household tasks in the United States today, most often they do so in a cultural context that associates homemaking with femininity. As Shelton and England (this volume) point out, this helps to explain why the wife, even when she holds all the economic bargaining chips, still does most of the household work. Similarly, the strong normative expectation that a man must be able to support his family in order to marry helps us understand why a couple might not marry if their pooled earnings, but not the male's individual earnings, are sufficient and secure enough to provide support for the new family.

WHY HAS MARRIAGE CHANGED?

The chapters in this volume indicate several sets of changes thought to be related to the dramatic changes in marriage and union formation during the last half century within most of the world's economically developed countries. Marriage has become less affordable at early ages as the educational requirements for making a good living have been extended and those not obtaining a college education have had increased difficulty establishing themselves in careers. Gendered expectations within marriage have not caught up with the demands for wives' economic contributions to households, reinforcing the barriers that joblessness and low earnings create for men's marriage and increasing the costs of marriage to women. Normative changes have reduced the costs of not marrying by greatly increasing tolerance for pursuing sexual activity, intimate coresident relationships, and parenthood while single. New contraceptive methods reduced the risks of becoming pregnant as a result of nonmarital sex. High divorce rates have reduced the returns to marriage by undermining its permanence. Each of these changes has helped to set the stage for delayed marriage, increased nonmarriage, and the emergence of alternative forms of intimate unions such as nonmarital cohabitation.

Economic Opportunities for Men. Research has consistently demonstrated that whether and when a man marries is closely tied to the adequacy and stability of his earnings. There are two major reasons for this. One is the normative imperative that a man should be able to support his family. The second is that decisions about marriage depend on the prospective partner's ability to judge whether a man is likely to satisfy this imperative in the long run (Oppenheimer, this volume). Thus, it is not surprising that marriage tends to occur after the completion of education (Kiernan, this volume) and often years after. One of the best predictors of whether a man will marry is whether he has a job (Goldscheider and Waite, 1986). Further, the difficulty that young men have in achieving and sustaining full-time, year-round employment and earnings above the poverty level is strongly related to the timing of marriage (Oppenheimer, this volume). We do not know whether the difficulty of achieving career and earnings stability has increased over time. We do know, however, that men with a high school education or less have experienced declines in real earnings over recent decades (Oppenheimer, 1994) and that increases in cohabitation have occurred disproportionately in this group (Bumpass and Lu, 1999; Lehrer, this volume). Taken together, these two trends suggest that cohabitation does not place the same requirement on men, that they be able to assume the primary breadwinner role, as does marriage (Cherlin, this volume).

Economic Opportunities for Women.   One of the most striking behavioral and normative shifts during recent decades has been the wholesale movement of women, including married women and mothers, into the labor force. In 1950, 24% of married women and 51% of single women worked for pay; by 1994 labor force participation had grown to 61 and 67%, respectively (Teachman et al., 1999). This movement is associated with changes in opportunities, in particular the growth of service-sector and professional jobs attractive to women, changes in normative beliefs about married women's employment, economic necessity in the face of rising standards of living and declining or stagnant real wages, women's increasing concern about the possibility of divorce, and a growing desire among women for activities that fit their interests and training and that are valued by others (Spain and Bianchi, 1996). As women's employment levels approached those of men, so did their wages (Oppenheimer, 1994); increasing wage parity may, however, have been due more to the increasing inequality in men's wages than to growth in women's wages (Bernhardt et al., 1995).

The implications for marriage of the increased economic power of women are widely debated. In traditional economic models of marriage, the benefit of marriage (and hence the motivation to marry) is seen as deriving from specialization (Becker, 1991). Men put all their effort in paid employment, where they have the relative advantage, while women focus on home production, where their relative advantage is greater. The wife's investments in the home are seen as making the man more productive in his work, producing what has come to be known as the "marriage premium"—married men are paid more than unmarried men (Gray and Vanderhart, this volume). The husband's concentration on work allows the wife to produce a quality home environment. According to these specialization models, the larger the wage gap between men and women, the greater the gains to marriage and the more likely marriage will occur. Conversely, the decline in marriage can be linked to the improvement in women's economic position relative to men (Moffitt, this volume; Gray and Vanderhart, this volume). When both marital partners are employed, the gains to specialization and the incentive to marry are reduced.

Others argue to the contrary that women's earnings power now facilitates marriage rather than discouraging it. In recent studies, the earnings of females have been *positively* associated with the propensity to marry, parallel to earlier and continuing effects of men's earnings (Goldscheider and Waite, 1986). Symmetric rather than specialization models of gains to marriage may be more consistent with today's marriage patterns (see Oppenheimer, this volume; Cherlin, this volume). In symmetric marriages, both spouses are engaged in breadwinning and both tend the home, although not necessarily in equal proportions. Such symmetry provides insurance against the loss or incapacity of a single breadwinner (Oppenheimer, this volume) and may be more efficient in the long run than an arrangement in which each spouse is totally specialized.

Gendered Roles within the Family.   Another often-cited reason for declining marriage rates and increasing cohabitation is the "second shift" (Hochschild, 1989). The substantial increase in the time women spend in paid employment has not been matched by a proportional shift in the time their husbands spend in homemaking (Shelton, this volume). Women may be reluctant to marry because they recognize that they will have to shoulder the primary responsibility for household work in addition to working outside the home. Some scholars have suggested that the future of marriage depends on achieving a more equitable division of household labor between men and women (Goldscheider and Waite, 1991). Cherlin (this volume) suggests that one of the "latent functions" of cohabitation is to allow women to assess the willingness and ability of a potential husband to contribute to work inside the home.

A related aspect of gender relations within marriage is the power differential between men and women. The male power advantage in marriage derives from traditional gender roles, the male earnings advantage, and, occasionally, the threat of physical violence. Its influence is evident in household negotiations: husbands' attitudes about the division of household labor have a stronger influence than do wives' attitudes on the work the husband and wife perform in the home (Shelton, this volume). As England (this volume) points out, however, women's power disadvantage may not be a realistic deterrent to marriage: male dominance affects single women as well as married women. The heavy load of paid work plus homemaking may be more of a problem for women who remain single, particularly if they want children. Marriage provides some help with household chores, and access to the (on average) higher earnings of a man.

Family Norms, Values, and Attitudes.   The constellation of norms, values, and attitudes concerning behaviors related to sexuality and the family has been transformed over recent decades. The changes we have seen are fundamentally intertwined with the transformation in marriage behaviors. Scholars disagree about the causal effects of normative change on behavior. On the one hand, societal disapproval of a behavior tends to reduce the chances it will occur by raising the social costs of engaging in it; on the other hand, shifts in the prevalence of behaviors can influence attitudes toward them. Guy Moors (this volume) demonstrates that on the individual level, values and attitudes are predictive of the family forma- tion choices people make, while at the same time choices made—whether to cohabit, marry, live separately from parents, or have a child—have the effect of reinforcing or negating earlier-held attitudes.

It is also common for both ideational change and behavioral change to arise simultaneously from other changes in the environment, such as changes in technology and economic conditions that make new behaviors possible and even adaptive. Akerlof et al. (1996) argue that the develop- ment of oral contraceptives and legal access to abortion triggered changes in norms and behavior by making it less possible for women to say no to sex outside of marriage. However, this view is also overly simple, because ideational and behavioral change can also influence the direction of tech- nological development. Childcare centers developed in response to women's movement into the workforce; the development of birth control technologies responded to an increased demand for control over repro- duction. It seems most productive to view norms, values, and attitudes as interdependent and mutually influential with other factors driving changes in marriage (Axinn and Thornton, this volume).

Ideational factors can influence behavior at several levels. A broadly held cultural norm (e.g., that a man must be able to support his family in order to marry) creates a context that defines the relations between eco- nomic opportunities and marriage behavior. If the norm changes, these relationships may also change as specific behaviors take on new meaning. Shared norms, values, and meanings also factor into the calculus of "rational choice" by influencing the social costs and rewards for engaging in particular behaviors. Interaction of individuals at the dyadic, group, and institutional levels can contribute to the evolution of attitudes and val- ues at the individual and social levels and lead to behavioral change.

In recent decades, attitudes toward family issues have changed dra- matically in some domains and remained relatively stable in others. Among the most significant change has been a steady increase in tolerance toward sexual behavior outside of marriage. In the United States, disap- proval of nonmarital sex, cohabitation, and childbearing declined steadily during the 1970s and 1980s, and remained low in the 1990s (Axinn and Thornton, this volume). These changes have reduced the social costs of enjoying intimate relationships and parenthood outside of marriage, and thus have reduced the incentives to marry. In doing so they have made the delay of marriage and the choice of nonmarriage more feasible.

In other domains, changes have been mixed. Disagreement with the idea that "men should achieve in the workplace while women care for home and family" has increased steadily (Axinn and Thornton, this volume). On the other hand, as noted above, the attitude toward the male breadwinner role in marriage seems to have remained unchanged. Gendered expectations of female behavior have changed more, but primarily in terms of increased tolerance for a variety of roles: homemaking and nurturing of the young are still firmly linked to a female identity, and even in couples with egalitarian attitudes women still do most of the household chores (Shelton, this volume). Expectations of gendered relations in marriage have changed, but still tend toward traditional models when compared to the more egalitarian expectations that define cohabitation. Finally, despite the dramatic change in marriage behavior, Americans have continued to value marriage strongly. Since the 1970s, there has been virtually no change in the proportion of young people who see married people as happier than unmarried people (Axinn and Thornton, this volume), and the proportion of high school seniors who claim that a good marriage is "quite or extremely important" to them has held steady at over 90% for women and over 85% for men (Thornton, 1989).

Increasing Divorce Rates. Another factor that may contribute to increases in delayed or foregone marriage is the substantial increase in divorce that occurred during the 1970s and 1980s. Today, young brides or grooms in the United States face at best an even chance that their marriage will last "until death do us part." As Waite and Gallagher (2000) suggest, it is the permanence of marriage that gives individuals confidence to invest in their marriages and to reap gains from marriage. Economic specialization and joint investment—whether in houses, cars, children, friends, or simply deep emotional attachments to each other—are risky strategies for relationships that may not last. Increasing divorce rates reduce the returns to marriage by making it riskier for individuals to invest in marriage. The lower the returns to marriage, the more likely are individuals to defer marriage and perhaps to forego it entirely.

Another consequence of high divorce rates is the large numbers of children who experience a parental divorce. These children, it turns out, are more likely to choose cohabitation before marriage, and are more likely to divorce themselves (Amato and Booth, 1997). Increasing divorce rates in one generation thus set off an echo in the next, fed by individuals whose first-hand experience teaches them to be wary of the permanence of marriage.

WHY DOES MARRIAGE VARY ACROSS GROUPS?

Focusing on trends in marriage and cohabitation can obscure the great variability within our society and across societies in the timing, prevalence, and meaning of marriage. Understanding group differences at a given point in time can provide perspectives on the importance of changing economic, cultural, and institutional factors that support marriage.

Education plays a crucial role in influencing union formation. Men who end their education at or before high school graduation tend to marry at earlier ages than men who attend college. College-educated men marry at high rates during the late twenties but by age 30 are still less likely than high school graduates or high school dropouts to have married (Raley, this volume). As Moffitt (this volume) demonstrates, different educational groups within the United States have experienced significant differences in the growth of male and female wages in recent decades, leading to increasing economic inequality within our population. He suggests that declining marriage rates for the more highly educated are a story of increasing female wages, whereas declining rates for the less educated are a story of decreasing male wages.

Belinda Tucker's (this volume) analysis of ethnic and racial differences in attitudes relating to marriage underscores the joint influence of norms and economic opportunities. Tucker finds that black, Hispanic, and white urban Americans value marriage equally; however, marriage has declined most precipitously in the black population. Large economic disparities between the races explain a large part of this difference, as do the lower availability of marriageable black men (because of higher mortality and incarceration rates) and lower levels of educational attainment. However, Tucker also finds that economic concerns loom larger in blacks' expectations and values about marriage. African-Americans are more likely to emphasize economic security and a promising earnings trajectory as a criterion for male marriageability, and this magnifies the effect of economic disadvantage on marriage.

Hispanic populations are also economically disadvantaged but have much higher rates of marriage than do African-Americans (Raley, this volume). Oropesa and Gorman (this volume) stress the importance of examining the cultural values brought by various immigrant groups to our country. Groups of Hispanic origin tend to have strong promarriage and profamily values (including an emphasis on male dominance within marriage). Asians also hold more traditional, profamily values, whereas immigrants of European origin are more similar to (but still more traditional than) native-born Americans. Among Hispanic and European immigrants, increasing exposure to American mainstream culture tends to weaken family values.

Religious institutions influence the marriage and cohabitation behavior of individuals by shaping and reinforcing norms and values (Lehrer, this volume). Among religious groups, Mormons and Fundamentalist Protestants marry earliest and are least likely to preface marriage with cohabitation. Jews are most likely to delay marriage and to cohabit before marrying. Closely associated with these differences in union formation are differences among religious communities in the importance placed on higher education and in values concerning nonmarital sex, marriage, divorce, gender roles, and childbearing.

Governments also influence union formation through their policies. Marriage penalties embedded in the tax system may discourage marriage (Waite and Gallagher, 2000), as may welfare programs that restrict eligibility to the unmarried. Women's marriage rates are lower, and cohabitation higher, in states with more generous benefits under Aid to Families with Dependent Children (Lichter et al., 1991; Moffitt et al., 1998).

Cross-national variation in marriage patterns is likely to be linked to national religious and other cultural traditions. Such traditions often support national policies and programs that directly or indirectly influence marriage behavior. But those policies and programs may have independent effects on family formation choices. The relatively low levels of cohabitation, nonmarital fertility, and divorce in southern European countries, together with low marriage and marital fertility rates, have been attributed to the lack of state support for employed parents (see Kiernan, this volume).

ORGANIZATION OF THE VOLUME

The four parts of this volume provide a sampling of research describing and explaining how the formation of intimate sexual unions has changed over time and how it varies across populations and groups. Part I focuses on demographic trends and population differences. R. Kelly Raley describes recent trends and differentials in marriage, cohabitation, and other intimate unions in the United States; Kathleen Kiernan provides an international perspective on the variations in trends among industrialized nations; and Catherine Fitch and Steven Ruggles examine historical trends and differentials in patterns of marriage in the United States since 1850.

In Part II, three papers provide theoretical perspectives on marriage and union formation. Martin Daly and Margo Wilson discuss insights from evolutionary psychology; Robert Pollak discusses the development of economic theories of marriage; and Andrew Cherlin suggests new approaches to understanding patterns of marriage and cohabitation, synthesizing themes from sociological and economic theory.

The six papers in Part III focus on norms, attitudes, and values related to marriage and cohabitation, and the process of relationship commitment. William G. Axinn and Arland Thornton describe changes in attitudes about marriage, family, and sexuality over recent decades in the United States. M. Belinda Tucker reports on values and expectations among black, white, and Hispanic urban Americans. R. S. Oropesa and

Bridget K. Gorman discuss the values of immigrant groups to the United States and the impact of assimilation on values. Guy Moors examines the ways in which individuals' family values and behavioral choices influence each other over time. Evelyn Lehrer analyzes and interprets differences in the United States among religious groups in marriage and cohabitation. Finally, Catherine A. Surra and Christine R. Gray identify the ways couples develop personal commitment in their relationships, focusing on social support and interpersonal perceptions.

Papers in Part IV examine the underlying bargain made in marriage and the extent to which it is constrained by external economic factors or changing norms within marriage. Valerie Kincade Oppenheimer discusses the effect of young men's difficulty in establishing career maturity on their marriage prospects, and Robert A. Moffitt evaluates the consistency of traditional microeconomic theories of marriage with recent trends and differentials in male and female wages and marriage rates. Paula England asks whether, given the female disadvantage in marriage, women still benefit by choosing to marry over remaining single. Beth Ann Shelton examines explanations for the gender gap in household work, which results in the "second shift" noted above. Jeffrey S. Gray and Michel J. Vanderhart examine the sources of the "marriage premium" in men's wages and the reasons underlying recent declines in this wage advantage. Finally, Linda J. Waite demonstrates the continuing robustness of other advantages in marriage: married men and women remain more highly satisfied with various aspects of their lives than singles, and these differences have not diminished over time.

The scientists contributing these papers represent a range of disciplines: sociology, demography, economics, history, social psychology, and evolutionary psychology. Their collective message is that there have been powerful forces reshaping marriage and intimate unions in recent years. Although scientists usually focus on the impact of one or another causal factor, it is most likely the confluence, interaction, and mutual reinforcement of changes in many domains—economic, technological, cultural and social—that have brought us to where we are today.

What is perhaps most remarkable, in the face of all these changes, is that marriage continues to be highly valued, indeed viewed as the most desirable form of intimate relationship (Axinn and Thornton, this volume; Cherlin, this volume). A future challenge for research is to "unpack" the meaning and benefits of marriage so as to understand this better. How does marriage provide for the needs of individuals and families in ways that other union forms do not? What are the social, cultural, and institutional forces supporting the value of marriage in the face of so much change? Another challenge for research is to improve our understanding of the social, economic, and cultural barriers to the formation of satisfying and enduring intimate unions, by any name, and the ways in which these barriers might be overcome. Whether our concern is the welfare of children, the self-fulfillment of adults, or the moral health of our society, improved knowledge of the processes underlying marriage and other intimate unions is of the utmost relevance.

REFERENCES

Akerlof, George A., Janet L. Yellen, and Michael L. Katz. 1996. "An Analysis of Out-of-Wedlock Childbearing in the United States." *Quarterly Journal of Economics* 111:277–317.

Amato, Paul R., and Alan Booth. 1987. *A Generation at Risk: Growing up in an Era of Family Upheaval*. Cambridge, MA: Harvard University Press.

Becker, Gary S. 1991. *Treatise on the Family*. Cambridge, MA: Harvard University Press (enlarged edition).

Bernhardt, Morris, M., and Handcock. 1995. "Women's Gains, Men's Losses: A Closer Look at the Shrinking Gender Gap in Earnings." *American Journal of Sociology* 101(2):302–328.

Blood, Robert O., and Wolfe, Donald M. 1960. *Husbands & Wives: The Dynamics of Married Living*. Glencoe, IL: Free Press.

Blumstein, Phillip, and Pepper Schwartz. 1983. *American Couples: Money, Work, Sex*. New York: William Morrow.

Bumpass, Larry, and Hsien-Hen Lu. 2000. "Trends in Cohabitation and Implications for Children's Family Contexts in the United States" *Population Studies* 54, forthcoming March.

Department of Health and Human Services. 1995. *Report to Congress on Out-of-Wedlock Childbearing*. Hyattsville, MD: National Center for Health Statistics.

England, Paula, and George Farkas. 1986. *Household, Employment and Gender: A Social, Economic, and Demographic View*. New York: Aldine de Gruyter.

Fishbein, M., and I. Ajzen. 1975. *Belief, Attitude, Intention and Behavior*. Reading, MA: Addison-Wesley.

Forste, Renata, and Koray Tanfer. 1996. "Sexual Exclusivity Among Dating, Cohabiting, and Married Women." *Journal of Marriage and the Family* 58:33–47.

Goldscheider, Francis K., and Linda J. Waite. 1986. "Sex Differences in the Entry into Marriage." *American Journal of Sociology* 92(1):91–109.

Goldscheider, Francis K., and Linda J. Waite. 1991. *New Families, No Families? The Transformation of the American Home*. Berkeley: University of California Press.

Hochschild, Arlie. 1989. *The Second Shift*. New York: Viking Penguin.

Homans, G. C. 1961. *Social Behavior: Its Elementary Forms*. New York: Harcourt, Brace and World.

Inglehart, Ronald. 1997. *Modernization and Postmodernization: Cultural, Economic and Political Change in 43 Societies*. Princeton: Princeton University Press.

Lichter, Daniel T., Felicia B. LeClere, and Diane K. McLaughlin. 1991. "Local Marriage Markets and the Marital Behavior of Black and White Women." *American Journal of Sociology* 96(4):843–867.

Moffitt, Robert A., Robert Reville, and Anne E. Winkler. 1998. "Beyond Single Mothers: Cohabitation and Marriage in the AFDC Program." *Demography* 35(3):259–278.

Oppenheimer, Valerie K. 1994. "Women's Rising Employment and the Future of

the Family in Industrial Societies." *Population and Development Review* 20(2):
293–342.

Pope, Hallowell, and Charles W. Mueller 1976. "The Intergenerational Transmission of Marital Instability: Comparisons by Race and Sex." *Journal of Social Issues* 35:112–125.

Rindfuss, Ronald, and A. VanDenHeuvel. 1990. "Cohabitation: A Precursor to Marriage or an Alternative to Being Single?" *Population and Development Review* 16:703–726.

Saluter, Arlene F., and Terry A. Lugaila. 1998. "Marital Status and Living Arrangements: March, 1996." *Current Population Reports* P20-496. Washington, DC: United States Department of Commerce.

Spain, Daphne, and Suzanne M. Bianchi. 1996. *Balancing Act: Motherhood, Marriage and Employment among American Women.* New York: Russell Sage.

Teachman, Jay. D., Karen A. Polonko, and John Scanzoni. 1999. "Demographics and Families." Pp. 39–76 in *Handbook of Marriage and the Family.* New York: Plenum Press.

Thornton, Arland. 1989. "Changing Attitudes Toward Family Issues in the United States." *Journal of Marriage and the Family* 51(4):873–893.

Ventura, Stephanie J., Joyce A. Martin, Sally C. Curtin, and T. J. Matthews. 1999. "Births: Final Data for 1991." *National Vital Statistics Reports* 47(18). Hyattsville, MD: National Center for Health Statistics.

Waite, Linda J., and Maggie Gallagher. 2000. *The Case for Marriage.* New York: Doubleday.

Weiss, Yoram. 1997. "The Formation and Dissolution of Families: Why Marry? Who Marries Whom? And What Happens Upon Divorce?" Pp. 81–123 in *Handbook of Population and Family Economics,* Vol. 1A, edited by Mark R. Rosenzweig and Oded Stark. Amsterdam: North Holland.

I

TRENDS IN MARRIAGE
AND COHABITATION

2

Recent Trends and Differentials in Marriage and Cohabitation: The United States

R. KELLY RALEY

Over the past 30 years, we have seen a dramatic transformation of American family life. The most prominent features of the transformation center on the formation of intimate relationships between men and women. Age at first marriage is rising and the proportions of women expected to never marry have increased slightly. Cohabitation is becoming a normative life experience. Most first sexual experiences occur before marriage or cohabitation.

My primary objective in this chapter is to document recent trends and differentials in marriage and cohabitation in the United States. I also examine trends in the types of relationships within which first sexual experience occurs. Although the analyses are descriptive, my focus on particular trends and differentials is informed by leading explanations for changes in American family life.

RECENT TRENDS IN THE TIMING OF FIRST MARRIAGE AND FIRST UNION

Since the marriage boom and the accompanying baby boom of the 1950s and early 1960s, the age at which young adults first marry has climbed steadily. A good indicator of the pace of marriage is the age at which half the population has married for the first time. For women born in the late 1930s, this age was 20 years and 7 months. Women born less than two decades later, in the early 1950s, had pushed the timing to 21 years and 6 months, almost a year later than their older counterparts (Sweet and Bumpass, 1987).

At the same time, cohabitation before marriage became increasingly common. Although only 7% of the women born in the late 1940s cohabited before age 25, this figure increased to 37% of the women born in the early 1960s (Bumpass and Sweet, 1989). Among never-married 25–29 year olds, 17% were currently cohabiting in the late 1980s and 23% in the early 1990s (Bumpass and Sweet, 1995). Because of these increases in cohabitation, young adults were forming first unions (coresidential partnerships) in the mid-1980s at the same age as they had in the early 1970s, despite rapid declines in marriage. For example, the percentage of women who married by age 25 dropped 23 percentage points (from 79 to 66%) during this period. The corresponding decline in the likelihood of ever marrying or cohabiting was only 4 percentage points. Similar changes occurred in men's marital timing and cohabitation (Bumpass et al., 1991).

To update these trends, I use data from the 1995 National Survey of Family Growth (NSFG). Figure 2.1 shows cohort life table estimates of marriage "survival" (i.e., nonmarriage) among women born between 1950–1954 and 1965–1969.[1] Nearly 70% of women in the 1950–1954 birth cohort had married by the age 25; this proportion decreased to 53% for the 1965–1969 birth cohort.

To provide more recent estimates of marriage timing, I constructed a period life table using the June 1995 Current Population Survey, calculating age-specific marriage probabilities between January 1992 and January 1995.[2] The dashed line in Figure 2.1 shows that similar to the results reported above, 51% of women marry by age 25, while 88% are estimated ever to marry (data not shown).

Figure 2.2 shows parallel trends in women's first union formation (marriage or cohabitation), estimated from cohort life tables using NSFG data. The age at first union has increased more slowly than the age at marriage; that is, cohabitation in some ways substitutes for previously earlier ages at marriage. Even so, young adults form first unions at later ages now than in earlier years. These results imply that as noted in previous research, first unions are more likely now than in the past to be informal.

Bumpass and Sweet (1989), analyzing data from the National Survey of Families and Households, reported that among those born in 1945–1949 who had formed a union by age 25, about 9% of women and 16% of men had cohabited. Among those born 15 years later, these figures increased to 49% for both men and women. Table 2.1 presents findings for women, using the National Survey of Family Growth. The first column shows the percentage of women who had not formed a union by age 25. (I use age 25 as the cutoff point to compare experiences of younger cohorts, who had not reached older ages before the survey, with those of older cohorts.) The next three columns report the percentage of women with each of three types of first union experience by age 25: marriage without cohabitation,

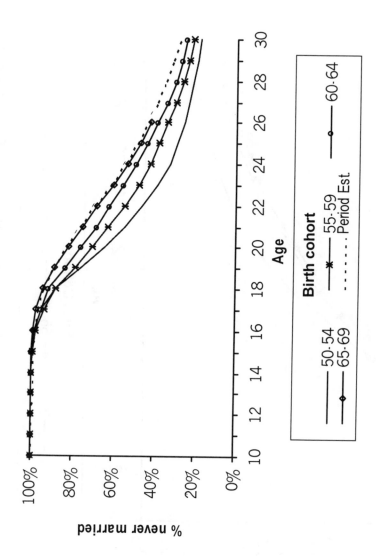

Figure 2.1. Women's survival to first marriage by birth cohort. *Source:* National Survey of Family Growth, 1995.

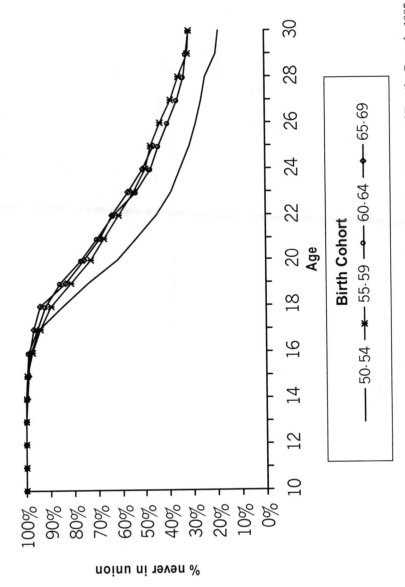

Figure 2.2. Women's survival to first union by birth cohort. *Source:* National Survey of Family Growth, 1995.

Table 2.1. Estimates of First Union Type before Age 25 by Birth Cohort

	All Women:	Women in Union by Age 25				
Birth Cohort	No Union by Age 25	Marriage[a]	Marriage after Cohabitation	Cohabitation No Marriage	Cohabit First (%)	Unweighed (N)
1950–1954	23	59	12	6	24	1770
1955–1959	26	46	17	12	38	2148
1960–1964	29	37	19	15	48	2148
1965–1969	32	31	23	15	55	1750

Source: National Survey of Family Growth, 1995.
[a]Marriage includes only women whose first union began with marriage. To calculate trends in marriage, ignoring cohabitation sum the marriage column with the marriage after cohabitation column.

cohabitation with subsequent marriage, and cohabitation without marriage. Presenting the latter two types of experience combined, the fourth column shows results similar to those reported by Bumpass and Sweet (1989). Similar trends are found for those who entered a first union in their late twenties (analyses not shown).

The behavioral data show that cohabitation before first marriage has become the norm. Attitudinal data support this inference; about half of young adults approve of nonmarital cohabitation—54.1% of 18–24 year olds and 48.8% of 25–29 year olds in 1987–1988 (Sweet, 1989). Many young adults see cohabitation as providing an opportunity for couples to "be sure they are compatible before marriage" (Bumpass et al., 1991). Although Table 2.1 suggests that marriage after cohabitation is more common than cohabitation without marriage, only half of cohabiting unions result in marriage, and this probability has been decreasing recently (Bumpass and Lu, 2000).

RACE DIFFERENTIALS

Receiving as much attention as the overall trends in marriage and cohabitation, the divergence of marriage patterns by race remains, for the most part, an enigma. Since the 1950s, black women's marriage rates have declined much more steeply than white women's (Bennett et al., 1989; Cherlin, 1992; Mare and Winship, 1991; Tucker and Mitchell-Kernan, 1995). White women's cohabiting unions were more likely than those of black women to end quickly in marriage (Manning and Smock, 1995; Schoen and Owens, 1992). As a result, the divergence by race in age at first union is only about half the divergence in marriage (Raley, 1996). To update trends in marriage by race, I use the Current Population Survey (CPS), which has a large sample of black women.[3] Figure 2.3 shows trends in marriage for white and black women separately. For the 1950–1954 cohort, 72% of white women and only 56% of black women were married by age 25. There was a strong divergence in marriage patterns for the 1955–1959 birth cohort (who married in the late 70s and early 80s). The probability of white women marrying by age 25 declined four points to 68%, compared to the decline of 15 points to 41% for black women.

Women born in the 1960s continued to experience declines in marriage, but the gap between blacks and whites was the same for the 1965–1969 cohort as it was for the 1955–1959 cohort. Given that marriage continues to decline, period estimates probably overstate the percentages of women in their early twenties who will actually marry at each age. Because race differences do not appear to be increasing, however, period estimates can provide good approximations of difference in black and white women's marriage probabilities. At the marriage rates for 1992–1995, about 60% of white women and about 30% of black women will marry by age 25. This 30 point gap narrows only slightly by age 50, at which time 92% of white women and 66% of black women will have ever married.[4]

As stated above, black–white differences in the timing of first union are smaller than differences in timing of first marriage. Only the NSFG provides data on cohabitation, so estimates of union timing are based on smaller samples than are the above estimates for marriage timing. Figure 2.4 shows, not surprisingly, that the trend in union formation for white women resembles that for all women, declining slightly but much less so than marriage. For black women, the 1950–1954 cohort is again distinct. Black women born in the early 1950s formed first unions at considerably younger ages than black women born later in the decade. For subsequent cohorts, there has been no increase in the timing of first union. As a result, race differences in the timing of first union have become slightly smaller over the 1955 to 1969 birth cohorts.

Figure 2.5 shows race differences in first union type. As stated above, more than half of all unions forming before age 25 begin informally. For blacks, this figure is more than two thirds. In addition, these unions are less likely to result in marriage than are first cohabiting unions of white women (Manning and Smock, 1995). Race differentials in cohabitation experience are not, however, consistent with attitudes toward cohabitation; African-Americans are no more likely than whites to approve of non-marital cohabitation (Carter, 1993; Sweet, 1989). Recent research shows that economic instability reduces marriage likelihoods more than cohabitation (Clarkberg, 1999). This might explain some of the race difference in first union type. Of course, economic instability can be only a partial

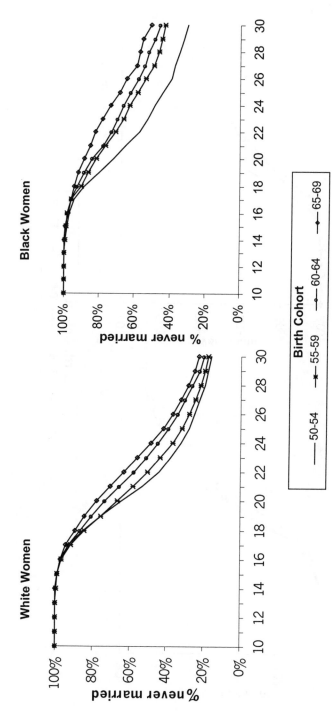

Figure 2.3. Women's survival to first marriage by race. *Source:* June Current Population Survey, 1995.

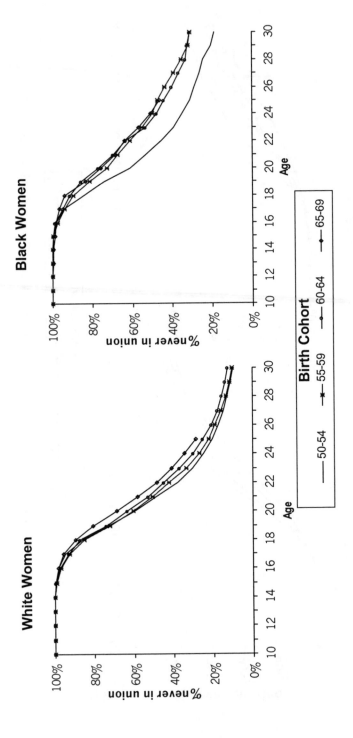

Figure 2.4. Women's survival to first union by race. *Source:* National Survey of Family Growth, 1995.

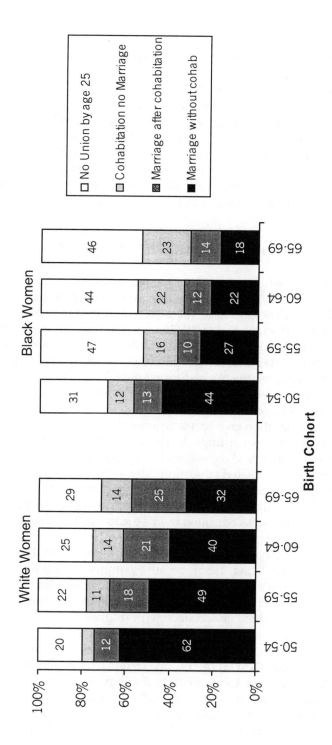

Figure 2.5. White–black differences in union experiences by age 25. *Source:* National Survey of Family Growth, 1995.

explanation, because cohabitation has increased among all socioeconomic groups (Bumpass et al., 1991).

Trends in marriage and cohabitation have not yet run their course. The age at marriage continues to rise and an increasing proportion of unions begin with cohabitation. However, the racial divergence in marriage that began with women marrying in the late 1950s and that accelerated for women marrying in the 1970s and early 1980s (Cherlin, 1992) does not continue to grow. Whereas between the 1960s and the early 1980s African-American marriage patterns were clearly changing more rapidly than white marriage patterns, this is less true in the late 1980s and early 90s.

SOCIOECONOMIC DIFFERENTIALS

The most successful explanations for the race differential in marriage involve variations on William J. Wilson's hypothesis that declines are the direct result of declines in stable, lucrative employment opportunities for young black men (Lichter et al., 1991, 1992; Schoen and Kluegel, 1988). Wilson (1987) argues that shifts in the industrial structure toward service jobs and away from manufacturing industries harmed the employment prospects of young, relatively uneducated men. This in turn decreased the pool of eligible (i.e., employed) young men available for marriage. As a result, marriage rates of both men and women declined. This is primarily a class-based rather than race-based argument.

On the one hand, low earnings clearly constrain men's marriage opportunities. Oppenheimer and colleagues (1997) show striking differentials in marriage rates by completed education. Men with a high school degree or less have lower marriage rates once they have completed their schooling compared to men with some college or more. The authors argue that this relationship is due to less educated men's greater difficulty obtaining stable work with a nonpoverty wage. On the other hand, young adults from high socioeconomic backgrounds marry at a later age than those of lower status (Michael and Tuma, 1985), because parents' education is a strong predictor of children's education and current school enrollment decreases the likelihood of marriage. Thus, school enrollment delays marriage, but better job opportunities associated with higher levels of education increase marriage rates following graduation.

Ideally, I would use data from the 1988–1989 National Survey of Families and Households (NSFH) to examine trends in men's marriage timing by completed education. Unfortunately, the sample of men in the NSFH is not large enough to permit this level of disaggregation. The 1990 Census includes a large enough population to do the analysis, but does not ask about age at first marriage, information necessary for a life table analysis.

The Census does have information on current marital status, including whether the respondent was ever married. Figure 2.6 shows differences in the proportions never married by age and current level of education. The graph is truncated at age 30 because the current status of young adults is the most likely to represent recent trends in marriage.

It is no surprise that men who achieve higher levels of education marry later. Men with no high school degree appear to have a higher likelihood of marrying in their teens, but by the mid-twenties the proportion ever married does not continue to increase. Having only a high school diploma is also associated with earlier marriage, with the timing shifted into the early 20s. Among college graduates, only 44% had married by age 25 and 70% by age 30. This 26 point difference is larger than for any of the other education groups, indicating that college-educated men have higher marriage rates after age 25 than less educated men. The increased economic opportunities associated with higher levels of education do not, however, offset the negative effects of school enrollment. By age 30, men with college degrees still lag behind men with less education in their likelihood of marriage.

Increases in cohabitation have further complicated the relationship between socioeconomic status and marriage. Men and women of lower socioeconomic status might choose cohabitation over marriage, because instability in economic resources leads to instability in relationships. Seeming to provide evidence for this interpretation, Bumpass and colleagues (1991) show that those with lower levels of education are more likely to have cohabited in their early 20s than are those who attend or completed college. The less educated are also more likely, however, to marry in their early 20s. The question remains whether the choice of cohabitation or marriage is associated with education.

Figure 2.7 shows NSFG data on trends in first union type by age 25 separately for women with a high school degree and those with a college degree. The white section of each bar indicates the proportion never in a union. Clearly, there is a negative association between education and early union formation. The proportion of the bar that is gray indicates the portion of women who cohabited before age 25. For the 1950–1954 cohort, 16% of those with just a high school education cohabited before age 25. A similar proportion (18%) of the college-educated women had cohabited by that age.

Over time, the proportion of first unions that began informally increased more steeply among the less educated. For the youngest cohort of women, education is negatively associated with the likelihood that a first union begins with cohabitation. Another component of the education differential is that union formation rates consistently dropped among the more highly educated women, but have remained relatively stable among

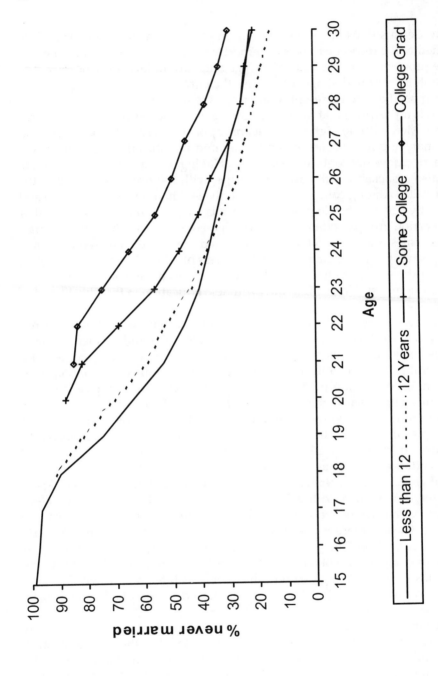

Figure 2.6.   Men's marriage survival by age and education. *Source:* 1990 Census Public Use Microdata, men aged 15–20.

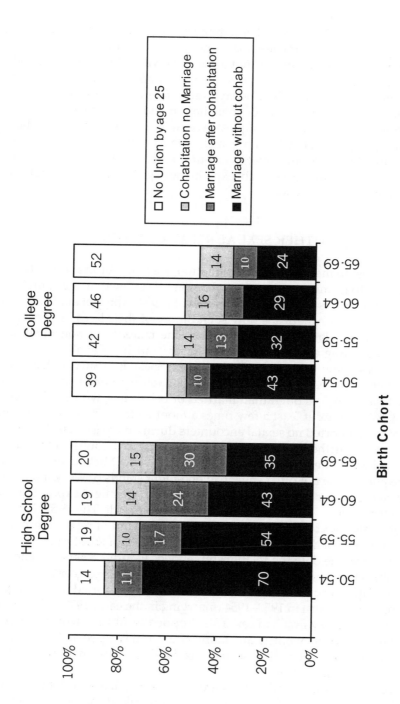

Figure 2.7. Women's first unions before age 15: marriage and cohabitation. *Source:* National Survey of Family Growth, 1995.

the least educated. That is, cohabitation has increased to offset declines in marriage more among the less than among the well educated.

Approval of cohabitation is not associated with education; approval is at least as high among the college educated as among those with no college experience (Sweet, 1989). The behavioral differential must therefore stem from the relative advantages of cohabitation and marriage within education groups. Less educated couples have higher rates of divorce (Martin and Bumpass, 1989). Furthermore, men with low levels of education have more difficulty establishing stable, full-time employment (Oppenheimer et al., 1997). These differences might explain the negative association between education and cohabitation.

OTHER SEXUAL RELATIONSHIPS

In contrast to marriage and cohabitation, we know little about relationships prior to forming a coresidential union. We know that age at first sexual intercourse has decreased (Michael et al., 1994; Abma et al., 1997). This might mean that Americans now spend more of their lives in noncoresidential sexual relationships. Then again, the majority of noncohabiting, unmarried young adults might not be having much sex at all.

Analyses of the 1992 National Health and Social Life Survey (Laumann et al., 1995) showed that unmarried, not-cohabiting women age 18–59 do indeed have sex less often than married or cohabiting women. But more than 40% have sex at least a few times a month. Only 27% of women and 19% of men reported no sexual encounters during the past year (Laumann et al., 1994). Furthermore, most individuals not in a coresidential union have had only one sexual partner in the past year (Michael et al., 1994). Single persons do not often engage in one-night stands or weekend flings.

Since the age at first intercourse has declined, we might expect that the character of first sexual relationships has changed. The NSFG asked respondents about their first sexual partner, the kind of relationship they had at the start of their sexual relationship, the date of the start of the relationship, and the date the relationship ended. Figure 2.8 shows trends in type of first sexual relationship.[5] Clearly a shrinking proportion of first relationships involve couples who are already married or engaged. Among women born in 1950–1954 (marrying in the early 1970s), 23% were married when they first had sex. This dropped to 10% for women born in the 1960s. Instead, women are more often initiating sexual activity in "steady" relationships. First sexual relationships with men whom they have just met remain rare (2.5%).

Clearly as sexual relationships are increasingly likely to begin before marriage, the stability of these relationships should decrease. For women

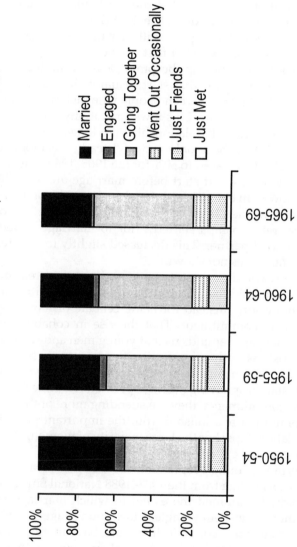

Figure 2.8. Type of relationship with first sex partner at first sex. *Source:* National Survey of Family Growth, 1995, women who had sex before age 25.

born 1950–1954, more than 70% of first sexual relationships were intact after 5 years. This decreased to 50% for the most recent cohort (analysis not shown). Figure 2.9 shows trends in the duration of first sexual relationships for relationships that start casually and for those that start as a "steady" relationship. Note that these relationships are not necessarily monogamous or continuous. The NSFG simply asks the respondent whether she is still having sex with her first sexual partner and, if not, when she last had sex with her first partner.

Are "steady" relationships becoming less committed, and how do they compare to relationships that start casually? By "casual" I mean sexual relationships that start between people who just met, go out occasionally, or are just friends. Figure 2.9 shows that, if anything, "steady" relationships and even "casual" relationships are longer-lived now than before. For the 1950–1954 cohort, only 40% of "steady" relationships were intact after a year. This increased to 60% for the 1965–1969 cohort. Is this because sexual relationships that start before marriage are more likely to end in marriage now than before? Additional analyses showed that this is not the case. Among women born between 1950 and 1954, 22% of those whose first sexual relationships started prior to marriage ended up marrying their first sexual partner. This decreased slightly to 17% for women born 1965–1969 (analyses not shown).

In some ways, these results parallel data on increasing cohabitation. Although young adults are forming life-long commitments more slowly, they are not opting instead for being celibate or having sexual relationships with no commitment. That the rise in cohabitation "offsets" the decline in marriage reminds us that young men and women are still forming relationships with some similarities to marriage. These findings on first sexual relationships demonstrate that young women do not prefer one-night stands or having multiple partners. As Americans delay making long-term commitments, they are spending more of their early life course in less committed relationships. But the important point is that they are having relationships. For the large majority of women, this is true even for the earliest sexual experiences.

Furthermore, young people continue to hold favorable attitudes toward marriage. Using data from the 1987–1988 National Survey of Families and Households, I examined the extent to which marriage is viewed as an improvement over being single. Most young (age 20–29) adults believe they would be more economically secure, have more emotional security, a better sex life, and a higher standard of living if they were married. Although marriage is not viewed so favorably in terms of freedom, independence, or relationships with friends and parents, on balance more than two-thirds think they would be happier married than single (analyses not shown). Singles in steady relationships favor marriage more strongly than

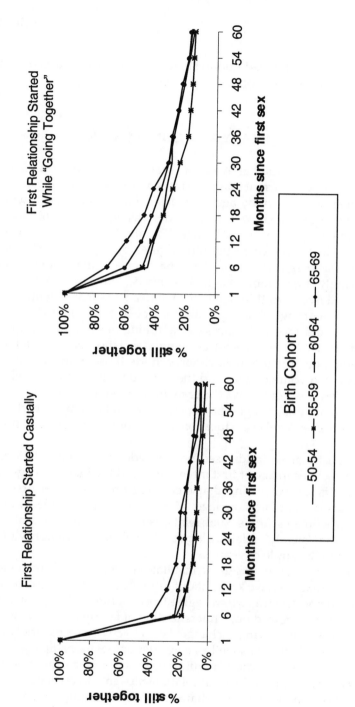

Figure 2.9. Trends in duration of first sexual relationship. *Source:* National Survey of Family Growth, 1995.

do singles in general. Steady nonresidential relationships are, obviously, often a first step toward a potential marriage.

SUMMARY AND CONCLUSION

The analyses presented above show that the age at first marriage continues to rise. Given current marriage rates, we expect that only about half of all women will marry by age 25. Black–white differences in women's marriage are large and show no signs of decreasing. Whereas 60% of white women are expected to marry by age 25, only 30% of black women are expected to do so. The corresponding figures by age 50 are 92 and 66%. Education is also associated with later marriage and union formation.

Increasingly, first unions begin informally. Now over half of white women's and over two-thirds of black women's first coresidential unions begin before marriage. Consequently the age at first union is increasing only slightly and race differences in the timing of union formation have remained stable. There is also a growing association between education and cohabitation. For the most recent cohorts those with less education cohabit at much younger ages and their first unions are more likely to be informal. This was not always the case. In the past, less educated women also married at younger ages. So, among women born in the early 1950s, those with higher levels of education were more likely to cohabit before marriage.

Finally, the analyses addressed noncoresidential sexual relationships. Given the declines in age at first intercourse and the increased age at first marriage, it is not surprising that increasing proportions of first sexual relationships start before marriage. More surprising is the level of commitment in women's first sexual relationships. Most first sexual experiences occur in "steady" relationships and a substantial minority of them last for at least a couple of years.

Recent trends in marriage, cohabitation, and sexual relationships demonstrate that what we know about intimate sexual unions can quickly become outdated. Even as we struggle to incorporate cohabitation into our analyses of marriage and our understanding of family life, the reasons for cohabitation and its meaning change. Sexual activity increasingly occurs in steady nonresidential as well as coresidential relationships. An understanding of the "ties that bind" requires us to shift our starting point to the formation of romantic and sexual relationships in adolescence, as well as to keep our eye on the changing character of cohabitating unions and marriages, and their socioeconomic and cultural variation.

Table 2.2.　Data Sources and Sample Sizes

	National Survey of Family Growth (NSFG)	June Fertility Supplement to Current Population Survey (CPS)
Year collected	1995	1995
Total sample	10,847	47,410
Age (years)	15–44	15–65
Sex	Women	Women
Cohabitation information	Yes	No

Table 2.3.　Sample Sizes with Age Restrictions

	National Survey of Family Growth	June Fertility Supplement to Current Population Survey
Total		
Birth cohort		
1950–1954	1770	5516
1955–1959	2148	6107
1960–1964	2148	6047
1965–1969	1750	5149
White		
Birth cohort		
1950–1954	1301	4558
1955–1959	1750	5022
1960–1964	1509	4887
1965–1969	1182	4134
Black		
Birth cohort		
1950–1954	370	604
1955–1959	453	661
1960–1964	515	681
1965–1969	457	609

ACKNOWLEDGMENTS

This chapter has benefited from the helpful comments of Elizabeth Thomson, Christine Bachrach, Linda Waite, Michelle Hindin, and two anonymous reviewers. Jenifer Bratter provided assistance with the management and analysis of computerized data files. This research was conducted using the facilities at the Population Research Center at the University of Texas, which is funded through HD-06160, a P30 grant by the National Institute of Child Health and Human Development.

NOTES

1.   These estimates were compared to estimates derived from the June Current Population Survey (CPS) and the 1992–1994 reinterview of the National Survey of Families and Households (NSFH). The NSFG produces results that are all but identical to the CPS. The 1965–1969 cohort in the NSFH had lower marriage rates than in the other two data sets, but the earlier cohorts match up to the CPS and NSFG. The results from NSFG are presented because these data also have information on cohabitation. See Tables 2.2 and 2.3 for more information on the data sources.

2.   Thus for these analyses an individual is represented three times if she has never married in 1992 and does not marry by 1995. Similar to all life table techniques, an individual is not represented in the data after experiencing the terminal event, in this case marriage.

3.   The estimates for the NSFG and CPS are very similar, although the gap between the 1950–1954 cohort and the other cohorts in timing of first marriage is slightly larger for the women in the NSFG compared to those in the CPS.

4.   This last estimate, for black women, is based on a sample with less than 100 women in every age group. Although using a 3-year window ameliorates some of the problems with sample size, it is still cause for some caution. A published estimate (Bennett et al., 1989) of the proportion of black women expected ever to marry for the cohort of women born in the 1950s is 75%. Given the downward trend-line, the estimate here of 66% seems reasonable.

5.   The NSFG includes women born as late as 1980. I do not extend this analysis of relationship type to the younger women who are still in their teens at the time of the interview. Their first sexual relationships are biased toward relationships begun at a relatively young age.

REFERENCES

Abma, Chandra J., William D. Mosher, Linda S. Peterson, and Linda J. Piccinino. 1997. *Fertility, Family Planning, and Women's Health: New Data from the 1995 National Survey of Family Growth.* National Center for Health Statistics. Vital Health Stat 23(19).

Bennett, Neil, David Bloom, and Patricia Craig. 1989. "The Divergence of Black and White Marriage Patterns." *American Journal of Sociology* 95(3):692–722.

Bumpass, Larry, and Hsien-Hen Lu. 2000. "Trends in Cohabitation and Implications for Children's Family Contexts." *Population Studies*, in press.

Bumpass, Larry, and James Sweet. 1989. "National Estimates of Cohabitation." *Demography* 24(4):615–625.

Bumpass, Larry L., and James A. Sweet. 1995. Cohabitation, Marriage, and Nonmarital Childbearing and Union Stability: Preliminary Findings from NSFH2. NSFH Working Paper No 65. Madison: University of Wisconsin, Center for Demography and Ecology.

Bumpass, Larry, James Sweet, and Andrew Cherlin. 1991. "The Role of Cohabitation in Declining Rates of Marriage." *Journal of Marriage and the Family* 53:913–927.

Carter, Wendy Y. 1993. "Attitudes Toward: Premarital Sex, Non-marital Childbearing, Cohabitation, and Marriage Among Blacks and Whites." NSFH Working Paper No. 61. Madison: University of Wisconsin, Center for Demography and Ecology.

Cherlin, Andrew. 1992. *Marriage, Divorce, and Remarriage*. Cambridge, MA: Harvard University Press.

Clarkberg, Marin. 1999. "The Price of Partnering: The Role of Economic Well-Being in Young Adult's First Union Experiences." *Social Forces* 77(3):945–968.

Laumann, Edward O., John H. Gagnon, Robert T. Michael, and Stuart Michaels. 1994. *The Social Organization of Sexuality: Sexual Practices in the United States.* Chicago: University of Chicago Press.

Lichter, Daniel T., Felicia B. LeClere, and Diane K. McLaughlin. 1991. "Local Marriage Markets and the Marital Behavior of Black and White Women." *American Journal of Sociology* 96(4):843–867.

Lichter, Daniel T., Diane K. McLaughlin, George Kephart, and David J. Landry. 1992. "Race and the Retreat from Marriage: A Shortage of Marriageable Men?" *American Sociological Review* 57(6):781–799.

Martin, Teresa Castro, and Larry L. Bumpass. 1989. "Recent Trends in Marital Disruption." *Demography* 26(1):37–51.

Manning, Wendy, and Pamela J. Smock. 1995. "Why Marry? Race and the Transition to Marriage Among Cohabitors." *Demography* 32:509–520.

Mare, Robert D., and Christopher Winship. 1991. "Socioeconomic Change and the Decline of Marriage for Blacks and Whites." Pp. 175–202 in *The Urban Underclass,* edited by C. Jencks and P.E. Peterson. Washington DC: The Brookings Institution.

Michael, Robert T., and Nancy Brandon Tuma. 1985. "Entry into Marriage and Parenthood by Young Men and Women: The Influence of Family Background." *Demography* 22(4):515–544.

Michael, Robert T., John H. Gagnon, Edward O. Laumann, and Gina Kolata. 1994. *Sex in America: A Definitive Survey*. New York: Little, Brown.

Oppenheimer, Valerie Kincade, Matthijs Kalmijn, and Nelson Lim. 1997. "Men's Career Development and Marriage Timing During a Period of Rising Inequality." *Demography* 34(3):311–330.

Raley, R. Kelly. 1996. "A Shortage of Marriageable Men? A Note on the Role of Cohabitation in Black-White Differences in Marriage Rates." *American Sociological Review* 61(6):973–983.

Schoen, Robert, and James R . Kluegel. 1988. "The Widening Gap in Black and White Marriage Rates: The Impact of Population Composition and Differential Marriage Propensities." *American Sociological Review* 53:895–907.

Schoen, Robert, and David Owens. 1992. "A Further Look at First Unions and First Marriages." Pp. 109–117 in *The Changing American Family,* edited by S.J. South and S.E. Tolnay. Boulder, CO: Westview.

Sweet, James A. 1989. "Differentials in the Approval of Cohabitation." NSFH Working Paper No. 8. Madison: University of Wisconsin, Center for Demography and Ecology.

Sweet, James, and Larry Bumpass. 1987. *American Families and Households*. New York: Russell Sage Foundation.

Tucker, M. Belinda, and Claudia Mitchell-Kernan. 1995. "Trends in African American Family Formation: A Theoretical and Statistical Overview." In *The Decline in Marriage Among African-Americans,* edited by M. Belinda Tucker and Claudia Mitchell-Kernan. New York: Russell Sage Foundation.

Wilson, William J. 1987. *The Truly Disadvantaged: The Inner City, the Underclass, and Public Policy*. Chicago: University of Chicago Press.

3

European Perspectives on Union Formation

KATHLEEN KIERNAN

INTRODUCTION

In the recent past marriage heralded the start of a first union for most couples in Europe. There were identifiable stages in the development of a relationship: courtship, engagement, and ultimately the marriage ceremony that was followed by the couple setting up home together. Now there is more flexibility in becoming a couple and whether they coreside. Here we examine these developments for a range of European countries. Our analysis includes a review of recent trends in marriage and cohabitation. We also use recently available data from the European Fertility and Family Surveys to examine the extent to which women are not forming partnerships and how this has changed over time, the extent to which they are living in noncoresidential intimate relationships, the type of first partnership in terms of whether it commences with marriage or cohabitation and if the latter whether it converts into a marriage, and the duration of cohabiting unions. As well as transnational comparisons we examine subgroup variation according to educational level, religious observance, and experience of parental divorce. In the final section we highlight some of the policy responses that there have been to these developments.

MARRIAGE TRENDS

Since the late 1960s and early 1970s marriage rates in most European countries have declined. Younger generations of Europeans have been marrying less and among those who marry the trend has been to do so at older ages and over a wider range of ages than was common among their recent predecessors. In broad outline, the decline in marriage rates began in Sweden and Denmark in the late 1960s, the Northern European countries, then spread through most of Western Europe in the early part of the

40

1970s, and became evident in the Southern European countries (Spain, Italy, Portugal, and Greece) around the mid-1970s. Since the 1980s, the decline in marriage rates continued in most European countries but at a slower pace.

To illustrate some of these changes we can compare the mean age at first marriage among women in 1975, which is generally close to the lowest average age observed in the twentieth century for many countries, with the most recently available data (Table 3.1). After World War II the general trend in European marriage rates had been to a younger and more universal marriage pattern, which reached its zenith during the 1960s and early part of the 1970s (Festy, 1980). Since then the mean age at marriage has generally risen in most countries. It is noticeable from Table 3.1 that in many countries the average age at marriage has increased by between 2 and 4 years regardless of the starting position. In the mid-1970s the average age of first time brides in most West European nations was clustered in the 22 to 24 year range whereas in the mid-1990s it is now clustered in the later twenties, in the range 26 to 29 years.

Table 3.1. Mean Age at First Marriage among Women Marrying in 1975 and in 1995

Average Age	Countries 1975	Countries 1995
29	—	Denmark, Iceland, Sweden
28	—	Belgium
27	—	Finland, Ireland, Netherlands, Norway, Spain, Switzerland, West Germany
26	—	Austria, East Germany, France, Italy, Luxembourg, United Kingdom
25	Sweden	Greece, Portugal
24	Ireland, Italy, Switzerland, Spain	
23	Denmark, Finland, Luxembourg, Portugal, Austria	
22	West Germany, France, Greece, Iceland, Netherlands, Norway, Poland, United Kingdom	Bulgaria, Czech Republic, Hungary, Poland
21	Belgium, Bulgaria, East Germany	
20	Czechoslovakia, Hungary	

Source: Council of Europe, Recent Demographic Developments in Europe, 1997.

It is clear from the simple data shown in Table 3.1 that there is a good deal of intra-European diversity in marriage ages. In 1995 the highest values were recorded in the Nordic countries of Sweden, Denmark, and Iceland (with an average at marriage among women of 29 years). The lowest values were to be seen in the Eastern European countries of Bulgaria, the Czech Republic, Hungary, and Poland, with an average age at marriage of around 22 years. Until very recently there has been little change in marriage rates in Eastern Europe, with rates beginning to decline only during the 1990s. Given that average age at marriage tends to correlate closely with overall proportions that ultimately marry, the degree of diversity across Europe suggests that marriage is more salient in some countries than in others.

COHABITATION

One of the important engines behind the decline in marriage rates and a movement to a later age at marriage is the rise in cohabitation that has occurred, particularly since the beginning of the 1980s, in many European countries. However, it should be emphasized that men and women living together outside marriage is certainly not new. Prior to the 1970s it was largely statistically invisible and probably socially invisible outside of the local community or social milieu. In some European countries there were subgroups that were probably more prone to cohabitation than others: the very poor; those whose marriages had broken up but were unable to obtain a divorce, as there was no such legislation, or it was more stringent than now, or it was very expensive to obtain a divorce; certain groups of rural dwellers; and groups ideologically opposed to marriage.

The form of cohabitation that came to the fore during the 1960s in Sweden and Denmark, and during the 1970s in other Northern and Western European countries, North America, and Australia and New Zealand, is new, and could be aptly termed "nubile cohabitation," whereby young people predominantly in their twenties and early thirties live together either as a prelude to, or as an alternative to, marriage. Additionally, with the growth in divorce "postmarital cohabitation" is also likely to have become more prevalent with the divorced cohabiting either in preference to, or as a prelude to, remarriage. Unfortunately in many data sources it is difficult to distinguish between the "nubile" form and "postmarital" cohabitation. However, the increased prevalence of cohabiting unions is likely to lie behind much of the decline in first marriage and remarriage rates that have occurred in many European countries in recent decades.

To date, data on cohabitation tend to be scarce and generally emanate from ad hoc surveys, which can make comparative analyses problematic, as sample sizes, coverage, and definitions may vary. However, in recent years more information from standardized questionnaires has become available for analysis, and here we make use of data from Eurobarometer Surveys and the UN Economic Commission for Europe Fertility and Family Surveys.

MARITAL STATUS DISTRIBUTIONS

To provide a perspective on the incidence of cohabiting and marital unions across a range of European nations we used data from a series of Eurobarometer Surveys carried out in the 15 member States of the European Community in 1996. Eurobarometer Surveys are primarily opinion surveys covering a range of topics relevant to the European Community and carried out under the auspices of the administration of the European Community. These surveys contain very basic demographic information on the respondents, including information on marital status in which "living as married" is one of the categories; the others are the more conventional ones of single, married, divorced, separated, and widowed. Such marital status distributions may not be as accurate as those obtained in dedicated family and fertility surveys but they probably reflect the relative position of different European countries in these developments. The 1996 survey had relatively large samples per country, typically in the range 3000–6000 respondents, depending on the size of the population of the particular country.

Figure 3.1 shows the proportions of women aged 25–29 years in the 15 European Community countries who were cohabiting, married, single, or separated/divorced/widowed at the time of the survey in 1996. In these data we cannot differentiate between never-married and postmarital cohabitants but assume that at the younger ages the former is likely to be the most prevalent. It is clear from Figure 3.1 that there is a good deal of diversity across European states in the incidence of cohabitation. Cohabitation is strikingly most common in the Nordic countries of Denmark, Sweden, and Finland, and France also has relatively high proportions cohabiting. For example, in these four countries around 30% of women aged 25–29 years are cohabiting. There is also a middle group of countries, which includes the Netherlands and Belgium, Great Britain, West and East Germany, and Austria, with levels of cohabitation between 8 and 16% among the group of women aged 25–29. At the other extreme is the set of Southern European countries and Ireland, where cohabitation is seemingly much rarer, with around 3% or less cohabiting.

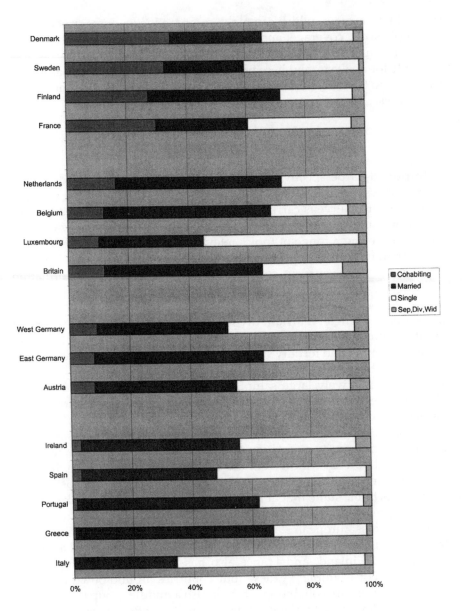

Figure 3.1. Marital status distribution of women aged 25–29 in 1996.

It is also clear from these data that there is a good deal of variation in the proportions of women in marital unions. The Southern European countries of Greece and Portugal exemplify one extreme where over 60% of women in their late twenties are married. However, we also see that within the set of Southern European countries there is a remarkable difference in the behavior of Italian and Spanish women as compared with the Portuguese and Greek women: over 60% of the Italian women are single and 50% of Spanish women are single compared with around one in three of the Portuguese and Greek women. It would seem that not only are men and women in Spain and Italy avoiding parenthood, they are also not forming partnerships either, at least in their twenties. In the Nordic countries of Denmark, Sweden, and Finland (Norway voted not to join the European Union and is therefore not included in such surveys) as well as in France, broadly speaking the proportions in the three main marital status groups are similar at around a third cohabiting, a third single, and a third married. Marriage is seemingly most popular in the Western European countries: notably in Great Britain, Ireland, the Netherlands, and Belgium. An important question with respect to changing patterns of union formation is whether the rise of cohabitation and nonpartnering is part of the same development. From the perspective of European countries and the data presented here, the answer seems to be sometimes "yes" and sometimes "no."

UNION FORMATION: EVIDENCE FROM THE EUROPEAN FERTILITY AND FAMILY SURVEYS

The cross-sectional information from the Eurobarometer Surveys has shown that there is a great deal of intra-European diversity in the extent of cohabiting unions, marital unions, and being single. Now we proceed to examine the formation of unions in more detail using data from the European Fertility and Family Surveys (FFS), which were carried out in the main in the first half of the 1990s under the auspices of the UN Economic Commission for Europe. In the analyses that follow we have confined our attention to the women in the samples. Over 20 countries participated in this enterprise and here we make use of data from those currently available for analysis. These countries along with the dates of interview and the age range of the respondents are shown in Table 3.2. In the main the surveys took place during the first half of the 1990s, the exceptions being Norway and Finland, and the Polish and to a lesser extent the Hungarian surveys took place in a period of major transition in Eastern Europe. Thus the timing and elapsed time for some of the surveys need to be borne in mind when making comparisons across countries. In the following

Table 3.2. UN ECE Fertility and Family Surveys: Year of Interview and Age Range

Country	Year	Age Range
Norway	1988/89	20–43[a]
Finland	1989/90	22–51
Sweden	1992/93	23–43[a]
France	1994	20–49
Germany	1992	20–39
Austria	1996	20–54
Switzerland	1994/95	20–49
Italy	1995/96	20–49
Spain	1994/95	18–49
Hungary	1993	18–41
Poland	1991	18–49
Latvia	1995	18–49
Lithuania	1994/95	18–49

[a]Specific cohorts, see text.

analyses the countries have been divided into four sets: the Nordic set includes Norway, Finland, and Sweden; the Western European set includes Austria, Switzerland, France, and Germany (Germany has been subdivided into East and West given their different history for much of the post-war period); the Southern European set includes Italy and Spain; and the Eastern European set includes Latvia, Lithuania, Poland, and Hungary. The FFS data sets include a core of questions common to all countries and others that were asked in some countries but not others. All countries included men and women in their samples and, except for Norway and Sweden, information was collected on men and women in the same age range. These two countries collected information for specific birth cohorts. In Sweden the cohorts were a sample of women born in 1949, 1954, 1959, 1964, and 1969 and men born in 1949, 1959, and 1964, and in Norway the years for women were 1945, 1950, 1955, 1960, 1965, and 1968 and for men 1945 and 1960. More detailed information including the questionnaires can be found in the Fertility and Family Surveys Questionnaire and Codebook (United Nations, 1992) and in the country reports.

NEVER-PARTNERED

Our earlier examination of the Eurobarometer data showed that there are marked variations in the proportions of single people across European nations. However, reporting oneself as single does not necessarily carry the implication of never having been in a union, as single as a civil status means never married but in common usage it has come increasingly to mean being "currently without a partner," and used by the separated and divorced as well as the never married to describe their partnership status. The Fertility and Family Surveys included a partnership history that incorporated dates of marriages and any other coresidential heterosexual intimate relationships, which allowed us to examine a range of issues, including the extent to which people have never lived with a partner and how this may have changed over time.

Figure 3.2 shows the proportions of women in the age groups 25–29 and 35–39 years who had never been in a coresidential partnership by the time they were aged 25 years. Focusing in on those aged 25–29 years, it is apparent that there is marked variation in the proportions of women who have never partnered, with lows in the Nordic countries of around 10% and in the Eastern European countries of 10–14%, and highs of 40% or more in West Germany and Italy. We can also ascertain whether there has been a decline in the propensity to form partnerships over time by comparing the proportions never partnered by age 25 among those who were aged 25–29 at the time of the survey and among those 10 years older, those aged 35–39 at the time of the survey. An examination of the lower half of the graph shows that in all the countries from Switzerland down to Sweden the proportions never partnered by age 25 has changed very little over the decade encompassed by the two age groups 25–29 and 35–39. This is also the case in many of the Eastern European countries. This implies that the marked change in the never-married population we have seen in many Northern and West European countries has less to do with the avoidance of partnerships and more to do with the replacement of marital unions by cohabiting unions.

The countries where there has been a marked decline in the proportions forming partnerships by age 25 are the two Southern European countries of Spain and Italy, and West Germany. In Spain and Italy it is a long-established tradition that young people live at home with their parents until they marry and the welfare regimes of these two nations is more family than state based, as is the case in many Northern and Western countries (Rehr, 1998). Thus, in a period of high youth unemployment and rising educational participation at the tertiary level as has occurred in these Southern European countries it is probably not surprising that marriage tends to be delayed. Moreover, parents may be less willing to assist with the establishment of an independent household if the partnership is cohabitation rather than a legal marriage.

Having never partnered does not imply lack of intimate relationships. The FFS tried to capture information on noncoresidential partnerships by asking those in noncoresidential unions whether they were "currently having an intimate relationship with someone who lives in a separate

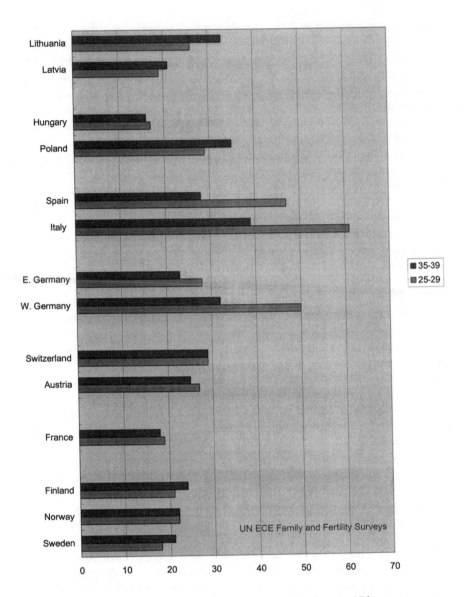

Figure 3.2. Percentage of women with no partnership by age 25 by age group.

household." These questions attempted to capture the extent of "living apart together" (LATS) in the population. Table 3.3 shows the proportions of never-partnered women answering yes to this question for the set of countries that included it on their interview schedule, and in parentheses the proportions in the age group who had never partnered. From Table 3.3 we see that with the exception of Poland, between a third and one-half of the never partnered reported that they were in an intimate noncoresidential partnerships. There was also a general tendency for higher proportions of the never partnered currently in their twenties compared with those in their thirties to report they were in an intimate relationship with someone who lived elsewhere. The women were also asked whether they were living separately because they "wanted to" or because they "had to," or both. The final column in Table 3.3 shows the percentage who responded that they "wanted to," and it is apparent there was a good deal of variation across nations in the responses to this question. Over 70% of the West German and over 60% of the Swiss respondents said that this

Table 3.3. Percentage of Never-Partnered LATS Women[a]

| | Age Group | | | | |
Country	20–24 (%)	25–29 (%)	30–34 (%)	All Ages 20–39 (%)	Want to (%)
France	38	32	19	32	29
Never partnered	(40)	(11)	(7)	(15)	
Austria	49	41	45	45	48
Never partnered	(48)	(16)	(5)	(19)	
Switzerland	54	47	45	47	63
Never partnered	(50)	(15)	(6)	(13)	
West Germany	43	47	34	42	72
Never partnered	(72)	(35)	(18)	(12)	
East Germany	38	33	24	34	45
Never partnered	(51)	(16)	(10)	(8)	
Spain	39	41	28	37	26
Never partnered	(70)	(31)	(12)	(28)	
Italy	47	56	41	46	40
Never partnered	(86)	(46)	(17)	(41)	
Latvia	47	49	41	44	—[b]
Never partnered	(41)	(13)	(5)	(15)	
Hungary	44	42	22	40	40
Never partnered	(30)	(10)	(4)	(11)	

[a]Percentage of women answering "Yes" to question: "are you currently having an intimate relationship with someone who lives in a separate household" according to age group and among those living apart the percentage responding that they are living apart because they "want to." Percentage never partnered by age group shown in parentheses.
[b]No information collected.

arrangement was a choice rather than a constraint, whereas only 26% of the Spanish and 29% of the French respondents said that they wanted to live in this way. In the other countries around 4 of 10 stated that they wanted this kind of living arrangement. There were no consistent differences across nations in the ways men and women responded to this question. In France, Switzerland, Spain, and Italy women were more likely than men to express that living apart was through choice whereas in Austria, West Germany, and Hungary there was little difference between the responses for the two sexes and in East Germany the reverse was the case.

TYPE OF FIRST PARTNERSHIP

We now focus on those women who have had a partnership and examine the type of first partnership according to type of first union: namely whether the respondents married directly with no cohabitation, whether they cohabited and then married, or whether they cohabited and the union had dissolved or was continuing at the time of the interview. Table 3.4 shows the proportions falling into these three groups among women aged 25–29 and 35–39 at the time of the survey.

Table 3.4. Type of First Partnership among Women with a First Partnership According to Age Group at the Time of the Survey

Country	Age Group 25–29			Age Group 35–39		
	Married Directly	Cohabited and Married	Cohabited	Married Directly	Cohabited and Married	Cohabited
Sweden[a]	7	41	52	8	62	30
Norway[a]	24	40	35	62	30	7
Finland	17	43	40	31	46	23
France	12	30	58	48	34	19
Austria	19	41	40	30	42	28
Switzerland	19	44	37	30	52	18
West Germany	16	38	46	38	33	29
East Germany	15	35	50	21	26	53
Italy	86	8	6	91	5	4
Spain	80	8	12	91	4	5
Latvia	50	34	17	67	26	8
Lithuania	75	9	16	78	10	12
Hungary	76	14	10	84	9	7
Poland	95	3	2	96	3	1

[a]Sweden birth cohorts 54 and 64 and Norway birth cohorts 50 and 60.

It is clear from Table 3.4 that among the most recent generation, those aged 25–29, that for the majority of women in Eastern and Southern European countries marriage still heralds the start of a first partnership, whereas this is the case only for a minority in the Nordic and Western European nations. In these latter two regions, cohabitation typically initiates a first union and around 30–40% of first unions were cohabitations that had converted into a marriage with the same partner.

To assess the extent of change over time we can compare the experiences of women aged 25–29 at the time of the survey with those aged 35–39. With respect to the probability of marrying directly, we see that not marrying directly was already well established and at a very low level among the older generation of Swedish women. There have also been some noticeable declines in other countries. For example, in Norway the proportion marrying directly was 24% among those aged 25–29 years (cohort 1960) but had been of the order of 62% among the generation born 10 years earlier (cohort 1950). Similarly in France we see a marked decline from 48% in the earlier generation to 12% among the younger one, and in West Germany a decline from 38 to 16% over the two generations. A somewhat slower pace of change is to be seen in the other countries such as Switzerland and Austria. Among the countries with over 70% marrying directly we see signs of change in Hungary and Spain, but this is less the case in Poland, Lithuania, and Italy. These data highlight not only the diversity across European nations but also the differential pace of change across nations.

DURATION OF COHABITING UNIONS

How long do first partnerships that commenced with cohabitation last? This is not a question with a straightforward answer as estimates of the duration of cohabiting unions need to take into account exit through marriage and exit through dissolution, and for those unions that continue, censoring at the time of the interview. We used life table analysis to estimate the proportions of cohabitations that had converted into marriages or dissolved by a specified time from the start of the union. For those countries where cohabitation is more prevalent Table 3.5 shows the proportions that had converted into marriages and had dissolved within 2 and 5 years for women aged 25–29 and those aged 35–39 at the time of the survey. There is some variation in the propensity to marry across nations and age groups. Sweden exhibits the lowest conversion to marriage with only one in three cohabitations having become marriages within 5 years of the start of the partnership. In most other countries one in two cohabitations have converted to marriages by the fifth anniversary of the union. In many

Table 3.5. Proportions (Derived from Life Table Analysis) of First Cohabiting Unions That Had Converted to Marriages or Dissolved by 2 and 5 Years of Start of Union by Age of Woman

	Married		Dissolved	
Country	2 years	5 years	2 years	5 years
Sweden				
1964[a]	7	30	13	28
1954	15	38	7	15
Norway				
1960[a]	26	51	12	22
1950	62	77	4	9
Finland				
25–29	31	53	9	20
35–39	44	62	6	11
France				
25–29	20	33	9	20
35–39	39	58	4	11
Austria				
25–29	26	53	6	15
35–39	28	48	4	10
Switzerland				
25–29	34	57	11	24
35–39	36	64	7	14
West Germany				
25–29	29	50	11	22
35–39	31	49	5	11
East Germany				
25–29	27	44	7	17
35–39	21	27	5	12

[a]Birth cohorts.

countries there are indications of a decline in the propensity to marry over time, most noticeably in Norway and France, whereas in other countries there is little sign of change, for example, West Germany, and in other signs of an increase, for example, East Germany. Turning to the extent to which cohabiting unions dissolve we see that among the most recent generation, those aged 25–29, that in most countries around 1 in 10 had dissolved by the second anniversary of the start of the union and by the fifth anniversary one in five to one in four unions had dissolved. Elsewhere (Kiernan, 1999) we have examined the dissolution rates of different types of first partnerships in more detail for 10 Western European nations and shown that in all the countries couples who cohabited before marrying their first partner were no more likely to divorce than those who marry without cohabiting. The most fragile partnerships were cohabiting unions that did not convert into marriages.

SUBGROUP DIFFERENCES

So far we have dwelt on cross-national variation in union formation behavior but there are also likely to be distinct variations within nations and between subgroups of the population. The FFS surveys included only a limited amount of background information on the respondents, but we were able to examine three important dimensions, namely, variation according to educational level, religious observance, and experience of parental separation.

Table 3.6 shows the proportions who married directly according to level of education divided into three levels. This is a relatively crude categorization, with level 3 broadly encompassing the graduate group, level 2 a middle group with secondary education, and level 1 a group with presecondary education. The proportions in these three educational groups varies across nations as indicated in the final column of Table 3.6, which shows the proportions of women who had attained graduate or equivalent status. Perusal of Table 3.6 shows that there are no simple observations to be made or a generalizable pattern to be seen with respect to union

Table 3.6. Proportions Married Directly According to Level of Education among Women with a First Partnership and Aged 20–39 Years at the Time of the Survey

Country	Level 1	Level 2	Level 3	Proportion Level 3 (%)
Sweden	10	5	8	33
Finland	14	18	20	17
Norway	—	9	10	50
France	16	9	8	18
West Germany	22	14	21	13
East Germany	21	17	16	30
Austria	22	20	16	19
Switzerland	46	15	20	14
Italy	87	84	79	9
Spain	82	73	65	15
Latvia	—	50	49	20
Lithuania	—	75	74	39
Hungary	77	73	64	13
Poland	95	96	97	14

formation and educational level. In some countries there is little association between educational level and propensity to marry directly as opposed to commencing with a cohabitation, whereas in other countries there is some evidence that those with the lowest level are more likely to marry directly and in yet others there is a curvilinear relationship, with the least educated and the most educated being more likely to marry directly. In Italy, Spain, and Hungary at younger ages (not shown here) there is some indication of cohabitation being most common among the elite group of graduates. This inconsistency in findings in relation to education has been noted by Carmichael (1995) in his extensive review of the literature on cohabitation. Moreover, he points to the research findings for various countries that show educational participation rather than level of educational qualifications has a greater impact on the propensity to cohabit.

Turning to religion Table 3.7 shows the proportions of women who married directly according to whether they attended church on some occasions versus those who reported that they practically never did. From the last column we see that there was some variation in the proportions who responded in this way; as might be expected nonattendance was rare in Italy and Poland and more common in East Germany and Sweden. However, within a given country we see that the proportions who married directly were more likely to attend church than their contemporaries who had commenced their first partnership with a cohabitation. Thus, across Europe cohabitation appears to be associated with the more secular groups within a population.

Table 3.7. Proportions Married Directly According to Some Church Attendance versus None among Women Who Had a Partnership and Aged 20–39 Years at the Time of the Survey[a]

Country	Some Attendance at Church	Never Attends Church	Reporting Never Attended Church (%)
Sweden	12	4	66
Finland	25	14	35
Norway	50	23	67
West Germany	32	16	43
East Germany	23	14	77
Switzerland	31	14	41
Italy	90	81	9
Spain	90	80	53
Latvia	60	51	31
Hungary	82	73	44
Poland	96	88	7

[a]France, Austria, and Lithuania did not include this question.

The final background factor examined is one that is pertinent to changing patterns of union formation, namely, whether there had been experience of parental separation or divorce. There is evidence for the United States and Great Britain [McLanahan and Bumpass, 1988; Thornton, 1991 (United States); Kiernan, 1992] that children who experience parental divorce are more likely to cohabit and have children outside of marriage.

The Fertility and Family Surveys included a question on whether the parents of the respondents had ever separated or divorced and the age at which this occurred. Table 3.8 shows the proportions of women who had married directly according to whether they had experienced parental divorce during childhood. It is clear that in all these countries the proportions marrying directly are invariably higher among those who did not experience parental divorce during childhood than among those who did. This applies in Northern European, Western European, Eastern, and Southern European countries, in countries where marrying directly is rare and cohabitation is normative as in Sweden, and in countries where marrying directly is normative and cohabitation is relatively rare such as Italy. All these differences were statistically significant at the 5% level or less. The preference for cohabiting among children who experienced a parental separation or divorce may well represent reluctance on the part of young

Table 3.8. Percentage Married Directly by Experience of Parental Separation or Divorce at Age 16 or under among Women Aged 20–39 Years at the Time of the Survey

	Married Directly		
Country	*Parental Divorce Yes (%)*	*Parental Divorce No (%)*	*Parental Divorce (%)*
Sweden	3	7	14
Finland[a]	16	21	8
France	14	29	18
West Germany	17	26	14
East Germany	12	18	21
Austria	8	25	13
Switzerland	16	24	14
Italy	65	88	4
Spain	67	86	6
Latvia	46	62	26
Lithuania	72	77	21
Hungary	66	81	17
Poland	85	96	5

[a]Finland did not ask age at parental divorce. Norway did not include a question on parental divorce.

people with such an experience to make a permanent commitment, such as that enshrined in legal marriage. Alternatively, given the experience of parental separation they may want to be more certain about committing to a permanent relationship and may take longer in the search for their ideal partner or in testing the strength of the relationship via cohabitation before committing to marriage. This consistency of the association between parental separation and cohabitation across nations suggests that this finding could be added to the litany of robust associations with respect to contemporary demographic behavior.

POLICY RESPONSES

Links between spouses in the past were deemed to be of sufficient importance that marriages and divorces were included within the scope of vital registration systems. The rise of cohabitation has eroded this public acknowledgment and moreover raises policy questions about the links between partners and their children and their interface with the public domains of life. Many European countries are recognizing that changes are underway and that marriage law, practices, and values and the assumptions on which policies are built are being evaluated. To date there have been a variety of policy responses to the emergence of cohabitation in different European countries.

At the beginning of 1998 the Netherlands, a country with intermediate levels of cohabitation and low rates of nonmarital childbearing, instituted the formal registration of partnerships for both heterosexual and homosexual couples, which made legally registered cohabitation functionally equivalent to marriage, except that cohabiting couples do not have the right to adopt. In the early 1990s, Denmark had instituted the legal registration of homosexual partnerships, but the Netherlands is the first country in Europe to formalize heterosexual cohabitation.

In France, which in terms of cohabitation levels is the most Nordic in that the rise of cohabitation and nonmarital childbearing has followed a trend similar to the developments in the Nordic countries, the government is instituting Civil Solidarity Pacts (PACS), which will allow homosexual and heterosexual couples to enter legal agreements that will give unmarried couples and siblings (coresiding for a minimum of 3 years) inheritance, tax, health, and tenants' rights broadly equivalent to those now held by married couples. In France, the PACS were originally conceived as meeting the demands of gay organizations for a form of legally recognized marriage ceremony. However, to avoid homophobic attacks from the right wing the government broadened the idea to include heterosexuals.

In Sweden, Finland, and Denmark, a more pragmatic approach has been taken. Over time family law has come to be applied to married and cohabiting couples in the same way, recognizing that legislation developed to meet the needs of married couples is also suited to the needs of unmarried couples (Bradley, 1996). In Britain, the Lord Chancellor's Department is due to report on issues pertaining to cohabitation, but the main focus is likely to be on property issues and the proposal in the 1998 Green Paper on the Family (British Government, 1998) that unmarried fathers who register the birth of their child with the mother be given the same automatic rights as married fathers has at present not been executed. Currently, unmarried fathers need a special court order to acquire such rights and very few fathers take advantage of this. In Germany, the protection of the family enshrined in the constitution applies only to marriage and not to "marriage-like partnerships" (Ditch et al., 1996), which implies a principled commitment not to accord equal status to married and cohabiting relationships, although private law could be changed. So just as the phenomenon of cohabitation is diverse and complex the responses to date have been equally variable, suggesting that there are few simple straightforward solutions to this development in family life.

CONCLUSION

This analysis of recently available data on union formation has shown that there is a marked variation in the ways men and women are forming partnerships across European nations. In Southern European countries marriage is still the preeminent marker for entry into first union, whereas in most West and Northern European countries cohabitation has eclipsed marriage as the marker for first partnership, and in the Nordic countries and France long-term cohabitation has become more prevalent. Most European countries appear to be experiencing changes in the ways that men and women become couples, but whether countries are on a trajectory to an ultimate destination where marriage and cohabitation are largely indistinguishable or even where cohabitation overtakes marriage as the dominant form of union awaits the future.

ACKNOWLEDGMENTS

The Economic and Social Research Council UK provided the funding for this project through Grant No. L315 25 3015. The ESRC Data Archive supplied the Eurobarometer data. The Fertility and Family Survey data were supplied by the Population Activities Unit at the UN Economic Commission for Europe at Geneva.

Thanks are also due to the Advisory Group of the FFS programme of comparative research and Statistics Sweden for permission granted under identification Number 06 to use the FFS data on which this study is based.

REFERENCES

Bradley, D. 1996. *Family Law and Political Culture: Scandinavian Laws in Comparative Perspective.* London: Sweet and Maxwell.

British Government. 1998. *Supporting Families: A Consultation Document.* London: Stationery Office.

Carmichael, G. 1995. "Consensual Partnering in the More Developed Countries." *Journal of the Australian Population Association* 12(1):51–86.

Council of Europe. 1997. *Recent Demographic Developments in Europe.* Strasbourg: Council of Europe.

Ditch, J., H. Barnes, and J. Bradshaw. 1996. *A Synthesis of National Family Policies 1995.* Brussels: Commission of the European Communities.

Festy, P. 1980. "On the New Context of Marriage in Western Europe." *Population and Development Review* 6(2):311–315.

Kiernan, K. 1992. "The Impact of Family Disruption in Childhood on Transitions Made in Young Adult Life." *Population Studies* 46(2):213–234.

Kiernan, K. 1999. "Cohabitation in Western Europe." *Population Trends* 96:25–32.

McLanahan, S., and L. Bumpass. 1988. "Intergenerational Consequences of Family Disruption." *American Journal of Sociology* 94:130–152.

Rehr, D. 1998. "Family Ties in Western Europe: Persistent Contrasts." *Population and Development Review* 24(2):203–234.

Thornton, A. 1991. "Influence of Marital History of Parents on the Marital and Cohabitational Experiences of Children." *American Journal of Sociology* 96:868–894.

United Nations. 1992. *Questionnaire and Codebook Fertility and Family Surveys in Countries of the ECE Region.* New York: United Nations.

4

Historical Trends in Marriage Formation: The United States 1850–1990

CATHERINE A. FITCH and STEVEN RUGGLES

The dramatic rise of marriage age and decline in proportion marrying since the 1960s have captured the attention of both academics and the media. It is sometimes forgotten that the 1960s were an exceptional period with respect to marriage behavior. This chapter puts recent changes in marriage patterns into historical perspective by assessing trends and differentials in marriage behavior in the United States over the very long run. Like the studies of Rodgers and Thornton (1985) and Haines (1996), our aim is mainly descriptive. We have expanded on the work of these authors in three dimensions. First, through the use of new data sources and new methods we have extended the series of basic measures of marriage formation backward to the mid-nineteenth century and forward to 1999. Second, we present more precise measures of marital behavior than previous studies of long-run trends in marriage formation. In particular, we present a consistent series of estimates for median age at first marriage, distribution of first marriage age, and proportion never marrying from 1850 through 1999 for native-born whites and from 1870 through 1990 for blacks. Finally, to assess the role of socioeconomic status in marriage formation, we examine the relationship between occupation and male marital status between 1850 and 1990.

DATA AND METHODS

The United States was very late to gather vital statistics on marriage; it was not until 1920 that marriage data were systematically collected from all the states. Even today, the data collected from marriage certificates provide a poor source for studying differentials in marriage patterns because some states gather very limited information. For example, 16 states do not even inquire about the race of the bride and groom, which makes a national analysis of the dramatic race differentials in marriage age impossible using vital statistics. Published tabulations of data from marriage certificates are also highly limited in scope and frequency. For the period after 1990, the National Center for Health Statistics has published no marriage statistics except raw counts of the monthly number of marriages in each state.

Accordingly, analysis of trends and differentials in marriage patterns in the United States must rely on census and survey tabulations of marital status by age. Such data allow calculation of two key measures of marriage behavior: the indirect median age at marriage and the proportion never marrying. The indirect median yields an unbiased age-independent measure of age at first marriage.[1] As described by Shryock and Seigal (1980), the indirect median is calculated in three steps. Step 1 estimates the proportion of people who will ever marry during their lifetime; we calculate this figure as the proportion of persons aged 45–54 who are not married, separated, widowed, or divorced. Second, this proportion is divided in half. The third and final step determines the current age of people at this half-way point through interpolation. For example, if we calculate that 90% of people will eventually marry, one-half of this proportion is 45%; the median age at marriage, then, is the age at which 45% of the population has married. We also measure the age at which 10, 25, and 75% of the population have married according to the same methodology (Shryock and Seigel, 1980; U.S. Bureau of the Census, 1975).

This analysis is based on the Integrated Public Use Microdata Series (IPUMS). The IPUMS consists of individual-level national samples of census data from 1850 to 1990 (with the exception of 1890 and 1930). When possible, we have used published tables from the 1890 and 1930 Census to fill these gaps.[2] Because of rapid changes over the past decade, we have also included data from the 1999 Current Population Survey (CPS).[3]

In the 1850, 1860, and 1870 census years, the census did not inquire about marital status. Fortunately, we do not need to know the exact marital status of individuals in order to compute the basic measures of nuptiality; we simply estimate the proportion of persons who were never married (single) and the proportion who are ever married (including the married, divorced, and widowed population) for each age. To do this, we created family interrelationship variables in the IPUMS, using a probabilistic approach to identify spouses and children within the household. We used 17 characteristics such as surname, sequence of enumeration, age, and birthplace (Ruggles et al., 1998) to infer ever-married status. The American census has always been taken on a *de jure* basis, so spouses are ordinarily listed as present in their usual place of residence even if they are temporarily absent. Widowed persons usually can be identified by the presence of children. The childless widowed or divorced population, however, cannot be identified in this way. Moreover, some never-married persons living with children are incorrectly identified as ever married. Analysis of the 1880 census suggests that this slippage has minor effects on estimates of marriage age, and requires only modest adjustments of age-specific proportions married (Fitch, 1998).

Unlike previous studies, our analysis excludes persons born outside the United States. Our main measure, the indirect median age at first marriage, is based on the concept of a synthetic cohort: age differences in the proportion ever married are treated as if they were changes over the life course. We need to know the marital status of the population at each age, but at the peak marriage ages many foreign-born immigrants had not yet arrived. If there were any association between marital status and immigration, the problem would be compounded. Thus, because the foreign-born population spent part of their life outside of the area of observation, they can bias the results of synthetic cohort measures.

In addition, for the period prior to 1870 our analysis excludes blacks. Although most slaves entered enduring marital unions, formal marriage was prohibited, and the 1850 and 1860 censuses did not enumerate the slave population with sufficient detail to study marriage patterns. Moreover, the free black population is subject to the same sort of biases as the foreign-born population, and the samples of free blacks are too small to produce conclusive results.[4]

MARRIAGE AGE BEFORE 1850

In one of the landmark essays of historical demography, John Hajnal (1965) revealed that the historic marriage pattern of Western Europe differed dramatically from that of other parts of Europe and from the rest of the world. This "European Marriage Pattern," as Hajnal termed it, was characterized by very late marriage for both men and women and by high proportions of individuals never marrying. At least as far back as the eighteenth century, Hajnal demonstrated, the mean age at first marriage for Western-European women generally varied from 24 to 27, and for men from 26 to 30. About a sixth of the European population never got married at all.

Hajnal explained the European marriage pattern by reference to the economic system, land availability, and family. Before the Industrial Revolution, Western-European couples were generally required to achieve economic independence before they were allowed to marry. In other parts of Europe and elsewhere in the World, Hajnal maintained, such economic independence was not a prerequisite to marriage; in many areas young couples were incorporated into large joint-family households together with parents and married siblings. This kind of family was exceedingly rare in Western Europe. Instead, couples often delayed marriage until the prospective bridegroom inherited the family farm. Decreasing land availability significantly constrained the economic opportunities of young couples. The problem was compounded when mortality began to decline in the late nineteenth century, since the previous generation stayed alive longer and an increasing number of siblings survived to adulthood (Hajnal, 1965).

According to the consensus of scholarly opinion, the timing and rate of marriage in the United States differed from that of Western Europe from the outset, even though the bulk of immigrants came from Western Europe. Observers as early as Ben Franklin noted the distinction between the European colonies in North America and European marriage patterns. After a discussion of births, deaths, and marriages in the colonies, Franklin concluded

> Hence marriages in *America* are more general and more generally early, than in *Europe*. And if it is reckoned there, that there is but one marriage per annum among one hundred persons, perhaps we may here reckon two; and if in *Europe* they have but four Births to a marriage (many of the marriages being late) we may here reckon eight. (Franklin, 1755, quoted in Haines, 1996:16)

The difference, according to Franklin and later scholars, was not the adaptation of a non-Western European model of family and economic structure (incorporating young couples into large households) but instead the bountiful economic opportunity offered young men either through cheap land or from wage labor in urban areas (Easterlin, 1976; Landale, 1989a,b; Leet, 1977; Yasuba, 1962).

We lack sufficient reliable data for the colonial period or for the United States as a whole before 1850 to make confident generalizations about either age at first marriage or about proportions never marrying. There are scattered estimates of marriage age from particular communities, mainly in New England, that suggest a mean age at marriage of perhaps 25.5 for men and 22.0 for women in the eighteenth century (Wells, 1992; Haines, 1996). These figures, however, are seriously biased downward by methodological problems.

The problems with the colonial estimates are twofold. First, unlike the measures of marriage age used by Hajnal and others (including the SMAM and indirect median), the measures of marriage age used in the colonial studies are not age independent. Because of very high fertility and high mortality (by modern standards) in the colonial period, the population was extremely young. Compared with the age-independent measure of marriage age used by Hajnal, this problem alone would bias the colonial estimates of age at marriage downward by at least half a year, and perhaps as much as a year. Second, the colonial estimates are subject to severe migration censoring, a technical problem Ruggles has explored in detail (Ruggles, 1992, 1999). We expect that migration censoring could bias the colonial estimates of marriage age downward by an additional 1 to 3 years.

For these reasons, we do not believe that the existing evidence for North America before 1850 is sufficient to confirm Franklin's hypothesis. If anything, we think the fragmentary colonial evidence suggests a broad similarity between North America and Western Europe.

MEDIAN AGE AT MARRIAGE AMONG WHITES, 1850–1998

Figure 4.1 shows our estimates of median age at first marriage for native-born whites from 1850 through 1999 (Table 4.1 in the appendix presents the underlying statistics). In 1850, native-born white men married at a median age of 25.3 and women at 21.3. These figures are somewhat lower than Hajnal's figures cited above, but that is partly because we are measuring the median rather than the mean, and median age at marriage is generally about a year and a half earlier than the mean age. Using Hajnal's method (1953), we estimate that the mean age at marriage for white Americans was 26.6 for men and 22.9 for women in 1850. Thus, marriage age for men in the mid-nineteenth century was close to the European marriage pattern, but for women it was probably slightly younger. For both men and women, marriage in mid-nineteenth century America generally took place at a significantly later age than in most countries outside of Western Europe (Haines, 1996; Hajnal, 1965).

Median age at marriage remained stable for white women from 1850 through 1870 but dropped noticeably for men after the Civil War. By 1890, however, marriage age for whites of both sexes rose still further to a peak of about 26 years for men and 22 for women. In a study of regional differences in the timing and incidence of marriage, Hacker reports a sharp decline in marriage age between 1860 and 1870 among Southern men and an increase among Southern women, presumably due to high wartime mortality (Hacker, 1999). Other researchers argue that the increase in age at first marriage at the end of the century was related to declining availability of land, which restricted opportunities for family formation (Easterlin, 1976; Landale, 1989a,b; Leet, 1977; Yasuba, 1962).

During the early decades of the twentieth century, marriage age among whites dropped substantially for men and somewhat less dramatically for women. Overall, white male age at first marriage fell by about 2 years between 1890 and 1930. This is probably associated with the growth of well-paid wage labor employment for men. In the rapidly industrializing

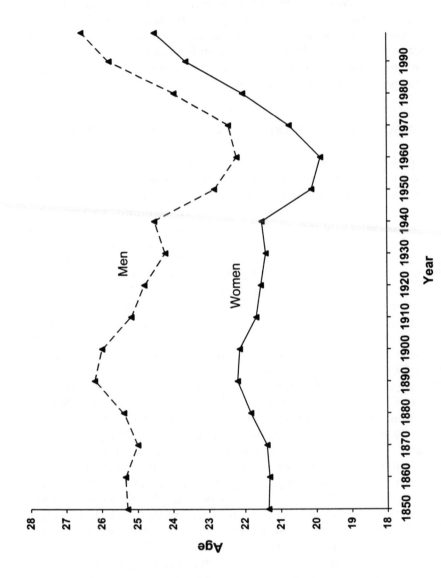

Figure 4.1. Median age at first marriage: native-born whites by sex, 1850–1999.

economy, young native-born white men increasing could find jobs that provided sufficient income to support a family.

There was a slight uptick in marriage age for whites during the depression, but after World War II there was an unprecedented marriage boom. The median age at marriage fell by 2.3 years for white men and 1.5 years for white women in just two decades. By 1960, median age at marriage was just 22 for white men and under 20 for white women. Again, this change was driven at least in part by the postwar economic expansion, which increased opportunities for young men dramatically, particularly in contrast with their depression-era childhood (Easterlin, 1980).

The most dramatic changes in white marriage age have occurred in the decades since 1960. White female age at first marriage has been rising by about 1 year per decade for the past 39 years. The increase for men started a decade later than it did for women, but since 1970 the trend has been virtually the same. By 1999, marriage age for both men and women actually exceeded the peak reached at the turn of the century.

MEDIAN AGE AT MARRIAGE AMONG BLACKS, 1870–1998

The long run trends in marriage age among blacks, shown in Figure 4.2 (and recorded in Table 4.2 of the appendix), differ dramatically from those of whites. From 1870 through 1940, the trends in black age at marriage for both men and women followed the trends for whites quite closely, but blacks on average were married about 2 years younger than whites. Earlier marriage among blacks may reflect lower expectations about life course economic opportunity; blacks often remained farm tenants throughout their lives and even nonfarm blacks experienced little upward occupational mobility (Landale and Tolnay, 1991; Sobek, 1997). Thus, black men and women had little incentive to delay marriage until they achieved economic success.

After 1940, black trends in marriage age diverged dramatically from those of whites. Whereas marriage age for whites plummeted during this period, there was essentially no postwar marriage boom for blacks. In fact, among black men the median age at marriage was rising slightly from 1940 to 1960. Among black women, there was a very slight dip in marriage age in 1950, but by 1960—the nadir of marriage age for whites—black female marriage age was as high as it had ever been.

By 1960, the historic race differential in marriage age had reversed: blacks were marrying slightly later than whites, not earlier. After 1970 marriage age rose substantially faster for blacks than for whites, and by 1990 blacks were marrying at a median age of 27.3 among women and 28.6 among men. As we will discuss later, the reasons behind the recent rise of

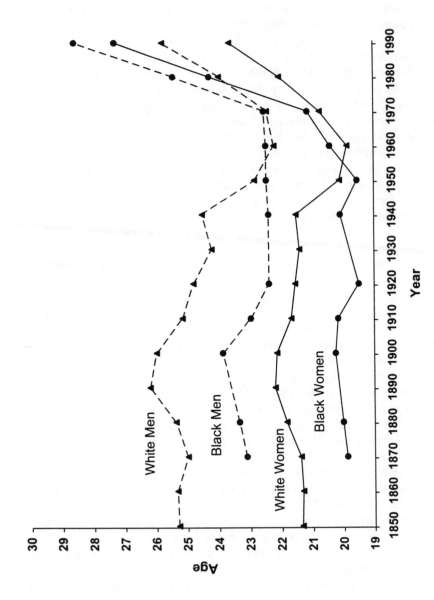

Figure 4.2.   Median age at first marriage: blacks and native-born whites by sex, 1850–1990.

marriage age are doubtless similar for blacks and for whites, but it is not yet clear why the increase was greater for blacks. Although the number of cases in the Current Population Survey data does not provide conclusive results for 1999, preliminary statistics suggest that the rate of increase in marriage age may have slowed considerably.[5]

DISTRIBUTION OF FIRST MARRIAGE

Age at first marriage is not fully described by the median. The census provides sufficient information to estimate the *distribution* of marriage ages. We assess the age at which 10, 25, 50, and 75% of the population had married in each census year.[6] The marriage age distributions are presented separately for native-born white men and women, and black men and women in Figures 4.3 through 4.6 (and Tables 4.1 and 4.2 of the appendix). These figures suggest that prior to 1950 the distribution of marriage age was relatively stable and quite broad for all four groups. The 10th and 25th percentiles in particular remained almost constant before World War II; the only exceptions to this stability were subtle fluctuations at the 50th and 75th percentiles.

For whites, however, the marriage boom in the postwar period was accompanied by a closer distribution of marriage age and the smallest difference between the 10th and 75th quartiles throughout the whole period. In 1960 the interquartile range for white women was only 3.5 years, compared to an average of nearly 6 years in previous decades. The interquartile range for white men decreased from an average of almost 7 years to 4.5 years. By 1980, however, the distribution had returned to prewar levels for both men and women. In the past three decades, the distribution has broadened further and ages for all percentiles have risen to unprecedented levels. Several investigators have argued that the United States became a more age-graded society during the course of the twentieth century (see discussion in Stevens, 1990). With a continuous series of observations throughout the course of the century, our analysis modifies that interpretation of life course transitions. The extremely narrow marriage age distribution of the postwar period now appears a short-run anomaly.

Among blacks, by contrast, there was little narrowing of the distribution of marriage after World War II. This trend is related to the absence of a marriage boom among blacks. The distributional data for blacks also highlights the magnitude of the marriage bust for blacks since 1970. Only 10% of black women in 1990 had married by age 20; before 1970, over half had married by that age.

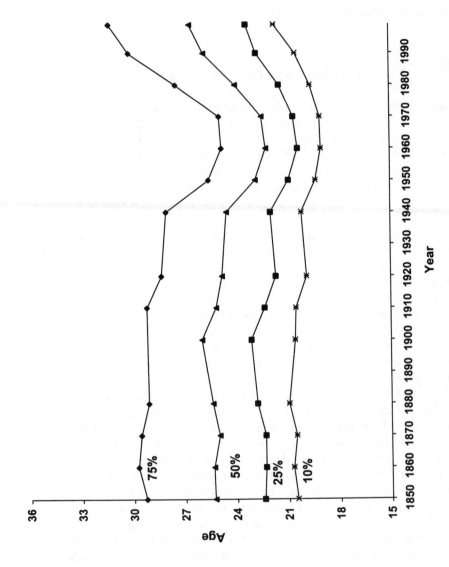

Figure 4.3.   Age at which 10, 15, 50, and 75% of native-born white men have married, 1850–1999.

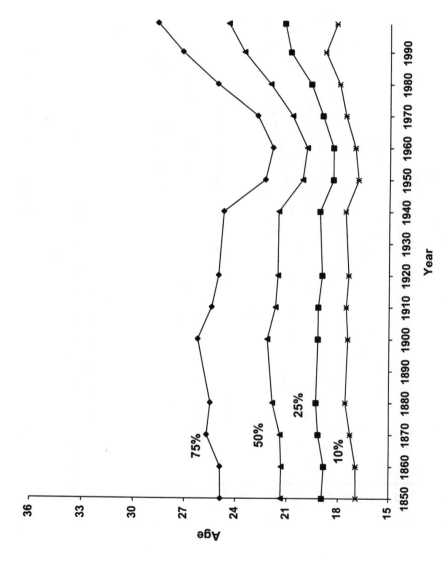

Figure 4.4. Age at which 10, 25, 50, and 75% of native-born white women have married, 1850–1999.

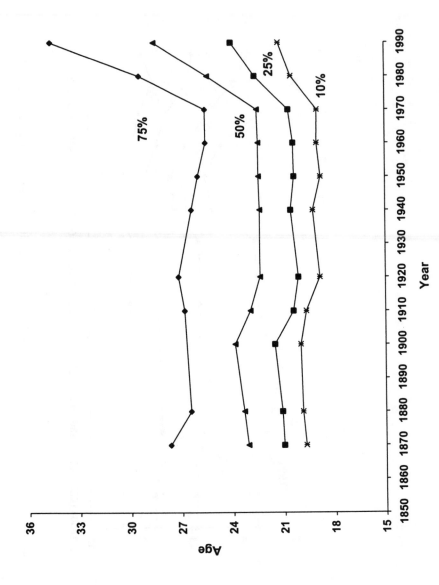

Figure 4.5.   Age at which 10, 25, 50, and 75% of black men have married, 1870–1990.

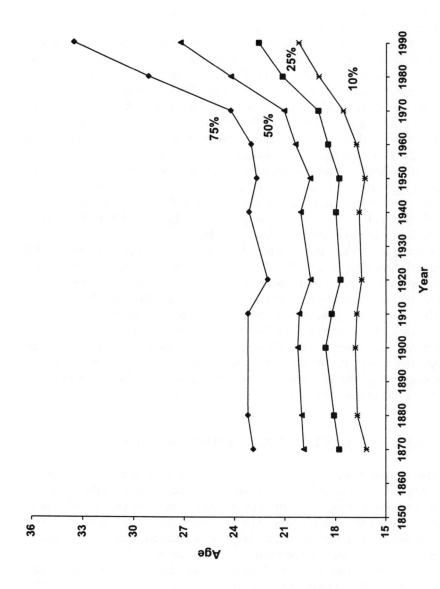

Figure 4.6. Age at which 10, 25, 50, and 75% of black women have married, 1870–1990.

PROPORTION NEVER MARRYING

A key indicator of the Northwestern European marriage pattern, as described by Hajnal, was the high proportion of men and women who remained never married. We measure nonmarriage as the percentage of individuals ages 45 to 54 listed as single. As seen in Figure 4.7, the proportion of whites never married follows a pattern similar to the trend in age at first marriage with a 20 to 30 year lag. For example, the peak in proportion never married was 1920 for white men and women; this same cohort of individuals married late in 1890 and 1900. These similarities suggest that determinates of marriage patterns have strong cohort effects, and that if the marriage age for a cohort is late, the proportion never married also will be high. If this statement is true, we could hypothesize that marriage age for women was on the rise prior to 1850 and that it was fairly stable for white men at that time. Similarly, given the recent dramatic rise in marriage age, it is likely that an unprecedented proportion of the current generation will never marry (Bloom and Bennett, 1990).

Among blacks the proportion never marrying, as seen in Figure 4.8, does not significantly lag behind the trends in median age at marriage. For black women in particular, consistently low proportions of never marrying and an early age at first marriage mark the period from 1870 to 1950. At the same time, these measures fluctuated more significantly for black men, but without evidence of the cohort effect demonstrated by whites. Since 1960, marriage was declining for all age groups of blacks and the proportion never marrying rose simultaneously with the median age at marriage. Thus, the recent rise in nonmarriage among blacks is apparently a period rather than the cohort effect (Table 4.3).

OCCUPATIONAL DIFFERENTIALS

The chronological patterns we have described suggest that marriage formation was powerfully influenced by economic circumstances. Several analysts have argued that changes in male economic opportunity since 1970 hindered the establishment of households and thus contributed to the unprecedented delay in marriage. Some of these studies, particularly those concerning race differentials, have demonstrated a significant connection between male economic circumstances and marriage timing (Bennett et al., 1989; Fossett and Kiecolt, 1993; Lichter et al., 1991, 1992; Oppenheimer, 1994; Oppenheimer et al., 1997; Testa and Krogh, 1995; Wilson and Neckerman, 1987). Unlike previous research our analysis will assess the effects of male occupational status on marriage for the entire period from 1850 through 1990 using the IPUMS. Because occupations

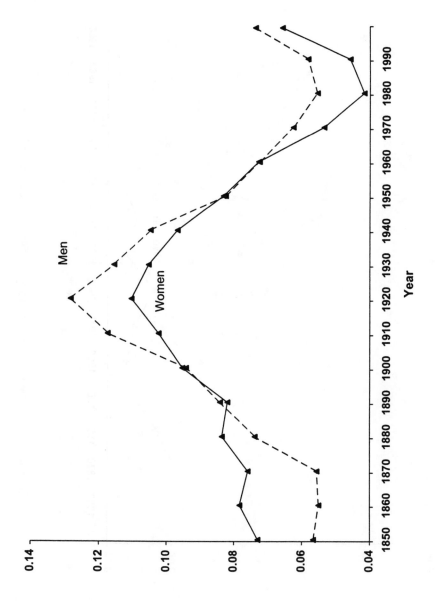

Figure 4.7. Proportion never married ages 45–54: native-born whites by sex, 1850–1999.

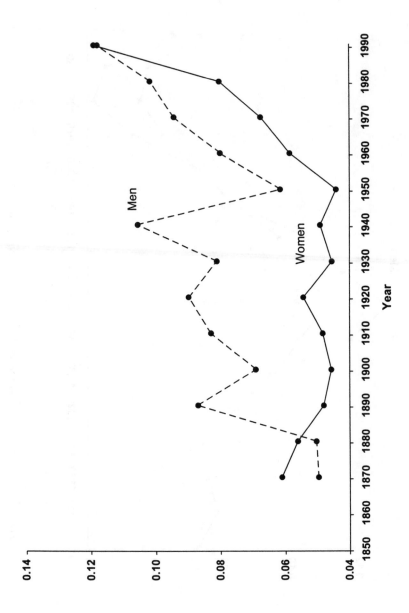

Figure 4.8. Proportion never married ages 45–54: blacks by sex, 1870–1990.

change over the life course, measures of marriage formation based on a synthetic cohort—such as the indirect median age at marriage—are inappropriate. Instead, we simply measure the percentage of men aged 22–27 who are never married.[7] Figure 4.9 shows the percentage of white and black men aged 22–27 never married in each year from 1850 through 1990.[8] The chronological trends for the percentage never married closely follow the trends in median age at first marriage. Note in particular that there was a pronounced marriage boom among whites in the decades following World War II, but virtually no marriage boom among blacks.

Figure 4.10 shows the percentage never married among 22- to 27-year-old whites broken down into five occupational categories: persons not in the labor force (including students), farm workers, and three categories of nonfarm workers. The nonfarm occupations are coded into three groups, based on the median earnings of each occupational title in 1950. Occupations with median 1950 earnings of $2000 or less are classified as "lower nonfarm," those with earnings between $2000 and $2600 are "middle nonfarm," and those with earnings of more than $2600 are "higher nonfarm."

As would be expected, young white men not in the labor force were more often unmarried than were any other group. Farm workers married earlier than nonfarm workers until 1920, perhaps because farming was a family enterprise that depended on female labor (Landale, 1989a). Differences among the three nonfarm occupational groups were modest. In the nineteenth century, those with low-earning occupations married earliest, but by 1900 there was a clear inverse relationship between occupational status and marriage age: those in the highest-paying jobs married earliest, and those with the poorest jobs delayed marriage longest. The marriage boom described earlier is evident in all five occupational groups.

The occupational patterns of marriage for black men, shown in Figure 4.11, are very similar: Those out of the labor force were most often unmarried and in the early period farm workers were usually married. The nonfarm patterns are less clearcut than the comparable patterns for whites, partly because of the small number of cases in the middle- and high-earnings groups before the mid- twentieth century. Nevertheless, in most years the lowest earning group did marry slightly later than the higher earning groups. The most striking result in Figure 4.11 is that the postwar marriage boom is clearly visible in every occupational group except for farmers, although by 1950, farmers represented a small minority of the black population. How, then, can we explain the absence of a marriage boom among black men as a whole?

The answer is revealed in Figure 4.12, which illustrates the occupational distribution of young black men from 1880 through 1990. In 1940, farming was still a major occupation for blacks, employing 31.7% of young men. With the introduction of automated cotton harvesters and other

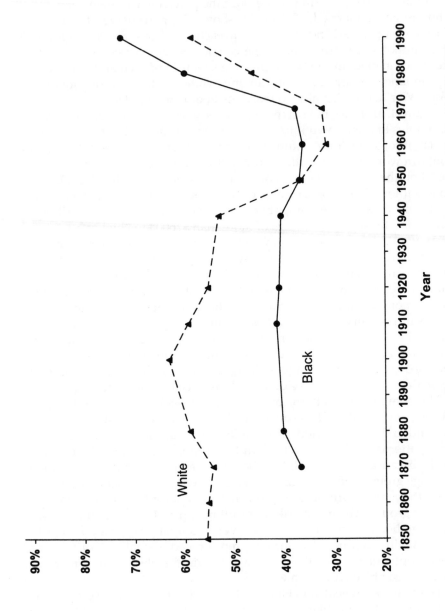

Figure 4.9. Percentage never married: black and native-born white men ages 22–27, 1850–1990.

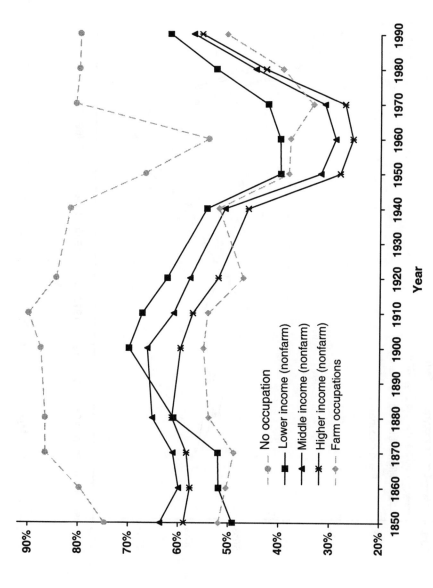

Figure 4.10. Percentage never married: native-born white men ages 22–27, by occupational group, 1850–1990.

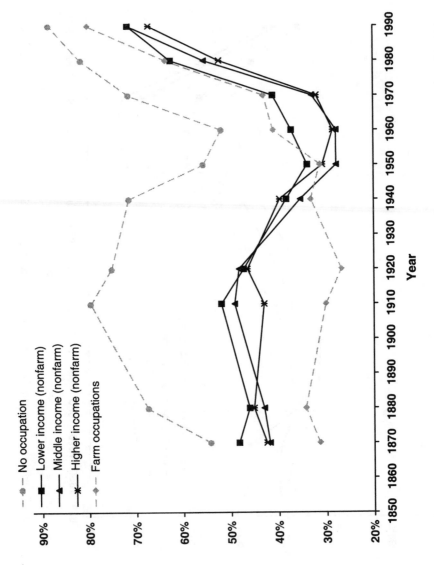

Figure 4.11. Percentage never married: black men ages 22–27, by occupational group, 1870–1990.

improvements in agricultural productivity, millions of blacks—many of them sharecroppers—were forced off the land (Grossman, 1989). By 1960, only 6.5% of young blacks remained on the farm. Many of the displaced farm workers found employment in the nonfarm sector, but millions were forced out of the labor market altogether. The percentage of young black men not in the labor force rose from 9.5% in 1940 (a depression year) to 16.8% in 1950 and to 22.3% in 1960.

The shift in the occupational composition of the black population explains the paradox of a marriage boom within each occupational group but no marriage boom for African-Americans as a whole. Were it not for the compositional shift from farming to nonworkforce, we would see a pronounced postwar marriage boom for blacks as well as for whites. During the economic boom of the 1960s, young blacks fared slightly better. By 1970 only 16.8% were not in the labor force and growing numbers of young blacks entered the middle and upper occupational groups. Since then, however, the employment situation for young blacks has worsened. By 1990, an all time high of 25.3% of young black men were not in the labor force. The grim economic prospects for young black men throughout the postwar period clearly have played a major role in the declining likelihood of marriage among blacks.

Employment trends for young whites were significantly different, as shown in Figure 4.13. The drop in agricultural employment for whites was both earlier and more gradual than it was for blacks. There was a slight increase in the percentage not in the labor force after the war, but this partly reflected a huge increase in higher education. Between 1940 and 1960, the most notable shift for young whites was the growth in higher earning nonfarm occupations—the occupational group most associated with early marriage. This trend, however, ceased after 1970. Between 1980 and 1990 employment of young whites in lower-earning jobs once again began to grow, which helps to explain the rise in marriage age during this period.

Changing female occupational structure also had profound implications for the dramatic change in marriage age for both blacks and whites since 1970. The independence theory of marriage formation posits that women will delay marriage if other more attractive alternatives are present (Goldsheider and Waite, 1986; Waite and Spitze, 1981). The growth of women's educational attainment, job opportunities, and wages since 1970 has substantially decreased women's economic dependence on a spouse. Because female labor force participation is often contingent on marital status we cannot carry out individual-level analysis measuring the affect of occupation on marriage behavior. Several studies, however, that have used longitudinal data and contextual analysis also show that the rise of female employment and the increase in female wages afforded many

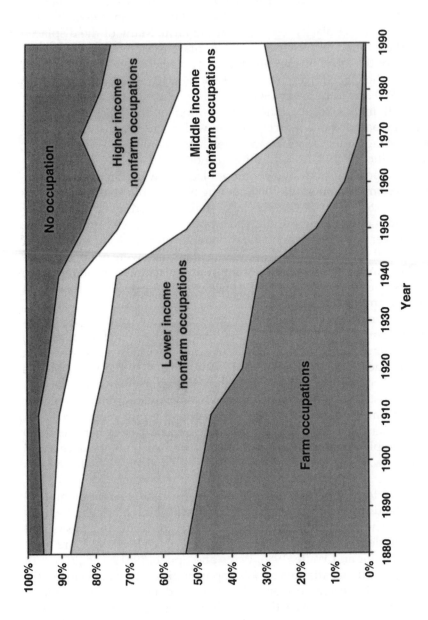

Figure 4.12. Occupational distribution of black men ages 22–27, 1880–1990.

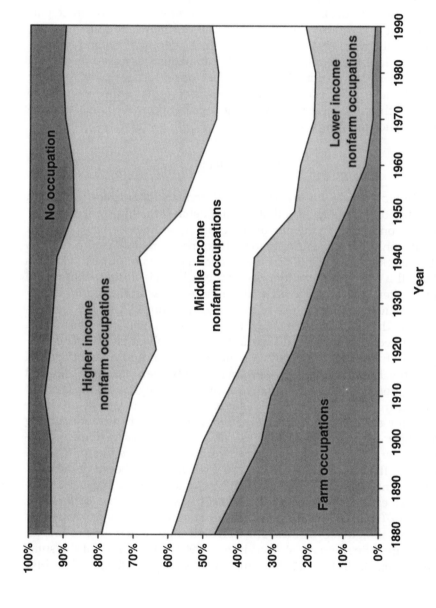

Figure 4.13. Occupational distribution of native-born white men ages 22–27, 1880–1990.

women the possibility of delaying marriage (McLanahan and Casper, 1995; Preston and Richards, 1975; Waite and Spitze, 1981).

In addition, the decline of young male wage rates and workforce participation after 1970 also contributed to delayed marriage (Lichter et al., 1992; Oppenheimer, 1994; Oppenheimer et al., 1997; Wilson and Neckerman, 1987). To date, no analyses have simultaneously assessed the impact of changing male and female employment opportunities over the long run. We believe that taken together these factors have the potential to explain much of the increase in marriage age between 1960 and the mid-1990s, but such analysis is beyond the scope of this study.[9]

SUMMARY

This broad overview of trends and differentials in marriage formation in the United States suggests that marital behavior is highly sensitive to economic conditions. In the nineteenth century, white Americans married fairly late, only slightly earlier than their counterparts in Western Europe. The United States in the late nineteenth century may not quite fit Hajnal's model of the West European marriage pattern, but it is closer to that model than to Eastern Europe or to virtually anywhere else in the world. In any case, it is plausible that the rise of marriage age from 1870 to 1890 reflects a decline in the availability of land. From a peak in 1890, white age at marriage declined gradually until 1930 and precipitously after 1940. The marriage boom for whites coincided with the economic boom, and both ended shortly after 1970. By 1999, whites were marrying even later than they had at the beginning of the century. This long-run view highlights the fact that the period from 1950 to 1970 is a historic anomaly, and an inappropriate baseline for research on marriage patterns. The long-run trends among blacks differ significantly from those of whites. Blacks married significantly earlier than did whites and were ultimately more likely to marry throughout the period from 1870 to 1940. The marriage boom of the postwar period had virtually no impact on blacks, apparently because of economic dislocations that occurred as blacks were forced out of farming. Between 1970 and 1990 black marriage age shot up more than 6 years, to a level higher than that of whites. The CPS data suggest that the rise in marriage age may finally have slowed in the 1990s, but because of the small number of blacks in the CPS, we must await Census 2000 for a definitive measure.

APPENDIX

See Tables 4.1, 4.2, and 4.3.

Table 4.1. Age at Which 10, 25, 50, and 75% of Native-Born White Men and Women Have Married, United States, 1850–1999

	10%	25%	50%	75%	Interquartile Range
Native-born white men					
1850	20.7	22.3	25.3	29.7	7.4
1860	20.5	22.3	25.0	29.6	7.2
1870	20.5	22.3	25.0	29.5	7.2
1880	21.0	22.8	25.4	29.1	6.3
1900	20.6	23.1	26.0		
1910	20.5	22.3	25.2	29.2	6.9
1920	19.9	21.7	24.8	28.3	6.6
1940	20.2	22.0	24.5	28.0	6.1
1950	19.3	20.9	22.8	25.5	4.6
1960	19.0	20.4	22.2	24.8	4.4
1970	19.1	20.6	22.4	24.9	4.3
1980	19.6	21.4	23.9	27.4	6.0
1990	20.5	22.7	25.8	30.1	7.4
1999	21.7	23.3	26.6	31.3	8.0
Native-born white women					
1850	17.0	18.8	21.3	24.9	6.0
1860	17.3	19.2	21.4	25.7	6.5
1870	17.3	19.1	21.2	25.5	6.4
1880	17.6	19.3	21.8	25.5	6.2
1900	17.4	19.2	22.1		
1910	17.5	19.2	21.7	25.4	6.2
1920	17.4	19.0	21.5	25.0	6.0
1940	17.6	19.1	21.5	24.7	5.6
1950	16.9	18.3	20.1	22.3	4.0
1960	17.0	18.3	19.9	21.9	3.5
1970	17.6	19.0	20.7	22.8	3.8
1980	18.0	19.6	22.0	25.1	5.5
1990	18.8	20.8	23.6	27.2	6.3
1999	18.1	21.2	24.5	28.6	7.4

Sources: Integrated Public Use Microdata Series; Current Population Survey (Basic Monthly Survey, January–July, 1999).

Table 4.2.   Age at Which 10, 25, 50, and 75% of Black Men and Women Have Married, United States, 1870–1990

	10%	25%	50%	75%	Interquartile Range
Black men					
1870	19.7	21.0	23.1	27.7	6.6
1880	19.9	21.1	23.3	26.5	5.3
1900	20.0	21.5	23.9		
1910	19.7	20.4	23.0	26.8	6.4
1920	18.9	20.1	22.4	27.1	7.0
1940	19.3	20.6	22.4	26.4	5.8
1950	18.8	20.4	22.4	26.0	5.6
1960	19.0	20.4	22.5	25.5	5.1
1970	19.0	20.7	22.5	25.6	4.9
1980	20.5	22.6	25.4	29.4	6.8
1990	21.2	24.0	28.6	34.7	10.7
Black women					
1870	16.2	17.8	19.9	22.9	5.1
1880	16.7	18.1	20.0	23.2	5.1
1900	16.8	18.6	20.3		
1910	16.8	18.3	20.2	23.2	5.0
1920	16.5	17.7	19.5	22.0	4.3
1940	16.6	18.0	20.1	23.2	5.1
1950	16.3	17.8	19.5	22.7	4.9
1960	16.8	18.5	20.4	23.0	4.6
1970	17.6	19.1	21.1	24.3	5.2
1980	19.0	21.2	24.3	29.2	8.0
1990	20.2	22.6	27.3	33.6	11.0

Source: Integrated Public Use Microdata Series.

Table 4.3. Percentage of Native-Born Whites and Blacks Never Married, Ages 45–54 by Sex, United States 1850–1998

	Native-Born White		Black	
	Men	*Women*	*Men*	*Women*
1850	5.7	7.3		
1860	5.5	7.8		
1870	5.6	7.6	5.0	6.1
1880	7.4	8.3	5.0	5.6
1890	8.4	8.2	8.7	4.8
1900	9.4	9.5	6.9	4.6
1910	11.7	10.2	8.3	4.8
1920	12.8	11.0	9.0	5.4
1930	11.5	10.5	8.1	4.6
1940	10.5	9.7	10.5	4.9
1950	8.2	8.3	6.1	4.4
1960	7.3	7.3	8.0	5.8
1970	6.3	5.4	9.4	6.7
1980	5.6	4.2	10.2	8.0
1990	5.8	4.6	11.8	11.9
1999	7.4	6.6		

Sources: Integrated Public Use Microdata Series; Current Population Survey (March Survey and Basic Monthly Survey January–July, 1999); "Marital Conditions," Table 82 in *Report on Population of the United States at the Eleventh Census: 1890* (Washington, DC: G.P.O, 1895); "Marital Conditions," Table 5, Chapter 11 in *Population, Volume II of the Fifteenth Census of the United States: 1930* (Washington, DC: G.P.O., 1933).

NOTES

1.   We prefer the indirect median measure of marriage to the singulate mean age at marriage (SMAM) widely used by historians, because it provides more precise period estimates when marriage age is changing rapidly (Fitch, 1998). The indirect median may differ slightly from the true median age at marriage because the proportion of people who will ever marry is estimated based on the population aged 45–54 at the time of the census, and this may not accurately predict the proportion of younger people who will eventually marry. For the period before 1950, we can evaluate the magnitude of this error because we know the actual proportion of the population that eventually did marry. In practice, the difference between the period-based indirect median and the true cohort median age at marriage is generally less than two-tenths of a year, but in theory the error could go as high as half a year in periods of very rapid change.

2.   In Figure 4.1, the age at marriage for 1890 and 1930 represents an adjustment of the published Census Bureau marriage age figures for the total population (U.S. Bureau of the Census, 1975). We have adjusted these figures based on the difference between the age at marriage of native-born whites and total population in the surrounding census years.

3.   We used all basic monthly surveys available for 1999 (January–July), but we have sufficient cases to study only the native-born white population. Our analysis of the black population will not extend to 1999.

4.   We also exclude persons who were neither white nor black. Although by 1999 the white–black dichotomy excludes significant portions of the population, these are the only two racial groups large enough throughout the 120-year period to produce accurate statistics. Most native-born Hispanics are included in the white population, although some are classified as blacks.

5.   We calculated the median age at marriage as 29.9 for men and 29.1 for women when using 5-year age groups in the interpolation step. Although this technique allows us to make an estimate with the limited number of cases in the 1999 CPS, Shryock and Seigel (1980) warn that indirect medians based on 5-year intervals are much less precise.

6.   We attempted to measure the 90th percentile of marriage age as well, but we found that the slope of the marriage curve is so gradual at higher ages that short-run period disturbances have the potential to bias the results significantly. In 1900, the sample with the smallest number of cases, we also excluded the 75th percentile because of the volatile fluctuations in percentage married at the older ages.

7.   We chose years 22 to 27 as the age range because it includes the median age at first marriage for native-born white men for all years between 1850 and 1990.

8.   We have excluded 1900 for blacks because the 1900 public use sample does not provide enough cases to analyze this subpopulation.

9.   This contradicts the statement by Ruggles (1997) that first marriages were not greatly affected by female workforce participation. We now think that preliminary analysis was incorrect. We are in the process of carrying out a new geographic analysis of the effects of male and female economic opportunity on the proportion of young men and women entering marriage. The new analysis uses better economic measures than the work reported earlier and focuses exclusively on the economic opportunities of young people.

REFERENCES

Bennett, Neil G., David E. Bloom, and Patricia H. Craig. 1989. "The Divergence of Black and White Marriage Patterns." *American Journal of Sociology* 95:692–722.

Bloom, David E., and N. Bennett. 1990. "Modeling American Marriage Patterns." *Journal of the American Statistical Association* 85:1009–1017.

Easterlin, Richard A. 1976. "Factors in the Decline of Farm Fertility in the United States: Some Preliminary Research Results." *Journal of American History* 63:600–614.

Easterlin, Richard A. 1980. *Birth and Fortune: The Impact of Numbers on Personal Welfare*. New York: Basic Books.

Fitch, Catherine A. 1998. "Marriage Age in Nineteenth Century United States." Presented at the annual meeting of the Population Association of America, Chicago, IL.

Fossett, Mark A., and K. Jill Kiecolt. 1993. "Mate Availability and Family Structure Among African Americans in U.S. Metropolitan Areas." *Journal of Marriage and the Family* 55:288–302.

Goldscheider, Frances K., and Linda J. Waite. 1986. "Sex Differences in the Entry to Marriage." *American Journal of Sociology* 92:91–109.

Grossman, James R. 1989. *Land of Hope: Chicago, Black Southerners, and the Great Migration*. Chicago: University of Chicago Press.

Hacker, J. David. 1999. *The Human Cost of War: White Population in the United States, 1850–1880*. Ph.D. dissertation, Department of History, University of Minnesota, Minneapolis, MN.

Haines, Michael R. 1996. "Long-Term Marriage Patterns in the United States from Colonial Times to the Present." *The History of the Family* 1:15–39.

Hajnal, John. 1953. "Age at Marriage and Proportion Marrying." *Population Studies* 7:111–136.

Hajnal, John. 1965. "European Marriage Patterns in Perspective." Pp. 101–138 in *Population in History*, edited by D. V. Glass and D. E. C. Eversley. Chicago: Aldine.

Landale, N. S. 1989a. "Agricultural Opportunity and Marriage: The United States at the Turn of the Century." *Demography* 26:203–217.

Landale, N.S. 1989b. "Opportunity, Movement, and Marriage: U.S. Farm Sons at the Turn of the Century." *Journal of Family History* 14:365–386.

Landale, Nancy S., and Stuart E. Tolnay. 1991. "Group Differences in Economic Opportunity and the Timing of Marriage: Blacks and Whites in the Rural South, 1910." *American Sociological Review* 56:33–45.

Leet, Don R. 1977. "Interrelations of Population Density, Urbanization, Literacy, and Fertility." *Explorations in Economic History* 14:388–401.

Lichter, Daniel T., Felicia B. LeClere, and Diane K. McLaughlin. 1991. "Local Marriage Markets and the Marital Behavior of Black and White Women." *American Journal of Sociology* 96:843–867.

Lichter, Daniel T., Diane K. McLaughlin, George Kephart, and David J. Landry. 1992. "Race and the Retreat from Marriage: A Shortage of Marriageable Men?" *American Sociological Review* 57:781–799.

McLanahan, Sara, and Lynne Casper. 1995. "Growing Diversity and Inequality in the American Family." Pp. 1–46 in *State of the Union: America in the 1990s*, Vol. 2, edited by R. Farley. New York: Russell Sage Foundation.

Oppenheimer, Valerie K. 1994. "Women's Rising Employment and the Future of Families in Industrial Societies." *Population and Development Review* 20: 293–342.

Oppenheimer, Valerie K., Matthijs Kalmijn, and Nelson Lim. 1997. "Men's Career Development and Marriage Timing During a Period of Rising Inequality." *Demography* 34:311–330.

Preston, Samuel H., and Alan Thomas Richards. 1975. "The Influence of Women's Work Opportunities on Marriage Rates." *Demography* 12:209–222.

Rodgers, Willard L., and Arland Thornton. 1985. "Changing Patterns of First Marriage in the United States." *Demography* 22:265–279.

Ruggles, Steven. 1992. "Migration, Marriage, and Mortality: Correcting Sources of Bias in English Family Reconstitutions." *Population Studies* 46:507–522.

Ruggles, Steven. 1997. "The Rise of Divorce and Separation in the United States, 1880–1990." *Demography* 34:455–466.

Ruggles, Steven. 1999. "Limitations of Family Reconstitution." *Continuity and Change* 14:105–130.

Ruggles, Steven, Matthew Sobek, et al. 1998. *Integrated Public Use Microdata Series*. Minneapolis: Minnesota Historical Census Project, University of Minnesota.

Shryock, Henry S., and Jacob S. Siegel. 1980. *The Methods and Materials of Demography*, Vol. 1. Washington, DC: U.S. Government Printing Office.

Sobek, Matthew. 1997. *A Century of Work: Gender, Labor Force Participation, and Occupational Attainment in the United States, 1880–1990*. Ph.D. dissertation, Department of History, University of Minnesota, Minneapolis, MN.

Stevens, David A. 1990. "New Evidence on the Timing of Early Life Course Transitions: The United States 1900 to 1980." *Journal of Family History* 15:163–178.

Testa, Mark, and Marilyn Krogh. 1995. "The Effect of Employment on Marriage among Black Males in Inner-city Chicago." Pp. 59–95 in *The Decline in Marriage among African-Americans: Causes, Consequences, and Policy Implications*, edited by M.B. Tucker and C. Mitchell-Kernan. New York: Russell Sage Foundation.

U.S. Bureau of the Census. 1933. *Fifteenth Census of the United States: 1890, Population*, Vol. II. Washington, DC: U.S. Government Printing Office.

U.S. Bureau of the Census. 1975. *Historical Statistics of the United States: Colonial Times to 1970*. Washington, DC: U.S. Government Printing Office.

U.S. Census Office. 1895. *Report on Population of the United States at the Eleventh Census: 1890*. Washington, DC: U.S. Government Printing Office.

Waite, Linda, and Glenna D. Spitze. 1981. "Young Women's Transition to Marriage." *Demography* 18:681–694.

Wells, Robert V. 1992. "The Population of England's Colonies in America: Old English or New Americans?" *Population Studies* 46:85–102.

Wilson, William J., and Kathryn M. Neckerman. 1987. "Poverty and Family Structure: The Widening Gap between Evidence and Public Policy." Pp. 63–92 in *The Truly Disadvantaged: The Inner City, the Underclass, and Public Policy*, edited by W.J. Wilson. Chicago: University of Chicago Press.

Yasuba, Yasukichi. 1962. *Birth Rates of the White Population in the United States, 1800–1860*. Baltimore: Johns Hopkins University Press.

II

PERSPECTIVES ON HOW UNIONS ARE FORMED

5

The Evolutionary Psychology of Marriage and Divorce

MARTIN DALY and MARGO I. WILSON

The principal aims of the conference from which this volume arose were to understand changing marital practices, particularly in the United States, and to predict future developments on the basis of recent trends in marriage, cohabitation, and divorce. Nevertheless, this chapter's primary focus is the relatively timeless and cross-culturally general attributes of marriage. Our rationale for this emphasis is a conviction that sound interpretation and prediction of contemporary short-term vicissitudes in marital behavior must be founded in a sound theoretical understanding of the marital relationship.

Marital alliance entails a joint investment in the affectional, reproductive, economic, domestic, and kinship domains associated with the partnership. The strength of the alliance depends on each partner's perception of the benefits and costs of continuing or terminating it, and these perceptions are grounded in a peculiar calculus that is affected by shared interests in the welfare of children, sexual fidelity, pressures from collateral kin, and the opportunity costs of marital decisions. The theoretical framework that seems to us most useful for understanding the effects of these factors and how they interact is an evolutionary psychological one. This approach is unfamiliar to many social scientists and thus requires a brief introduction.

EVOLUTIONARY PSYCHOLOGY

If psychology is the science concerned with how the brain/mind processes information and generates behavior, then evolutionary psychology is simply that part of psychological science that is conducted with active attention to contemporary theory and research in evolutionary biology. The label "evolutionary psychology" does not refer to a unitary, falsifiable theory. Like "social psychology" or "cognitive psychology," it refers to a field within which alternative theories vie (Barkow et al., 1992; Bock and Cardew, 1997; Crawford and Krebs, 1998; Daly and Wilson, 1988a,b,c, 1997, 1999; McBurney and Gaulin, 2000).

Why should we, as psychologists, pay heed to developments in evolutionary biology? Because the human brain/mind is a magnificently complex, functional device comprised of countless subsidiary devices with distinct subsidiary adaptive functions, and evolutionary biology is the science that addresses both the definitional criteria of adaptive functioning and the processes by which adaptive complexity arises and persists in living creatures. For example, evolutionary biology is the science that addresses why two sexes exist and in what aspects of their morphology and psychology they might be expected to differ (Daly and Wilson, 1983; Michod and Levin, 1988). A sophisticated acquaintance with evolutionary biology can be a great aid to psychologists and social scientists in their efforts to generate fruitful hypotheses and to avoid blind alleys.

The complexity of people and other living things requires an explanation. Pre-Darwinian thinkers such as Paley (1802) could think of only one: that one or more creatures analogous to ourselves, but unimaginably more powerful, must have designed and created us. Such creationist theories have at least two flaws that make them scientifically worthless: they merely shift the unexplained complexity to invisible creators, thus solving nothing, and they are devoid of testable implications that would enable one to choose among the numerous competing versions, whose claims for credence invariably rely on bald assertions of authoritative revelation. Nevertheless, for want of a better idea, even biologists were creationists until 1858, when Charles Darwin and Alfred Russel Wallace presented a new, naturalistic theory to the Linnaean Society.

Darwin and Wallace (1858) noted that random variation is ceaselessly generated among individuals within a species (albeit by processes not then understood), and that this variation is then winnowed by nonrandom differential survival and reproduction. The result, they argued, is that the more successful forms proliferate while their alternatives perish, and this could generate an accumulation of increasingly complex functional "design" over generations, without the assistance of any sentient designer. Analogizing this process to the selective breeding practiced by farmers intent on improving their stock, Darwin called it "natural selection." All the processes that this theory entails have since been abundantly confirmed (see, e.g., Endler, 1986; Freeman and Herron, 1998). No other viable explanation for complex adaptation in the living world has been proposed, nor is there any apparent need for one. Like other fundamental theories such as the atomic theory, the theory of evolution by selection has attained the status of "fact."

Darwin's contemporary, the sociologist Herbert Spencer, epitomized the natural selective process as "survival of the fittest," and the phrase stuck. However, the Darwinian process is not merely a matter of differential longevity. Over generations, it is successful attributes that "survive," not individuals, and this sort of long-term survival requires successful reproduction. An imaginary example may clarify this point. Suppose that there were a novel mutation that had the effect of turning a handsome stag into a pacifist, devoid of all inclination to butt heads for mating rights. This new variety of male would save energy and avoid injury, relative to his fellows, and would therefore be likely to outlive them. But so what? If the stag produces no sons, the pacifism-inducing mutation cannot proliferate to become the new standard of long-lived staghood.

The point is that the Darwinian process has designed the adaptive attributes of living creatures on the basis of a single, peculiar criterion of successful functioning: *outreproducing competing variants*, which usually means one's same-sex, same-species rivals. More precisely, selection favors those variants that are most successful in promoting Darwinian *"fitness": the posterity of the organism's particular set of genes in competition with their alleles*. This is the bottom line to which our evolved attributes were "designed" to contribute.

Evolutionary psychologists attempt to analyze mind and behavior into their natural, functional subsystems, guided by the recognition that fitness maximization has been the historical arbiter of all aspects of organismic design. That is, they are adaptationists and selectionists. Adaptationism in psychology is nothing new. Elucidating the functional designs of organisms and their constituent parts has been the cornerstone of biological discovery for centuries (Mayr, 1983), and like other life scientists, psychologists partition their subject matter (mind and behavior) into distinct functional entities: processes such as brightness compensation, sound localization, memory encoding and retrieval, object recognition, eye–hand coordination, and so forth. Unfortunately, however, although effective psychological scientists have always been adaptationists, they have seldom let an understanding of natural selection inform their adaptationism, and have therefore wandered down many garden paths, imagining that the hierarchy of adaptive functions is organized to maximize things like happiness, or self-esteem, or even a comatose quiescence, rather than what it is actually organized to maximize, namely fitness.

Women and Men in Evolutionary Perspective

With this brief introduction to evolutionary psychology as background, consider the human animal in comparative perspective. Its first noteworthy feature, for present purposes, is that *Homo sapiens* reproduces sexually. Many creatures do not, and the fact of sexual reproduction has immediate implications. Unlike ourselves, asexual organisms produce offspring that are genetically identical to the mother, with the result that the resource allocations and other exigencies that best serve maternal fitness are necessarily optimal for offspring fitness, too, since the mother's and the offspring's fitnesses are isomorphic. In sexual reproducers, by contrast, the lack of genetic identity between parent and offspring makes "parent–offspring conflict" (Trivers, 1974) endemic: the resource allocations and other states of affairs that would maximize parental fitness are not identical to those that would maximize the fitness of any one offspring.

A mother is equally related to all her young, so if they are of equal quality and expected reproductivity, they are equally promising contributors to her fitness, and we may expect maternal motives to have evolved so as to bestow resources where presently available cues predict that they will most enhance the youngster's expected fitness. From the offspring's perspective, however, one's self is twice as effective a contributor to one's own fitness as one's (full) sibling, and one should therefore have evolved to prefer that resources go to a sibling rather than to self only when they impart at least twice as great an increment to the sib's expected fitness as to one's own. This criterion becomes even more stringent if the sibling is a mere half sib. The "expected" fitness effects in this argument refer of course to average effects in ancestral generations, and may or may not constitute valid expectations in rapidly changing modern environments; for further discussion of this important point, see Crawford (1998), Daly and Wilson (1999), and Irons (1998).

The result is that in sexual reproducers, the attributes of parents and offspring necessarily evolve not simply to complement one another, but also, to some degree, to counter one another, with young inclined to covet a larger share of parental resources than their parents (or siblings) are inclined to permit. The implications of this conflict for maternal and infantile physiology and psychology have been best expounded by Haig (1993), who showed how significant components of the morphology and physiology of pregnant women and their fetuses are dedicated to a struggle between them, a struggle that is apparently more intense and costly when the paternity of successive young changes and the fetus therefore manifests adaptations that discount the value of the mother's future reproduction more extremely (Trivers and Burt, 1999).

Besides engendering parent–offspring conflict, sexual reproduction introduces an additional social relationship, namely that of mates. From an evolutionary perspective, mates have a deep commonality of interest grounded in shared reproduction: since each gains equal fitness from the eventual reproduction of their common offspring, they are likely to have evolved to evaluate alternative actions and states of affairs similarly, insofar as those actions and states of affairs have had predictable effects on their children's prospects. However, the fact that both parties gain fitness from the same young also entails a potential for conflict: either can gain if the other can be manipulated to invest more in their joint project (Winkler, 1987).

The second thing to note about *Homo sapiens* in comparative biological perspective is that people are dioecious: individuals come in two varieties, female and male, and successful reproduction requires one of each. Not all sexually reproducing creatures are dioecious, and the considerations discussed above, including that of the potential for parasitic exploitation of a mate's efforts, apply to monomorphic hermaphrodites (e.g., Fischer, 1988) just as they do to dioecious animals like ourselves. The additional twist that dioecy adds is the evolution of two distinct morphs, with distinct attributes, which, like those of parent and offspring, are partly complementary and partly antagonistic (Gowaty, 1997; Rice, 1996; Trivers, 1972).

In dioecious organisms, the female is, by definition, the sex that produces the larger gamete: eggs are bigger than sperm. So when internal fertilization (the union of parental gametes inside one parent's body) evolved—as it has done in many independent lineages—it has almost always been within the female rather than the male. This in turn set the evolutionary stage for the sexually differentiated elaboration of additional modes of internal nurturance, such as mammalian pregnancy and lactation, with females literally left holding the babies. This sexual differentiation of the evolved mechanisms of "parental investment" (Trivers, 1972) engenders an asymmetry in opportunities for parasitic exploitation of a mate's reproductive efforts: females commonly invest vastly more time and energy in nurturing each offspring than do males, who can disappear after conception and still gain the full fitness benefit of successfully raised young. Various sex differences in the psychophysiological paraphernalia that we call "sexuality" follow logically from this asymmetry, as discussed briefly below and at length by Symons (1979).

In other words, insofar as reproductive effort can be partitioned into the pursuit of matings versus parental investment (Trivers, 1972; Low, 1978), male mammals commonly specialize in the former and females in the latter. Thus, the principal factor limiting male fitness is often the number of mating partners, whereas female fitness seldom profits analogously from sheer number of mates and is instead limited by nutrient availability. Since the minimal time and energy cost of producing a viable offspring is usually much lower for males than females, maximal reproductive potential is higher. The variance in fitness then tends to be higher in males than females ("effective polygyny"; see Daly and Wilson, 1983:151–152), and the proportion who die without having reproduced is also higher,

engendering more intense male–male competition and the selective favoring of specialized weaponry for same-sex combat and relatively costly,
dangerous, competitive inclinations in males. Moreover, in species in
which males are anatomically and psychologically specialized for violent
competition, and their fitness depends on the frequency and exclusivity of
mating access, males may also apply their violent abilities to the task of
direct aggressive control of the females themselves. It is also noteworthy—
and without an evolutionary perspective, paradoxical—that the extent to
which males are larger and more heavily armed than females tends to
be correlated, across species, with excess male vulnerability to external
threats of starvation, disease, and even predation, as the demands of intrasexual competitive prowess compromise male design efficiency with
respect to other aspects of the species' ecological niche (e.g., Gaulin and
Sailer, 1985).

Of course, the preceding paragraph's typological sketch of mammalian
mating systems and sex differences must be qualified by the recognition of
substantial diversity. Effective polygyny—defined as the ratio of male fitness variance over female fitness variance—is highly variable. The extent
to which males grow larger than females, die younger, have higher fitness
variance, and so forth varies even among closely related species, and these
various aspects of sexual differentiation are apparently strongly correlated
with one another. Most notably, wherever pairs remain together and care
for their young cooperatively—as foxes and various monkeys and beavers
and a smattering of other mammals do—these sex differences are diminished or abolished.

One reason why such biparental care is atypical among mammals is
that males are vulnerable to "cuckoldry" and hence to unwitting investment in young sired by rivals. This consideration tends to make paternal
investment evolutionarily unstable, by reducing its expected fitness
returns relative to those attainable from the pursuit of additional mates.
Nevertheless, there are at least a few mammalian species in which males
invest substantially in their young, and *Homo sapiens* is obviously one of
them. So the third thing to note about our species in comparative perspective—and the first in which we differ from closely related species—is that
people form mateships of some stability, with biparental care of young.
Our nearest relatives, the great apes, cleave much closer to the mammalian
stereotype above, with males very much larger than females and parental
investment predominantly or solely maternal.

The human animal is by no means an exemplary monogamist, however.
The prevalence of adulterous fantasy and action proves that marriage does
not abolish interest in the opposite sex, and the same is implied by the
ubiquity of countermeasures to adultery (e.g., Wilson and Daly, 1992a).
Moreover, the ethnographic record reveals that men tend to be ardent

polygamists when the opportunity presents itself: in the majority of known human societies—including all those that subsist by foraging, as all people did until the relatively recent invention of agriculture—most marriages are (at least serially) monogamous, and yet some men of high status manage to have multiple wives simultaneously (Betzig, 1986).[1]

Many human sex differences can be interpreted as evolutionary vestiges of a selective history as an effectively polygynous species, that is, one in which male fitness has been more variable than female fitness and intrasexual competition has thus been more intense among males. These vestiges include sex differences in body size, in maturation schedules, in intrasexual combat, and in rates of senescence. In all these attributes, the sexes differ more in human beings than in monogamous mammals, but less than in extremely polygynous mammals such as bison or sea lions or our cousins, the great apes. The likely implication is that our species evolved under conditions of *slight* effective polygyny. More specifically, we may conclude that pair formation with biparental care is an ancient hominid adaptation, even though competitively ascendant men continued to be polygamists. Not only is that the most straightforward interpretation of our various slight but significant sexual dimorphisms, it is also what is implied by the ethnographic record of marital polygamy, as summarized above.

MARITAL ALLIANCE AS A NEGOTIATED EXCHANGE

Details vary across cultures, but marriage is essentially universal: individual women and men in all societies form socially recognized alliances, indefinite in duration but ideally permanent, which entail sexual and other entitlements and obligations, and which are deemed the appropriate or ideal context in which to produce and raise children. Its ubiquity suggests that marital alliance is an ancient arrangement that is in some sense instantiated in our evolved human nature, as does the instability of the alternative practices that are occasionally invented by utopian revolutionaries.

When evolutionists discuss marriage in the broader context of animal mating systems, they often encounter the objection that human marriage is an economic institution, and is thus unique. This objection is naive. Mates cooperate in many animal species and they often divide tasks. One may gather food for both, for example, while the other prepares a nest or guards the young; such exchanges of benefits are as "economic" as the reciprocities of human couples. More importantly, the economic function of marriage is not more fundamental than its reproductive function. As is the case for any animal, the basic "economic" motives of human beings exist and assumed their modern forms as means to the end of reproduction.

There *is* something unusual about human marriage as compared to the mateships of other animals, although it is an aspect of the institution whose salience has waned in the modern west: the involvement of third parties. Parents and other relatives exert considerable influence on marital timing and mate choice in traditional, face-to-face societies, where a marriage may even cement an alliance between clans. Although even familial politics may not be entirely unique to the human case since analogous things happen in some birds (Emlen et al., 1995), the political scrimmaging that surrounds human marital alliance is surely unrivalled.

Anthropologists often characterize marriage as a contract between kin groups, whereby a woman, with all her sexual, reproductive, and productive potential, is bestowed by her natal group in exchange for benefits from the groom and his kinsmen (e.g., Lévi-Strauss, 1969). Murdock (1967) tabulated the cultural practices of 860 societies, and noted that a net transfer of valuable goods ("bridewealth") and/or services from the groom's family to the bride's family was characteristic of marriage in 580 (67%) of them. A net flow of wealth in the opposite direction ("dowry") was customary in only 3% of societies, and in the remaining 30%, no asymmetrical transfer of wealth was essential or typical. Modern industrial societies, where the importance of kinship has largely withered, fall into this last group, but they often retain vestiges of the culture of bridewealth, such as a father "giving" his daughter in marriage. The negotiation of bridewealth is transparently concerned with value received for value given. In many societies, only a down payment is made at the time of the marriage itself, with the balance due when children are produced, and in the event of prolonged childlessness, it is common for the groom's family to demand either that the bridewealth be refunded or the bride replaced. Moreover, although bridewealth is often idealized as invariant in a given society, it is in practice negotiable, and a principal determinant of the price that is actually paid is the woman's expected future fertility (Borgerhoff Mulder, 1995).

Although the reverse practice of dowry is much rarer, it warrants a few words here, since its very existence can be misread as proof that the direction of ancillary resource flow in marital transactions is arbitrary. Dickemann (1981) noted that dowry is predominantly an upper-class phenomenon in highly stratified societies, by which families compete to place their daughters in high status marriages where they may produce high status sons who will have many children, often by many women. Gaulin and Boster (1990) refined this analysis by showing that dowry is confined to that minority of highly stratified societies in which even men at the top are restricted to one legal wife. Most societies permit polygamous marriage to those men who can afford it, and rich, powerful men often acquire several wives, but in a few societies in which wealth and status differentials are sufficient to support extreme polygyny, monogamy is nevertheless enjoined by law. High status men in these societies may sire many bastards, but only the one legitimate wife can bear an heir who will inherit his father's wealth and standing, so families compete and pay for the privilege of marrying a daughter to such a man so that she will become the mother of his heirs (probably de facto polygynists in their turn). But if this is the explanation for dowry, to what can we attribute socially imposed monogamy? To answer this question, we must first note that it appears never to occur in simple foraging, horticultural, or pastoral societies. Rules enforcing monogamy have arisen only in large-polity, complex, role-differentiated societies such as ours. Alexander (1975) and Betzig (1986) have argued that socially imposed monogamy arose only where between-group competition (particularly warfare) had developed to such a degree that leaders needed the diverse skills of many followers, whose support they could enlist only by foreswearing polygyny and harem holding, and offering a wife-in-every-bed bargain instead.

MARRIAGE AS A REPRODUCTIVE UNION

In most human societies and throughout most of human history, at least since the invention of agriculture and possibly before, getting a bride required a substantial transfer of resources to her kinsmen. Having acquired a wife, to what is a man entitled? His proprietary rights may include control of the fruits of her labor, but this is far from universal. What a husband gains in all societies is *legitimate sexual access to his wife and the opportunity to sire her children*, and in most cases these rights are exclusive (or his to bestow).

Some anthropologists have been so impressed by the labor value of children and by the utility of having a large kin group as to theorize that it is not the opportunity to sire their wives' children that men value, but the opportunity to claim them as kin once they are born. In an extreme version of this argument, Paige and Paige (1981) proposed that the reason why public acknowledgments of paternity exist is to establish paternal entitlements against rival claimants. But this theory is refuted by the ethnographies, in which it is hard to find even an anecdote about two men claiming paternity of a disputed child, whereas *denials* of fatherhood and its obligations abound. Men are profoundly concerned that the children in whose welfare they invest are their own, and they are often enraged to discover otherwise (Wilson, 1987; Daly and Wilson, 1988a, c).

In referring to marriage's reproductive function, we are not talking merely of its historical origins. Whether negotiated by kin groups or the partners themselves, marriage is a contract whereby a man acquires sexual and reproductive rights while his wife acquires some entitlement to his resources for the support of herself and her children (Irons, 1983; Wilson and Daly, 1992a).

Marital inclinations and behavior continue to exhibit signs of "design" for reproduction. Youth has always affected a woman's *mate value* (her statistically expected contribution to her partner's fitness) more than a man's, for example, while social status and wealth have greater impact on a man's mate value than a woman's; accordingly, men everywhere place more emphasis on a potential marriage partner's youth than do women (Kenrick and Keefe, 1992), whereas women everywhere emphasize a candidate's social standing more than do men (Buss, 1989). The fit between emotions and marital alliance's reproductive function is even clearer when we consider responses to infidelity. Adultery by either partner threatens the other's expected fitness, but for slightly different reasons: a woman whose mate is a polygynist or philanderer suffers a diminution of his investments in her children and herself, whereas a man with an adulterous mate risks misdirecting his parental investments to enhance rivals' fitness. It might thus be anticipated that the sexual jealousy of women and men would be qualitatively different, with male jealousy more focused on the sexual act and female jealousy focused on the alienation of the partner's attention and material resources, and that is exactly what a diversity of evidence indicates (Buss et al., 1992; Buunk et al., 1996; Daly et al., 1982; Teisman and Mosher, 1978).

Betzig (1989) proposed that insight into why people marry might be gained by considering why they divorce. Reviewing information from 160 societies around the world (the "Standard Cross-Cultural Sample"), she found that sexual infidelity was by far the most widely cited motive for divorce, and infertility ranked a clear second. Betzig concluded that the predominant grounds for marital dissolution imply that the predominant motive for marriage is to reproduce.

Betzig also noted that it is usually only female infidelity that warrants divorce. A sexually asymmetrical response to adultery is of course widespread, and Daly et al. (1982) have argued that it is in fact cross-culturally universal, claims to the contrary notwithstanding. There *are* ethnographic reports of adulterous men being punished more severely than women, and these have repeatedly been invoked as proof that double standards of sexual misconduct are readily reversed and therefore arbitrary (e.g., Whyte, 1978). But this interpretation is wrong, for in *every* such case, the severely punished men were adulterers not by virtue of their own marital status, but because they dallied with married women (Daly et al., 1982). There are in fact *no* reversed double standards in the ethnographic record: no case has been described in which sexual contact with someone other than one's spouse is deemed a greater offense when committed by a married man than by a married woman. Wherever law has been codified, it has included an offense of unlawful sexual contact with a married woman; it is usually characterized as a property offence against the husband, entitling him to damages just as any other unauthorized misuse of his property that reduces its value might do (Wilson and Daly, 1992a). Only in the nineteenth century did some legal codes begin to treat adultery by man and wife similarly, but even where the law has become gender neutral, there remains a substantial sex difference in actual responses to infidelity, with men much more likely than women to respond to a partner's infidelity both with violence (Daly and Wilson, 1988b) and by terminating the relationship (Daly and Wilson, 1983; Buckle et al., 1996).

MARITAL CONFLICT

By affording a general theory about what marriage and the sentiments that motivate it are organized to achieve, an evolutionary perspective also provides guideposts for the investigation of marital conflict, because it suggests particular situational, demographic, and other factors that are likely to threaten mate solidarity. Our own research on the marital relationship has mainly entailed using this approach to discover risk factors for marital violence, on the assumption that even extreme violence can be viewed as the tail of a distribution of the intensity of conflict, and that factors that exacerbate or mitigate marital conflict will be associated with greater or lesser rates of spousal assault and homicide. In other words, we have treated murder and assault as conflict "assays." It seems plausible that marital dissolution can be treated as another such assay, and hence that risk factors for marital violence will often have parallel impacts on rates of divorce. For example, female youth, common-law as opposed to registered marital status, a big age disparity in either direction, and the presence of children of prior unions are risk factors for spousal homicide, and each of these factors is associated with elevated rates of divorce, too (Becker et al., 1977; Daly and Wilson, 1988b; Daly et al., 1997).

If marriage is correctly interpreted as an evolved aspect of human sociality, with a basic reproductive function, then certain expectations about the sources of marital conflict would seem to follow. We have argued that marriage engenders solidarity because (both extant and potential) offspring contribute similarly to both partners' fitness, but if marital harmony derives ultimately from correlated expected fitnesses, then marital disharmony may be expected to be evoked by (ancestral) cues of a threat to that correlation. Regrettably, there are several such threats.

The most dangerous source of marital conflict is adultery. We have already mentioned the asymmetry in this issue; when Samuel Johnson's friend and biographer James Boswell ventured that "there is a great

difference between the offence of infidelity in a man and that of his wife,"
Dr. Johnson replied "The difference, sir, is boundless. The man imposes no
bastards upon his wife" (Boswell, 1779:1035). As noted previously, infidelity, particularly by the wife, topped the list of reasons for divorce in Betzig's (1989) cross-cultural review, and it also tops the list of motives for
both uxoricide and nonlethal wife assault (Daly and Wilson, 1988b; Wilson
and Daly, 1996; Wilson et al., 1995). More generally, in samples of well-
described spousal homicides from a wide range of societies, *male sexual
proprietariness* appears to have been the dominant motivating factor in a
large majority (usually over 80%) of cases (Daly and Wilson, 1988c). By this
term, we encompass men's preemptive concerns both that their wives
might be adulterous and that they might wish to quit the marriage even
when no particular male rival is involved. In either case, men often explain
or justify their violence as a response to intolerable loss: "if I cannot have
her, no one shall." The reason we said "spousal homicides" and not just
"uxoricides" in remarking on the dominant motivational status of these
issues is because they also predominate even when the wife is the eventual
killer: the majority of such cases, worldwide, are apparently reactions to
male accusations and assaults arising from sexual proprietariness (Wilson
and Daly, 1992b, 1993, 1996).

Both parties may wish to end an unsatisfactory marriage, but it is probably more often the case that the inclination to separate is asymmetrical, at
least at first. Staying in a marriage must always entail opportunity costs
(foregone options), so asymmetrical inclinations to separate may be
expected whenever one party (X) feels that his or her own "mate value"
exceeds that of the partner (Y), since if these perceptions have any validity
at all, the implication is that Y has done better than her or his expected outcome of reentering the marriage market. These potential conflicts are tem-
pered by the uncertainties and start-up costs associated with divorce and
remarriage, by the efficiencies and trust that can build up over time in a
reciprocal partnership, and, once children are produced, by the couple's
joint interest in their welfare and by a well-founded apprehension that the
children's interests are usually best served by marital stability.

What one is giving up by staying married cannot of course be known
directly, but must be inferred from perceptions of the available marriage
market, among other things. These perceptions—or perhaps we should
say these intuitive semistatistical inferences—are not necessarily accurate,
and there is some evidence that contemporary mass media may distort
them in ways that act against marital stability. Kenrick and colleagues
(1989, 1994) have shown that perusing photographs of physically attractive members of the opposite sex (versus abstract art in a control condition) induced men, but not women, to downgrade their judgments of their
current partners' attractiveness and to profess lower levels of love and

commitment. Looking at pictures of successful, socially dominant persons of the opposite sex produced similar effects in women, but not in men. It thus appears that exposure even to an artificial pool of candidates for imagined heterosexual attention may be sufficient to influence what are in effect one's evaluations of how well one has done in the mating market, although further research on the duration and other aspects of these effects is obviously needed. At present, we can only wonder whether the endless barrage of beautiful winners on television and in magazines is having cumulative effects on marital dissatisfaction and unrest.

Citing cross-cultural evidence that the median duration of marriages ending in divorce is about 4 years, Fisher (1992) proposed that human sentiments have evolved to bring about serial monogamy, with couples inclined to stay together only long enough to "complete a successful lactation." This argument attracted a good deal of popular press, but it never had a sound basis in fact or in theory. The distribution of marital durations before divorce exhibits no bump indicative of a "four-year itch," nor is there any evidence that couples are apt to divorce when their first child is a toddler. Quite the contrary in fact. The marriages that dissolve after only a few years duration are predominantly the childless ones, and successful reproduction reduces rather than raises the marital-duration-specific likelihood of divorce (Becker et al., 1977; Waite and Lillard, 1991). As for the supposed theoretical rationale, the hypothetical benefit of serial mating is "bet-hedging" by diversifying offspring genotypes, but there is no reason to think that such a benefit would ever have been substantial in human evolution and good reason to propose that it would be more than offset by costs to maternal fitness incurred as a result of reduced relatedness and cooperativeness within her brood. Moreover, all evidence indicates that marital instability damaged the life prospects of dependent children in ancestral societies, as it does today (Daly and Wilson, 1996, 1998). An evolved psychological adaptation specifically designed to effectuate separation while children are still dependent is utterly implausible.

A third source of marital conflict derives from the fact that personal reproduction is only one component of expected fitness. One's impacts on the reproduction of one's relatives affect fitness, too (Hamilton, 1964), and since mates have separate kindreds in whom they are likely to retain benevolent interests, each may then resent the other's "nepotistic" investments of time, attention, and material resources. This is the evolutionary theoretical gloss on a widely recognized source of marital friction: in-laws. Betzig (1989) placed in-law problems fifth on her list of causes of divorce in the ethnographic record. This issue is hardly ever invoked as a primary motivational factor in spousal homicide, but complaints of excessive attention to her natal family are often identified as causal factors in wife assault (e.g., Counts et al., 1992).

Asymmetries of relatedness are at the root of another source of marital disharmony besides the in-law problem: either party to the marriage may have children of a prior union, and when they do, the two are likely to disagree about their resource entitlements (e.g., Hobart, 1991; Messinger, 1976). The presence of stepchildren constitutes a major risk factor for spousal homicide (Daly et al., 1997; Brewer and Paulsen, 1999), for nonlethal wife assault (Daly et al., 1993), and for divorce (Becker et al., 1977; White and Booth, 1985).

Finally, we must consider the dissatisfaction that derives from inequitable contributions to a marriage. One partner, usually the wife, is apt to be disgruntled when unequal power within the relationship sustains an asymmetry of investment in the joint venture that she finds unacceptable and irremediable. This is, in a sense, the issue that we referred to earlier as the potential for male parasitism of female reproductive investments, and evolutionists might argue that it is analytically inseparable from the conflicts over expenditures of extrapair mating effort and nepotistic effort discussed above. Why, after all, should either parent be inclined to shirk in the rearing of their children, other than to save oneself for the pursuit of these alternative fitness-promoting activities?

Conflicts about inequitable workloads are rarely listed as motivational factors in spouse murders, although we have read police notes on cases in which wives killed husbands who used force to usurp the wives' wages for extramarital pursuits. In cases of nonlethal wife abuse, accusations of female sloth are frequently cited as being of relevance (Dobash and Dobash, 1979), and conflicts over labor and investment are also germane to divorce: according to Betzig's (1989) review, "economics"—which she elaborates as encompassing laziness and failure to provide expected material resources—is the fourth-ranked cause of divorce in the ethnographic record. (Number three is "personality," which refers to a vague catch-all category of incompatibility or chronic disagreement, rather than a particular substantive issue. Thus, economics could be deemed the third ranking conflict domain leading to divorce after infidelity and infertility.)

IMPLICATIONS AND CONCLUSIONS

What does this evolution-minded view of the cross-culturally general aspects of marriage suggest about contemporary and future marital behavior in developed countries? As the influence of family members and the state diminishes, and as individual women and men become freer agents in an open marriage market, both the appeal of marriage and its stability are likely to reflect the perceived value of "commodities" in that market. Where evolutionary psychology may be able to help is in characterizing those subjective commodities.

We suggested earlier that marital instability is countered by the perceived costs of marriage market reentry, by efficiencies and trust that are slowly built up in a long-standing partnership, and by couples' shared interest in their children's welfare. With easier access to divorce and reduced familial interference and condemnation, the first of these is likely to have lost some power in contemporary society, but the second may have gained some. The effect of children is probably the most powerful of the three, and its impact must have been diminished by reductions in family size and by delayed childbearing. Rasmussen (1981) has gone so far as to argue that the human psyche is specifically adapted to fall out of love with (to disengage from) a mate if a long-term sexual relationship is fruitless, because this was an ancestral cue of infertility and selection will have favored betting that the infertile party is the partner rather than oneself and trying elsewhere.

If it is true that marriage, from a woman's perspective, entails granting some exclusivity of sexual and reproductive rights to a man in exchange for his commitment to invest in her and in her children, then the bargain will sour when husbands are undependable sources of investment. If men only sporadically possess the material resources that wives want, women are apt to prefer to retain their autonomy and their right to multiple suitors, with the result that marital-like unions are informal and unstable, paternity confidence is low, and men are more inclined to invest the little they have in mating effort than in their putative offspring (e.g., Flinn and Low, 1986). Moreover, if men lack the means to uphold their part of the marital bargain, they are apt to resort to coercive threats and violence in their attempts to maintain exclusive control of wives and girlfriends who no longer value them, which ironically raises their net costliness in the women's eyes and may thus elevate incentives to leave the relationship (Wilson and Daly, 1992b). Thus, economic trends that make the trajectory of men's income unpredictable are likely to induce marital instability, too.

The unreliability of employment income will generally go hand in hand with income inequality, and a large body of research in the social and health sciences suggests that many social problems are more tightly linked with inequity per se than with average levels of material welfare (e.g., Wilkinson, 1996). We are not aware, however, of any attempt to assess whether recent increases in income inequality have had any effect on marital (in)stability, net of the effects of concurrent social trends. To some extent, women have always married because letting the best available suitor lay claim to them is making the best of a constrained set of choices. If men of considerable means are legally restricted to one wife, many women may prefer unregistered relationships with well-to-do de facto polygynists over marriage with impecunious bachelors, despite the risks that flow from the "other woman's" lack of legal entitlements. Whether de facto polygyny has been growing as income inequality has grown may warrant investigation.

To the extent that marital stability is affected by men's perceptions of the likely consequences of withdrawing their material support from their families, real improvements in the social supports provided for single mothers and their children are likely to have the unfortunate side effect of weakening men's incentives to be investing fathers. The prevalence of single parenthood in modern Sweden suggests that combining a high level of personal freedom with a social safety net can have a surprising negative effect on the inclination to marry. Thus, although economic inequity is a likely source of marital instability, as argued above, more socialistic policies cannot necessarily be expected to reverse the trend.

The increasing presence of women in the workplace may be having several consequences. One is that they are less dependent on men and can demand more in exchange for the lost autonomy of marriage, or opt out of marriage altogether (although it must of course be noted that relatively affluent working women are not the main source of recent increases in "out-of-wedlock" childbirth). Another is that modern women often move in social spheres of which their mates know little, which may incline some men to see their wives and girlfriends as insufficiently monitored to warrant committing resources to marriage and putative progeny, and thus tip the men over into a more promiscuous "serial courtship" modus operandi. In addition, workplace interactions between the sexes take place outside the purview of both parties' mates and are likely to provide temptations toward both affairs and more permanent rearrangements that were rarer in most societies of the past. Finally, a working wife may also face marital conflict reflecting her partner's anxiety that her marriage market value could be improving relative to his own.

Obviously, there are many reasons why the institution of marriage is under stress in the modern world. But considering human sociality in evolutionary and cross-cultural perspective also suggests that marital alliance is so much a part of the human adaptation that the satisfactions of marital partnership are no more likely to be abandoned as obsolete than is competitive status striving, or parental love.

NOTE

1.   The point here is not that "woman" is monogamous while "man" is polygamous (as a bit of doggerel attributed to Dorothy Parker would have it), for

although there is abundant evidence that women are *less* polygamously inclined than men (e.g., Buss, 1994), they certainly possess such inclinations and there is growing evidence that women's adulterous and polyandrous inclinations exhibit adaptive design (e.g., Bellis and Baker, 1990; Gangestad and Thornhill, 1997).

REFERENCES

Alexander, Richard D. 1975. "The Search for a General Theory of Behavior." *Behavioral Science* 20:77–100.

Barkow, Jerome H., Leda Cosmides, and John Tooby. 1992. *The Adapted Mind: Evolutionary Psychology and the Generation of Culture.* New York: Oxford University Press.

Becker, Gary S., E.M. Landes, and R.T. Michael. 1977. "An Economic Analysis of Marital Instability." *Journal of Political Economy* 85:1141–1187.

Bellis, Mark A., and Robin R. Baker. 1990. "Do Females Promote Sperm Competition? Data for Humans." *Animal Behaviour* 40:997–999.

Betzig, Laura L. 1986. *Despotism and Differential Reproduction: A Darwinian view of History.* Hawthorne, NY: Aldine de Gruyter.

Betzig, Laura L. 1989. "Causes of Conjugal Dissolution: A Cross-cultural Study." *Current Anthropology* 30:654–676.

Bock, Gregory R., and Gail Cardew, eds. 1997. *Characterizing Human Psychological Adaptations.* Ciba Foundation Symposium 208. Chichester: Wiley.

Borgerhoff Mulder, Monique. 1995. "Bridewealth and Its Correlates: Quantifying Changes over Time." *Current Anthropology* 36:573–603.

Boswell, James. [1779] 1953. *Life of Johnson,* edited by R.W. Chapman. Oxford: Oxford University Press.

Brewer, Victoria E., and Derek J. Paulsen. 1999. "A Comparison of U.S. and Canadian Findings on Uxoricide Risk for Women with Children Sired by Previous Partners." *Homicide Studies* 3:317–332.

Buckle, Leslie, Gordon G. Gallup, and Zachary A. Rodd. 1996. "Marriage as a Reproductive Contract: Patterns of Marriage, Divorce, and Remarriage." *Ethology and Sociobiology* 17:363–377.

Buss, David M. 1989. "Sex Differences in Human Mate Preferences: Evolutionary Hypotheses Tested in 37 Cultures." *Behavioral & Brain Sciences* 12:1–49.

Buss, David M. 1994. *The Evolution of Desire.* New York: Basic Books.

Buss, David M., Randy J. Larsen, Drew Westen, and Jennifer Semmelroth. 1992. "Sex Differences in Jealousy: Evolution, Physiology, and Psychology." *Psychological Science* 3:251–255.

Buunk, Bram P., Alois Angleitner, Viktor Oubaid, and David M. Buss. 1996. "Sex Differences in Jealousy in Evolutionary and Cultural Perspective." *Psychological Science* 7: 359–363.

Counts, Dorothy C., Judith K. Brown, and Jacquelyn C. Campbell, eds. 1992. *Sanctions and Sanctuary: Cultural Perspectives on the Beating of Wives.* Boulder, CO: Westview Press.

Crawford, Charles. 1998. "Environments and Adaptations: Then and Now." Pp. 275–302 in *Handbook of Evolutionary Psychology,* edited by Charles Crawford and Dennis Krebs. Mahwah, NJ: Erlbaum.

Crawford, Charles, and Dennis Krebs, eds. 1998. *Handbook of Evolutionary Psychology.* Mahwah, NJ: Erlbaum.

Daly, Martin, and Margo Wilson. 1983. *Sex, Evolution and Behavior*, 2nd ed. Belmont, CA: Wadsworth.

Daly, Martin, and Margo Wilson. 1988a. "The Darwinian Psychology of Discriminative Parental Solicitude." *Nebraska Symposium on Motivation* 35:91–144.

Daly, Martin, and Margo Wilson. 1988b. "Evolutionary Social Psychology and Family Homicide." *Science* 242:519–524.

Daly, Martin, and Margo Wilson. 1988c. *Homicide*. Hawthorne, NY: Aldine de Gruyter.

Daly, Martin, and Margo Wilson. 1996. "Violence against Stepchildren." *Current Directions in Psychological Science* 5:77–81.

Daly, Martin, and Margo Wilson. 1997. "Crime and Conflict: Homicide in Evolutionary Psychological Perspective." *Crime and Justice* 22:251–300.

Daly, Martin, and Margo Wilson. 1998. *The Truth about Cinderella: A Darwinian View of Parental Love*. London: Weidenfeld & Nicolson.

Daly, Martin, and Margo Wilson. 1999. "Human Evolutionary Psychology and Animal Behaviour." *Animal Behaviour* 57:509–519.

Daly, Martin, Margo Wilson, and Suzanne J. Weghorst. 1982. "Male Sexual Jealousy." *Ethology and Sociobiology* 3:11–27.

Daly, Martin, Lisa Singh, and Margo Wilson. 1993. "Children Fathered by Previous Partners: A Risk Factor for Violence against Women." *Canadian Journal of Public Health* 84:209–210.

Daly, Martin, Karen A. Wiseman, and Margo Wilson. 1997. "Women with Children Sired by Previous Partners Incur Excess Risk of Uxoricide." *Homicide Studies* 1:61–71.

Darwin, Charles, and Alfred Russel Wallace. 1858. "On the Tendency of Species to Form Varieties; and on the Perpetuation of Varieties and Species by Natural Means of Selection." *Journal of the Linnaean Society of London (Zoology)* 3:45–62.

Dickemann, Mildred. 1981. "Paternal Confidence and Dowry Competition: A Biocultural Analysis of Purdah." Pp. 417–438 in *Natural Selection and Social Behavior*, edited by Richard D. Alexander and Donald W. Tinkle. New York: Chiron Press.

Dobash, R. Emerson, and Russell P. Dobash. 1979. *Violence against Wives*. New York: Free Press.

Emlen, Steven T., Peter Wrege, and Nathalie J. Demong. 1995. "Making Decisions in the Family: An Evolutionary Perspective." *American Scientist* 83:148–157.

Endler, John A. 1986. *Natural Selection in the Wild*. Princeton, NJ: Princeton University Press.

Fischer, Eric A. 1988. "Simultaneous Hermaphroditism, Tit-for-Tat, and the Evolutionary Stability of Social Systems." *Ethology and Sociobiology* 9:119–136.

Fisher, Helen. 1992. *Anatomy of Love: The Natural History of Monogamy, Adultery, and Divorce*. New York: Simon & Schuster.

Flinn, Mark V., and Bobbi S. Low. 1986. "Resource Distribution, Social Competition, and Mating Patterns in Human Societies." Pp. 217–243 in *Ecological Aspects of Social Evolution*, edited by Daniel I. Rubenstein and Richard W. Wrangham. Princeton, NJ: Princeton University Press.

Freeman, Scott, and Jon C. Herron. 1998. *Evolutionary Analysis*. Upper Saddle River, NJ: Prentice Hall.

Gangestad, Steven W., and Randy Thornhill. 1997. "The Evolutionary Psychology of Extrapair Sex: The Role of Fluctuating Asymmetry." *Evolution and Human Behavior* 18:69–88.

Gaulin, Steven J.C., and James Boster. 1990. "Dowry as Female Competition." *American Anthropologist* 92:994–1005.

Gaulin, Steven J.C., and Lee D. Sailer. 1985. "Are Females the Ecological Sex?" *American Anthropologist* 87:111–119.

Gowaty, Patricia A. 1997. "Sexual Dialectics, Sexual Selection, and Variation in Reproductive Behavior." Pp. 351–384 in *Feminism and Evolutionary Biology,* edited by Patricia A. Gowaty. New York: Chapman & Hall.

Haig, David. 1993. "Genetic Conflicts in Human Pregnancy." *Quarterly Review of Biology* 68:495–532.

Hamilton, William D. 1964. "The Genetical Evolution of Social Behaviour. I and II." *Journal of Theoretical Biology* 7:1–52.

Hobart, Charles. 1991. "Conflict in Remarriages." *Journal of Divorce & Remarriage* 15:69–86.

Irons, William. 1983. "Human Female Reproductive Strategies." Pp. 169–213 in *Social Behavior of Female Vertebrates,* edited by Samuel Wasser. New York: Academic Press.

Irons, William. 1998. "Adaptively Relevant Environments versus the Environment of Evolutionary Adaptedness." *Evolutionary Anthropology* 6:194–204.

Kenrick, Douglas T., and Richard C. Keefe. 1992. "Age Preferences in Mates Reflect Sex Differences in Reproductive Strategies." *Behavioral & Brain Sciences* 15:75–133.

Kenrick, Douglas T., Sara E. Gutierres, and L. Goldberg. 1989. "Influence of Popular Erotica on Judgments of Strangers and Mates." *Journal of Experimental Social Psychology* 25:159–167.

Kenrick, Douglas T., Steven L. Neuberg, Kirstin L. Zierk, and Jacquelyn M. Krones. 1994. "Evolution and Social Cognition: Contrast Effects as a Function of Sex, Dominance and Physical Attractiveness." *Personality & Social Psychology Bulletin* 20:210–217.

Lévi-Strauss, Claude. 1969. *The Elementary Structures of Kinship.* Boston: Beacon Press.

Low, Bobbi S. 1978. "Environmental Uncertainty and the Parental Strategies of Marsupials and Placentals." *American Naturalist* 112:197–213.

Mayr, Ernst. 1983. "How to Carry Out the Adaptationist Program?" *American Naturalist* 121:324–334.

McBurney, Donald, and Steven J.C. Gaulin. 2000. *The Evolved Mind.* Upper Saddle River, NJ: Prentice Hall.

Messinger, Louise. 1976. "Remarriage Between Divorced People with Children from Previous Marriages: A Proposal for Preparation for Remarriage." *Journal of Marriage and the Family* 2:193–199.

Michod, Richard E., and Bruce R. Levin, eds. 1988. *The Evolution of Sex.* Sunderland, MA: Sinauer.

Murdock, George P. 1967. *Ethnographic Atlas.* Pittsburgh: University of Pittsburgh Press.

Paige, Karen E., and Jeffery M. Paige. 1981. *The Politics of Reproductive Ritual.* Berkeley, CA: University of California Press.

Paley, William. 1802. *Natural Theology; or Evidences of the Existence and Attributes of the Deity, Collected from the Appearances of Nature.* London: Fauldner.

Rasmussen, Dennis R. 1981. "Pair-bond Strength and Stability and Reproductive Success." *Psychological Review* 88:274–290.

Rice, William R. 1996. "Sexually Antagonistic Male Adaptation Triggered by Experimental Arrest of Female Evolution." *Nature* 381:232–234.

Symons, Donald. 1979. *The Evolution of Human Sexuality.* New York: Oxford University Press.

Teismann, Mark W., and D.L. Mosher. 1978. "Jealous Conflict in Dating Couples." *Psychological Reports* 42:1211–1216.

Trivers, Robert L. 1972. "Parental Investment and Sexual Selection." Pp. 134–179 in *Sexual Selection and the Descent of Man 1871–1971*, edited by Bernard Campbell. Chicago: Aldine.

Trivers, Robert L. 1974. "Parent-Offspring Conflict." *American Zoologist* 14:249–264.

Trivers, Robert L., and Austin Burt. 1999. "Kinship and Genomic Imprinting." In *Genomic Imprinting*, edited by Rolf Ohlsson. Heidelberg: Springer.

Waite, Linda J., and Lee A. Lillard. 1991. "Children and Marital Disruption." *American Journal of Sociology* 96:930–953.

White, Lynn K., and Alan Booth. 1985. "The Quality and Stability of Remarriages: The Role of Stepchildren." *American Sociological Review* 50:689–698.

Whyte, Martin K. 1978. *The Status of Women in Preindustrial Societies.* Princeton, NJ: Princeton University Press.

Wilkinson, Richard G. 1996. *Unhealthy Societies: The Afflictions of Inequality.* London: Routledge.

Wilson, Margo I. 1987. "Impacts of the Uncertainty of Paternity on Family Law." *University of Toronto Law Review* 45:216–242.

Wilson, Margo, and Martin Daly. 1992a. "The Man Who Mistook His Wife for a Chattel." Pp. 289–322 in *The Adapted Mind*, edited by Jerome H. Barkow, Leda Cosmides, and John Tooby. New York: Oxford University Press.

Wilson, Margo, and Martin Daly. 1992b. "Who Kills Whom in Spouse Killings? On the Exceptional Sex Ratio of Spousal Homicides in the United States." *Criminology* 30:189–215.

Wilson, Margo, and Martin Daly. 1993. "Spousal Homicide Risk and Estrangement." *Violence & Victims* 8:3–15.

Wilson, Margo, and Martin Daly. 1996. "Male Sexual Proprietariness and Violence against Wives." *Current Directions in Psychological Science* 5:2–7.

Wilson, Margo, Holly Johnson, and Martin Daly. 1995. "Lethal and Nonlethal Violence against Wives." *Canadian Journal of Criminology* 37:331–361.

Winkler, David W. 1987. "A General Model for Parental Care." *American Naturalist* 130:526–543.

6

Theorizing Marriage

ROBERT A. POLLAK

INTRODUCTION

Equilibrium and efficiency are central concerns in economics. In rational actor models, equilibrium is defined by the requirement that individuals, taking as given the choices of others, choose the best alternative available to them, evaluated according to their preferences and their perceptions of the consequences. In this chapter, I discuss equilibrium and efficiency in marriage markets. The equilibrium of a marriage-market model should predict who will marry and who will not, and identify the key variables that determine marriage and nonmarriage. It may also predict who will marry whom (i.e., the pattern of assortative mating), the timing of marriage (e.g., age at first marriage), divorce, and remarriage. The efficiency of the marriage market has received less attention. Economists say that an equilibrium is efficient if no individual can be made better off without someone else being made worse off. Under certain conditions (e.g., the rational actors' perceptions of the consequences are accurate), the definition of equilibrium implies that no rational actor could do better for himself or herself by making a different choice, given the choices made by others. But even if perceptions are accurate and marriage-market equilibrium is efficient from the perspective of marriage-market participants, it may be inefficient from a broader perspective that includes the well-being of their children. More specifically, unless marriage-market participants take full account of the interests of their children, marriage-market equilibrium will be inefficient.

I begin with the simplest marriage-market models, two-sex demographic models, which are built up from "mating rules" that are postulated directly rather than derived from the behavior of rational actors. I then turn to matching and search models, the two types of rational-actor models from which mating rules may be derived. I next consider the two explanatory categories that underlie rational actor models: preferences and opportunities. Finally, I discuss two alternative definitions of efficiency—a narrow definition that restricts attention to the individuals who are marriage-market participants, and a broader definition that also includes their children.

REDUCED-FORM DEMOGRAPHIC MODELS

Demographic models provide the simplest equilibrium models of marriage. Yet nondemographers are often surprised to learn that classical stable population theory (CSPT), demographers' standard model of fertility, is a one-sex model. CSPT postulates an age-specific fertility schedule for women and an age-specific mortality schedule for women. These two schedules, in conjunction with the very strong assumptions that both of these schedules remain constant over time, imply an equilibrium growth rate and an equilibrium age distribution for the female population.

Demography's two-sex problem (see Pollak, 1986, 1990) is the problem of introducing men into this one-sex, female-based model. The two-sex problem is often motivated by discussing the effect on fertility of a "marriage squeeze"—an imbalance between the female and male populations of marriageable age brought about, for example, by wars that disproportionately reduce the number of marriageable men or by baby booms that, because woman typically marry older men, increase the number of marriageable women years before they increase the number of marriageable men. Common sense suggests that a marriage squeeze is likely to reduce age-specific fertility rates for women but CSPT, because it assumes that all vital rates remain constant, cannot accommodate this common sense conclusion.

Demography's two-sex problem is solved, in a formal sense, by the "Birth Matrix-Mating Rule" (BMMR) model introduced in Pollak (1986). [Feeney (1972), in an unpublished doctoral dissertation, presents a two-sex model with the same basic structure, but without satisfactory proof of the existence of equilibrium.] The BMMR model has three components:

- a birth matrix, which indicates the number of offspring born to each possible type of union (e.g., the union of a female of age i and a male of age j);
- a mating rule, which indicates the number of unions of each type as a function of the number of females in each age category and the number of males in each age category; and
- age-specific mortality schedules for males and females.

Under relatively weak assumptions, the BMMR model determines equilibrium growth rates and equilibrium age distributions for the female and male populations. It also determines who marries whom or, more specifically, the age patterns of assortative mating. The model assumes that all fertility is marital fertility and all unions are monogamous, although both of these assumptions are easy to relax. The BMMR model accommodates our common sense conclusion about the effect of a marriage squeeze because it allows changes in the age structure of the population (e.g., shortages of marriageable men relative to marriageable women caused by wars or baby booms) to change the number of unions; although the birth matrix (i.e., the number of births to each type of union) remains constant, changes in the number of unions imply changes in the number of births and, hence, changes in the implied age-specific female fertility rates.

MATCHING MODELS AND SEARCH MODELS

Whether we interpret "unions" narrowly or broadly, the mating rule of the BMMR model is not a full-blown theory of marriage or union formation but a reduced form, presumably reflecting the requirements of equilibrium in the "marriage market." The "marriage market" metaphor is useful because it suggests the notions of choice, competition, and equilibrium, and, hence, the important role that the analytical tools of economics must play in a theory of marriage. (The earliest use of the phrase "marriage market" recorded in the *Oxford English Dictionary* is from *Punch* in 1850. "Marriage mart" is apparently older; Lord Byron used the phrase in *Don Juan* in 1823.)

"Unions" in the BMMR model can be construed narrowly to mean legally sanctioned, formal marriage or broadly to include not only formal marriage but also cohabitation, consensual unions, etc. From a formal modeling standpoint, the interpretation of "marriage" or "mating" makes no difference. Putting empirical meat on bare theoretical bones, however, requires examining individual's preferences and opportunities, and these depend, for example, on whether we define "marriage" to include or exclude cohabitation. Same-sex marriage is an exception to the assertion that the interpretation of marriage makes little differences; because matching and search models usually assume two distinct groups (e.g., men and women; students and colleges), the analysis of same-sex marriage requires different analytical tools.

Economists have two approaches to modeling competition and equilibrium in marriage markets, one based on matching and the other based on search. Both matching and search models begin with the preferences of individuals and analyze their implications for marriage-market equilibrium, but they make different assumptions about the information available to and the alternatives faced by marriage-market participants. Matching models are nonstochastic and timeless; they implicitly assume that complete and accurate information about potential spouses is instantaneously and costlessly available to all marriage-market participants. Search models, in contrast, are stochastic and dynamic; they recognize explicitly that individuals have less than complete and accurate information about potential spouses, and that acquiring more and better information requires resources and takes time; search models often emphasize the role of impatience or, more formally, positive time preference.

Matching Models. A substantial literature now exists on matching models, following the line of analysis begun by Gale and Shapley (1962). Roth and Sotomayor (1990) provide the definitive exposition of matching models. Mortensen (1988) and Weiss (1997) provide accessible introductions to both matching and search approaches. Becker's *Treatise on the Family* (1981; enlarged edition, 1991) relies primarily on matching models in its initial analysis of the marriage market (Chapters 3 and 4), but informally revisits many of these issues from a search perspective in its subsequent discussion of marriage and divorce (Chapter 10).

A "one-to-one matching" assigns at most one man to every woman and at most one woman to every man. In the marriage-market context, an individual who is paired with a member of the opposite sex is said to be "married." "At most" is crucial to the definition of a one-to-one matching. On the one hand, it rules out polygamy and polygyny. On the other, it leaves open the possibility that some men and some women (perhaps many men and many women) will remain unmarried. Although I restrict my attention to one-to-one matchings, generalization to "many-to-one" matchings are relatively straightforward and can be used to analyze the matching of students to colleges and the matching of workers to firms as well as polygamous and polygynous marriages. The wide range of applications of matching models was suggested by the title of Gale and Shapley's classic paper "College Admissions and the Stability of Marriage."

The equilibrium concept for one-to-one matching models, a "stable matching," is defined by two properties: (1) no married individual prefers being unmarried to his or her current assignment and (2) no two individuals of opposite sexes prefer being married to each other to their current assignments. Preferences play a key role in the definition of a stable matching. It is assumed that each man has a ranking of all the women and that each woman has a ranking of all the men; remaining unmarried is treated as an additional alternative ranked by men and by women. Under relatively weak assumptions about the internal consistency of individuals' preferences (e.g., transitivity), at least one stable matching exists; without strong additional assumptions, however, more than one stable matching may exist—that is, equilibrium need not be unique. A simple example illustrates the possibility of multiple equilibria. Suppose there are two men $\{m_1, m_2\}$ and two women $\{w_1, w_2\}$ whose preference rankings are given by

m_1	m_2		w_1	w_2
w_1	w_2		m_2	m_1
w_2	w_1		m_1	m_2

and that every individual would prefer being married with the lowest ranked individual of the opposite sex to being unmarried. Under these assumptions, it is easy to verify that the matchings $\{(m_1, w_1), (m_2, w_2)\}$ and $\{(m_1, w_2), (m_2, w_1)\}$ are both stable matchings. That is, $\{(m_1, w_1), (m_2, w_2)\}$ is stable because the men have been assigned the women they most prefer; hence, switching partners cannot make either man better off. Similarly, $\{(m_1, w_2), (m_2, w_1)\}$ is stable because the women have been assigned the men they most prefer; hence, switching partners cannot make either woman better off. Pollak (1994) provides some discussion of the implications of multiple equilibria for the role of norms and institutions in determining which equilibrium will be realized.

Although matching models can be used to analyze who remains unmarried, who marries, and who marries whom, the analysis has tended to focus on who marries whom and the implied pattern of "assortative mating." Indeed, in theoretical work the issue of who remains unmarried is often bracketed by assuming that there are equal numbers of women and men, and that each individual's preferences are such that remaining unmarried is ranked below all possible marriages. In empirical work, attention is often restricted to those women and men who marry; the resulting analysis is contaminated by selection bias and, of course, cannot shed light on who remains unmarried.

Search Models. In a search model, when two individuals meet in the marriage market, they must decide whether to marry or to continue searching, balancing the attractiveness of marriage now to a particular individual against the expected value of remaining unmarried and continuing to search. Economists are most familiar with search models in the context of labor markets, although some of the modeling assumptions that simplify the analysis of labor markets are less attractive in the context of marriage markets. For example, many labor-market models assume that a worker's consumption opportunities and job offer prospects do not change as search duration increases, assumptions that imply that a worker's optimal decision rule for accepting or rejecting job offers is a "reservation wage" that does not change as search duration increases. This "stationarity" conclusion and the assumptions that lead to it are problematic for labor markets and even more problematic for marriage markets. (To justify stationarity, economists often assume that economic agents' remaining life expectancy is independent of their age, so that mortality, if it occurs at all, is like radioactive decay.)

The simplest marriage-market models assume that the alternatives encountered in the marriage market are individuals of the opposite sex, that each man has a ranking of all women, and that each woman has a ranking of all men. Nothing is said about the origin or nature of these preference rankings. The matching models of Becker (1973, 1981) modify these simplest models by explicitly introducing a single consumption good. Becker's matching model, an application of the Koopmans–Beckmann (1957) assignment model, assumes that individuals care whom they marry only in so far as it affects their consumption; thus, from the standpoint of the marriage-market participants, the alternatives encountered in the marriage market are, in effect, the consumption levels corresponding to particular marriages. Furthermore, Becker assumes "transferable utility," which, loosely speaking, implies that transferring a unit of the consumption good from one individual to another is equivalent to transferring a unit of utility (a "util") from one individual to another. [Bergstrom (1997) and Weiss (1997) discuss transferable utility.] Potential marriages are thus like potential partnerships, producing a surplus that can be divided between the spouses or partners.

Becker assumes that prospective spouses, when they meet in the marriage market, can make binding costlessly-enforceable agreements regarding allocation and distribution within marriage. This assumption, together with the assumption of transferable utility, ensures that competition in the marriage market leads to an "efficient" matching, which, under these assumptions, implies an assignment of spouses that maximizes total output. An alternative formulation, building on the bargaining models of marriage of Manser and Brown (1980) and McElroy and Horney (1981), assumes that prospective spouses, when they meet in the marriage market, cannot make binding agreements but recognize that allocation and distribution within marriage are determined by a "bargaining game" that spouses play after they have married. [Lundberg and Pollak (1996) survey the literature on bargaining models of marriage.]

When bargaining takes place after marriage, the alternatives encountered in the marriage market are marriage to a particular individual, but marriage-market participants recognize that marriage will be followed by bargaining and anticipate the outcome that can be expected to emerge from bargaining within marriage. The inability of prospective spouses to make binding agreements does not alter the logic of competition and equilibrium in matching or search models. As Lundberg and Pollak (1993) show in their analysis of a marriage model without binding agreements, it does open the possibility that marriage markets might yield "inefficient" matches relative to the matches that would be realized if binding, costlessly enforceable agreements were possible.

PREFERENCES, OPPORTUNITIES, AND RATIONAL ACTOR MODELS

Like virtually all economic or rational actor models, matching and search models emphasize choice. The starting point is the assumption that individuals can evaluate, compare, and rank the alternatives available to them and that they choose the one that is best in light of their preferences. Neither type of model, however, attempts to provide an account of the self-interest that underlies choice. Beyond formal consistency requirements, matching models and search models are silent about individuals' preferences for the alternatives they encounter in the marriage market.

In surveying the economics literature on marriage and divorce, Weiss (1997) discusses four economic motives for choosing marriage over non-marriage. (Weiss also recognizes noneconomic motives for marriage.) The first, increasing returns, refers to household production and "economies of scale" whose realization depends on household size. The second, imperfect capital or credit markets, exploits the superior information, monitoring, and enforcement advantages of family relationships to reduce the transaction costs of borrowing and lending. The third, sharing collective or household public goods, emphasizes lumpy consumer durables and on the noneconomic side, "both partners enjoy[ing] the same child." Fourth, risk sharing or insurance, like capital or credit market motives, exploits the information, monitoring, and enforcement advantages of family arrangements relative to market or government insurance and risk sharing arrangements. As Weiss acknowledges, the motives that depend on the transaction costs apply not only to marriage but also to other family-based arrangements.

An essential insight of the rational actor model is that incentives matter: changes in incentives cause individuals to change their behavior in predictable directions. Changes in opportunities can be manifested as changes in prices or wages, or as changes in household technology. In the household production context, an increase in the price of a market good is likely to cause an individual to reduce consumption of those commodities for which the good is an important input. For example, if mothers' time is an important input into the production of children, then the household production model predicts that an increase in women's wage rates, which the household production model interprets as the price of time, is likely to reduce the production of children. By the same reasoning, the model predicts that women with higher wage rates (e.g., those with more education or "human capital") are likely to have fewer children. Of course these predictions are hedged: for example, the new home economics recognizes that higher wages have "income effects" that may outweigh their "substitution effects," so that an increase in women's wage rates might increase rather than decrease the number of children. A more sophisticated analysis also recognizes both "unobserved heterogeneity" and the endogeneity of wages. For example, high-wage women may differ from low-wage women in ability, preferences, or other unmeasured dimensions, and these differences may cause differences in wages; a researcher may mistakenly attribute the observed differences in behavior (e.g., nonmarital fertility, marriage, marital fertility, divorce, remarriage, investments in children's human capital) to differences in wages even if the real cause of differences in both wages and behavior is (unobserved) differences in ability and preferences.

Another essential insight of the rational actor model is that an individual's decisions are interrelated and, hence, cannot be analyzed separately, one decision at a time. Thus, decisions regarding marriage must be analyzed in conjunction with other behaviors such as nonmarital fertility, marital fertility, divorce, remarriage, human capital accumulation, and labor force participation. The rational actor model assumes that individuals are forward looking; they recognize that their choices today have predictable, although not perfectly predictable, consequences for the future.

The rational actor model offers two explanatory categories, preferences and opportunities, but it provides little guidance for disentangling their contributions to changes in behavior. In "De Gustibus Non Est Disputandum," Stigler and Becker (1977) provide an authoritative statement of the orthodox position among neoclassical economists that economics should treat preferences as fixed and exogenous. Their claim is not that preference change cannot "explain" changes in behavior, but rather that it can explain too much: any change in behavior, whether caused by changes in opportunities or by changes in preferences, can be attributed to preference change.

In more recent work, Becker and his collaborators recognize the importance of preference formation and change. Their work builds on earlier work by economists, much of it outside the neoclassical tradition [e.g., the Marxists, Veblen, Galbraith, Gintis, Bowles, and Gintis; Bowles (1998) survey this literature] as well as more recent work in consumer demand analysis [Houthakker and Taylor, Pollak, Pollak and Wales; Pollak and Wales (1992, Chapter 4) survey this literature]. Becker (1992, 1996) provides an expansive view of preference formation, recognizing the roles of parents and other family members and of others ("peer pressure"). By postulating specific mechanisms of preference formation, these models avoid the Stigler–Becker critique that preference change can explain "too much."

To what extent do recent changes in patterns of marriage, divorce, fertility, and childrearing reflect changes in preferences—that is, changes in the way individuals rank alternatives—and to what extent do they reflect changes in the set of alternatives or opportunities available? Explanations usually emphasize either cultural variables (e.g., preferences, values, ideology) or economic variables, including underlying technological variables (e.g., prices, wages, particularly women's wages, welfare payments, the spread of computers). Preston (1986), Lesthaeghe and Surkyn (1988), and Pollak and Watkins (1993) reject this "either–or" view and recognize both economic and cultural variables. Pollak and Watkins (1993) discuss the difficulties of disentangling preferences or culture-based explanations from economic or opportunity-based explanations in the context of the fertility transition, but much of that discussion extends readily to marriage. Following Pollak and Watkins (1993), I conclude this section by making four points:

1. The relative importance of cultural variables and economic variables should be an empirical question, but this requires specifying "culture" as something other than a "residual."

2. Economic variables are presumably susceptible to policy (e.g., tax policy, welfare policy). Cultural variables may also be susceptible to policy (e.g., advertising campaigns) but evidence on the ability of policy to alter behavior by influencing culture is scarce. The issues here are similar to those that arise in attempting to encourage couples to limit their fertility (e.g., by subsidizing condoms or by persuading couples that small families are more desirable than large families).

3. Dynamic interactions between economic and cultural variables may be important. One can tell a plausible story and write down a tractable model (e.g., of interdependent preferences) in which economic variables influence cultural or preference variables (e.g., as women's wage rates rise, women's participation in the market increases; as more women participate in the market, preferences shift to make women's participation in the labor force a more acceptable alternative for other women and more acceptable to men). Cultural variables (e.g., redefinitions of socially acceptable gender roles for women) presumably can affect economic variables (e.g., human capital accumulation, labor force participation).

4. It may be impossible, in principle, to disentangle cultural and economic influences. That is, some cultural explanations may provide an alternative to rational actor explanations "by denying the

validity of a dichotomous classification scheme that distinguishes between opportunities and preferences. To borrow a metaphor from chemistry, such cultural explanations are not simply mixtures of opportunities and preferences, but new compounds whose elements—opportunities and preferences—are bonded together to form a new molecule with distinct characteristics" (Pollak and Watkins, 1993).

EFFICIENCY

An equilibrium is said to be efficient with respect to a particular group if no member of that group can be made better off without making some other group member worse off. In the marriage-market context, a threshold distinction is between efficiency from the standpoint of marriage-market participants and efficiency from the standpoint of a broader group that also includes the children of marriage-market participants. A broader notion of efficiency considers not only marriage but also related choices such as marital and nonmarital fertility, divorce, remarriage, and investment in children's human capital, choices that cannot be separated from marriage-market choices in a rational actor model.

Waite (1995), in her PAA presidential address, focuses on the connection between marriage and the well-being of marriage-market participants. Presenting data on several dimensions of well-being, she concludes that marriage is good for both husbands and wives. Although conceding that some of the apparent benefits of marriage reflect selection, Waite argues that many of the apparent benefits are real. Yet, Waite asks: "If marriage produces all these benefits for individuals, why has it declined?" (p. 499).

Her answer is that marriage has declined because the returns to marriage have declined, for both men and women (e.g., "because of increases in women's employment, there is less specialization by spouses" and because "high divorce rates decrease people's certainty about the long-run stability of *their* marriage, and thus may reduce their willingness to invest in it"). She also asserts that the benefits of marriage "are *not* well known outside the research community" and declares her belief that "social scientists have an obligation to point out the benefits of marriage."

Waite presents no evidence, however, that individuals underestimate the benefits they would derive from marriage. Neither the fact that not all adults marry nor the recent decline in marriage implies that individuals underestimate the benefits they would derive from marriage or overestimate the costs. Economists are professionally skeptical of claims that social scientists or policymakers are better able to judge the self-interest of individuals than the individuals themselves.

If, as Waite (1995) suggests, marriage-market participants are unaware of the benefits that they would derive from marriage, then marriage-market equilibrium will be inefficient even from the perspective of marriage-market participants. The "revealed preference" arguments that economists often use to analyze efficiency involve two steps: first, they infer preferences from observed choices and, second, they equate preference with well-being. Thus, an individual who chooses alternative X and rejects alternative Y "reveals" a preference for X over Y. (Think of X and Y as multidimensional alternatives, involving, for example, not only marriage but also nonmarital and marital fertility, divorce, etc.) Furthermore, if we evaluate well-being in terms of preferences, then we can conclude that the individual who chooses X is better off with X than he or she would have been with Y.

Revealed preference arguments rest on the twin assumptions that individuals' preferences deserve deference ("consumer sovereignty") and that individuals are sufficiently well informed that their decisions reflect not only their preferences but also the constraints they actually face. Sen (1977) discusses the philosophical issues raised by equating preference with well-being. Kahneman et al. (1999) survey the psychological issues raised by equating preference, as economists understand the term, with satisfaction or well-being. Philipson and Hedges (1998) deal with the informational issues, elaborating the self-selection arguments of Heckman, to argue that participants in experiments (e.g., clinical trials, job training programs) are often better able to evaluate the effectiveness of "treatments" than outside investigators; hence, they argue, that data on the difference between the attrition rates of treatment and control groups should be utilized in estimating treatment effects.

Arguments that equilibrium is inefficient from a standpoint that recognizes the well-being of children rest on a different foundation than arguments that consider only the well-being of marriage-market participants. If we accept consumer sovereignty and equate well-being with choice, then arguments based on the well-being of marriage-market participants must rely on claims that individuals misperceive the consequences of their own actions. On the other hand, arguments based on the well-being of children can appeal not only to misperception, but also to the economist's traditional rationale for government intervention, externalities.

Externalities arise when one individual's well-being is affected by the behavior of others, and these effects are not mediated through markets. Air and water pollution are classic examples of negative externalities: the behavior of polluters affects those living nearby, but polluters do not pay their neighbors for the right to pollute. [Readers familiar with Coase (1960) will recognize that the situation is more complex and more symmetric than this sentence suggests.] Positive externalities are less prominent in the economic literature, perhaps because they are less common; the classic example is a beekeeper whose bees pollinate a nearby apple orchard.

Economists usually follow Becker (1981) and assume that parents' preferences reflect their children's well-being; more precisely, Becker assumes that parents are "altruistic" in the sense that their preferences include the utilities of their children. The appeal to "parents' preferences," however, masks two crucial issues. First, Becker's model is a "common preference model"—the family behaves like an individual with a single preference ordering. Lundberg and Pollak (1996, 1999) discuss the theoretical and empirical problems with common preference models and advocate replacing them with models in which husbands and wives have distinct preferences that are reconciled by bargaining. A bargaining approach is also necessary if we are to understand results such as those reported in Thomas (1990), which purport to show that children do better when their mothers control a larger fraction of family resources. An approach that recognizes the separate preferences of husbands and wives also facilitates the comparison of the well-being of children in a single-parent (e.g., female-headed) family with what their well-being would have been in a two-parent family because it allows us to compare parental behavior in single-parent families with parental behavior in two-parent families.

Because adults are the decision makers in the rational actor model, the well-being of children depends on the extent to which adults' preferences and values give weight to the needs of children. Decisions about fertility, marriage, and divorce reflect adults' resources and preferences with whatever weight they give to their children's well-being. The altruist model assumes that parents care about their children's well-being, but it makes no assumption about "how much" they care. If the parents are "rich enough and altruistic enough," to borrow a phrase from Behrman et al. (1995, Introduction), then parents will allocate sufficient resources (e.g., time and money) to the child to provide the child with the wealth-maximizing level of human capital. [The issues this raises are discussed in Becker and Murphy (1988) (reprinted Becker, 1991, Chapter 11 Supplement), in Behrman et al. (1995, Chapter 5), and in Lundberg and Pollak (1999).] To the extent that the decisions of men and women regarding fertility, marriage, and divorce affect the number of children who fail to receive the wealth-maximizing level of human capital, these decisions create externalities (e.g., by affecting the probability that children will graduate from high school or from college).

McLanahan and Sandefur (1994) provide evidence that children who grow up with both biological parents are likely to do better in a variety of dimensions (e.g., the probability of high school graduation, the probability of involvement in crime, or the probability of a teen-age nonmarital pregnancy) than when they grow up with a single parent or a stepparent.

Dan Quayle, when he was Vice President, launched the "family values" debate in the popular media in 1992 by attacking the television program "Murphy Brown" whose title character had a child out-of-wedlock. In an article entitled "Dan Quayle Was Right," Whitehead (1993) summarizes for a nonprofessional audience the social science research on the apparent consequences for children of nonmarital childbearing and divorce. To the extent that these correlations between family structure and outcomes for children reflect underlying causal connections—and the extent to which they do is an open question—they have profound implications for public policies affecting the incentives to marry and remain married.

CONCLUSION

Matching models and search models envision equilibrium in the marriage market in different ways, each emphasizing issues that the other deemphasizes or ignores. Matching models assume that marriage-market participants have full information, while search models focus on imperfect information and information acquisition. In both matching and search models, however, marriage-market participants are assumed to behave rationally in light of their preferences and the opportunities they believe are available to them. Thus, for both types of models, the explanatory categories of the rational actor model, preferences and opportunities, provide a taxonomy for analyzing marriage-market behavior.

In evaluating the efficiency of marriage-market equilibrium, we distinguish between the perspective of marriage-market participants and a broader perspective that includes other affected individuals such as children. If, as Waite (1995) suggests, marriage-market participants are unaware of the benefits that they would derive from marriage, then marriage-market equilibrium will be inefficient even from the narrow perspective of marriage-market participants. If, as McLanahan and Sandefur (1994) suggest, family structure affects the life-chances of children, and if the interests of marriage-market participants do not coincide with those of their children, then the marriage market creates externalities. These externalities imply that the marriage-market equilibrium will be inefficient from a broad perspective that includes not only the well-being of adults but also the well-being of children.

ACKNOWLEDGMENTS

This chapter draws heavily on Pollak (1997). I am grateful to the John Simon Guggenheim Memorial Foundation and the John D. and Catherine T. MacArthur Foundation for financial support, to Thomas K. Burch and particularly Elizabeth

Thomson for helpful comments, and to Joanne Spitz for editorial assistance. An earlier version of this paper was presented at an NIH conference, "Ties that Bind: Perspectives on Marriage and Cohabitation," Bethesda, Maryland, June 29–30, 1998.

REFERENCES

Becker, Gary S. 1973."A Theory of Marriage: Part I." *Journal of Political Economy* 81:813–846.

Becker, Gary S. 1981. *Treatise on the Family*. Cambridge, MA: Harvard University Press. (Enlarged edition, 1991.)

Becker, Gary S. 1992. "Habits, Addictions, and Traditions." *Kyklos* 45:327–345.

Becker, Gary S. 1996. *Accounting for Tastes*. Cambridge, MA: Harvard University Press.

Becker, Gary S., and Kevin M. Murphy. 1988. "The Family and the State." *Journal of Law and Economics* 31:1–17.

Behrman, Jere R., Robert A. Pollak, and Paul Taubman. 1995. *From Parent to Child: Inequality and Immobility in the United States*. Chicago: University of Chicago Press.

Bergstrom, Theodore C. 1997. "A Survey of Theories of the Family." Pp. 21–79 in *Handbook of Population and Family Economics*, Vol. 1A, edited by Mark R. Rosenzweig and Oded Stark. Amsterdam: North-Holland.

Bowles, Samuel. 1998. "Endogenous Preferences: The Cultural Consequences of Markets and Other Economic Institutions." *Journal of Economic Literature* 36:75–111.

Coase, Ronald. 1960. "The Problem of Social Cost." *Journal of Law and Economics* 3:1–44.

Feeney, Griffith M. 1972. "Marriage Rates and Population Growth: The Two-Sex Problem in Demography." Ph.D. dissertation, University of California, Berkeley.

Gale, David, and Lloyd Shapley. 1962. "College Admission and the Stability of Marriage." *American Mathematical Monthly* 69:9–15.

Kahneman, Daniel, Edward Diener, and Norbert Schwarz, eds. 1999. *Well-Being: The Foundations of Hedonic Psychology*. New York: Russell Sage Foundation.

Koopmans, Tjalling C., and Martin Beckmann. 1957. "Assignment Problems and the Location of Economic Activities." *Econometrica* 25:53–76.

Lesthaeghe, Ron, and Johan Surkyn. 1988. "Cultural Dynamics and Economic Theories of Fertility Change." *Population and Development Review* 14:1–45.

Lundberg, Shelly, and Robert A. Pollak. 1993. "Separate Spheres Bargaining and the Marriage Market." *Journal of Political Economy* 101:988–1010.

Lundberg, Shelly, and Robert A. Pollak. 1996. "Bargaining and Distribution in Marriage." *Journal of Economic Perspectives* 10:139–158.

Lundberg, Shelly, and Robert A. Pollak. 1999. "Bargaining in Families." University of Washington, Seattle, WA. Unpublished manuscript.

Manser, Marilyn, and Murray Brown. 1980. "Marriage and Household Decision-Making: A Bargaining Analysis." *International Economic Review* 21:31–44.

McElroy, Marjorie B., and Mary J. Horney. 1981. "Nash-Bargained Household Decisions: Toward a Generalization of the Theory of Demand." *International Economic Review* 22:333–349.

McLanahan, Sara, and Gary Sandefur. 1994. *Growing up with a Single Parent: What Hurts, What Helps.* Cambridge, MA: Harvard University Press.

Mortensen, Dale T. 1988. "Matching: Finding a Partner for Life or Otherwise." Pp. S215–S240 in *American Journal of Sociology*, Vol. 94, Supplement, *Organizations and Institutions: Sociological and Economic Approaches to the Analysis of Social Structure*, edited by Christopher Winship and Sherwin Rosen. Chicago: University of Chicago Press.

Philipson, Tomas, and Larry V. Hedges. 1998."Subject Evaluation in Social Experiments." *Econometrica* 66:381–408.

Pollak, Robert A. 1986. "A Reformulation of the Two-Sex Problem." *Demography* 23:247–259.

Pollak, Robert A. 1990. "Two-Sex Demographic Models." *Journal of Political Economy* 98:399–420.

Pollak, Robert A. 1994. "Taking Power Seriously," Washington University in St. Louis, MO. Unpublished manuscript.

Pollak, Robert A. 1997. "Theories of Marriage." *Proceedings of the GeneralPopulation Conference of the International Union for the Scientific Study of Population* 2:905–917.

Pollak, Robert A., and Terence J. Wales. 1992. *Demand System Specification and Estimation*, New York: Oxford University Press.

Pollak, Robert A., and Susan Cotts Watkins. 1993. "Cultural and Economic Approaches to Fertility: Proper Marriage or *Mésalliance*?" *Population and Development Review* 19:467–496.

Preston, Samuel H. 1986. "Changing Values and Falling Birth Rates." Pp. 176–195 in *A Population and Development Review*, Vol. 12, Supplement, *Below-Replacement Fertility in Industrial Societies: Causes, Consequences, Policies*, edited by K. Davis, M. S. Bernstam, and R. Ricardo-Campbell.

Roth, Alvin E., and Marilda A. Oliveira Sotomayor. 1990. *Two-sided Matching: A Study in Game-Theoretic Modeling and Analysis.* Cambridge, MA: Cambridge University Press.

Sen, Amartya. 1977. "Rational Fools: A Critique of the Behavioural Foundations of Economic Theory." *Philosophy and Public Affairs* 6:317–344.

Stigler, George J., and Gary S. Becker. 1977. "De Gustibus Non Est Disputandum." *American Economic Review* 67:76–90.

Thomas, Duncan. 1990. "Intra-Household Resource Allocation: An Inferential Approach." *Journal of Human Resources* 25:635–664.

Waite, Linda. 1995. "Does Marriage Matter?" *Demography* 32:483–507.

Weiss, Yoram. 1997. "The Formation and Dissolution of Families: Why Marry? Who Marries Whom? And What Happens upon Divorce." Pp. 81–123 in *Handbook of Population and Family Economics*, Vol. 1A, edited by Mark R. Rosenzweig and Oded Stark. Amsterdam: North-Holland.

Whitehead, Barbara Dafoe. 1993. "Dan Quayle Was Right." *Atlantic Monthly* 271: 47–84.

7

Toward a New Home Socioeconomics of Union Formation

ANDREW J. CHERLIN

Although most people in the developed world marry for love, they don't marry *only* for love. Rather, most people also make rational calculations about the costs and benefits of marrying the individuals they love. Is he or she likely to maintain steady employment? Be generous and fair-minded? Good with children? Willing to share the housework? If the answers to questions such as these are unsatisfactory, people often will not marry the objects of their love. Consequently, social scientists have found that theories of rational decision making can help explain the marriage choices that individuals make. For example, many studies show that in the United States, young men who are employed are more likely to marry than are young men who are unemployed. Social scientists would explain this pattern as follows: in American society, married men are expected to contribute substantially to their family's income. Most young women consider whether the financial benefits a potential partner could bring are sufficient to justify a marriage. If not, they usually wait for an improvement in earning potential or look for someone else.

This chapter reviews the rational decision-making approach to studying union formation (by which I mean the formation of either marital or cohabiting unions) since its introduction in the mid-twentieth century and suggests some new directions. I focus mainly on the United States. Since mid-century, rational decision-making theories of the process of entry into first marriage have been dominated by a model first advanced in sociology in the 1950s by Talcott Parsons (Parsons and Bales, 1955) and in economics in the 1960s by Gary Becker (1965, 1981). It is a model of role specialization and the gains to trading money and services with a spouse: marriage is said to be most advantageous when the woman specializes in home production and the man specializes in labor market production. Whether or not the assumptions of the theory are correct, it has led to predictions that seem to fit the workings of the marriage market—until recently, at least. For example, the theory is consistent with the example discussed above: it predicts than employed men should be more likely to marry because they can offer women a higher level of income and are therefore more attractive as marriage partners.

But recent evidence suggests that another key prediction of the specialization and gains-to-trade model is no longer accurate: women with greater labor market potential, according to the theory, should be less likely to marry. This prediction follows from the idea that wives specialize in housework and child care and obtain most of their income from their husbands. If so (and it *was* so for most women when Parsons and Becker first developed their theories in the mid-twentieth century), then women who can earn good incomes themselves would gain less economically from marrying. Put otherwise, women with higher earnings would need to marry less in order to have an adequate income. Therefore they should be less likely to marry than women who could not earn much on their own. But data I will review in this chapter show that, contrary to the theory, women with greater labor market potential are now *more* likely to marry.

Moreover, since the 1970s, cohabitation outside of marriage, which had previously been confined to the poor, has become increasingly common and acceptable among the general population. It has emerged as an important part of the union formation process, often preceding first marriages and sometimes substituting for them. Any theory of union formation must take it into account explicitly. Yet the theorists of the specialization and gains-to-trade theory, who began writing the in 1950s and 1960s, never considered cohabitation as part of the process to be modeled.

The old paradigm in social science, then, is in need of revision. Some of its predictions are contradicted by recent data and it is silent on the important topic of premarital cohabitation. I believe that over the next decade, we will see the emergence of a new paradigm that better fits the facts. Already we can see the stirrings of new approaches. In this chapter I would like to review the recent research and to suggest some of the directions I think this new work will take. I will argue that it must combine both the rational choice approach that has been highly developed in economics and the social structural and cultural approaches of sociology. It must also draw on the insights of evolutionary psychologists. The existing rational decision-making theory is sometimes called the "new home economics," in contrast to the homemaker-oriented "home economics" courses prevalent in many universities in the 1950s and 1960s. I think we are beginning to see the transformation of the new home economics of marriage into a broader, new home socioeconomics of union formation.

FROM SPECIALIZATION TO SYMMETRY

In the mid-twentieth century, the typical marriage bargain was indeed one of specialization: women sought men who would earn enough to support a family, at least during the peak childrearing years, and men sought women who would raise their children and do the housework. Most married women did not work outside the home while they were raising children. Most men did little child care or housework. Even among African-American women, who have historically worked outside the home in larger numbers than have whites, a majority of wives did not work outside the home as recently as 1960.[1] Today, at the start of the twenty-first century, it is much more common for married women to work outside the home, although their wages still tend be less than their husbands' wages. And husbands are doing a greater share of the child care and housework, although wives still do the majority of it.

We might categorize contemporary marriages and partnerships as symmetrical rather than specialized. In 1973, British sociologists Michael Young and Peter Willmott wrote about the emergence of the "symmetrical family," in which the roles of husbands and wives were similar in that women did some market work and men did some home work (Young and Willmott, 1973). Symmetric does not yet mean identical, they cautioned, because men still do more in the labor market and less at home. Nevertheless, they argued that a transition to a different form of marriage had occurred.

THE GAINS TO TRADE MODEL

During the heyday of the breadwinner–homemaker marriage, social scientists developed theories to explain the sharp division of labor between wives and husbands. In sociology, Parsons and his colleague Robert F. Bales proposed that small groups, including families, functioned best when one person took on the role of "instrumental leader" and another took on the role of "socioemotional" leader (Parsons and Bales, 1955). In economics, Gary Becker argued that if women are more productive in home work than men, or men are more productive at paid work, the partners would maximize their utility if the man specialized in paid work and the woman specialized in home work (Becker, 1965). By trading income from paid work for child care and housework services, both the wife and husband would gain. These sociological and economic theories rested on an often unstated assumption that human evolution had selected women to be more productive at childrearing and emotional labor than men.

A key corollary of the specialization theories is that women with higher earning potential and a greater career orientation should be less likely than other women to marry both because they would have less to gain monetarily by marrying and because men would not prefer them. Jessie Bernard (1972) presented two tables for teenage women in 1960 that showed that teenagers with more income or better jobs were less likely to marry. (In the 1950s, teenage marriage was much more common than it is now.) However, there is no good empirical test of this hypothesis on nonteenagers using 1950s or even 1960s data that I know of. Studies based on 1970s data on women's educational attainment (an indicator of earnings potential) and marriage typically found modest positive effects of education on marriage probabilities or no effect (Cherlin, 1980; Sweeney, 1997; Waite and Spitze, 1981). Several recent studies suggest that the positive effect of women's education on marriage has become substantially stronger over time in the United States and Canada, in contradiction to the specialization theory's prediction (Goldscheider et al., 1998; Oppenheimer et al., 1995; Sweeney, 1997). Direct questions about preferences show comparable findings: unmarried men and women aged 19–35 in the 1987 National Survey of Families and Households were asked how likely it would be for them to marry partners with particular characteristics. Neither men nor women were very willing to marry someone who was "unlikely to hold a job." In fact, men were much more willing to marry a woman who was "not good looking" than to marry one who was unlikely to hold a job (South, 1991).

Thus, whether or not Becker's gains-to-trade model and Parsons and Bales's small-group dynamics theories predicted which young women were more likely to marry in the mid-twentieth century, they are strongly contradicted by recent data. To be sure, the Becker model still helps to explain trends over time because it predicts that as women's earning potential increases relative to men, the gains to marriage will decline and marriage rates should fall. This has indeed occurred: the median age at marriage has been increasing since 1960 and is now 27 for men and 25 for women; and 10% of women aged 40–44 in 1996 had never married, compared to 5% in 1970 (U. S. Bureau of the Census, 1998).[2] But on an individual level, the model no longer predicts well which women are more likely to marry. And neither the Becker nor the Parsons and Bales models addresses premarital cohabitation at all.

BEYOND GAINS TO TRADE

Men's Declining Earnings. Why, then, has an increasingly positive association emerged between women's earning potential and their likelihood of marrying? The best-developed explanation is Valerie Kincade

Table 7.1. Percentage Never Married for U. S. Men, Age 30, by Education: 1970, 1980, and 1990

	College Degree	Some College	High School Degree	Less Than High School Degree
1970	16	13	10	15
1980	24	17	16	21
1990	33	28	27	33

Source: Tabulations by R. Kelly Raley from U. S. Bureau of the Census public use microdata files.

Oppenheimer's argument that the declining earning potential of young men underlies the shift (Oppenheimer, 1988; Oppenheimer et al., 1995, 1997; Oppenheimer and Lew, 1995). Because she is contributing a chapter to this volume, I will not describe her views in detail. Her basic thesis is that as young men's earnings have declined, they have come to prefer women with whom they can pool earnings rather than women who will not work for pay.

It is a persuasive argument for which Oppenheimer has amassed considerable evidence, and I accept its importance. But it is unlikely to be the sole explanation for the trends in union formation. Consider trends in age at marriage for men with different levels of education. Oppenheimer's thesis implies that increases in age at marriage should be much greater among men who have not attended college than for men who have attended college because the former group has suffered a substantial decline in economic fortunes whereas the latter group, by and large, has not. Table 7.1 shows the percentage ever married for men at age 30, by educational attainment, for 1970, 1980, and 1990.[3] As the reader can see, sharp drops in the percentage ever married occurred among all groups, not just the less well educated. In fact, the beginning and ending figures for college graduates are nearly identical to the figures for men without a high school degree. These numbers suggest that factors other than the declining fortunes of non-college-educated men contributed to the delay in marriage.

Fertility Decline. What other factors, in addition to declining economic opportunities for young men, might account for the shift toward later marriage and the symmetrical family? I would suggest that one important factor is the long-term decline in fertility, interrupted only by the 1950s baby boom.[4] In this process the economic benefits of having children have declined and the costs of raising them have increased. Parents therefore have fewer children and invest more resources in them. This change increases women's attachment to the labor force because the period of time when young children are home has shortened and the need to supply more income for college education and other expenses has increased. Women and men postpone marriage while both invest in increasing their earning potential through education and work experience. In support of this argument, long-term trends for the twentieth century reveal that age at marriage was lower during the baby boom than before or since (Cherlin, 1992).

Material Aspirations and Cultural Change. Young and Willmott suggest that increasing aspirations for a higher standard of living may be responsible, in part, for the shifting marriage bargain. They ascribe this materialism to a democratic culture in Great Britain (and by extension in the United States) in which increases in national income allow the upper classes to obtain new goods (such as, currently, the home computer). These goods then diffuse through the population, as the VCR has recently done. A greater emphasis on consumption within the home requires a larger income and creates pressure for women to work for pay. It also increases investment in earning potential prior to marriage for women and men. This argument shades into a more general explanation based on the long-term growth of individualism in Western societies—a development that is related to industrialization but also involves independent, cultural change. Several theorists of the timing of fertility declines, both historically in Europe and currently in developing countries, have contended that cultural change has had important independent affects on people's childbearing preferences (Cleland and Hobcraft, 1985).

Women's Bargaining Power and Cohabitation. I would like to advance another possible explanation for delayed marriage, one that is complementary to Oppenheimer's approach, in that it emphasizes women's resources (rather than men's) and it applies to better educated young adults more than to the poorly educated. My claim is that the bargaining position of women has improved and that women are using their improved bargaining position not just to search for men with higher earning potential but also to search for men who will share more equitably in home production: housework and child care. Moreover, women are incorporating premarital cohabitation into the search and bargaining processes because cohabitation provides a better opportunity to observe men's skills and preferences for home production.

The bargaining position of women has improved in part because of their greater earning potential, compared to men. Earnings data suggest that among women and men with some college education, women's earnings have increased faster than men's (Bianchi and Spain, 1996). Among the less well educated, women's earnings have been stagnant while the earnings of men have declined (Bianchi and Spain, 1996). In both cases, women's bargaining power relative to men has increased, but among the less well educated this change has more to do with men's declining labor market position than with women's gains.

The principle that the greater earning potential of women improves their bargaining position can be derived from several social scientific frameworks. In sociology, social exchange theory predicts that when women's alternative resources increase, their partners have less power in shaping the terms of a relationship (Cook et al., 1990). In social psychology, the concept of a comparison level for alternatives expresses a similar notion (Thibaut and Kelley, 1959). In game-theoretic economics, the minimum level of benefits a woman will accept before ending a relationship—her so-called threat point—increases when alternative sources of support increase (Weiss, 1997).

But I would add that the bargaining position of women also has improved because of better birth control technology (e.g., the birth control pill) and the availability of abortion. These technological advances have allowed women to have intimate relationships and residential partnerships with men without fear of pregnancy. They can therefore extend their search process to include trial relationships and partnerships prior to marriage.

During this search process, women may be looking for evidence not only of men's earning potential, as has been emphasized in the literature, but also of men's willingness to share housework and childrearing. This willingness is difficult to observe outside of an intimate relationship. Consequently, sexual relationships that involve regular overnight visits and cohabiting unions are valuable sources of information that can otherwise be obtained only indirectly. That women tend to prefer men who share the home tasks is suggested by the repeated finding that men with more egalitarian gender-role attitudes have higher marital satisfaction and are less likely to divorce (Amato and Booth, 1995; Bahr and Day, 1978; Blair, 1993; Kaufman, forthcoming; Perry-Jenkins and Crouter, 1992; Vannoy and Philliber, 1992), whereas women with more egalitarian attitudes have lower marital satisfaction and are more likely to anticipate a divorce (Huber and Spitze, 1983; Lye and Biblarz, 1993; Lueptow et al., 1989).

Clarkberg (1997) provides evidence that young women with high earning potential may be using cohabitation as a way to observe men's suitability for marriage. Using data from the 1972 to 1996 waves of the National Longitudinal Survey of the High School class of 1972, she reports that women with higher earning potential were more likely to cohabit than to marry, whereas men with higher earning potential were more likely to marry than cohabit. We know that married women tend to spend several more hours per week in housework than do cohabiting women (Shelton and John, 1993). This difference may be in part a selection effect (i.e., women who enjoy caring for children and maintaining a home may be more likely to marry), but it may also be that married women pay a house-work penalty that cohabiting women do not. Women who are most attractive on the marriage market economically may be able to use their position to bargain for a better household division of labor and may use cohabitation to observe whether that bargain is likely to be upheld.

This is not to say that a women's bargaining position is typically as strong as a man's. Women still earn substantially less, on average, than men. Women may also care more, on average, about emotional connections, altruism, and raising children than do men. England and Kilbourne (1990) suggest as much and argue that the different childhood experiences of girls and boys may be responsible for these adult differences. It is also possible that women's greater caring is a deep-seated tendency that has an evolutionary basis. Beutel and Marini (1995) analyzed data on the attitudes of high school seniors in the Monitoring the Future surveys between 1977 and 1991. Throughout the period, girls were more likely to express concern and responsibility for the well-being of others and were less likely to accept materialism and competition. In contrast to this lack of change, there were substantial changes in girls' attitudes toward gender roles and their occupational aspirations. Beutel and Marini argue that the persistent gender differences on orientation toward others most likely result from differences in socialization, although they acknowledge that "the possible influence of biological sex differences, particularly on orientation toward others, also needs to be ruled out" (p. 443). Whatever the reason, if women care more about emotional connection and children, they will be disadvantaged in their negotiations with men about home production because, in England and Kilbourne's words, "women do not bargain as far toward the margins of their power as men do" (England and Kilbourne, 1990:171).

Are Women Worse off?   A recent paper by Akerlof et al. (1996) goes even further, claiming that the introduction of the birth control pill and the legalization of abortion created a "technology shock" that has hurt women and children by reducing women's ability to marry. The argument is that men can now demand sex without commitment and can find some women willing to agree; therefore, women who wish to marry are disadvantaged because they can no longer trade sexual access for marriage. Nor can they convince men to marry them if they become pregnant. The result, say the authors, has been less marriage and more childbearing outside of marriage.

Without doubt, better contraception and abortion availability have contributed to sexual activity among unmarried individuals and to the growth of cohabitation. In that sense, the "technology shock" has had an impact. In addition, it may have weakened the bargaining position of women who have few other qualities attractive to men—in particular, women with low earning potential. But the authors do not consider the possibility that better birth control may have strengthened the bargaining position of women who have other desirable qualities—in particular, women with higher earning potential. For these women, the gains to marriage are lower and the costs, such as having to do most of the housework, remain. Men increasingly recognize the value of these women's earning power and want to become their partners. Contraception and abortion give these women greater control over their own fertility, which allows them to enter into intimate relationships with men and to better observe their partner's characteristics before committing to a marriage. Their choices and their satisfaction with their partners may be improved as a result. In other words, Akerlof et al. (1996) err in assuming that regular sexual access is the only bargaining chip women can play and that, having played it, marriage is the desirable result.

COHABITATION AND MARRIAGE

All this presumes that premarital cohabitation is an acceptable, common living arrangement that serves as an information-gathering stage in the process of marriage. Data now suggest that a majority of recent first marriages are preceded by a period of cohabitation. Prior to about 1970, cohabitation was rare outside of the poor. Today, there is little stigma attached to living with a partner outside of marriage, except among socially conservative religious groups.

But as widely noted as cohabitation is, it still provides a theoretical challenge. Observers differ about its meaning, and theorists of marriage formation have largely ignored it. To incorporate cohabitation, it is necessary to understand its cultural meaning and how the cultural meaning of marriage differs. I would argue that there are two key elements of the cultural meaning of cohabitation in the United States currently:

As a Long-Term Arrangement, Cohabitation Is Still Seen as Inferior to Marriage. Studies of adolescents and never-married young adults show that the vast majority still want to marry. In fact, the vast majority do marry: nearly 90% of whites and 70–75% of African- Americans (Cherlin, 1992). Even among African-Americans, marriage seems to be the preferred living arrangement, but individuals from low-income families often see it as not feasible. Frank F. Furstenberg, Jr. (1996) argues on the basis of a series of interviews with low-income African-Americans that marriage has taken on the status of a "luxury consumer item," whereas cohabitation is "the budget way" to start a family.

If cohabitation were becoming more acceptable as a long-term partnership arrangement, its average duration should be increasing. That is not, however, the case in the United States. In a recent analysis, Bumpass and Lu (1998) estimate that between 1987 and 1995, the expected duration of cohabiting unions remained virtually the same. A little more than half ended, either by marriage or separation, within 1 year. Eighty-three percent in 1995 (and 82% in 1987) had ended within 3 years. This short duration stands in contrast to Scandinavia, where long-term cohabiting unions have been much more common, and to other Western European nations, where average durations are somewhat longer than in the United States.

The typically short durations in the United States, along with expressed preferences for marriage, suggest that marriage is still the goal for most young adults and cohabitation is still seen as an intermediate status. There has been debate among American demographers on this point. Some have maintained that cohabitation is more like singlehood than marriage (Rindfuss and VandenHeuvel, 1990). For instance, the school enrollment rate of cohabiting young adults is more like the rate among single individuals than married individuals. But this debate can be resolved by introducing the concepts of manifest and latent functions, developed in sociology by Robert K. Merton (1968). A manifest function is a publicly stated, acknowledged one. A latent function is unacknowledged and unstated. The manifest function of cohabitation is to provide a satisfying intimate relationship; on a day-to-day level most cohabitors may think little about marriage. Nevertheless, the latent function is often as an information-gathering stage prior to a making a decision to marry; that is evident by virtue of the regularity with which cohabitation leads either to marriage (about half the time) or to a break-up within a short period of time.

To Marry, It Is Culturally Required that the Man Have the Capacity to Provide Steady Earnings. I have said earlier that it is now desirable for the woman to have good earning potential. I claim here that it is still *required* of men. They no longer need the capacity to wholly support a family but they do need the capacity to provide a substantial amount of support, usually more than half. This cultural requirement may even have an evolutionary basis in the responsibility of men in hunter–gatherer societies to provide protection and part of the food supply for mothers and children. It is the difficulty of fulfilling this cultural requirement, I believe, that underlies the sharp decline in marriage among African-Americans. It is not simply a matter of the wages of women increasing relative to the wages of men, which has occurred to a greater extent among African-Americans than among whites, but also a matter of a lack of confidence that men will be able to provide an acceptable level of earnings over a long-term period.[5]

WHY MARRY?

Given the acceptability of cohabitation, and the greater demands marriage makes on men's earning capacity, it might reasonably be asked why most Americans bother to marry at all. The benefits of income pooling and increasing returns to scale can be obtained just as well by cohabiting. The same is true for regular sexual activity. Moreover, we have seen above that the economic gains to marriage have been reduced as women's wages have risen relative to men's. I would argue that marriage still bestows two kinds of benefits that are lacking in cohabiting unions: enforceable trust and social status.

Enforceable Trust.   Economists such as Pollak (1985) have argued that marriage reduces the transaction costs of enforcing the agreements of wives and husbands. One such cost is the ease of monitoring the behavior of one's partner. For example, evolutionary psychology suggests that monitoring the sexual fidelity of one's partner should be particularly important to men, who otherwise cannot be certain that they are the fathers of their partners' children. To be sure, cohabiting unions provide the benefits of close monitoring of behavior without the commitment of marriage. But marriage is still superior in lowering the risk that one's partner will break the agreements that have been made. At a wedding I attended recently, the minister said, "Will all of you witnessing these promises do all in your power to uphold these two persons in their marriage?" The assembled families and friends of the bride and groom said in unison, "We will." Families and friends do not make these promises when people begin a cohabiting union—indeed there is no public ceremony. Typically, most family members and friends are not upset if the cohabiting union ends. In contrast, family and friends still regard the end of a marriage as unfortunate, particularly if children are involved. And we know that the dissolution rate for cohabiting unions is higher than the rate for marriages.

The public commitment and the involvement of friends and relatives create an enforceable trust that is not present in cohabiting unions. It allows couples to have more confidence that their investments in the union will be recouped. These investments include, in addition to sexual fidelity, raising children. England and Farkas (1986) argue that raising children is a "relationship-specific investment." A wife's time and effort devoted to raising a couple's children are valuable to her husband. But should the marriage end, they are not valuable to other potential husbands because the children are not his. In contrast, men's investment in paid work, which is typically greater than their investment in home work, would be valuable to other women because it increases the amount of money men can bring to a remarriage.

The public commitment of marriage also gives couples more confidence that they will benefit from increasing returns to scale. For example, two people living together usually can afford a nicer house than either could purchase alone. However, there are many up-front costs to home owner-ship, such as closing fees and renovations, that only recoup their value after several years of ownership. The enforceable trust of marriage makes individuals more confident that their up-front investments in goods such as houses will pay off in the long run.

We know that marital unions are more stable than cohabiting unions. Still, enforceable trust is not as strong as it was in the middle of the twen-tieth century, when the stigma of divorcing was greater and when family and friends worked harder to keep a marriage together. It could be that over the next few decades the social pressure to remain married will decline even further; if so, the expectation would be to see more cohabita-tion and less marriage than today.

Social Status. Being married, I would argue, still conveys the cultural benefit of increased social status. It signifies that the partners have suc-cessfully fulfilled their adult social roles. Marriage has long been seen as a mark of successful adulthood for women because of its association with childbearing. But it also is crucial for defining what it means to be an adult male in American society (Nock, 1998). Psychoanalytic theories of gender differences (Chodorow, 1978) suggest that men define themselves by sep-arating from their birth family more than women do. Marriage has been the culturally approved way for men to achieve this separation in adult-hood. It leads to noticeable changes in their public behavior: married men spend more time with relatives or at religious services and events, and less time with friends and at bars or taverns, than they did before they married (Nock, 1998). It is the way that men in American society have taken on the culturally prescribed roles of wage earner, father, and public citizen. To be sure, it is no longer as necessary to be married to fulfill these roles; but marriage still bestows considerable prestige.

WHO BENEFITS?

It is too simplistic to say that women, or men, as a group have benefitted or suffered from the changes in union formation. The changes in the labor market and in the culture since mid-century have improved the bargaining position of the growing number of women with substantial earning power—those with college educations, for example. Their earning poten-tial is attractive to men, and they can use their market strength to bargain for a better division of household labor. The availability of effective

contraception and of abortion and the acceptance of premarital sexual relationships have also benefitted them. They can use regular sexual relationships and cohabitation as ways of observing at close range whether a potential spouse is likely to share in home production.

Women with little earning potential, on the other hand, may have lost
ground due to the social changes of the past few decades. Because of the
decline in the earnings of blue-collar men, it is more difficult for them to
find men who meet the cultural expectations of becoming steady-earning
husbands. As Akerlof et al. (1996) suggested, these women may have been
disadvantaged by the ease at which men can obtain regular sexual relationships without making a long-term commitment. And they are less able
to support themselves through government assistance due to the erosion
in welfare benefits since the mid-1970s and to the new time-limits welfare
receipt.

For men, the winners and losers may have been just the opposite. Young
men with high earning potential do not have the power in the union formation market that they used to. More of them see the need to pool
incomes with a wife, which means they may be asked to do more work at
home in return. They have lost ground relative to their privileged position
in the specialized, breadwinner–homemaker marriage of mid-century. On
the other hand, it is possible that men with low earning power may have
gained: the cultural changes mean that they often can have children and
regular sexual relationships without having to live up to the cultural standard required in order to be married.

TOWARD A NEW PARADIGM

How should we think about union formation? During the second half
of the twentieth century, the basis of intimate unions in the United States
changed from specialization and household production at mid-century to
income pooling and household consumption by the end. At mid-century,
almost all unions except among the poor were marriages; they were characterized by high fertility (by twentieth century standards) and ample
home production. By and large, women married young, had children relatively quickly, and spent a great deal of time raising children, cooking
meals, and cleaning their homes. Studies have shown that women's time
spent in housework did not decline during the first half of the century,
despite the introduction of labor-saving devices such as the vacuum
cleaner and the washing machine (Vanek, 1974).

But since mid-century, married women have become more and more
important as sources of family income. In part, income pooling has been a
response to stagnant male incomes since the 1970s and to rapidly rising

housing prices. Nevertheless, income pooling also reflects rising material expectations: larger homes, two cars rather than one, two (or three) televisions, VCRs, home computers, and so on. And at the same time home production has declined: fewer children are being raised, more meals are being eaten out of the home, and less time is spent in housework, even counting increases in husbands' contributions (Robinson and Godbey, 1997).

From Gains-to-Trade to Bargaining. When specialization and household production dominated, it was reasonable to theorize that the glue holding unions together was the gain that the partners accrued from trading what they produced in their complementary roles. The theory assumed that the interests of husbands and wives were identical (and, in the language of economics, could therefore be represented by a single utility function). Another assumption, usually implicit, was that evolution had made women better at raising children and men better at working outside the home. According to this model, there was little for husbands and wives to bargain over because social roles inside and outside the house were so strictly (and naturally) divided by gender.

By the end of the century, however, there was much greater variability in the kinds of tasks it was acceptable for women and men to do. And it became clear (as the divorce rate rose spectacularly in the 1960s and 1970s) that the interests of women and men in intimate unions were not identical. Rather, partners establish their roles through a process of bargaining. Theories of bargaining will, I believe, become the dominant approach to understanding union formation and dissolution in the early twenty-first century.

As I stated earlier, social psychology, sociology, and economics all have produced versions of bargaining theories that are similar at their core. All assume that the actors have different interests and preferences, that they negotiate roles and responsibilities, and that individuals with more attractive alternatives outside the relationship can often bargain for a greater share of the rewards inside the relationship. These principles have been applied to married couples. For example, as noted earlier, husbands' investments in earning power can be easily transferred to other marriages, whereas wives' investments in raising their husbands' children cannot be easily transferred. Therefore, husbands typically have better alternatives outside their marriage than wives and are in a stronger bargaining position (England and Kilbourne, 1990). The same principles can be applied to the process of negotiation that leads to cohabitation and then to marriage.

Bargaining models are most advanced in economics, where a large literature exists in the field of game theory (Kreps, 1990). As a general framework, bargaining models seem promising. Indeed, there have already been many applications to marital bargaining (for a review, see Lundberg and Pollak, 1996). Yet despite considerable mathematical sophistication, the literature typically is concerned with simple bargaining situations that lack the complexity of real-world decisions about cohabiting and marrying. The gap between the models and real life suggests the complexities and constraints of the bargains between would-be partners and spouses. It also leaves open the question of whether social scientists will ever be able to construct bargaining models that adequately reflect the full range of complexities and constraints.

Still, the game-theoretic literature offers insights. It demonstrates that bargaining can sometimes result in an agreement that is less than optimal for both persons, particularly when there are constraints on information, or when it is costly to search for alternatives, or when external factors (such as social norms) limit the accepted ways of playing the game (Lundberg and Pollak, 1998). Thus, it is said, individuals often bargain using "bounded rationality": they reach a solution that is satisfactory but not necessarily optimal (Kreps, 1990).

The Social Context.   Because bargaining theorists recognize the complexity of human behavior, the intellectual distance between game/social exchange theorists and sociologists who study gender and social structure is less than might be thought. Bargaining theories cannot, as a rule, tell us what constraints exist on individual behavior or why these constraints exist. It does not probe the embeddedness of economic action in culture and social structure (Granovetter, 1985). Sociologists, therefore, still have much to tell us about the accepted ways of playing the games of courtship, cohabitation, and marriage. For example, it is important to understand why, in Sweden, cohabiting unions often last for many years whereas, in the United States, they tend to be of shorter duration—and even more important to determine whether the situation is changing in the United States. (So far, as I have noted, it has not.) More generally, sociologists, and perhaps evolutionary psychologists, can contribute to our understanding of the gendered nature of the typical bargain, which is most apparent in the deviations from what rational decision making would predict. For example, why it is that men seem so resistant to doing housework, even when their wives have substantial earnings? Do men commonly feel that it is necessary to limit housework in order to affirm their masculinity? (Berk, 1985).

These are the outlines of the ways of thinking about union formation that seem most promising. There is still some life in the specialization model, but it is becoming less useful as the work and personal experiences of men and women continue to change. Newer theoretical approaches are promising but still developing. Social scientists who would contribute to these emerging perspectives on union formation face several challenges. Their theories must include cohabitation, not just marriage—and they must explain not just why people cohabit but why cohabitors marry. They must explain both change (e.g., women's earning potential) and resistance to change (e.g., men's work at home). They must deal with bargaining environments that are complex and constraining. If they can surmount these challenges, they will succeed in advancing our understanding of the changing nature of intimate unions.

NOTES

1.   In 1960, 42.9% of nonwhite women, aged 14 to 59 and married with husband present, were in the labor force—meaning that they worked for pay. For white women, the comparable percentage was 33.5% (U. S. Bureau of the Census, 1973).

2.   Valerie Kincade Oppenheimer and her colleagues have argued that declining gains to trade should affect the probability of ever marrying but not age at marriage (Oppenheimer et al., 1997). But declining gains to trade could result in a longer search process before finding a partner whose characteristics warrant cohabitation or marriage.

3.   I thank R. Kelly Raley for producing this table.

4.   Although this decline is itself influenced by labor market opportunities for women, I would argue that it is in part an exogenous result of larger historical forces such as the transformation from a familial (and usually agricultural) mode of production to a labor market mode of production.

5.   Wilson (1987, 1996) has written about the effects of joblessness on African-American men's "marriageability."

REFERENCES

Akerlof, George A., Janet L. Yellen, and Michael L. Katz. 1996. "An Analysis of Out-of-Wedlock Childbearing in the United States." *Quarterly Journal of Economics* 111:277–317.

Amato, Paul, and Alan Booth. 1995. "Changes in Gender Role Attitudes and Perceived Marital Quality." *American Sociological Review* 60:58–66.

Bahr, S. J., and R.D. Day. 1978. "Sex Role Attitudes, Female Employment, and Marital Satisfaction." *Journal of Comparative Family Studies* 14:53–67.

Becker, Gary S. 1965. "A Theory of the Allocation of Time." *Economic Journal* 75:493–517.

Becker, Gary S. 1981. *A Treatise on the Family*. Cambridge, MA: Harvard University Press.

Berk, Sarah Fenstermaker. 1985. *The Gender Factory*. New York: Plenum.

Bernard, Jessie. 1972. *The Future of Marriage*. New York: World Publishing Company.

Beutel, Ann M., and Margaret Mooney Marini. 1995. "Gender and Values." *American Sociological Review* 60:436–448.

Bianchi, Suzanne, and Daphne Spain. 1996. *American Women in Transition*. New York: Russell Sage Foundation.

Blair, S. l. 1993. "Employment, Family, and Perceptions of Marital Quaility." *Journal of Family Issues* 14:189–212.

Bumpass, Larry L., and Hsien-Hen Lu. 1998. "Trends in Cohabitation and Implications for Children's Family Contexts." Paper presented at the Annual Meeting of the Population Association of America, Chicago.

Cherlin, Andrew. 1980. "Postponing Marriage: The Influence of Young Women's Work Expectations." *Journal of Marriage and the Family* 42:355–365.

Cherlin, Andrew J. 1992. *Marriage, Divorce, Remarriage*. Cambridge, MA: Harvard University Press.

Chodorow, Nancy. 1978. *The Reproduction of Mothering: Psychoanalysis and the Sociology of Gender*. Berkeley, CA: University of California Press.

Clarkberg, Marin. 1997. The Price of Partnering: The Role of Economic Well-Being in Young Adults' First Union Experiences. BLCC Working Paper 97-11. Ithaca, NY: Cornell Employment and Family Careers Institute.

Cleland, John, and John Hobcraft. (Eds.) 1985. *Reproductive Change in Developing Countries: Insights from the World Fertility Study*. Oxford: Oxford University Press.

Cook, Karen, Jodi O'Brien, and Peter Kollock. 1990. "Exchange Theory: A Blueprint for Structure and Process." Pp. 151–181 in *Frontiers of Social Theory: The New Syntheses*, edited by George Ritzer. New York: Columbia University Press.

England, Paula, and George Farkas. 1986. *Households, Employment, and Gender: A Social, Economic, and Demographic View*. New York: Aldine.

England, Paula, and Barbara Stanek Kilbourne. 1990. "Markets, Marriages, and Other Mates: The Problem of Power." Pp. 163–188 in *Beyond the Marketplace*, edited by Roger Friedland and A. F. Robertson. New York: Aldine de Gruyter.

Furstenberg, Frank F., Jr. 1996. "The Future of Marriage." *American Demographics* June:34–40.

Granovetter, M. 1985. "Economic Action and Social Structure: The Problem of Embeddedness." *American Journal of Sociology* 91:481–510.

Goldscheider, Frances, Pierre Turcotte, and Alexander Kopp. 1998. "The Changing Determinants of First Union Formation in Industrialized Countries: The United States and Canada." Paper presented at the Annual Meeting of the Population Association of America, Chicago, April.

Huber, J., and G. Spitze. 1983. "Considering Divorce: An Expansion of Becker's Theory of Marital Instability." *American Journal of Sociology* 86:75–89.

Kaufman, Gayle. Forthcoming. "The Effect of Gender Role Attitudes on Men's and Women's Family Formation and Dissolution." *Journal of Family Issues*.

Kreps, David M. 1990. *Game Theory and Economic Modeling*. New York: Oxford University Press.

Lueptow, L. B., M. B. Guss, and C. Hyden. 1989. "Sex Role Ideology, Marital Status, and Happiness." *Journal of Family Issues* 10:383–400.

Lundberg, Shelly, and Robert A. Pollak. 1996. "Bargaining and Distribution in Marriage." *Journal of Economic Perspectives* 10:139–158.

Lundberg, Shelly, and Robert A. Pollak. 1998. "Bargaining in Families." Manuscript.

Lye, D. N., and T. J. Biblarz. 1993. "The Effects of Attitudes Toward Family Life and Gender Roles on Marital Satisfaction." *Journal of Family Issues* 14:157–188.

Merton, Robert K. 1968. *Social Theory and Social Structure*, enlarged edition. New York: Free Press.

Nock, Steven L. 1998. *Marriage and Men's Lives*. New York: Oxford University Press.

Oppenheimer, Valerie Kincade. 1988. "A Theory of Marriage Timing: Assortative Mating Under Varying Degrees of Uncertainty." *American Journal of Sociology* 94:563–591.

Oppenheimer, Valerie Kincade, and Vivian Lew. 1995. "American Marriage Formation in the 1980s: How Important Was Women's Economic Independence." Pp. 105–138 in *Gender and Family Change in Industrialized Countries*, edited by Karen Oppenheim Mason and An-Magritt Jensen. Oxford: Clarendon Press.

Oppenheimer, Valerie Kincade, Hans-Peter Blossfeld, and Achim Wackerow. 1995. "United States of America." Pp. 150–173 in *The New Role of Women*, edited by Hans-Peter Blossfled. Boulder, CO: Westview Press.

Oppenheimer Valerie Kincade, Matthijs Kalmijn, and Nelson Lim. 1997. "Men's Career Development an Marriage Timing During a Period of Rising Inequality." *Demography* 34:311–330.

Parsons, Talcott, and Robert F. Bales. 1955. *Family, Socialization, and the Interaction Process*. New York: Free Press.

Perry-Jenkins, M., and A. C. Crouter. 1990. "Men's Provider-Role Attitudes: Implications for Household Work and Marital Satisfaction." *Journal of Family Issues* 11:136–156.

Pollak, Robert A. 1985. "A Transaction Cost Approach to Families and Households." *Journal of Economic Literature* 23:581–608.

Rindfuss, Ronald R., and Audrey VandenHeuvel. 1990. "Cohabitation: A Precursor to Marriage or an Alternative to Being Single?" *Population and Development Review* 16:703–726.

Robinson, John, and Geoffrey Godbey. 1997. *Time for Life: The Surprising Ways Americans Use Their Time*. University Park, PA: Pennsylvania State University Press.

Shelton, B.A., and D. John. 1993. "Does Marital Status Make a Difference? Housework among Married and Cohabiting Women." *Journal of Family Issues* 14:401–420.

South, Scott. 1991. "Sociodemographic Differentials in Mate Selection Process." *Journal of Marriage and the Family* 53:928–940.

Sweeney, Megan. 1997. "Women, Men, and Changing Families: The Shifting Economic Foundations of Marriage." Annual Meeting of the Population Association of America, Washington, DC, March.

Thibaut, John, and Harold H. Kelley. 1959. *The Social Psychology of Groups*. New York: Wiley.

U. S. Bureau of the Census. 1973. "Employment Status and Work Experience." *1970 Census of the Population. Subject Reports*, PC(2)-6A.Washington, DC: U. S. Government Printing Office.

U. S. Bureau of the Census. 1998. "Marital Status and Living Arrangements: March 1996." *Current Population Reports*. Series P20-496. Washington, DC: U. S. Government Printing Office.

Vanek, Joann. 1974. "Time Spent in Housework." *Scientific American* 11:116–120.

Vannoy, D., and W. W. Philliber. 1992. "Wife's Employment and Quality of Mariage." *Journal of Marriage and the Family* 54:387–398.

Waite, Linda J., and Glenna Spitze. 1981. "Young Women's Transition to Marriage." *Demography* 18:681–694.

Weiss, Yoram. 1997. "The Formation and Dissolution of Families: Why Marry? Who Married Whom? And What Happens On Divorce?" Pp. 81–123 in *Handbook of Population and Family Economics*, edited by M. R. Rosenzweig and O. Stark. Amsterdam: Elsevier.

Young, Michael, and Peter Willmott. 1973. *The Symmetrical Family*. New York: Pantheon.

Wilson, William Julius. 1987. *The Truly Disadvantaged: The Inner City, the Underclass, and Public Policy.* Chicago: University of Chicago Press.

Wilson, William Julius. 1996. *When Work Disappears.* New York: Knopf.

III

VALUES, ATTITUDES, AND NORMS
ABOUT MARRIAGE

8

The Transformation in the Meaning of Marriage

WILLIAM G. AXINN and ARLAND THORNTON

INTRODUCTION

There have been dramatic changes in marital and childbearing behavior in the United States in the twentieth century. Although the central trends in family formation and dissolution have not been monotonic over the decades—with substantial booms and busts in marriage, divorce, and childbearing—family formation patterns today clearly differ from those of a century ago. Marriage rates are lower, age at marriage is higher, divorce is more widespread, marital fertility is lower, and nonmarital childbearing is more extensive today than at the beginning of the century. In the latter half of the century, as the timing of first marriages has been extended, the incidence of new living arrangements, such as premarital cohabitation and independent nonfamily living, has increased. These changes constitute a long-term transformation in marital behavior that coincides with equally dramatic changes in the meaning that individual Americans place on the institution of marriage. Unfortunately, we have very little documentation of the transformation in values, attitudes, and beliefs about marriage across the first part of the twentieth century. However, we do know a fair amount about changes in values, attitudes, and beliefs about marriage since the 1950s.

Attitudes toward marriage became significantly more negative in the United States between the mid-1950s and the mid-1970s. There was a dramatic increase in approval for remaining single, an increased negative orientation toward marriage, and a growing emphasis on the restrictions associated with marriage (Veroff et al., 1981). Although the vast majority of young people still expected to get married, the age at which they expected to make this transition also increased substantially over this period (Thornton and Freedman, 1982). In contrast, attitudes toward marriage have remained quite stable during the mid-1980s and 1990s

(Thornton and Young-DeMarco, 1999). But although the general disposition toward marrying remains stable, the meaning Americans place on this social relationship continues to change. In this chapter we discuss the ways that the meaning of marriage continues to evolve for Americans and the relationship of these changes to the social organization of marriage and family life.

We begin by sketching a theoretical framework illustrating the relationships between the changing social organization of marriage and the meaning individuals place on marriage as a social relationship. Then we briefly describe the stability in attitudes toward marriage, singlehood, and divorce through the late 1970s, the 1980s, and the early 1990s. Next we examine the dramatic changes in beliefs regarding the social meaning of marriage, emphasizing changes in attitudes toward childlessness, premarital sex, nonmarital cohabitation, premarital childbearing, marital childbearing, and the gender division of labor. Finally we discuss interrelationships among these changes and related aspects of the social organization of marriage.

THE SOCIAL ORGANIZATION OF
FAMILY AND MARRIAGE

One of the most important changes in Western societies during recent centuries has been the proliferation of social organizations and institutions that are not based on kinship relations (Coleman, 1990; Durkheim, 1984). With the creation and expansion of factories, schools, medical and public health organizations, police, commercialized leisure, the mass media, and other nonfamily organizations, the lives of individuals have been increasingly conducted within, and organized by, nonfamily institutions (Coleman, 1990; Ogburn and Tibbitts, 1933; Thornton and Fricke, 1987). Although families, of course, continue to be important organizations for individuals, numerous other institutions organize and influence their lives as well. Many social activities formerly associated closely with the family, such as work, socialization, consumption, leisure, protection, and residence, are more closely associated with nonfamily organizations now than they were previously (Coleman, 1990; Thornton and Fricke, 1987). As a result, today individuals spend more time than they did in previous centuries interacting with people who are not relatives, receive more of their resources and information from nonfamilial institutions, and experience more nonfamilial authority.

This reorganization of family life and the family's connections with the rest of society alters both family behaviors and values and beliefs regarding those behaviors. Together, the combination of changing behavior and changing attitudes and beliefs produces a transformation in the meaning of specific aspects of the family, such as marriage. Although the determination of cause and effect is difficult, we have good reasons to believe that the changes over time in beliefs and behaviors are closely related. Consider marriage as a specific example.

First, changes over time in attitudes toward marriage and related social activities are quite likely to affect individuals' marital behaviors. As described by the theory of planned behavior, we have strong theoretical reasons to expect that values, attitudes, and beliefs are important determinants of behavioral choices (Ajzen, 1988). A great deal of empirical research on marriage and related behavior supports this view. We know that those who feel positively about marriage marry more rapidly than those who do not (Axinn and Thornton, 1992), those with positive attitudes toward premarital sex are more likely to experience sex before marriage than those with negative attitudes (Ku et al., 1998), those who approve of premarital cohabitation are more likely to cohabit than those who do not (Axinn and Thornton, 1993), and those who are positive toward having many children enter childbearing more quickly than those who are not (Barber, 1998). Thus widespread changes in people's beliefs about marriage may be responsible, at least in part, for the long-term changes in marital behaviors.

Second, changes in marital experiences, and experiences with related behaviors, are likely to have important consequences for individuals' values, beliefs, and attitudes toward marriage. In fact, one of the most basic building blocks of our theories of the formation of values and beliefs is that individuals' experiences shape their values and beliefs (Mead, 1934; Ajzen, 1988). Of course, other social forces, such as religion, mass media, the legal system, family, and friends, are also likely to influence individuals' values and beliefs (Thornton, 1995). However, the composition of the content in messages from these sources is also strongly affected by the experiences of the individuals who compose that content. In general, the experience of a situation or condition is likely to make an individual more positive toward that situation or condition. The mechanisms that produce this relationship include cognitive consistency, learning, and the social influence of others (Axinn and Barber, 1997). Thus, as childbearing, sex, heterosexual coresidence, and the gender division of labor become increasingly organized outside of marriage, we also expect individuals' attitudes toward the organization of these activities outside marriage to become increasingly favorable.

In the United States in the past, a number of social activities were closely associated with marriage. These include sexuality, heterosexual coresidence, childbearing, childrearing, and the gender division of labor.

This linkage of these behaviors with marriage, however, has changed in recent decades. Just as many social activities were increasingly reorganized outside the family, childbearing, sex, heterosexual coresidence, and the gender division of labor began to be organized outside of marriage (Davis, 1984). We know that childbearing still occurs within marriage (Barber, 1998), sexual activity remains high in marriage (Waite, 1995; Waite and Gallagher, forthcoming), marital coresidence continues to be the most common adult living arrangement (Thornton et al., 1993), and marital relationships still affect the division of labor (Goldscheider and Waite, 1991). However, in the latter half of the twentieth century there have been dramatic increases in the extent to which these activities take place outside of marriage, in alternative social arrangements.

Sex, cohabitation, childbearing, childrearing, and a gendered division of labor have been closely tied to the meaning American's place on marriage as a social relationship. The expectation that sex, heterosexual cohabitation, childbearing, childrearing, and a gender division of labor are defining elements of marriage has changed. This change in attitude toward the organization of these activities within marriage constitutes a fundamental transformation in the meaning we place on marriage. The objective of this chapter is to examine this transformation in the meaning Americans place on marriage directly, by documenting trends in individuals' values, attitudes, and beliefs about marriage.

ATTITUDES TOWARD MARRIAGE, REMAINING SINGLE, AND DIVORCE

We use measures of attitudes and values from a variety of sources to describe the recent trends in Americans' views of marriage and related social activities. The four primary sources we use are "Monitoring the Future," the "General Social Survey," the "Intergenerational Panel Study of Parents and Children," and the "National Survey of Families and Households." Information from these four primary sources is also supplemented by published data from other sources.

Monitoring the Future (MTF) is a survey of a nationally representative sample of high school seniors in the United States that has been collected every year since 1976 by the Survey Research Center at the University of Michigan. To facilitate our presentation of information from this source, we provide data only from 1976–1977, 1985–1986, and 1993–1994.[1] The General Social Survey (GSS), with some exceptions, has been conducted annually since 1972 by the National Opinion Research Center of the University of Chicago. It is a nationally representative study of the English-speaking, noninstitutionalized population of the United States ages 18 and over. Because the sample was limited to the noninstitutionalized population, thereby omitting a large number of young people in college dormitories and other institutions, we restrict our analysis of these data to those aged 24 or older. The Intergenerational Panel Study of Parents and Children (IPS) is a survey of white mothers who gave birth in 1961 in the Detroit Metropolitan area and their children.[2] The mothers were interviewed by the Survey Research Center of the University of Michigan twice in 1962 and then again 1963, 1966, 1977, 1980, 1985, and 1993. The children born in 1961 were interviewed in 1980, when they were aged 18, and then again in 1985 and 1993. We use information from the panel of both son/daughter and mother interviews in our presentation below. The National Survey of Families and Households (NSFH) is a nationally representative survey of the noninstitutionalized population aged 18 and over directed by the University of Wisconsin and conducted by the Institute of Survey Research at Temple University. It was first conducted in 1987–1988 with a follow-up approximately 5 years later.[3]

Detailed descriptions of the differences among these data sources are provided elsewhere (Thornton and Young-DeMarco, 1999), so we do not repeat that discussion here.[4] Our aim is to document the general trends over time in beliefs about marriage and related social activities. The absolute values of these attitude measures vary across data sources because of important differences in question wording, response alternatives, sampling, and the precise date of measurement. For our purpose, we focus on the trends over time represented in each of the different data sources.

Marriage versus Remaining Single

First, we examine trends over time in views of marrying versus remaining single. Specifically, respondents were asked whether they agree or disagree with the statement that "Married people are happier than those who go through life without getting married." Table 8.1 presents the trends in the fraction of respondents who agree with this statement. The first row of Table 8.1 comes from the MTF surveys. The left-hand side of Table 8.1 presents data for women and the right hand side presents data for men. The data for women indicate that women's attitudes toward marriage, as measured by this specific item, have remained quite stable from the mid-1970s to the mid-1990s. In the 1990s 58.5% of women reported agreeing that married people are happier, and in the mid-1970s 59.5% felt the same way. In the right-hand side of the first row, we see that men's attitudes

Table 8.1. Attitudes toward Marriage

	Women			Men		
Item and Data Source	Mid-1970s	Mid-1980s	Mid-1990s	Mid-1970s	Mid-1980s	Mid-1990s
Percentage who agree (or are neutral) that married people are happier than people who do not marry						
Monitoring the Future	59.5	58.5	58.4	63.1	64.7	72.1
Intergenerational Panel Study[a]		54.9	52.1		62.1	59.3

Source: Thornton and Young-DeMarco (1999, Table 2).
[a]Son/daughter sample.

toward marriage remained quite stable from the mid-1970s through the mid-1980s, but there was a slight increase from the 1980s to the 1990s in the percentage who agreed with the statement that married people are happier. As we discuss below, this increase in the view that married people may be happier cannot be confirmed from other data sources.

The second row of Table 8.1 presents responses to a similar statement from the son/daughter sample in the IPS. The left-hand side of the second row shows that the percentage of women who agreed that married people are happier has remained relatively stable from the mid-1980s to the mid-1990s in this survey as well. The right-hand side of the second row shows that in this study the level of men's agreement with the statement that married people are happier has actually declined slightly. That is, sons in the IPS have become a little less positive toward marriage during the same time interval that young men in MTF have become a little more positive toward marriage. Both these differences are statistically significant, although neither difference is substantively large. Overall we fail to find strong or consistent evidence of trends in young people's attitudes toward marriage between the mid-1970s and the mid-1990s.

An exploration of attitudes toward marriage as reflected in other specific measures demonstrates a similar pattern. The percentage who feel that there are few good marriages these days has remained stable in MTF data from the mid-1970s to the mid-1990s among both men and women (Thornton and Young-DeMarco, 1999, Table 2). Likewise, the fraction of young men and women participating in the MTF study who said that having a good marriage is extremely important and definitely prefer to have a mate remained quite stable from the 1980s into the 1990s (Thornton and Young-DeMarco, 1999, Table 2). Thus, there is little evidence of any dramatic shifts in attitudes toward marriage between the mid-1970s and the mid-1990s (also, see Glenn, 1996).

Marital Dissolution

We find similar stability in attitudes toward divorce over these decades. Table 8.2 presents trends in responses to questions related to divorce from three different studies. In the first row of Table 8.2 we show the percentage of MTF respondents who say once married, it is very likely they would stay married. There is no significant trend over time for either men or women. In fact, for men the percentage who say it is very likely they will remain married is precisely the same in the mid-1970s as in the mid-1990s.

The second row of Table 8.2 shows the percentage of NSFH respondents who say marriage is for a lifetime. Here too we find that for both men and women, the percentage who say marriage is for a lifetime is almost the same in the mid-1990s as it was in the mid-1980s. The third row of Table 8.2 shows the percentage of mothers in the IPS who agree with the statement that parents should stay together even if they do not get along. Agreement with this statement implies no tolerance of divorce when children are present, and as shown in Table 8.2, the level of tolerance among mothers in this study has remained quite stable (and high) from the mid-1970s to the mid-1990s.

Table 8.2. Attitudes toward Divorce

	Women			Men		
Data Source and Item	*Mid-1970s*	*Mid-1980s*	*Mid-1990s*	*Mid-1970s*	*Mid-1980s*	*Mid-1990s*
Monitoring the Future						
Percentage saying very likely they would stay married	65.8	66.3	62.6	56.7	54.9	56.7
National Survey of Families Households						
Percentage saying marriage is for a lifetime		72.1	73.2		77.9	78.4
Intergenerational Panel Study[a]						
Percentage agreeing (or neutral) that parents should stay together even if they do not get along	19.6	17.9	17.3			

Source: Thornton and Young-DeMarco (1999, Table 3).
[a]Mother sample.

Thus, we find stability in attitudes toward divorce from the mid-1970s through the mid-1990s in all three of these studies.

ATTITUDES TOWARD PREMARITAL SEX, NONMARITAL COHABITATION, CHILDBEARING, AND THE GENDER DIVISION OF LABOR

In contrast to the stability in attitudes toward marriage and divorce from the mid-1970s to the mid-1990s, we find significant differences between the 1990s and 1970s in attitudes toward premarital sex, nonmarital cohabitation, childbearing, and the gender division of labor. Next we document some of these changes, beginning with attitudes toward premarital sex.

Premarital Sex

The view that premarital sex constitutes inappropriate behavior declined from the mid-1970s to the mid-1980s. The percentage of adult women participating in the GSS who say that premarital sex is always or almost always wrong declined from 56 to 44% during this time period while the comparable decline for adult men was from 46 to 33% (row 1 of Table 8.3). Similarly, among teenage men participating in the 1979 National Survey of Young Men and the 1988 and 1995 National Surveys of Adolescent Males, the number saying that premarital sex was never okay

Table 8.3.   Attitudes toward Premarital Sex

Data Source and Item	Women			Men		
	Mid-1970s	Mid-1980s	Mid-1990s	Mid-1970s	Mid-1980s	Mid-1990s
General Social Survey						
Percentage who say premarital sex is always or almost always wrong	56.4	44.4	42.1	46.0	33.2	31.9
National Survey of Families Households						
Percentage who disagree that it is allright for unmarried 18 year olds to have sex		65.6	60.0		53.8	48.6

or okay only if the couple plans to marry declined from 45% in 1979 to 20% in 1988 (Ku et al., 1998).

Although the trends between the mid-1970s and the mid-1980s are consistent across data sets and age groups, trends during the subsequent years seem to vary by data source, question wording, and age of respondents. Looking first at adults in the GSS (Table 8.3), we see that the number disapproving of premarital sex was remarkably similar in the mid-1990s and mid-1980s (differences not statistically significant). However, among adult respondents in the NSFH, the number who disapproved of unmarried 18 year olds having sex declined by several percentage points during this same time period (Table 8.3). Interestingly, disapproval of premarital sex increased rather than decreased among teenagers from the late 1980s to the early 1990s. Whereas in 1988 20% of teenage men in the National Survey of Adolescent Males said that premarital sex was never okay or okay only if the couple plans to marry, by 1995 the number had grown to 29% (Ku et al., 1998). The explanation for these differences in trends across questions, data sources, and age groups is not clear.[5] It does appear, however, that the dramatic and pervasive trends toward approval of premarital sex through the mid-1980s have not continued for all age groups after the mid 1980s. The decline in approval of premarital sex among teenage men in the early 1990s could be particularly important if it continues.[6] As Ku et al. (1998) report, premarital sexual attitudes and behavior are closely related, and the decline in approval of premarital sex can largely account for declines in premarital sexual experience during the same period.

It should be noted, however, that although the various data sources provide different estimates of the trends in the late 1980s and the early 1990s, they are remarkably consistent in showing greater approval of premarital sex in the mid-1990s than in the mid-1970s. This is true even among teenagers as the reported increase in approval across the 1980s was much larger than the reported decline in approval between 1988 and 1995 (Ku et al., 1998).

Although we might expect that the greater acceptance of premarital sex in the 1990s than the 1970s would have been accompanied by increased acceptance of extramarital sex, this trend has not occurred. Instead, attitudes toward extramarital sex have been negative throughout this period, and the modest change that has occurred has been toward increased disapproval (Thornton and Young-DeMarco, 1999, Table 7). So although Americans are now more tolerant of sex before marriage than in the 1970s, this permissiveness does not extend to sex with multiple partners while married.

Sex, of course, remains a fundamental dimension of married life (Waite, 1995; Waite and Gallagher, forthcoming), but as we have seen, marriage is no longer the only socially accepted relationship within which sexual relations may occur. Many Americans accept the idea of sexual relationships among the unmarried, and the prevalence of this tolerance has grown. As acceptance of premarital sex has grown, one dimension of the meaning of marriage, as the exclusive socially acceptable relationship for sexual activity, has also changed.

Nonmarital Cohabitation

Values, attitudes, and beliefs about heterosexual nonmarital cohabitation have become substantially more accepting in recent decades. Table 8.4 displays trends in attitudes toward cohabitation from three different studies. The first row of Table 8.4 shows that the percentage of MTF respondents who agree that living together is a good idea increased dramatically throughout the period from the mid-1970s to the mid-1990s for both men and women. In fact, there are statistically significant increases in this fraction both from the mid-1970s to the mid-1980s and then again from the mid-1980s to the mid-1990s (also, see Schulenberg et al., 1995).

Other studies demonstrate the same increase in acceptance of nonmarital cohabitation between the mid-1980s and the mid-1990s. Row 2 of Table 8.4 shows the percentage of NSFH respondents who agree that living together without being married is all right and row 3 shows the same percentages from the son/daughter sample of the IPS. In both cases we see a

Table 8.4.   Attitudes toward Nonmarital Cohabitation

	Women			Men		
Data Source and Item	*Mid-1970s*	*Mid-1980s*	*Mid-1990s*	*Mid-1970s*	*Mid-1980s*	*Mid-1990s*
Monitoring the Future						
Percentage agreeing living together is a good idea	33.0	39.3	51.2	46.9	53.1	61.6
National Survey of Families Households						
Percentage agreeing that living together is all right		16.0	19.8		23.0	23.6
Intergenerational Panel Study[a]						
Percentage agreeing that living together is all right		56.6	64.2		69.4	71.8

Source: Thornton and Young-DeMarco (1999, Table 5).
[a]Son/daughter sample.

significant increase in the fraction of women who believe cohabitation is all right and a more modest increase in the fraction of men who believe cohabitation is all right. Today marriage is not the only acceptable route to coresidence for many American couples. This is another dimension in which the meaning of marriage continues to change in our society.

Childbearing

We examine two ways to think about attitudes and values regarding the intersections between marriage and childbearing in the United States. One is the extent to which people believe that in order to have a child couples should be married. The second is the degree to which people believe that married couples should have children. In Table 8.5 we provide data about trends in American's views of these two dimensions of childbearing and marriage.

Table 8.5A displays the percentage of MTF respondents who say they believe unmarried childbearing is destructive to society. These data indicate that there have been significant declines in the fraction of women who

Table 8.5. Attitudes toward the Intersection of Marriage and Childbearing

	A: Attitudes toward Premarital Childbearing					
	Women			*Men*		
Data Source and Item	*Mid-1970s*	*Mid-1980s*	*Mid-1990s*	*Mid-1970s*	*Mid-1980s*	*Mid-1990s*
Monitoring the Future Percentage who say childbearing outside of marriage is destructive to society	23.1	17.2	14.8	20.2	17.3	17.2
	B: Attitudes toward Childlessness					
	Women		*Men*			
Data Source and Item	*1985*	*1993*	*1985*	*1993*		
Intergenerational Panel Study[a] Percentage who say all couples who can have children ought to have children	32.8	21.9	40.5	30.6		

Source: Thornton and Young-DeMarco (1999, Table 8).
[a]Son/daughter sample.

believe unmarried childbearing is destructive to society between the mid-1970s and the mid-1980s and again between the mid-1980s and the mid-1990s. The fraction of men who believe this is destructive to society also declined over the same period, although this decline was not statistically significant. Thus the negative stigma individuals attribute to having a child outside of marriage appears to be declining across recent decades (also, see Schulenberg et al., 1995).

These results are very consistent with the findings of Ku et al. (1998) from the National Survey of Young Men and the National Survey of Adolescent Men. In these studies adolescent males were asked their views about the best resolution to a pregnancy for an unmarried girl. Between 1979 and 1995, the percentage recommending marriage, abortion, and adoption all declined substantially, while the percentage suggesting that the mother have the baby and the father help to support it increased dramatically from 19 to 59%. Increased support for unmarried childbearing has also been reported by Pagnini and Rindfuss (1993).

Table 8.5B shows the percentage of the son/daughter sample from the IPS who say that all couples who are able to have children should have children. This percentage has also been declining. The fraction of both men and women who said that all married couples who can have children should have children declined significantly between the mid-1980s and the mid-1990s. This indicates that the view that married couples should also be parents also seems to be weakening. Thus, the meaning of marriage is continuing to evolve so that the activities of childbearing and childrearing are less often seen as fundamentally tied to marriage.

Gender Division of Labor

Most economic explanations of marital behavior focus on the value of marriage as a relationship that provides the stability to allow men and women to specialize and trade (Becker, 1976, 1991; Davis, 1984). If men and women divide labor so that one sex works in the nonfamily economy for pay and the other sex cares for the home and family, marriage provides a valuable social arrangement to ensure that each benefits from the others' activities (Durkheim, 1984). In the United States in the early 1950s there was widespread agreement that men should work in the nonfamily economy while women worked in the home where they cared for the family. However, in the four decades since there have been by dramatic changes in views of this division of labor.

These changes have continued through the 1990s. Table 8.6 displays trends in the percentage of respondents from all four studies who disagree with a statement saying that men should achieve in the workplace while women care for the home and family. The trends are dramatic for both males and females in all four studies. The first row displays results from

Table 8.6. Attitudes toward Men Working While Women Care for Home and Family

	Women			Men		
Item and Data Source	Mid-1970s	Mid-1980s	Mid-1990s	Mid-1970s	Mid-1980s	Mid-1990s
Percentage who *disagree* that men should achieve in the workplace while women care for home and family						
Monitoring the Future	42.1	64.3	74.4	17.3	32.2	39.7
General Social Survey	33.9	51.2	66.8	29.0	49.0	60.1
National Survey of Families and Households		21.8	31.6		17.0	27.8
Intergenerational Panel Study[a]		65.7	69.0		62.1	68.2

Source: Thornton and Young-DeMarco (1999, Table 1).
[a]Son/daughter sample.

MTF. It shows significant increases in the percentage who disagree with the statement about the gender division of labor both between the mid-1970s and the mid-1980s and between the mid-1980s and the mid-1990s for both women and men. Although the levels are a bit different, the percentages for the GSS, displayed in row 2, follow exactly the same pattern. Neither the NSFH nor the son/daughter sample of the IPS has measures from the mid-1970s, but they both show the same pattern of change between the mid-1980s and the mid-1990s as the other studies. Americans are continuing to grow less likely to believe that men should achieve in the workplace while women care for the home and family.

These results mark another dimension in which the meaning of marriage is continuing to change. Economic independence and interdependence are still closely associated with marriage (Bulcroft and Bulcroft, 1993; Oppenheimer, 1994), but views of the gender division of this interdependence continue to change. In recent decades Americans are becoming less and less likely to believe that the only appropriate gender division of labor for couples is men working outside the home and women working inside the home.

FEEDBACK LOOPS WITHIN THE MARRIAGE SYSTEM

Endorsements of marriage have remained stable through the period from the mid-1970s to the mid-1990s, as evidenced by the stability in both attitudes toward marriage and attitudes toward divorce. However, the meaning of marriage is continuing to evolve. Over time marriage is less often seen as the only acceptable social relationship for sex or coresidence, it is less often considered fundamentally tied to childbearing and child-rearing, and a gender-based division of labor is less likely to be seen as the only means of economic interdependence among couples. These changes in attitudes, values, and beliefs about many of the social activities closely associated with marriage are closely interrelated with changes in marital behaviors. In fact, as discussed earlier, these changes in attitudes, values, and beliefs are likely to be both causes and consequences of changing marital behavior. As a result, these attitudes, values, and beliefs probably form a key set of mechanisms that connects the evolving changes in many different dimensions of marriage and related behaviors. There are multiple ways that these evolving changes in various dimensions of the meaning of marriage may be interrelated.

First, the rapid rise in divorce during the 1960s and 1970s was accompanied by extensive publicity, and knowledge of this family trend became widespread. A particularly important aspect of the publicity was information about the negative psychological, social, and economic consequences that can be associated with divorce. These developments may have led to some questioning of the institution of marriage and decreased confidence in marriage as a way of life (Weitzman, 1985; Thornton, 1991).

Second, an extensive body of research shows that children of divorced parents have more positive attitudes toward premarital sex and are more sexually experienced (Thornton and Camburn, 1987; Ku et al., 1998). Given this empirical relationship and plausible theoretical reasons for expecting an effect of divorce on children's attitudes toward premarital sex, it also seems likely that the historical trend in divorce would have contributed to the trend toward more approving attitudes toward premarital sex.

Third, it is likely that the growing concerns about the viability of marriage and the increased acceptability of premarital sex played a major role in the rapid increase in unmarried cohabitation. With concerns about success in marriage young people may have become attracted to the idea that they could live together without being married in order to obtain additional information about their compatibility. If they found that they were incompatible, they could break up the relationship without the trauma of divorce. This orientation may have been a major contributor to a rapid substitution of marriage with cohabitation by many young Americans. This hypothesis is buttressed by microlevel data showing that children of divorced parents have substantially higher cohabitation rates and lower marriage rates than children from continuously married families, indicating that growing up in a family with divorced parents could lead to choosing cohabitation rather than marriage (Thornton, 1991). Furthermore, attitudes toward premarital sex, cohabitation, and divorce appear to be key mechanisms linking parental divorce to children's cohabiting behavior (Axinn and Thornton, 1992, 1993, 1996).

Fourth, this adjustment to concern about success in marriage may actually lead to higher rates of dissolution. A rapidly growing body of empirical data suggests that cohabitation may increase rather than decrease the rate of union dissolution. Cohabiting unions have been shown to have high rates of dissolution, and the divorce rate among married couples who had previously cohabited is substantially higher than the rate among couples who had not cohabited prior to marriage (Bumpass and Sweet, 1989). Once again, changes in attitudes toward marriage, divorce, and childbearing associated with cohabiting experiences may be an important part of the link between premarital cohabitation and subsequent marital and divorce behavior. These attitudes may select those already most likely to divorce for cohabiting arrangements (Axinn and Thornton, 1992; Lillard et al., 1995), and cohabiting experiences may also reshape individuals' attitudes (Axinn and Thornton, 1992; Axinn and Barber, 1997).

Fifth, delayed marriage, increased divorce, and the rise in nonmarital cohabitation are linked to changes in childbearing behavior through a variety of mechanisms as well. Childbearing is less common among cohabiting couples than among married couples, but more common among cohabiting couples than among those who remain single (Bachrach, 1987; Manning, 1995). A substantial fraction of births occurring to those who are not married occur to those who are cohabiting (Bumpass and Lu, 1999). Again, attitudes, values, and beliefs surrounding marriage and associated social activities, such as sex, childbearing, and childrearing, are implicated as an important element connecting these various family behaviors. For example, cohabiting experiences substantially reduce fertility preferences (Axinn and Barber, 1997). This may be part of the link between cohabitation and childbearing behavior.

Finally, the evolution in the meaning of marriage and related social activities is closely linked across the generations. Delayed marriage in one generation is associated with delayed marriage in the next generation (Thornton, 1991), reduced childbearing in one generation is associated with reduced childbearing in the next generation (Axinn et al., 1994), and divorce in one generation is associated with an increased risk of marital dissolution in the next (McLanahan and Bumpass, 1988). Premarital sexual activity, nonmarital cohabitation, and nonmarital childbearing are probably linked across the generations as well. Furthermore, attitudes, values, and beliefs about marriage and related social behaviors appear to be a key element in this intergenerational connection. The attitudes and values of mothers have a strong impact on their children's premarital sex, cohabiting, marriage, marital childbearing, and premarital childbearing behaviors (Axinn and Thornton, 1992, 1993; Barber, 1998; Thornton and Camburn, 1987). Much of these effects are explained by the close association between the attitudes and values of mothers and their children (Axinn and Thornton, 1996), but substantial effects of mothers' attitudes and values remain, even after taking their children's own attitudes and values into account (Axinn and Thornton, 1993; Barber, 1998). In fact, mothers' attitudes and values regarding marriage, related social activities, and the intersection between these social activities and nonfamily social activities have dramatic influences on their children's cohabitation, marriage, premarital childbearing, and marital childbearing behavior that cannot be explained by their children's own attitudes and values (Axinn and Thornton, 1993; Barber, 1998).

Attitudes and values about the meaning of marriage have important consequences for marital behavior beyond the fact they are themselves affected by experiences. Furthermore, attitudes and values have strong intergenerational consequences, affecting the behavior of both individuals and their children. As a result, the recent changes in attitudes and values documented here are likely to continue to shape marital behavior for some time to come. Thus, although the majority of social science research on marriage continues to focus primarily on the role of economic consequences of recent changes in social organization, we argue research should also attend to the attitudinal and value consequences of those changes.

NOTES

1. For each of these 2-year periods we average together data from respective individual years.

2. Because of the changing focus of this study and its increasing geographical dispersion, it has been known by different names over the years. Starting as a study of the fertility behavior of Detroit women in 1962, the study was originally titled Family Growth in Detroit. With the widening geographical distribution of the sample and the expansion of the content in 1980, the study was renamed the Study of American Families. Since the study is not representative of the larger national population, we have more recently referred to the project as the IPS of Parents and Children.

3. Although efforts were made to interview young people living in dorms and other group quarters via their connections to other households, we limit our analyses of the NSFH data to those aged 29 and over by the first wave of the survey.

4. That more detailed discussion addresses key differences in study design among the various data sources that may affect interpretation of our results. One key difference is that some of these data come from longitudinal panel studies, in which the same respondents are interviewed repeatedly over time (IPS and NSFH), and some of the data come from repeated cross-sectional studies, in which

new respondents are interviewed at every time point (MTF and GSS). These design differences allow some insight into whether differences by age, period, or cohort generate observed differences over time (Thornton and Young-DeMarco, 1999). Unfortunately, discussion of these complex issues is beyond the scope of the current brief treatment of the topic.

5. For example, the design differences discussed in Note 4 may produce some of these differences.

6. This decline may, at least in part, have been fueled by recent increases in the incidence and awareness of human immunodeficiency virus (HIV) and related sexually transmitted diseases.

REFERENCES

Ajzen, I. 1988. *Attitudes, Personality, and Behavior*. Chicago: Dorsey Press.

Axinn, W. G., and J. S. Barber. 1997. "Living Arrangements and Family Formation Attitudes in Early Adulthood." *Journal of Marriage and the Family* 59(3): 595–611.

Axinn, W. G., and A. Thornton. 1992. "The Relationship Between Cohabitation and Divorce: Selectivity or Causal Influence?" *Demography* 29(3):357–374.

Axinn, W. G., and A. Thornton. 1993. "Mothers, Children, and Cohabitation: The Intergenerational Effects of Attitudes and Behavior." *American Sociological Review* 58:233–246.

Axinn, W. G., and A. Thornton. 1996. "The Influence of Parents' Marital Dissolutions and Children's Family Formation Attitudes." *Demography* 33(1):66–81.

Axinn, W. G., M. Clarkberg, and A. Thornton. 1994. "Family Influences on Family Size Preferences." *Demography* 31(1):65–79.

Bachrach, C. 1987. "Cohabitation and Reproductive Behavior in the U.S." *Demography* 24:623–637.

Barber, J. S. 1998. "Ideational Influences on the Transition to Parenthood: Attitudes Toward Childbearing and Competing Alternatives." Unpublished manuscript, Institute for Social Research, University of Michigan.

Becker, G. S. 1976. *The Economic Approach to Human Behavior*. Chicago: University of Chicago Press.

Becker, G. S. 1991. *A Treatise on the Family*. Cambridge, MA: Harvard University Press.

Bulcroft, R. A., and K. A. Bulcroft. 1993. "Race Differences and Attitudinal and Motivational Factors in the Decision to Marry." *Journal of Marriage and the Family* 55:338–355.

Bumpass, L.L., and H. Lu. 1999. "Trends in Cohabitation and Implications for Children's Family Contexts in the U.S." Center for Demography and Ecology Working Paper No. 99-15, University of Wisconsin–Madison.

Bumpass, L. L., and J. A. Sweet. 1989. "National Estimates of Cohabitation: Cohort Levels and Union Stability." *Demography* 26(4):615–625.

Coleman, James S. 1990. *Foundations of Social Theory*. Cambridge, MA: Harvard University Press.

Davis, K. 1984. "Wives and Work: The Sex Role Revolution and Its Consequences." *Population and Development Review* 10(3):397–417.

Durkheim, E. 1984. *The Division of Labor in Society*. New York: Free Press.

Glenn, N. D. 1996. "Values, Attitudes, and American Marriage." Pp. 15–33 in *Promises to Keep: Decline and Renewal of Marriage in America,* edited by D. Popenoe, J. B. Elshtain, and D. Blankenhorn. Lanham, MD: Rowman and Littlefield.

Goldscheider, F. K., and L. J. Waite. (1991). *New Families, No Families? The Transformation of the American Home.* Berkeley: University of California Press.

Ku, L., Sonenstein, F. L., Lindberg, L. D., and Bradner, C. H. 1998. "Understanding Changes in Sexual Activity Among Young Metropolitan Men: 1979–1995." *Family Planning Perspectives.* 30(6):256–262.

Lillard, Lee A., Michael J. Brien, and Linda J. Waite. 1995. "PreMarital Cohabitation and Subsequent Marital Dissolution: Is It Self-Selection?" *Demography* 32(3): 437–458.

Manning, W. D. 1995. "Cohabitation, Marriage, and Entry into Motherhood." *Journal of Marriage and the Family* 57:191–200.

McLanahan, S. S., and L. L. Bumpass. 1988. "Intergenerational Consequences of Family Disruption." *American Journal of Sociology* 94:130–152.

Mead, G. H. 1934. *Mind, Self and Society: From the Standpoint of a Social Behaviorist.* Chicago: University of Chicago Press.

Ogburn, W. F., and C. Tibbitts. 1933. "The Family and Its Functions." *Recent Social Trends in the United States,* the President's Research Committee of Social Trends, Report 1, 1:661–708. New York: McGraw-Hill.

Oppenheimer, V. K. 1994. "Women's Rising Employment and the Future of the Family in Industrial Societies." *Population and Development Review* 20:293–342.

Pagnini, D. L., and R. R. Rindfuss. 1993. "Divorce of Marriage and Childbearing: Changing Attitudes and Behavior in the United States." *Population and Development Review* 19:331–347.

Schulenberg, J., J. G. Bachman, L. D. Johnston, and P. M. O'Malley. 1995. "American Adolescents' Views on Family and Work: Historical Trends from 1976–1992." Pp. 37–64 in *Psychological Responses to Social Change: Human Development in Changing Environments,* edited by P. Noach, M. Hofer, and J. Youniss. Berlin: Walter de Gruyter.

Thornton, A. 1989. "Changing Attitudes Toward Family Issues in the United States." *Journal of Marriage and the Family* 51:873–893.

Thornton, A. 1991. "Influence of the Marital History of Parents on the Marital and Cohabitational Experiences of Children." *American Journal of Sociology* 96(4):868–894.

Thornton, A. 1995. "Attitudes, Values, and Norms Related to Nonmarital Fertility." Pp. 201–216 in *Report to Congress on Out-of-Wedlock Childbearing.* Hyattsville, MD: U. S. Department of Health and Human Services. DHHS Pub. No. (PHS) 95-1257.

Thornton, A., and D. Camburn. 1987. "The Influence of the Family on Premarital Sexual Attitudes and Behavior." *Demography* 24(3):323–340.

Thornton, A., and D. S. Freedman. 1982. "Changing Attitudes Toward Marriage and Single Life." *Family Planning Perspectives* 14:297–303.

Thornton, A., and T. E. Fricke. 1987. "Social Change and the Family: Comparative Perspectives from the West, China, and South Asia." *Sociological Forum* 2(4):746–772.

Thornton, A., and L. Young-DeMarco. 1999. "Trends in Attitudes toward Family Issues in the United States: The 1980s and 1990s." Unpublished paper, Institute for Social Research, The University of Michigan.

Thornton, A., L. Young-DeMarco, and F. Goldscheider. 1993. "Leaving the Parental Nest: The Experience of a Young White Cohort in the 1980s." *Journal of Marriage and the Family* 55:216–229.

Veroff, J., E. Douvan, and R. Kulka. 1981. *The Inner American*. New York: Basic Books.

Waite, L. J. 1995. "Does Marriage Matter?" *Demography* 32(4):483–507.

Waite, L. J., and M. Gallagher. Forthcoming. *The Case for Marriage*. Cambridge, MA: Harvard University Press.

Weitzman, L. J. 1985. *The Divorce Revolution*. New York: Free Press.

9

Marital Values and Expectations in Context: Results from a 21-City Survey

M. BELINDA TUCKER

Due to greater marital delay, higher divorce rates, and an increased tendency among some groups to never marry, marital prevalence in the United States has declined quite dramatically over the past several decades (Raley, 1998; Saluter and Lugaila, 1998). Despite this substantial change in marital behavior, there is consistent evidence that Americans continue to hold the institution of marriage in high regard (Thorton, 1989). This positive valuation of marriage seems to hold across ethnic and racial groups, despite significant differences in family formation behavior (Tucker and Mitchell-Kernan, 1995d). Compared to the general population, African-Americans marry later, are about twice as likely to divorce, and are less likely to marry ever, yet blacks' views of the importance of marriage are similar to those held by members of other ethnic groups (Heiss, 1997; Tucker and Mitchell-Kernan, 1995c). The gap between family formation behavior and expressed personal values is, therefore, greater among African-Americans than for the general population.

Not surprisingly, research and theory have focused on understanding the more observable change in family formation behavior, rather than the increasing gap between values and conduct. Though insight into the former should inform our interpretations of the latter, a focus on actions independent of the contextual values—particularly at the societal rather than individual level—may result in the misspecification of behavioral models. That is, behavior can be meaningfully interpreted only when we understand the belief systems that surround the act.

Explanations of changing marital behavior and, in particular, racial divergence have been offered primarily by sociologists and family economists who have variously cited family values, economics, demographic shifts, changing gender roles, and cultural differences as causative (e.g., Cherlin, 1998; Darity and Myers, 1995; Guttentag and Secord, 1983; Lichter et al., 1992; Morgan et al., 1993; Oppenheimer, 1988; Wilson, 1987, 1996).

166

These interpretations of societal change have focused primarily on aggregate level processes. At the same time, psychological studies of the changing nature of romantic involvements (e.g., greater likelihood of divorce) have given inadequate consideration to the impact of structural forces. An understanding of the apparent inconsistency between marital beliefs and behaviors, however, requires a conceptual and methodological framework that incorporates both levels of analysis. In this chapter I report data from a research program (Tucker and Mitchell-Kernan, 1997) designed to examine how family formation attitudes and behaviors are related to both individual and contextual level processes, in order to better inform our understanding of ethnic-specific trends in family organization. Specifically, I will examine ethnic consistency and difference in family formation attitudes and determinants of marital expectancy.

INTERPRETING THE GAP BETWEEN MARITAL BEHAVIOR AND VALUES

Value Differentiation

Several conceptual perspectives offer insight into the apparent divergence between marital values and behavior. Thorton (1989) has shown that the constellation of attitudes about family formation in the United States has become considerably more heterogeneous and that Americans in general are far more accepting of a range of family types and behaviors. Reviewing studies of attitudes toward marriage from the late 1950s through the mid-1980s, he found no significant shifts in either the desire to marry or the desire to remain single or childless, and since 1960, no decline in the proportion of persons who expect to marry. However, he did observe a weakening in the "normative imperative" to marry, to remain married, to have children, to be faithful to one's spouse, and to differentiate male and female roles.

Relatedly, Barich and Bielby (1996) proposed that our fundamental conceptions of marriage have changed in recent years. Examining responses to student surveys between 1967 and 1994, they found that the romantic ideal associated with marriage has been maintained. Yet students became less likely to view marriage as necessary for having children or facilitating sexual gratification, which suggests that the significance of such factors for motivating marital entry has diminished. Notably, over the same period of time, there developed a greater emphasis on economic security as an expectation of marriage.

Recently, a number of historians and historical sociologists have presented evidence of long-standing distinctions in specific aspects of family organization among blacks and whites (such as the greater prevalence of child fosterage among African-Americans) (McDaniel, 1994; Morgan et al., 1993; Stevenson, 1996). Some view these behavioral differences as reflective of distinctive value orientations stemming from West African cultural retentions as well as adaptations to the harsh conditions of slavery and the lingering economic and social disadvantage in its aftermath. In certain other respects, however, black and white family formation behavior appears to be converging. Ruggles (1997) has noted that the magnitude of the differential in black and white nonmarital births has narrowed considerably over the last 40 years—due primarily to shifts in the behavior of whites.

Cross-Cultural Variations in Nuptiality

Long before the current debate over the source of racial differences in marriage behavior, Dixon (1971) constructed a theory to explain cross-cultural variation in marital entry. She argued that three factors mediated the relationship between social structure and nuptiality: (1) the availability of mates, (2) the feasibility of marriage, and (3) the desirability of marriage. This schema incorporates both structural elements (i.e., whether the environment includes persons eligible for mating from both demographic and economic perspectives) and attitudinal components (i.e., the value of marriage to the individual). Under this model, high marital valuation and desirability would lead to marriage only when both availability and feasibility are high.

As previously noted, this perspective may offer some insight into marital decline among African-Americans (Tucker and Mitchell-Kernan, 1995d). That is, the depressed economic circumstances of African-American men, in particular, coupled with the significant sex ratio imbalances characteristic of many black communities have led individuals to assess marital feasibility in personal terms as low. Attempts to empirically demonstrate the contributions of demographic and economic forces to the marriage behavior of African-Americans (and, in particular, racial differences) have demonstrated mixed success (e.g., Lichter et al., 1991; Tucker and Mitchell-Kernan, 1995b; Wood, 1995). Typically, however, such research has sought to explain marital behavior, but not the related attitudinal dimensions, including marital valuation, marital values, and expectation of marriage. Furthermore, attempts to link individual marital behavior to environmental conditions have failed to consider the fact that marriage behavior is not under volitional control. Since actual entry into marriage requires the cooperation of at least one other person, the expectation of marriage should better represent an individual's assessment of availability and feasibility, given the value placed on marriage, and, as such, may be more responsive to contextual facilitators and inhibitors.

Theory of Reasoned Action

On a more general level, the gap between attitudes and behavior is addressed by the social psychological theory of reasoned action (Ajzen and Fishbein, 1980) in which the intention to act is viewed as a function of one's attitude toward the behavior as well as normative beliefs concerning the expectations of others to perform the behavior (i.e., social pressure). Notably, the focus is on the development of behavioral intentions that are presumed to be antecedent to actual behavior. Although the theory enjoys widespread usage as a means of understanding health behavior, it has implications for the issue at hand. It could be argued that despite the favorable attitudes of all groups of Americans toward marriage, there has been a decline in the social pressure on people to marry, thus accounting for the decline in marriage. Under this perspective, the discrepancy could also result from a more complex set of attitudes toward marriage (including more stringent requirements for marriage, more discriminating mate selection criteria, or greater concern with the conditions under which marriage occurs such as a more secure economic base). This perspective is focused primarily on individual level processes. However, as Liska (1984) pointed out in his critique of the theory of reasoned action, most behaviors of interest are contingent on the cooperation of others, a number of environmental resources, and one's position in the social structure.

The Empirical Problem

Together, these three sets of perspectives suggest that an assessment of predictors of expected marital behavior should consider (1) the range and complexity of marital values that should inform marital behavior, (2) objective and perceived environmental barriers to marriage, including availability of viable mates, (3) feasibility of marriage in terms of personal resources, and (4) perceived social pressure to marry.

Studies of family formation typically rely on comparisons between persons who marry and who do not marry, without accounting for whether persons in the latter category have marriage as an unrealized goal. The particularly large gap between value placed on marriage and marital behavior among African-Americans suggests that within this population the number of persons with unrealized marital goals will be substantial. Therefore, research focused only on those who actually enter marriage may present a biased view of the kinds of factors that contribute to the ideological investment in marriage. It is also impossible to examine the gap between marital values and behavior within any given individual. That is, since we are concerned with those persons who highly value marriage, but do not marry, the behavior in question is somewhat nebulous (i.e., when does one finally "not" marry?). (I acknowledge the possibility of the less likely alternative—persons who do not value marriage, but marry any-way.) To address this concern, I focus on marital expectation, while con-trolling for the value placed on marriage.

ECONOMIC CONSTRAINTS ON
AFRICAN-AMERICAN MARRIAGE

Scholars focused on the more substantial decline in marriage among African-Americans have placed particular emphasis on the role of eco-nomic constraints. An argument popularized by Wilson (1987) holds that the increasing economic marginality of African-American men has made them less attractive as potential husbands and less interested in marrying, since they are constrained in their ability to perform the provider role in marriage (see also Darity and Myers, 1986/87, 1995). Indeed, there is ample evidence that the African-American population, and most particu-larly its men, has been hit especially hard by more recent economic downturns. In examining potential causes of black marital decline, Cher-lin (1998) notes that during the 1990–1991 economic recession, African-Americans were the only large racial–ethnic group to suffer a net loss of jobs (Sharp, 1993). Hill et al. (1993) points out that the five recessions between 1970 and 1990 resulted in a tripling of unemployment levels for blacks, which (unlike for whites) never returned to prerecession levels. He argues that this sharp increase in economic instability has contributed to marital instability, and shows that between 1970 and 1983, every one per-centage point rise in unemployment was accompanied by an equivalent rise in single-parent families. Though some studies support this notion (Hatchett et al., 1995; Testa and Krogh, 1995), others find that economic factors explain only a portion of black marital decline over the past 30 years (e.g., Ellwood and Rodda, 1991; Mare and Winship, 1991; Wood, 1995). Wilson (1996) now argues that the long-term impact of a decaying economy in the inner city has been the transformation of norms support-ing husband–wife families and the weakening of social sanctions against nonmarital births.

Though these notions have rarely been tested with Latino populations, high rates of marriage continue amid economic disadvantage and at least one study confirms the absence of an economic effect on marriage among Mexican-Americans (Oropesa et al., 1994). However, they also found that in several areas the direction of effects was exactly the opposite for immi-grant and native-born groups, suggesting that greater within-group heterogeneity makes unwise broad-based theorizing about Mexican-American marital behavior.

There is evidence that a decline in the economic circumstances of young American males of all races (Easterlin, 1980; Lichter et al., 1991) has affected overall marriage patterns. Oppenheimer (1988) argues that the delay in marriage that is now characteristic of American society is due to an elongated mate search strategy fueled primarily by uncertainty regarding male economic prospects. Still, there is a developing body of attitudinal literature that indicates that economics plays a greater role in the marital decision making of African-Americans compared to other ethnic groups (Bulcroft and Bulcroft, 1993; Tucker and Mitchell-Kernan, 1995c). These studies suggest that the attitudinal emphasis on the economic foundation of marriage is distinguishable from both contextual level indicators (e.g., unemployment levels) and personal resources (e.g., income). Furthermore, such attitudes may have an impact on marriage behavior over and above the objective indicators that are the subject of most economic and sociological inquiry.

METHOD

Sample and Procedures

From August 1995 through January 1996, telephone interviews were conducted with 3407 persons aged 18–55 in 21 cities in the United States selected to represent a range of specific community level variables, including size, ethnic proportions, sex ratio, and indicators of economic climate. The cities ranged in size from 101,000 to 7.3 million residents and represented all regions. Respondents included only those between the ages of 18 and 55, inclusive. African-Americans and whites were interviewed in all 21 cities, and Mexican-Americans were interviewed in three Western and Southwestern cities. African-Americans and whites were limited to those who lived in the United States for at least 6 of the first 12 years of their lives. The sample includes 1380 (40%) African-Americans, 228 (7%) Mexican-Americans, and 1700 (53%) whites. Field activities, including sampling and interviewing, were carried out by the Survey Research Center of the University of Michigan's Institute for Social Research. Sampling was conducted at the city level, which therefore excluded suburbs and geographic areas not located within city boundaries. A two-stage sample design was used to construct equal probability samples for each ethnic–racial subgroup while maintaining a relatively high proportion of residential numbers. The interview response rate for the total sample (i.e., the percentage of selected, eligible respondents who completed an interview) was 79.3%.

Analyses presented here were conducted either for the total sample or for the 2142 persons who were not married, of whom 970 (45%) were African-American, 115 (5%) were Mexican-American, and 1057 (49%) were white Americans. Table 9.1 summarizes the demographic characteristics

Table 9.1. Demographic Characteristics of the Sample

	Whites		African-Americans		Mexican-Americans	
	Male (839)[a]	*Female* (960)[a]	*Male* (516)[a]	*Female* (864)[a]	*Male* (90)[a]	*Female* (138)[a]
Age[b]	35.9 (9.17)[c]	36.9 (9.85)[c]	34.4 (10.03)[c]	35.3 (10.03)[c]	35.2 (10.29)[c]	32.9 (9.60)[c]
Education[b]	14.7 (2.47)[c]	14.6 (2.20)[c]	13.4 (2.10)[c]	13.5 (2.06)[c]	12.3 (2.32)[c]	12.1 (2.05)[c]
Personal income[b]	$44,222	$27,256	$27,293	$20,756	$25,839	$14,083
Married (%)	41	41	32	28	51	49
Parents (%)	43	54	63	78	68	83
Born in United States (%)	95	94	91	95	65	59

[a]Sample size.
[b]Mean values.
[c]Standard deviations.

of the total sample by ethnicity and gender. The groups are fairly comparable on age, although whites are most highly educated and have the highest incomes. Mexican-Americans are most likely and whites are least likely to be parents. Due to our sample selection restrictions, relatively few African-Americans and whites were foreign born, although a significant minority of the Mexican-American population was born outside the United States.

Measures

In this section I describe all of the key variables used to produce the results presented in this chapter, including family formation values used in the descriptive analyses, as well as predictors used in both the preliminary and more parsimonious final regression models. When appropriate, reliability coefficients (Cronbach αs) for the entire sample are presented (though in all cases coefficients for each ethnic group were very close to the overall value).

Family Formation Expectations, Values, and Perceptions. The dependent measure of marital expectancy consisted of the single question: "How likely do you think it is that you will ever marry?" (scored from 1 meaning "extremely unlikely" to 10 meaning "extremely likely"). Several indicators of family formation values were examined—all using the same response choices described above: "How important is being married to you?" "How important to you are romantic relationships in general?" "How important is it to you, personally to get married some day?" "How import is it to you to be married when you have children?" To assess the significance of economic considerations in relationships, respondents were asked to rate on a 10-point scale the importance of "having adequate income, that is having enough money" for a "successful marriage or serious committed relationship" (from "not important at all" to "extremely important"). Perceived social pressure to marry was determined by two indicators: "How much pressure have you felt from your family to get married" and "How much pressure do you feel from your friends to get married?" Response choices for both questions were a 10-point scale ranging from "no pressure" to "a great deal of pressure."

Questions concerning the costs and benefits of marriage are modified versions of those used by Bumpass and Sweet (1998) in the National Survey of Families and Households. Measures of the perceived socioemotional and economic benefits of marriage were constructed from a series of questions with the following stem: For each of the following areas, please tell me how you think your life might be different if you were married or living together with someone as married (scored on a 10-point scale from "much worse" to "much better"). The socioemotional benefits measure was constructed from responses in the areas of friendships, sex life, leisure time, sense of security, and practice of religion. The reliability coefficient for this measure was .87. The economic benefits measure consisted of the single item assessing whether one's standard of living would be improved through marriage.

Demographic Indicators. Measures also included the demographic characteristics of personal income, education, age, and parental status. Personal income was assessed by the question, "About how much income did you make in 1994 before taxes, that is what is the amount of money that you alone made last year? Please include all sources of income, including salaries, wages, social security, welfare, and any other income you received in 1994." Education was a categorical variable that combined total years of education with the highest degree received, resulting in a variable that ranged from 10 years, indicating that the participant did not complete high school, to 20 years, indicating an advanced degree. Age was measured by age in years at last birthday. Parenthood (which was more predictive than number of children in previous runs) was coded as "0" for no living children and "1" for at least one child.

Personal Resources. Indicators of personal resources included religiosity, social support, perceived poverty, and self-esteem. Although other religion indicators were tested, the item that emerged for use in final analyses was a single-item measure of religiosity: "Using a 1 to 10 scale, with 1 meaning not religious at all and 10 meaning extremely religious, how religious would you say you are?" The mean of three items from The

Provision of Social Relations Scale (Turner, 1992) was used to measure social support: perceived family support ("My family will always be there for me should I need them."), the existence of a confidante ("I have at least one friend or family member I could tell anything."), and social companionship ("When I want to go out and do things, I have someone who would enjoy doing these things with me."). The response scale ranged from 1 to 10 indicating not at all true to very much true. Since this question assessed different aspects of social support, which in theory could be unrelated to one another (i.e., support from friends versus support from family), we did not expect the combination of three variables to have high internal consistency. The Cronbach α for the measure was .59. Finally, perceived impoverishment consisted of mean scores from a three-item measure used by Pearlin and Johnson (1977) in their Chicago stress study. Respondents were asked how often they did not have money to afford (1) food, (2) clothing, or (3) medical care. A four-category response scale of "never, rarely, sometimes, or often" was used. The Cronbach α was .78. A six-item indicator, included in the National Survey of Black Americans (Jackson et al., 1980), was used to assess the self-acceptance aspect of self-esteem (Cronbach α = .76).

Gender Role Ideology. Traditional gender role ideology was a modification of questions used on the survey of Bumpass and Sweet (1998) and included the following items: "A woman's most important task in life should be having and raising children." "A man should earn a larger salary than his female partner." "Even though a woman works outside the home, her husband or partner should be the main breadwinner." The reliability coefficient for this measure was .76.

Contextual Measures. City level variables were derived from the 1990 Census Summary Tape Files 3 and 4 (STF3B, STF4B), in which information for Hispanics is extracted from the files of the Census-designated racial groups (i.e., whites, blacks, Asian/Pacific Islander, and American Indian/Alaskan Native). They included sex- and race-specific percentage unemployed, sex ratios, proportion of racial groups with some college, racial proportions in the population, proportions of the population that were divorced, race-specific median income, and proportions of the racial groups that were below the poverty level.

RESULTS

The analyses were conducted in several phases. First, I examined whether and how family formation values varied by ethnic group and gender, when controlling for age, education, and income. Next, I determined the sociodemographic, attitudinal, and contextual variables associated with expectations of marriage. In the interests of parsimony, only the final regression models from this phase are presented, each including age, education, and income as control variables, but omitting other variables that proved to be unrelated to the variable of interest in preliminary runs.

Ethnic Group and Gender Comparisons on Family Formation Values

Table 9.2 presents mean scores by ethnic group and gender when family formation attitudes were regressed on age, education, and income. Also presented are the F values testing for the main effects of ethnicity and gender. Note that although all respondents were asked the series of questions about the value of marriage generally, only noncohabitating singles (i.e., not currently married) were queried about their expectations of marriage and perceived benefits of marriage. Only respondents who had never married were asked about social pressure to marry.

Consistent with a number of other studies conducted over the past several decades, marital values of African-Americans, Mexican-Americans, and whites in our study are similar in a number of respects. There are no significant ethnic differences on expectation of marriage, the importance of marrying some day, and the importance of being married when having children, but Mexican-Americans and African-American men valued marriage significantly more highly than others. Men placed greater value on "long-term relationships" than did women, and Mexican-Americans as a group valued relationships more than other groups.

The greatest ethnic differences were observed for economic values. African-Americans believed most strongly that marital success is dependent on adequate financing. They were also substantially more likely than other ethnic groups to perceive the economic benefits of "marriage or living together with someone as married." whites were least likely to perceive socioemotional benefits of marriage. Unfortunately, since this question did not differentiate between cohabitation and legal marriage, perceived unique benefits of the latter cannot be assumed from these responses.

Finally, all groups reported very little pressure to marry from either family or friends. In all three ethnic groups, women were more likely than men to feel such pressure, and Mexican-American women perceived the greatest pressure to marry. But the means on a 1–10 scale were remarkably low for every group: 64% of single African-Americans, 58% of single Mexican-Americans, and 51% of single whites felt no pressure to marry from families. The respective figures for pressure from friends were 69, 64, and 60%.

Table 9.2. Marital Values Means by Ethnicity and Gender Adjusted for Age, Education, and Income

	African-American		Mexican-American		White American		F Values	
	Women	Men	Women	Men	Women	Men	Ethnicity	Gender
Expectation of marriage[a]	6.3	6.9	6.9	7.3	6.4	6.7	1.8	.8
Importance of Marriage[b]	7.1	7.5	7.8	7.8	7.0	7.1	7.7***	.5
Important of relationship[b]	7.7	8.1	8.2	8.4	7.6	7.9	6.0**	4.0*
Important to marry some day[b]	7.5	7.8	7.1	8.4	7.9	7.8	.7	3.3
Importance of being married when having children[b]	8.2	8.2	8.3	9.0	8.3	8.1	2.6	.8
Importance of income for marriage[b]	8.7	8.3	7.6	8.1	7.8	7.3	83.1***	.6
Perceived economic benefits of marriage[a]	4.5	4.0	2.7	2.9	3.3	3.2	34.6***	.2
Perceived socioemotional benefits of marriage[a]	6.9	6.7	7.0	6.8	6.4	6.3	21.1***	1.1
Perceived family pressure to marry[c]	2.8	2.5	3.7	2.5	2.2	2.5	.9	8.1*
Perceived friends pressure to marry[c]	2.6	2.3	3.5	2.6	2.4	1.9	4.9**	6.8*

[a]Single, noncohabitating respondents only (n = 1056–1255 women, 718–883 men).
[b]All respondents (n = 1943–1956 women, 1437–1443 men).
[c]Never married respondents only (n = 587 women, 504 men).
*$p < .05$; **$p < .01$; ***$p < .001$.

Single African-Americans—who make up a greater proportion of their ethnic group than either Mexican-Americans or whites—are most likely to have experienced no social pressure to marry.

Although most of the values questions were answered only by single persons, four items were asked of all respondents. We might therefore expect variation in responses on the basis of marital status. Further, since the three racial–ethnic groups in this study vary greatly in the likelihood that a member would be married or single, characteristics of those who occupy a given marital status category might also differ among the three groups. Table 9.3 presents mean values by ethnicity, gender, and marital status (i.e., currently married versus all singles), adjusted for age, education, and income. Not unexpectedly, among all three ethnic groups, persons who are married have more favorable attitudes about marriage and long-term committed relationships, and also believe more strongly that it is important to be married when one has children. Notably, white women did not differ on the basis of marital status in the value placed on being married to have children. Indeed, married white women were least likely of all married groups to endorse this value. Overall, ethnic differences were less strong than marital status differences, and they did not differ at all on the importance of marriage for having children. When ethnicity was a factor, unmarried whites expressed lower commitment to marriage than did either blacks or Mexican-Americans. In sharp contrast to these trends, no marital status differences emerged for the importance of having an adequate income for a successful marriage, but strong ethnic differences were apparent among both single and married persons. No ethnicity x marital status interactions were significant, demonstrating that similar trends in the association of marital status with values were evident across ethnic groups.

Predicting Marital Expectancy

A multilevel analysis was conducted by performing separate multiple regressions by gender, including all ethnic groups in the model with marital expectancy as the dependent variables and the set of independent variables described above. City-level indicators were added to the analyses, one at a time, after the individual-level models were determined. The regression program in the Stata statistical package was used because it provides "Huber–White" covariance matrices (producing robust standard errors) and permitted control for the effects of clustering (i.e., based on the use of 21 sites). Since the gender–ethnic differences in the models were of considerable theoretical significance, the final models are presented by ethnicity for women and men. Although analyses presented do not make distinctions on the basis of sexual orientation, respondents who considered themselves to be ineligible for marriage due to either religious reasons or sexual orientation were not asked questions concerning legal marriage.

Results of the regression analyses are presented in Table 9.4. To control its effects, "importance of marriage" is included in all four models. As expected, the variable most predictive of expectation of marriage (exclusive of value of marriage) is respondent age, with younger persons having higher expectations of marrying eventually. With the exception of African-

M. Belinda Tucker

Table 9.3. Whole Sample Marital Values Means by Ethnicity, Gender, and Marital Status Adjusted for Age, Education, and Income[a]

| | African-American | | Mexican-American | | White American | | F Values | | | |
| | | | | | | | Women | | Men | |
	Women	Men	Women	Men	Women	Men	Ethnicity	Marital Status	Ethnicity	Marital Status
Importance of marriage							5.1**	271.0***	5.5*	199.4***
Married	9.3	9.2	9.0	9.0	8.8	9.0				
Not married	6.3	6.6	6.4	6.5	5.7	5.8				
Importance of relationship							3.1*	74.6***	3.3*	23.3***
Married	8.5	8.5	8.7	8.7	8.2	8.3				
Not married	7.3	7.9	7.5	8.0	7.2	7.6				
Importance of being married when having children							.1	14.5***	3.6	10.9*
Married	8.7	8.8	8.8	9.2	8.1	8.6				
Not married	8.0	7.9	7.9	8.8	8.1	7.8				
Importance of income for marriage							48.7***	2.1	38.0***	2.3
Married	8.6	8.3	7.5	7.8	7.7	7.2				
Not married	8.7	8.3	7.7	8.4	7.8	7.4				

[a]There were no significant ethnicity × marital status interactions.
*$p < .05$; **$p < .01$; ***$p < .001$.

Table 9.4. Summary of Regression Analyses of Marital Expectation Including Value of Marriage

	Betas			
	African-American Women (n = 530)	African-American Men (n = 287)	White Women (n = 460)	White Men (n = 381)
Age	−.35***	−.25**	−.39***	−.38***
Education	.13**	.08	.09*	.13**
Income	.05	.14**	−.02	.10**
Never married	.06	.15*	.08	.08
Social support	.05	.15**	.01	.11
Self-esteem	.04	.02	.10**	.04
Religiosity	.09+	.03	.07*	−.008
Socioemotional benefits	.05	.05	.03	−.03
Economic benefits	.14***	−.03	−.01	.12***
Traditional gender role	.06	.01	.06	.09*
Importance of marriage	.31***	.26**	.36***	.41***
Divorce (city)	.10*			
White female unemployment				.08**
Black unemployment		−.12**		
R^2	.32	.26	.44	.50
Unique contribution of importance of marriage	.08	.07	.09	.14

*p < .05; **p < .01; ***p < .001.

American men, more highly educated persons were more likely to expect to marry. Yet, unlike all other groups, black men who had higher levels of social support were more likely to believe they would marry. Self-esteem and religion were predictive only for white women and only among white men did more traditional gender role orientation increase the expectation to marry.

Economic variables were predictive in a number of ways. Personal income is predictive of marital expectancy for men only. Further, among both African-American women and white men, believing that there are economic benefits from marriage is associated with higher expectancy. Although all of the contextual variables were tested individually in the models (not shown), the economic variables proved to be most salient. Black men who live in cities with higher levels of black unemployment are less likely to expect to marry. Indeed, both black female and black male unemployment were significant predictors, virtually equal in predictive ability. However, white men who live in cities in which white female unemployment is higher are more likely to expect to marry. White male unemployment level made no contribution to the model. One noneconomic contextual variable made a significant contribution to a model. African-American women who lived in cities with higher divorce levels had greater expectations of marriage.

DISCUSSION

Overall, the comparative findings demonstrate that all three racial–ethnic groups hold strong promarriage values, but that these values are particularly strong among African-Americans and Mexican-Americans. For half of the values examined, there were no ethnic differences. Where differences existed, they were in several cases precisely the opposite of what has been commonly assumed. In particular, when controlling for age, education, and income, African-American men expressed higher regard for the institution of marriage than did white men and were as likely as white men to expect to marry some day. Similarly, unmarried white women and men placed significantly less value on marriage than women and men of other groups; and married white women were least likely to believe that being married when having children was important.

Mexican-Americans valued marriage most highly—a circumstance that Orospesa et al. (1994) attribute to differences in cultural and religious orientation. Yet, the Mexican-American women in this study were least likely to believe that it is important to marry some day, whereas Mexican-American men endorsed this item most highly. A similar distinction between the marital beliefs of Latino men and Latinas was observed in the Southern California study conducted within this program of research (Tucker and Mitchell-Kernan, 1995c). This may reflect a growing ambivalence among some Latinas about marriage in the face of the conflicts generated through increased women's economic power and traditional gender-role beliefs (Melville, 1980; Pesquera, 1984; Vasquez and Gonzalez, 1981).

The most dramatic racial–ethnic differences were observed about the role of economics in marriage. African-Americans believed most strongly that having an adequate income was critical for marital success and were most likely to see an economic benefit to be derived from marriage. Overall, this was true regardless of marital status, although *single* Mexican-American men held beliefs similar to those of African-American men about the salience of an adequate income for marriage (further evidence that such views may contribute to marital reluctance or delay). African-American women placed greatest emphasis on the proper financing of marriage. Clearly, these data indicate that within this sample of urban blacks, marriage is highly valued, but coupled with the recognition that the financial requirements for marriage are substantial. Yet, there is a greater realization among African-Americans that being married can increase one's standard of living, though this was not true of single Mexican-American men. The distinction between the necessary financial underpinnings of marriage and the potential financial benefits to be derived may be related to the distinction between marital entry and maintenance. That is, individuals recognizing the pitfalls of insufficient finances in marriage would be reluctant to enter marriage without assurances of adequate funding. Once adequate funding exists, the gains to be had from such a partnership can be realized.

Finally, the results of the values analyses demonstrated quite clearly that social pressure to marry is now very low among all three ethnic groups. Using the interpretive framework of the theory of reasoned action, this substantial decline in the societal imperative to marry should have far reaching effects on marital behavior. It is interesting to note that though pressure to marry from both family and friends is greatest for Mexican-American women, they are also the group that expresses the highest degree of marital resistance (as noted above).

The multiple regression results proved revealing in a number of respects. The significant demographic variables show how one's position in the social structure informs marital values and assessments of feasibility. Younger and more highly educated persons have traditionally been more likely to marry. Older persons who have never married may be uninterested in marriage or resigned to never marrying. The fact that male earning power encourages marriage may reflect the continued strength of traditional ideology concerning male roles in this society. In other results from this project, we find that a substantial minority within all three ethnic groups still believes that men have primary responsibility for providing the financial support for families (Taylor et al., 1999).

The power of the economic predictors was also apparent in the regression results. Though recognition of the socioemotional benefits of marriage did not encourage marital expectancy in any group, among both African-American women and white men, those who believed that being married increased one's standard of living had greater expectations of marriage. Why does this result apply only to African-American women and white men? It may be that a presumption of economic betterment through marriage exists for both white women and black men—independent of marital decision making. That is, because of the advantaged economic position of white men generally (note the great discrepancy between white male personal income and all other incomes within this sample), white women have greater reason to believe that marriage will bring economic security. Similarly, black women have traditionally been economic coproviders in marriage, so black men would be more likely to assume that with marriage comes a working wife. Among both black women and white men, however, the economic contributions of a partner are less assured, and may therefore play a greater role in one's marital intentions and assessments of feasibility.

Interestingly, having been previously married affected marital expectations only among black men (lowering them). Black men were also more likely to want to marry if they had high levels of social support. In this context, social support may serve as an indicator of social integration. That is, African-American men who are more integrated into social networks may be more likely to view marriage as a viable option.

The significant contextual effects provide greater support for the critical role played by economics in marital expectation. African-American men who lived in cities in which black unemployment (both male and female) was low had greater expectations of marriage. This would support the notions of Wilson (1987) and Darity and Myers (1995), who assert that black marital decline stems in significant part from the decline in economic options for black men. The contextual effect of unemployment may also denote the level of economic uncertainty in the environment. Men who live in cities where unemployment is high have no reason to believe that their environment provides economic security sufficient to support a family.

Notably, the effect of contextual economics for white men is quite different. Those who lived in cities where joblessness was higher among white females (i.e., where women had greater need for economic support) displayed greater marital intent. This finding is coupled with the fact that white males with more traditional gender role orientations were more likely to expect to marry. Such men would view economic provision for women as a fundamental part of the male role. It would appear then that when these men are assessing the economic benefits of marriage, they include in their considerations the benefits for potential wives as well as their own economic role.

One noneconomic contextual finding emerged. African-American women who lived in cities where divorce levels were high were more likely to expect to marry. In previous analyses on this project, divorce levels in cities appear to be an indicator of mate availability. That is, cities with higher divorce levels have greater numbers of single middle-age adults. Notably, for black women, only overall divorce levels were associated with marital expectancy. Black divorce levels were completely unrelated to the outcome variable, which suggests that (in light of significant shortages of black men in many communities) African-American women may be broadening their pools of potentially eligible partners. Other evidence from this research program on interracial dating and marriage (Tucker and Mitchell-Kernan, 1995a; Taylor et al., under review) supports this view.

With respect to the recent dramatic change in marital behavior among African-Americans, these findings are suggestive of several possible scenarios. One, the findings could indicate that African-Americans are more sensitive to the economic underpinnings of marriage. This would be understandable, given the precarious economic circumstances that have historically characterized the African-American experience and the more recent postindustrial displacement of blacks in manufacturing jobs. Second, it could mean that the greater prevalence of divorce among blacks makes them more sensitive to the kinds of external/structural forces that threaten marital success. To the extent that economic problems figure prominently in African-American divorce, the shared wisdom in the population at large would warn against becoming involved in such situations in the first place. In their prospective study of marriage, Hatchett et al. (1995) found that black men who had provider role concerns had less stable marriages. That is, *concern* about economic provision (rather than the actual experience of economic crisis) was found to be sufficient to threaten, and indeed end, the marriages of African-American men. [See Bowman's (1988, 1990) cogent analyses of the negative psychological consequences of provider role strain among African-American men.] Finally, these findings may reflect an acknowledgment of the greater economic insecurity of African-Americans generally, and the potential impact of such insecurity on marriage. Such fears are well grounded. Layoff statistics from 1998 show that even during this period of general economic prosperity, blacks were twice as likely as whites to have lost their jobs—3.7% versus 1.8% of the civilian labor force (United States Bureau of Labor Statistics, 1999).

Brockman (1987) observed that the normative trend in many Caribbean countries to delay marriage until economic supports are stabilized and sufficient is becoming characteristic of many Western societies. If this is what is occurring among African-Americans, it would certainly support Oppenheimer's (1988) theory of marital timing—that marriage more generally in the United States is being delayed until more information about the economic potential of prospective husbands, in particular, is known. Yet, as Raley (1998) notes, marriage for a good many African-American women is not being simply delayed, but may not ever occur. In other words, when additional data regarding the economic potential of prospective husbands are secured, for many African-American women, it is not good news.

Although these findings are instructive, economics could be only one of a number of factors contributing to the decline of marriage among African-Americans. For example, in a dissertation completed using data from this study, Taylor (1998) found that gender role orientation is more predictive of marital views, in some circumstances, than either economic or availability factors. She also found that the gap between gender role orientations of African-American men and women is greater than the gap between white men and women, and that black men hold more traditional gender role views than white men. This holds true despite the fact that (as other studies show) black men are more likely to engage in household tasks and childrearing, and that black women contribute a greater share of the economic support of households than do white women.

The greater societal question (as well as other Western societies) is why the normative imperative to marry has declined. Although few respondents in this study felt pressured to marry, more African-Americans than others perceived *no* pressure to marry. It may be that the very pervasiveness of singlehood in black communities is propelling its greater acceptance—a self-perpetuating phenomenon. For African-American women, perhaps the increased recognition that marriage for many is unlikely and the existence of more successful, single role models (e.g., Oprah Winfrey) have contributed to a climate that is far more supportive of singlehood.

This study has significant limitations. The data are cross-sectional, and, as such, are incapable of informing causal processes. Also, the limited interview time necessitated by the telephone survey method constrains the type and amount of information that can be obtained. More in-depth questioning (perhaps through qualitative methods) may elicit more insight into the gap between marital values and behavior. Yet, the results of this study provide evidence that African-American perceptions of the role of economics in marriage are distinctive and likely influential in assessments of marital feasibility and intent—particularly in the context of economic uncertainty and a scarcity of economically viable African-American men.

ACKNOWLEDGMENTS

This research was supported by two grants from the National Institute of Mental Health: research Grant No. RO1 MH 47434 to M. Belinda Tucker and Claudia Mitchell-Kernan and Independent Scientist Award No. KO2 MH 01278 to M. Belinda Tucker. I gratefully acknowledge the assistance of Drs. Pamela L. Taylor and Saskia Subramanian and Student Research Program participants Billy Pieratt, Chanda Uppal, and Corbet Ma.

REFERENCES

Ajzen, Icek, and Martin Fishbein. 1980. *Understanding Attitudes and Predicting Social Behavior*. Englewood Cliffs, NJ: Prentice-Hall.
Barich, Rachel R., and Bielby, Denise D. 1996. "Rethinking Marriage: Change and Stability in Expectations, 1967–1994." *Journal of Family Issues* 17:139–169.
Bowman, Phillip. J. 1988. "Post-Industrial Displacement and Family Role Strains: Challenges to the Black Family." Pp. 75–96 in *Families and Economic Distress*, edited by P. Voydanoff and L. C. Maika. Newbury Park, CA: Sage.
Bowman, Phillip. J. 1990. "Coping with Provider Role Strain: Adaptive Cultural Resources Among Black Husband-Fathers." *Journal of Black Psychology* 16: 1–21.

Brockmann, C. Thomas. 1987. "The Western Family and Individuation: Convergence with Caribbean Patterns." *Journal of Comparative Family Studies* 18:471–480.

Bulcroft, Richard A., and Bulcroft, Kris A. 1993. "Race Differences in Attitudinal and Motivational Factors in the Decision to Marry." *Journal of Marriage and the Family* 55:338–355.

Bumpass, Larry L., and James A. Sweet. 1998. The National Survey of Families and Households. 29 September 1999. <http:www.icpsr.umich.edu/cgi/ab.prl?file=6906.

Cherlin, Andrew J. 1998. "Marriage and Marital Dissolution Among Black Americans." *Journal of Comparative Family Studies* 29:147–158.

Darity, William. A., Jr., and Samuel Myers, Jr. 1995. "Family Structure and the Marginalization of Black Men: Policy Implications." Pp. 263–308 in *The Decline in Marriage Among African Americans: Causes, Consequences and Policy Implications*, edited by M. B. Tucker and C. Mitchell-Kernan. New York: Russell Sage.

Dixon, Ruth. 1971. "Explaining Cross-Cultural Variations in Age of Marriage and Proportion Never Marrying." *Population Studies* 25:215–233.

Easterlin, Richard A. 1980. *Birth and Fortune: The Impact of Numbers on Personal Welfare*. New York: Basic Books.

Ellwood, David T., and David T. Rodda. 1991. *The Hazards of Work and Marriage: The Influence of Male Employment on Marriage Rates*. Working Paper No. H-90-5. Cambridge, MA: Malcolm Wiener Center for Social Policy, John F. Kennedy School of Government, Harvard University.

Guttentag, Marcia, and Paul F. Secord. 1983. *Too Many Women: The Sex Ratio Question*. Beverly Hills: Sage.

Hatchett, Shirley, Joseph Veroff, and Elizabeth Douvan, 1995. "Marital Instability among Black and White Couples in Early Marriage." Pp. 177–218 in *The Decline in Marriage Among African Americans: Causes, Consequences and Policy Implications*, edited by M. B. Tucker and C. Mitchell-Kernan. New York: Russell Sage.

Heiss, Jerold. 1997. "Values Regarding Marriage and the Family from a Woman's Perspective." Pp. 284–300 in *Black Families*, 3rd ed., edited by H. P. McAdoo. Thousand Oaks, CA: Sage.

Hill, Robert B., with Andrew Billingsley, Eleanor Engram, Michelene R. Malson, Roger H. Rubin, Carol B. Stack, James B. Stewart, and James E. Teele. 1993. *Research on African American Families: A Holistic Perspective*. Boston: William Monroe Trotter Institute, University of Massachusetts.

Jackson, James S., M. Belinda Tucker, and Gerald Gurin. 1980. *National Survey of Black Americans* [Machine Readable Data File]. Ann Arbor, MI: Institute for Social Research [Producer], Inter-University Consortium for Political and Social Research [Distributor].

Lichter, Daniel T., Felicia B. LeClere, and Diane K. McLaughlin. 1991. "Local Marriage Markets and the Marital Behavior of Black and White Women." *American Journal of Sociology* 96:843–867.

Lichter, Daniel T., Diane K. McLaughlin, George Kephart, and David J. Landry. 1992. "Race and the Retreat from Marriage: A Shortage of Marriageable Men?" *American Sociological Review* 57:781–799.

Liska, Allen E. 1984. "A Critical Examination of the Causal Structure of the Fishbein/Ajzen Attitude-Behavior Model." *Social Psychology Quarterly* 47:61–74.

Mare, Robert D., and Christopher Winship. 1991. "Socioeconomic Change and the Decline of Marriage for Blacks and Whites." Pp. 175–202 in *The Urban Under-*

class, edited by C. Jencks and P. Peterson. Washington, DC: The Brookings Institution.

McDaniel, Antonio. 1994. "Historical Racial Differences in Living Arrangements of Children." *Journal of Family History* 19:57–78.

Melville, Margarita B. 1980. *Twice a Minority: Mexican American Women*. St. Louis: Mosby.

Morgan, S. Philip, Antonio McDaniel, Andrew T. Miller, and Samuel H. Preston. 1993. "Racial Differences in Household and Family Structure at the Turn of the Century." *American Journal of Sociology* 98:799–829.

Oppenheimer, Valerie Kincade. 1988. "A Theory of Marriage Timing." *American Journal of Sociology* 94:563–591.

Oropesa, R.S., Daniel T. Lichter, and Robert N. Anderson. 1994. "Marriage Markets and the Paradox of Mexican American Nuptiality." *Journal of Marriage and the Family* 56(4), 889–908.

Pearlin, Leonard I., and Joyce S. Johnson. 1977. "Marital Status, Life Strains, and Depression." *American Sociological Review* 42:704–715.

Pesquera, Beatriz M. 1984. "'Having a Job Gives You Some Sort of Power': Reflections of a Chicano Working Woman." *Feminist Issues* 4:79–96.

Raley, R. Kelly. 1998. "Trends in Marriage and Union Formation." Paper presented at "The Ties the Bind: Perspectives on Marriage and Cohabitation" conference sponsored by the National Institute of Child Health and Human Development, Bethesda, MD.

Ruggles, Steven. 1997. "The Effects of AFDC on American Family Structure, 1940–1990." *Journal of Family History* 22:307–326.

Saluter, Arlene F., and Terry A. Lugaila. 1998. "Marital Status and Living Arrangements: March 1996." *Current Population Reports*, Series P-20, No. 496. Issued March 1998. <http://www.census.gov/population/www/socdemo/ms-la .html>

Stevenson, Brenda E. 1996. *Life in Black and White: Family and Community in the Slave South*. Oxford: Oxford University Press.

Taylor, Pamela L. 1998. "Attitudes toward Marriage among African American Singles: A Test of Four Perspectives." Ph.D. Dissertation, Department of Psychology, University of California, Los Angeles, Los Angeles, CA.

Taylor, Pamela L., M. Belinda Tucker, and Claudia Mitchell-Kernan. 1999. "Ethnic Variations in Perceptions of Men's Provider Role." *Psychology of Women Quarterly* 23:759–779.

Taylor, Pamela L., M. Belinda Tucker, and Claudia Mitchell-Kernan. Manuscript under review. "Interethnic Dating and Marriage in 21 U.S. Cities."

Testa, Mark, and Marilyn Krogh, 1995. "The Effect of Employment on Marriage Among Black Males in Inner-City." Pp. 59–95 in *The Decline in Marriage Among African Americans: Causes, Consequences and Policy Implications*, edited by M. B. Tucker and C. Mitchell-Kernan. New York: Russell Sage.

Thornton, Arland. 1989. "Changing Attitudes toward Family Issues in the United States." *Journal of Marriage and the Family* 51:873–893.

Tucker, M. Belinda, and Claudia Mitchell-Kernan. 1995a. "Interracial Dating and Marriage in Southern California." *Journal of Social and Personal Relationships* 12:341–361.

Tucker, M. Belinda, and Claudia Mitchell-Kernan. 1995b. "African American Marital Trends in Context: Towards a Synthesis." Pp. 345–362 in *The Decline in Marriage Among African Americans: Causes, Consequences and Policy Implications*, edited by M. B. Tucker and C. Mitchell-Kernan. New York: Russell Sage.

Tucker, M. Belinda, and Claudia Mitchell-Kernan. 1995c. "Marital Behavior and Expectations: Ethnic Comparisons of Attitudinal and Structural Correlates." Pp. 145–171 in *The Decline in Marriage Among African Americans: Causes, Consequences and Policy Implications*, edited by M. B. Tucker and C. Mitchell-Kernan. New York: Russell Sage.

Tucker, M. Belinda, and Claudia Mitchell-Kernan. 1995d. "Trends in African American Family Formation: A Theoretical and Statistical Overview." Pp. 3–26 in *The Decline in Marriage Among African Americans: Causes, Consequences and Policy Implications*, edited by M. B. Tucker and C. Mitchell-Kernan. New York: Russell Sage.

Tucker, M. Belinda, and Claudia Mitchell-Kernan. 1997. "Understanding Marital Decline among African Americans." *African American Research Perspectives* Winter, 40–45.

Turner, R. Jay. 1992. "Measuring Social Support: Issues of Concept and Method." Pp. 217–233 in *The Meaning and Measurement of Social Support*, edited by H. Veiel and U. Baumann. New York: Hemisphere.

U.S. Bureau of Labor Statistics. 1999. Table 28 Unemployed Persons by Reason for Unemployment, Race, and Hispanic Origin. 29 September, 1999. <http://stats.bls.gov/pdf/cpsaat28.pdf>

Vasquez, Melba J. T., and Anna M. Gonzalez. 1981. "Sex Roles among Chicanos: Stereotypes, Challenges, and Changes." Pp. 50–70 in *Explorations in Chicano Psychology*, edited by A. Baron, Jr. New York: Praeger.

Wilson, William Julius. 1987. *The Truly Disadvantaged*. Chicago: The University of Chicago Press.

Wilson, William Julius. 1996. *When Work Disappears: The World of The New Urban Poor*. New York: Knopf.

Wood, Robert G. 1995. "Marriage Rates and Marriageable Men—A Test of the Wilson Hypothesis." *Journal of Human Resources* 30:163–193.

10

Ethnicity, Immigration, and Beliefs about Marriage as a "Tie That Binds"

R. S. OROPESA and BRIDGET K. GORMAN

Recent changes in union formation norms and ethnic diversity are at the forefront of public attention. Among the most salient changes in union formation norms is the weakening normative imperative to marry that is occurring with greater tolerance of cohabitation, premarital sex, nonmarital childbearing, and divorce (Thornton, 1989). This weakening normative imperative has contributed to delays in marriage and increases in cohabitation. Between 1966 and 1996, the median age at first marriage increased from 23 to 27 for men and 20 to 25 for women, due in part to the growing prevalence of cohabitation (Bureau of the Census, 1998a; Bumpass and Sweet, 1989).

These changes are occurring alongside growing ethnic diversity. The white share of the population is declining, and over the next 50 years whites will shrink from approximately 70 to 59% of the total population. Whereas the black share will remain at 12%, Latinos and Asians will grow to 20 and 10% of the total population (respectively) due to increases in immigration (Edmonston and Passel, 1994). Moreover, both Asians and Latinos are relatively concentrated in the immigrant generation. Approximately 40% of all Latinos and two-thirds of Asians are foreign born (Edmonston and Passel, 1994). These trends are of interest because marriage is linked to ethnicity. Approximately 80% of adult whites are ever married, in comparison to 61% of blacks, 70% of Latinos, and 72% of Asians (Bureau of the Census, 1997, 1998b).

Previous empirical research on normative beliefs about marriage focuses on blacks and whites [Oropesa (1996) and Trent and South (1992) are limited exceptions]. Using the National Survey of Families and Households, we broaden the comparative focus to include Latinos and Asians, with special attention to how normative beliefs are shaped by nativity. Several questions are answered: How are normative beliefs about marriage associated with ethnicity and nativity? Why are normative beliefs associated with ethnicity and nativity? and How does exposure to American society shape normative beliefs? We conclude by asking whether normative beliefs vary among specific ethnic groups that are subsumed under panethnic labels such as "Latino."

THEORETICAL BACKGROUND

The Economic and Ideological Underpinnings of Normative Beliefs

An economic perspective on the gains to marriage provides a convenient starting point for insights into normative beliefs (Becker, 1991). Under the traditional breadwinner system, marriage is preferable to singlehood for producing superior "goods" such as companionship, sexual gratification, and children. The production of these goods requires inputs of both labor and income, as well as a principle for efficiently organizing productive responsibilities. One organizing principle is comparative advantage. Women assume responsibility for domestic production because of their reproductive advantage and men assume responsibility for generating income because of their advantage in the labor market. Marriage is also advantageous over singlehood because the marriage "contract" ensures the relative stability of joint production.

The incentives to support marriage under this system can be undermined in several ways, not the least of which is through economic change. One view is that growing economic opportunities for women undermine support for marriage. Economic opportunities diminish economic need as an incentive for women to marry. Another view is that marriage is undermined by circumstances that increase economic uncertainty surrounding the establishment of an independent household. Economic uncertainty reduces the attractiveness of commitments that limit one's flexibility to deal with economic hardship. Consistent with the uncertainty argument, the empirical evidence suggests that unemployment, low earnings, and low education hinder marriage transitions for both men and women (Easterlin, 1987; Goldscheider and Waite, 1986; Oppenheimer, 1994; Oppenheimer and Lewin, 1999; Oropesa et al., 1994; Waite and Spitze, 1981).

The erosion of normative support for marriage is also tied to contemporary ideological currents that promote personal freedom as the route to self-actualization (Bellah et al., 1985; Lesthaeghe, 1995). Individualistic ideologies reject the necessity of marital unions for the production of joint commodities. Nonmarital sexual activity, cohabitation, and childbearing are tolerated as matters of individual conscience in the quest for personal fulfillment. Such beliefs should promote tolerance of alternatives to marriage for self-actualization.

Similar sentiments are echoed in ideologies that depict marriage as an institution that reinforces nonegalitarian gender relations. Marriage is portrayed in some feminist discourse as subjecting women "to a set of obligations that interfere with their ability to function as full and equal participants in the rest of social, cultural, economic, and political life" (Chafetz, 1995:76). The feminist solution, according to the public, is for women to emphasize careers and "define autonomy and self-actualization as the major goals of their lives and to cease devoting all of their energies selflessly to others" (Chafetz, 1995:77). Thus, egalitarian gender ideologies should promote tolerance of alternatives to marriage for self-actualization.

Ethnicity and Nativity

The implications of the economic uncertainty argument are straightforward. Normative support for marriage should be strongest among whites and Asians if ethnic patterns reflect economic circumstances. According to *Current Population Surveys* (Bureau of the Census, 1997, 1998b), the unemployment rates for whites (4%) and Asians (5%) are low relative to Latinos (8%) and blacks (10%). The median earnings of male year-round full-time workers are also much higher for whites ($36,998) and Asians ($34,950) than Latinos ($22,950) and blacks ($26,001). This pattern is consistent with the relative concentrations of whites and Asians in managerial and professional occupations, as well as their greater educational attainment. Approximately 42% of Asians and 26% of whites age 25 and over have a college degree. These figures exceed those for Latinos (11%) and blacks (14%).

Such comparisons are incomplete without reference to nativity. Immigration from Latin America and Asia has contributed substantial numbers of the foreign-born to the U.S. population. Consistent with their origins in agricultural sectors, the working class, and the economically marginal populations of the origin societies, Latin American immigrants typically have small endowments of human capital. This contributes to differences in economic circumstances by nativity. The median earnings of foreign-born and native-born Latino men who are employed full-time, full-year are $19,760 and $28,190, respectively. Foreign-born Latino women typically earn about $15,974 and native-born women earn about $22,060. Nativity differences are also evident for education and occupation, with the foreign born less likely to have a college education and to be employed in managerial and professional occupations. These differences are not replicated for the unemployment rate (8% for the foreign born and 9% for the native born).

Asian immigrants have the classic profile of "brain drain" migrants— high levels of formal education and the ability to speak English well (Barringer et al., 1993). They also have a relatively high percentage of workers in professional occupations and relatively high incomes (Chiswick and Sullivan, 1995). In numerical terms, 43% of foreign-born Asians and 39% of native-born Asians (age 25+) have at least a bachelor's degree. Approximately one-third of both native-born and foreign-born Asians are employed in managerial and professional occupations. This contributes to relatively high median incomes for full-time, full-year foreign-born Asian workers—$33,800 for men and $24,980 for women. Both of these figures are more than $5000 less than those for their native-born counterparts. The unemployment rates for foreign-born and native-born Asians are 4 and 6%, respectively.

The picture is complicated further by the pattern of nativity differences among both blacks and non-Latino whites. Native-born and foreign-born blacks have the highest unemployment rates of any group (11 and 10%). Moreover, the occupational and earnings profiles of these two groups are somewhat similar. Although the black foreign born are more likely than the black native born to have a college education (23 vs. 13%), the percentages in managerial/professional occupations (e.g., 16 vs. 15% for men) and earnings are similar ($25,220 vs. $27,000 for men). Foreign-born whites are advantaged relative to native-born whites, as well as foreign-born Latinos and blacks. They typically have higher incomes and a greater likelihood of completing college and holding managerial/professional occupations.

The foregoing has important implications for expectations regarding beliefs about marriage. From a naive economic perspective, Latinos and blacks should be less likely and Asians should be as likely as non-Latino whites to hold pronuptial beliefs, given their relative circumstances. Foreign-born Latinos and blacks should be among the least pronuptial because they are mired in precarious socioeconomic circumstances. However, beliefs about marriage must be considered in relation to cultural heritages that are embodied in worldviews. Many immigrants originate in less developed countries plagued by economic uncertainty and limited opportunities, but marriage is relatively early and nearly universal because of pronuptial ideologies. This directs attention to the cultural heritages of foreign-born Latinos and Asians (see Foner, 1997).

In contrast to the United States, Latin American and Asian cultures are frequently described in terms of values that subordinate the needs of individuals to those of collectivities (Triandis, 1994). This is evident in the extent to which marriage and the family define obligations. Marriage is essential for a meaningful life, as well as for forging kinship ties that can be mobilized to deal with economic hardship. For example, Mexico is an exemplar of familistic and "machista" societies in Latin America. Mexican men allegedly are expected to be dominant in relations with women and retain some degree of sexual freedom after marriage. At the same time, prevailing values contribute to the strength of marital and familial bonds.

Strong family bonds and the protection of the family affirm manhood. Marriage, motherhood, and self-sacrifice for the family are celebrated as the highest achievements for women (Gonzalez de la Rocha, 1994; Tiano, 1994).

This description resonates with portrayals of Mexican-American culture. Williams (1990:27) suggests that Mexican-American culture traditionally promoted marriage as "part of God's plan for human beings." Blea (1992:72) claims that "across classes, the major life objective for women is marriage. . . . Chicanas have been socialized to believe that marriage, children, and the family are the most valued aspirations." Moreover, similar portrayals could be made of the cultural heritages of other Latin American immigrants. Because of this heritage, "Hispanics from many ethnic backgrounds tend to be more family-oriented than other Americans. Latino culture traditionally values maintaining good relationships with family members, caring for infirm relatives, and placing family needs above individual needs" (del Pinal and Singer, 1997:29).

Asian cultural orientations also reflect traditions that emphasize the importance of marriage and the family. Among Asians, marriage is "an expected event in the life of the family and young adult" (Fong, 1995:409). Lessinger (1995:111) suggests that "Indian and Indian immigrant women continue to believe marriage, childrearing and nurturing the family are their most fulfilling social roles." Kibria (1993) emphasizes the rejection of individualism by Vietnamese-Americans in favor of more flexible versions of traditional collectivist family ideals to deal with economic hardship and uncertainty. Marriage among Vietnamese-Americans remains a serious matter requiring the assent of one's parents because it is a vehicle for forging kinship ties. Divorce also is frowned on because of the belief that it has negative consequences for children and the family. Similarly, Nash (1995:848) describes Korean-Americans as valuing the "tight family bonds" that characterize families in Korea. Nevertheless, Korean immigrants have adapted to migration-related changes in family composition. Due to the impact of migration-induced family disruption in Korean-American communities, "the marriage bond has in some ways become stronger than filial piety" (Nash, 1995:848).

RESEARCH ISSUES

This research addresses several overlapping questions. The first question is: How are normative beliefs about marriage associated with ethnicity and nativity? According to the economic uncertainty argument, Latinos should be less supportive and Asians should be as supportive of marriage as whites. At the same time, such expectations are naive given cultural heritages that are consistent with collectivism. Cultural heritages may counteract economic uncertainty for Latinos and complement the economic advantages of Asians. Economic and cultural explanations converge to predict less normative support for marriage among blacks. Blacks should be less supportive of marriage due to economic disadvantage and the alleged development of a cultural repertoire that emphasizes bonds to the extended family over the marriage bond (Cherlin, 1992; Wilson, 1987).

Normative beliefs should also reflect differences in nativity. In general, the foreign born should offer less support than the native born for marriage because of economic disadvantage. Yet, this seems unlikely. The majority of immigrants come from countries where marriage remains culturally ingrained. In keeping with cultural heritages, the foreign born may offer the strongest normative support for marriage.

The second research question is: Why are normative beliefs about marriage associated with ethnicity and nativity? Ethnicity and nativity are examined both before and after controlling for economic and demographic characteristics (discussed below), as well as beliefs about familial responsibilities, gender roles, and nonmarital sexuality and childbearing. Nativity will also be highlighted in the analysis of ethnic differences, given disparities in the share of each ethnic group that is foreign born. Needless to say, the search for a universal explanation may be in vain. Trent and South (1992) conclude that black–white differences in attitudes toward family formation reflect economic differences, but Hispanic–white differences reflect cultural differences.

The third question is: How does exposure to American society shape normative beliefs? According to the classic assimilation perspective, exposure occurs across "generational time" and "chronological time" within the immigrant generation. The issue of generational time is addressed in the analysis of nativity differences. The issue of chronological time redirects attention to the attitudes of immigrants. Immigrants' attitudes should become increasingly similar to those of the native-born majority with exposure to the media and changes in human and cultural capital over time. An alternative scenario is assimilation into ethnic subcultures that are alienated from mainstream values (Portes and Rumbaut, 1996).

The last issue deals with the utility of panethnic designations such as "Latino." Oropesa (1996) argues that Latinos are not necessarily a homogeneous entity. Mexican-Americans tend to be more supportive of marriage than Puerto Ricans. We extend his study by examining additional indicators of normative support for marriage and additional groups with the inclusion of Cuban-Americans.

Data and Methods

This study utilizes the 1987 National Survey of Families and Households (NSFH). The NSFH is a national probability sample of 13,007 individuals, with oversamples of persons in several ethnic groups and types of living arrangements. Our analysis is based on 12,907 non-Latino white (N= 9414), Latino (N= 996), Asian (N= 124), and black (N= 2373) respondents. The loss of 100 cases is due to the exclusion of those who are not in the four ethnic groups of interest (e.g., American Indians) and whose status is unclear from their birthplace and ethnicity (e.g., whites born in Asia). Cases with missing data are not excluded to avoid erroneous inferences from the rejection of cases that are not missing completely at random. Instead, Bayesian procedures for the multiple imputation of missing data were employed (see Schafer, 1997). Five imputations were made to generate values for missing data, with the resulting five datasets analyzed by standard methods. The results were combined to yield estimates, standard errors, and p-values that incorporate uncertainty about missing data. Further, the data are weighted, with the weight adjusted to return the N for each ethnic group to its original size for significance tests.

Dependent Variables

Normative beliefs are attitudes about what individuals *should* do. The NSFH includes reactions to statements that measure normative beliefs about the desirability, permanence, and elasticity of the marriage bond. The *desirability* of creating a marriage bond is reflected in the view that "it's better for a person to get married than go through life being single." Belief in the *permanence* of the marriage bond is reflected in the view that "marriage is a lifetime relationship and should never be ended except under extreme circumstances." *Elasticity* refers to a marriage bond that can be "stretched" to provide freedom to pursue individual interests; that is, "in a successful marriage, the partners must have the freedom to do what they want individually." Reactions to these statements and the statements described below (with one exception) were measured with a five-point scale: (1) "strongly disagree," (2) "disagree," (3) "neither agree, nor disagree," (4) "agree," and (5) "strongly agree."

These statements provide insights into collectivistic and individualistic orientations toward marriage. Normative support for creating a marriage bond that lasts a lifetime and deemphasizes individual freedom is consistent with collectivism. Individualism is marked by tolerance of singlehood, divorce, and personal freedom.

Independent Variables

Ethnicity and Nativity.   Place of birth is used in conjunction with ethnicity to identify the foreign- and native-born segments of each ethnic group. Foreign-born whites are all white persons born in Europe and former European colonies. Foreign-born Asians are all Asians born in South,

Southeast, and East Asia. The foreign-born segment of the Latino popula-
tion was born in Latin America and the Spanish Caribbean (including
Puerto Rico). Foreign-born blacks are blacks born in Africa and the former
French and English possessions in the Caribbean.

Economic and Demographic Characteristics.   Economic circumstances
are described by family income, public assistance receipt during the previous 5 years, employment status (employed, not employed), years of education, and the poverty rate in the county of residence. Demographic controls include sex, age, the number of children borne or fathered, the age of
the youngest child in the household, marital status (married, cohabiting,
single—ever married, single—never married), residence with members of
the extended family, religion (Catholic, non-Catholic, none), and place of
residence (nonmetropolitan, metropolitan area).

Ideologies and Attitudes.   A summary index measures beliefs about
sexual intimacy and procreation. The standard scale was used to gauge
reactions to three statements: "It is all right for unmarried 18 year olds to
have sexual relations if they have strong affection for each other," "It is all
right for an unmarried couple to live together even if they have no interest in considering marriage," and "It is all right for an unmarried couple
to live together as long as they have plans to marry." Another item used a
seven-point scale to gauge approval of "women who have a child without
getting married." This was converted to a five-point scale to maintain consistency with the other items. The average score across these items com-
prises the Index of Tolerance. High values indicate tolerance of nonmarital
sexual intimacy and procreation. This scale is highly reliable (Cronbach's
$\alpha = .8$).

Two items measure gender ideologies: "If a husband and wife both
work full-time, they should share household tasks equally" and "It is
much better for everyone if the man earns the main living and the woman
takes care of the home and family." The latter variable is reverse coded (5
= strongly disagree, 1 = strongly agree). Interestingly, these variables are
uncorrelated with each other. Believing in the need for dual-earner couples to share household tasks is consistent with any position on the issue
of separate spheres for men and women.

Familism refers to familial obligations. The Index of Parental Obligations measures beliefs about parental support of adult children in times of
need. This index is created by averaging responses to the following statements: "Parents ought to help their adult children with college expenses,"
"Parents ought to provide financial help to their adult children when the
children are having financial difficulty," and "Parents ought to let their
adult children live with them when the children are having problems."
Cronbach's α is acceptable at .6.

The Index of Filial Obligations is created by averaging responses to the statements that "Children ought to provide financial help to aging parents when their parents are having financial difficulty" and "Children ought to let aging parents live with them when the parents can no longer live by themselves." These two items generate a reliability coefficient of .6 (Cronbach's α).

Caveats

Several caveats should be noted. First is terminology. We use "foreign born" and "immigrants" interchangeably to avoid redundancy, despite the fact that the latter is a subset of the former. "Ethnicity" is used instead of "race" because Latinos can be of any race. "Black" is preferred over "African-American" because the latter is a misleading designation for those born in the Caribbean (Waters, 1994).

Second, causal inferences from correlations between attitudes are inherently tenuous. Regardless, empirical evidence is necessary to shed light on the connections (or lack thereof) between normative beliefs about marriage and other normative beliefs that are part of the wider ideological landscape.

Third, small differences in parameter estimates may be statistically significant between groups with large Ns because the power of statistical tests is affected by sample size. In such cases, substantive and statistical significance should be distinguished. Similarly, the low power of tests for groups with small Ns may require a change in the significance criterion from .05 to .10 to reduce the chance of accepting a false null.

Lastly, this study builds on other studies of ethnic differences in beliefs about family formation by expanding the coverage of different dimensions of the marriage bond and "ethnonativity" groups. For example, Oropesa (1996) and Trent and South (1992) do not cover the full range of ethnic groups under consideration here. Trent and South (1992) also do not discuss immigrants because they exclude nativity from their analysis. In contrast to other studies, the "impacts" of attitudes about gender and familism are demonstrated as well.

RESULTS

How Are Normative Beliefs Associated with Ethnicity and Nativity? Why?

Tables 10.1 and 10.2 show how ethnicity and nativity affect normative beliefs about marriage. Table 1 presents means for the groups of interest.

Table 10.1. Means for Normative Beliefs by Ethnicity and Nativity[a]

	Non-Latino White			Latino			Asian			Black		
	Total (N = 9414)	Foreign Born (N = 320)	Native Born (N = 9094)	Total (N = 996)	Foreign Born (N = 496)	Native Born (N = 500)	Total (N = 124)	Foreign Born (N = 94)	Native Born (N = 30)	Total (N = 2373)	Foreign Born (N = 79)	Native Born (N = 2294)
Better to marry than stay single	3.44	3.66	3.43c	3.74***	3.96	3.50c	3.67*	3.80	3.19b	3.35***	3.84	3.33c
Marriage partners ...freedom	3.75	3.68	3.75	3.50***	3.50	3.51	3.64	3.51	4.12b	3.49***	3.38	3.49
Marriage is a lifetime commitment	3.99	4.08	3.99	4.05	4.09	4.00	4.11	4.19	3.80	3.87***	4.18	3.86b

[a]Cell entries are weighted means and percentages. Conventional asterisk notation is used for tests of significance across ethnic groups, with non-Latino Whites as the reference (*p < .05; **p < .01; ***p < .001). Letter superscripts are used for tests of significance for the contrast between the native born and the foreign born within each ethnic group (b, p < .01; c, p < .001). No differences are significant for p-values between .05 and .10.

Table 10.2. Ordinary Least-Squares Regressions[a]

	Better to Marry Than Stay Single			Marriage Partners . . . Freedom			Marriage Is a Lifetime Commitment		
	Model 1 b	Model 2 b	Model 3 b	Model 1 b	Model 2 b	Model 3 b	Model 1 b	Model 2 b	Model 3 b
White	—	—	—	—	—	—	—	—	—
Latino	.300***	.129**	.204**	-.241***	-.207***	-.206***	.059	-.004	-.103*
Asian	.236*	-.034	.127	-.108	-.055	-.133	.117	.018	.034
Black	-.087***	-.089***	-.032	-.258***	-.257***	-.272***	-.116***	-.117***	-.075**
Nativity (1 = foreign)	.419***	.357***	.194***	-.142***	-.070	-.085*	.141***	.131**	-.002
Sociodemographic									
Sex (1 = female)			-.277***			.075**			-.103***
Age			.006***			-.000			-.003***
Children born/fathered			-.007			-.005			.013*
Age of youngest child			-.002			.011***			-.010***
Single—never married			-.246***			-.059+			.027
Divorced			-.155***			-.092***			-.305***
Married			—			—			—
No religion			-.104**			.074*			-.224***
Non-Catholic			-.141***			.004			.104*
Catholic			—			—			—
Resides in non-SMSA			.051*			-.006			.042+
Extended family			.004			-.076*			.036

	Model 1	Model 2	Model 3
Economic			
Income	-.000	.000	-.000
Public assistance	-.010	-.040	.010
Employed	-.019	-.031+	-.010
County poverty	.001	.001	-.000
Education	-.006+	.020	-.089*
Attitudinal			
Index of Tolerance	-.047***	.208***	-.279***
If both work, should share	.031*	.056***	.120***
Better if man earns (5 = strongly disagree)	-.260***	.175***	-.168***
Index of Parent Obligations	.239***	.132***	.208***
Index of Filial Obligations	.045***	.111***	.138***
Intercept	3.425***	3.748***	3.985***
	3.17***	1.145***	3.741***

[a]All parameter estimates (*b*s) are unstandardized regression coefficients for the following models: Model 1 presents the bivariate coefficients; Model 2 includes ethnicity and nativity; Model 3 adds the sociodemographic, economic, and attitudinal variables.

+$p < .10$; *$p < .05$; **$p < .01$; ***$p < .001$.

Here we see significant ethnic differences in beliefs about the desirability of marriage. Latinos (3.7) and Asians (3.7) tend to believe more strongly than whites (3.4) in the desirability of marriage. The mean for blacks is lower than the mean for whites, but the difference is small.

Nativity differences are also evident. The foreign born (3.8) tend to believe more strongly than the native born (3.4) that marriage is desirable over singlehood (not shown). This relationship is replicated for each ethnic group. Foreign-born Latinos (4.0), Asians (3.8), blacks (3.8), and whites (3.7) tend to "agree" that marriage is preferable to singlehood. The native-born counterpart of each group is nearer to the midpoint of the scale.

The implications of nativity differences for ethnic differences can be determined with the unstandardized regression coefficients generated from a series of ordinary least-squares regression models in Table 10.2: Model 1 presents the bivariate results for ethnicity and nativity, Model 2 includes both nativity and ethnicity, and Model 3 includes all covariates. Models 1 and 2 suggest that nativity is partially responsible for the differences between whites, Latinos, and Asians on desirability. Because the foreign born tend to believe more strongly than the native born in the desirability of marriage and the foreign born comprise larger segments of the Latino and Asian populations, the parameter estimate for Latinos is reduced from .300 to .129 and the estimate for Asians declines from .236 to −.034 in Model 2. The addition of the other covariates slightly increases the parameter estimate for Latinos to .204 in Model 3. Thus, Latinos remain more pronuptial than whites after other variables are controlled. Asians are not significantly different from whites in Model 2 or Model 3.

The question remains as to what is responsible for the observed reduction in the parameter estimate for Latinos besides nativity. Additional analysis indicates economic and demographic characteristics are not responsible. The bivariate coefficient for Latinos changes from .300 to .265 ($p < .001$) in a model restricted to just the economic and demographic variables (not shown). The inclusion of attitudes in Model 3 reduces this coefficient further to .204 ($p < .001$). Latinos are more likely to believe in traditional gender roles and more likely to believe in obligations between family members. Those who hold traditional gender role ideologies and are familistic, in turn, feel it is better to get married. Normative support is also consistent with traditional views about sex and procreation, but the Index of Tolerance does not reduce the coefficient for Latinos.

The small negative bivariate parameter estimate for blacks in Model 1 (−.087, $p < .001$) is reduced to insignificance in Model 3 (−.032). In contrast to Latinos and Asians, this does not reflect nativity because most whites and blacks are native born. The reduction of the parameter estimate is primarily a function of age and marital status. Blacks tend to be younger than whites and are more likely to be single. Not surprisingly, those who are young and single tend to be less pronuptial than those who are older and married.

As for nativity, the bivariate regression coefficient is reduced from .419 in Model 1 to .357 with the addition of ethnicity in Model 2. The inclusion of the remaining covariates reduces the coefficient to .194 in Model 3. Additional analysis indicates that this reduction is due more to attitudes than economic and demographic circumstances. Nativity matters, in part, because of the fit between attitudes about marriage and attitudes about family responsibilities. The foreign born affirm familial obligations that are consistent with support for marriage. In addition, immigrants are more likely to believe in separate spheres for men and women. This belief, in turn, is positively associated with the desirability of marriage.

These models assume that the effects of both nativity and ethnicity are additive. Tests for interactions indicate that the association between nativity and desirability is generally not conditional on ethnicity. An exception is a significant interaction term for Latinos (.277, $p < .05$). Nativity has a greater effect for Latinos than whites, even after a variety of demographic, economic, and other attitudinal variables are controlled.

In addition to offering less normative support for the desirability of marriage, whites place greater emphasis than Latinos and blacks (but not Asians, see Table 10.1) on individual freedom within marriage. The multivariate results in Table 10.2 show that these differences are not due to demographic circumstances, economic circumstances, or differences in other attitudes. The estimates for Latinos are −.241 and −.206 in Models 1 and 3. The coefficient for blacks is −.258 in Model 1 and −.272 in Model 3 after all variables are controlled.

Table 10.2 also reveals that the foreign born believe somewhat less strongly than the native born in the need for individual freedom. The parameter estimate in Model 1 indicates a difference in means of −.142. This contrast remains significant in Model 3 (−.085). As might be expected from the similar means for the foreign and native born for every ethnic group except Asians, controlling for nativity does not alter conclusions about the role of ethnicity in Model 2. In contrast, controlling for ethnicity reduces the parameter estimate for nativity.

Attitudes about the permanence of the marriage bond tend to be similar across groups. Blacks are the only group that is significantly different from whites in Table 10.1. Although blacks tend to believe slightly less strongly than whites in marriage as a lifetime commitment, means near 4.0 indicate that the typical respondent in every ethnic group tends to view marriage as a lifetime commitment that should never be ended. Table 10.2 shows that both blacks and Latinos are slightly less "wedded" to the idea of commitment after all other variables are taken into consideration. Nevertheless, the small magnitude of these coefficients should be noted.

The parameter estimates for nativity indicate that the foreign born feel slightly more strongly than the native born that marriage is a lifetime commitment (Models 1 and 2), except when other covariates are taken into account in Model 3. A series of additional models (not shown) were explored to determine the source of the change in the parameter estimate from .141 to −.002. Nativity is significant in a model restricted to demographic variables with a value of .102 ($p < .05$) and is borderline significant with a parameter estimate of .079 ($p < .055$) in a model with the demographic and economic variables. Although this parameter estimate is reduced to .046 (p = n.s.) in a model that adds beliefs about whether men should be primarily responsible for earning a living, the Indexes of Parental and Filial Obligations also have roles to play. The inclusion of both indexes in a model with the demographic and economic predictors reduces the regression coefficient to −.004 (p = n.s.).

To this point, we have discussed the attitudinal, economic, and demographic variables primarily as control variables. Although space limitations preclude an extensive discussion, these variables are important for reasons other than their ability to shed light on the parameter estimates for nativity and ethnicity. For example, normative support for marriage (desirability and permanence) is consistent with disapproval of nonmarital sexual activity and procreation, as well as attitudes that emphasize familial obligations, separate spheres for husbands and wives, and the sharing of housekeeping responsibilities among dual earners. Normative support for individual freedom is positively associated with the Index of Tolerance, the belief that housework should be shared, and the rejection of separate spheres. Interestingly, advocacy of individual freedom increases with familism.

Gender and marital status are two demographic variables of interest. Women tend to feel less strongly than men about desirability and permanence, and slightly more strongly that marriages should provide partners with individual freedom. As for marital status, single and divorced respondents feel less strongly than married respondents about desirability. Divorced respondents also believe less strongly in individual freedom and are less positive that marriage should involve a lifelong commitment.

With one exception (education), no socioeconomic covariate is significant at the .05 level in Model 3 for any dependent variable. However, additional analysis reveals that the effects of employment and education are explained by other attitudes. The employed and more highly educated tend to feel less strongly about desirability and permanence, unless gender role attitudes are controlled. The highly educated and employed have less traditional views of marriage because they have less traditional views about separate spheres for men and women. This suggests that education is important for reasons besides economic security per se—"liberalizing" value changes that accompany educational attainment have implications for views about marriage.

Are Normative Beliefs about Marriage Associated with Exposure to American Society?

The consequences of exposure to American society can be approached in terms of both "generational time" and "chronological time." Generational time is discussed above in terms of nativity differences. The associations between beliefs and chronological time in the United States among the foreign born are shown with unstandardized regression coefficients in Table 10.3. Model 1 is limited to years of residence in the United States and

Table 10.3. Ordinary Least-Squares Regressions for the Foreign Born[a]

	Model 1	Model 2	Model 3
A. Better to Marry Than Stay Single			
Years of residence	−.015***	−.013***	−.007*
White		—	—
Latino		.371***	.228*
Asian		.161	.080
Black		.178	.213
B. Marriage Partners . . . Freedom			
Years of residence	.012**	.009*	.008*
White		—	—
Latino		−.241*	−.253*
Asian		−.189	−.146
Black		−.299*	−.378**
C. Marriage Is a Lifetime Commitment			
Years of residence	−.001	.002	.004
White		—	—
Latino		.103	−.003
Asian		.232	.046
Black		.194	.152

[a]All parameter estimates are unstandardized regression coefficients for the following models: Model 1 presents the coefficient for duration of residence in an equation with age, Model 2 adds ethnicity, and Model 3 adds the sociodemographic, economic, and attitudinal variables.
$^+p < .10$; $^*p < .05$; $^{**}p < .01$; $^{***}p < .001$.

age (those who are older are at risk of residing longer in the United States). Models 2 and 3 add ethnicity and the full set of covariates, respectively. Coefficients for age and the other covariates are omitted to preserve space.

These results support the assimilation hypothesis for two dependent variables. Although belief in permanence is unrelated to years of residence and ethnicity, desirability declines with years of residence in each model. Those who have been in the United States for longer periods tend to feel less strongly than those who have been in the United States for shorter periods that marriage is preferable to singlehood. Desirability among the foreign born also is not generally a function of ethnicity. Consistent with the interaction discussed earlier, Latinos are the only group that is significantly different from whites. Foreign-born Latinos tend to be more pronuptial than foreign-born whites. However, ethnicity does not play a role in the effect of duration of residence (Model 2). The reduction in the estimate for duration in the transition from Model 2 to Model 3 cannot be attributed to any single set of explanatory variables.

The association between duration of residence and elasticity is also consistent with the assimilation hypothesis. Time spent in the United States increases acceptance of the idea that marriage should provide room for individual freedom, both before and after other variables are controlled. Views about freedom are also related to ethnicity. Foreign-born Latinos and blacks less strongly believe in the need for individual freedom.

Do Normative Beliefs Vary among the Specific Groups That Are Subsumed Under Panethnic Designations?

The foregoing analysis uses panethnic designations to identify ethnic groups. Panethnic designations are required due to the absence of specific ethnic identifiers in the NSFH, sample size limitations, and the desire to treat groups consistently. At the same time, we might expect different subgroups that are subsumed under panethnic labels to have different orientations toward marriage on the basis of relative economic circumstances alone. For example, Mexican-Americans and Puerto Ricans are relatively disadvantaged and Cubans are among the most advantaged Latino groups. Fortunately, these subgroups can be identified in the NSFH.

Table 10.4 presents the means for Mexican-Americans, Puerto Ricans, and Cuban-Americans. These results point to significant variation in some attitudes. Cuban-Americans (4.1, $p < .10$) tend to score higher and Puerto Ricans (3.6, $p < .05$) tend to score lower on desirability than Mexican-Americans (3.8). In addition, Cubans (3.2, $p < .10$) and Puerto Ricans (3.3, $p < .01$) believe less strongly in the need for marriage to provide individual freedom (Mexican-Americans, 3.6). Nevertheless, the three groups

Table 10.4.   Means for Specific Latino Subgroups[a]

	Mexican-American			Puerto Rican			Cuban-American		
	Total (N = 629)	Foreign Born (N = 256)	Native Born (N = 373)	Total (N = 189)	Foreign Born (N = 118)	Native Born (N = 71)	Total (N = 43)	Foreign Born (N = 37)	Native Born (N = 6)
Better to marry than stay single	3.78	4.04	3.55[d]	3.57*	3.74	3.36[c]	4.06[+]	4.18	3.44
Marriage partners ... freedom	3.57	3.65	3.50	3.32**	3.18	3.51[b]	3.21+	3.31	2.75
Marriage is a lifetime commitment	4.11	4.17	4.06	4.00	4.03	3.96	4.05	4.09	3.82

[a] The significance of contrasts between ethnic groups is indicated by asterisk notation, with Mexican-Americans serving as the reference group: $^+p < .10$; $^*p < .05$; $^{**}p < .01$. Letter superscripts denote significant differences by nativity within each group: b, $p < .10$; c, $p < .05$; d, $p < .001$. The residual category of "other" Latinos is excluded here (N = 135).

share normative support for marriage as a lifetime commitment with means that exceed 4.0.

Nontrivial differences by place of birth are evident as well. Although too few U.S.-born Cubans were surveyed to merit discussion, those born in Mexico and Puerto Rico are more supportive than their U.S.-born coethnics of marriage over singlehood. The nativity differences for both groups are approximately one-half of a point.

SUMMARY AND CONCLUSIONS

Over the past several decades, considerable attention has been devoted to the impact of race on marriage, particularly with respect to broader economic and cultural changes confronting America. Indeed, issues related to the economic and cultural underpinnings of "black–white" differences in marriage have been debated extensively. However, the racial and ethnic composition of American society is changing. The Latino and Asian-American populations are growing rapidly due to immigration. This is important because Latinos, Asians, and immigrants are absent from most benchmark studies of normative beliefs about marriage.

Our research attempts to fill this void by answering several questions about the linkages between ethnicity, immigration, and normative beliefs about marriage. Drawing on both economic and cultural perspectives, the first question dealt with the nature of relationships. The economic perspective suggests that group differences in normative beliefs reflect group differences in economic uncertainty. Because Latinos (and blacks) typically face greater economic uncertainty than whites, they should believe less strongly in the desirability of marriage, the need to surrender individuality in a marriage, and the permanence of marriage. Asians and whites should hold similar attitudes because of similar economic circumstances. Greater uncertainty should also motivate the foreign born to believe less strongly in desirability, the need to surrender individuality, and permanence. In contrast, the cultural perspective suggests Latinos and Asians should believe more strongly in these normative beliefs due to the greater prevalence of immigrants with collectivistic cultural heritages among them.

The empirical results for the Latino–white contrast are consistent with the cultural model of greater collectivism for desirability and elasticity (consistent with Trent and South, 1992). Latinos tend to offer greater normative support for marriage over singlehood and less normative support for individual freedom within marriage. Although the Latino–white differential in elasticity is not substantially affected by the controls in multivariate models, the analysis provides additional support for the cultural perspective on desirability. Latinos are more likely than whites to be foreign born and the foreign born tend to believe more strongly than the native born in the desirability of marriage. The Latino–white gap also is related to the more traditional views of Latinos on familial obligations and gender. These relationships cannot be reduced to economic circumstances. Indeed, the bivariate results showed that Latinos and whites hold similar beliefs about the permanence of marriage despite dissimilar economic circumstances. In multivariate models, Latinos tend to offer slightly less normative support for permanence. The small magnitude of this difference should be emphasized.

The results for Asians are more difficult to evaluate, given their small Ns in the NSFH and the low power of statistical tests. Consistent with cultural arguments, Asians tend to feel more strongly than whites that marriage is desirable and nativity is partially responsible for this relationship. The signs of the parameter estimates also are consistent with the expectation that Asians offer less support for individualism in marriage and more support for marriage as a lifetime commitment. Nevertheless, significance tests cannot be ignored—Asians and whites do not differ in their attitudes about the elasticity and permanence of the marriage bond.

At first glance, the results appear consistent with the behavioral evidence of a greater retreat from marriage among blacks. In keeping with economic and cultural arguments, differences in means suggest that blacks offer relatively less normative support for marriage over singlehood and for marriage as a lifetime commitment. Blacks also believe less strongly in the need for individual freedom. Yet, a word of caution is necessary. The difference between blacks and whites is approximately .1 for both desirability and permanence. This suggests that the difference between these populations is small, perhaps trivial. Consequently, the black–white "marriage gap" is probably not due to differences in the normative beliefs examined here.

Another research question deals with the consequences of exposure to American society. This issue can be examined in terms of "generational time" and "chronological time." The generational approach was followed with the investigation of nativity differences (albeit discussed along with ethnic differences). Consistent with cultural perspectives that emphasize the greater sense of collectivism among immigrants, the foreign born believe more strongly than the native born in the desirability of marriage and less strongly in the need for individuality in marriage. This conclusion holds both before and after controls. The foreign born also believe more strongly in the permanence of marriage, until the aforementioned ideological factors are controlled. The foreign born are more likely than the native born to believe in commitment because they hold views about families and gender that are an ideological "fit" with traditional views of marriage.

Although these findings suggest that exposure across generational time promotes assimilation (or acculturation), they beg the question of what immigrants are assimilating into. The classic assimilation perspective assumes that the children and grandchildren of immigrants assimilate into a mainstream culture that spans ethnic groups. Recent challenges to this perspective raise the specter of assimilation into the subcultures of native-born coethnics that reject mainstream values. Additional analyses provide little evidence for the latter viewpoint. Native-born Latinos and Asians do not differ from native-born whites in their beliefs about desirability or the commitment entailed in marriage. The only significant differences occur for elasticity. Native-born Latinos are less concerned and native-born Asians are relatively more concerned about freedom. The final word awaits studies that can examine the second and third generations in different settings (e.g., inner cities).

The "chronological time" approach focuses on exposure to American society within the immigrant generation. With the passage of time in the United States, immigrants tend to feel less strongly that marriage is desirable over singlehood and more strongly that marriages should provide opportunities for individual freedom. The view that marriage requires a lifetime commitment is unaffected by duration of residence.

The last issue brings us full circle to the relationship between ethnicity and normative beliefs. For the most part, we have followed the standard approach by using panethnic categories. The "panethnic" approach is useful for summarizing broad patterns and is necessary to overcome data limitations. However, attention should be paid to the groups that constitute various panethnic categories for the same reason that panethnic groups are of interest in the first place—the circumstances of specific groups can vary greatly. For example, ethnic differences among Latinos suggest that Cuban-Americans are more pronuptial than Mexican-Americans. This may stem from migration-related class differences. In contrast to labor migrants from elsewhere in Latin America, (pre-Mariel) refugees from Cuba were disproportionately drawn from the skilled blue collar and white collar ranks of Cuba's middle/upper class (Portes and Bach, 1985). A definitive answer awaits future research.

In closing, this analysis sheds light on the roles of ethnicity and nativity in attitudes about marriage. In so doing, it confirms the importance of bringing Latinos and Asians into analyses. It also confirms the observation that "anyone who studies the family and neglects explicit consideration of migration processes . . . is likely to miss core aspects of family phenomena" (Jasso, 1997:64). This is because the ties that bind individuals in families through marriage are the same ties that facilitate the migratory journey

(Rumbaut, 1997). Indeed, family ties and normative support for marriage may be strengthened as a direct result of immigration policies that favor the admission of immigrants to the United States for family reunification. Future research should build on the present study to investigate how normative beliefs vary across a wide range of specific ethnic groups, generational statuses, and contextual circumstances. Such efforts are needed because American society is experiencing potentially divisive strains on many fronts that are associated with changing values in a multicultural environment. Our results suggest that the basis for division does not necessarily lie in the views of immigrants (or their native-born coethnics) toward marriage as a "tie that binds."

ACKNOWLEDGMENTS

The authors gratefully acknowledge the comments of the editors and an anonymous referee. This research was partially supported by NICHD Core Grant P30-HD28263 to the Population Research Institute at the Pennsylvania State University.

REFERENCES

Barringer, Herbert, Robert W. Gardner, and Michael J. Levin. 1993. *Asians and Pacific Islanders in the United States.* New York: Russell Sage.

Becker, Gary. 1991. *A Treatise on the Family,* 2nd ed. Boston, MA: Harvard University Press.

Bellah, Robert N., Richard Madsen, William M. Sullivan, Ann Swidler, and Steven M. Tipton. 1985. *Habits of the Heart: Individualism and Commitment in American Life.* New York: Harper & Row.

Blea, Irene I. 1992. *La Chicana and the Intersection of Race, Class, and Gender.* New York: Praeger.

Bumpass, Larry L., and James A. Sweet. 1989. "National Estimates of Cohabitation." *Demography* 26:615–625.

Bureau of the Census. 1997. *Current Population Survey: Annual Demographic File* [Computer File]. ICPSR Version. Washington, DC: U.S. Department of Commerce.

Bureau of the Census. 1998a. "Estimated Median Age at First Marriage, by Sex: 1890 to the Present." Internet (http://www.census.gov/population/socdemo/ms-la/tabms-2.txt).

Bureau of the Census. 1998b. *Current Population Survey: Annual Demographic File* [Computer File]. ICPSR Version. Washington, DC: U.S. Department of Commerce.

Chafetz, Janet Satlzman. 1995. "Chicken or Egg? A Theory of the Relationship between Feminist Movements and Family Change." Pp. 63–81 in *Gender and Family in Change in Industrialized Countries,* edited by Karen Oppenheim Mason and An-Magritt Jensen. Oxford: Clarendon Press.

Cherlin, Andrew J. 1992. *Marriage, Divorce, Remarriage.* Cambridge, MA: Harvard University Press.

Chiswick, Barry R., and Teresa Sullivan. 1995. "The New Immigrants." Pp. 211–270 in *The State of the Union*, Vol. 2, edited by Reynolds Farley. New York: Russell Sage.

del Pinal, Jorge, and Audrey Singer. 1997. "Generations of Diversity: Latinos in the United States." *Population Bulletin* 52. Washington, DC: Population Reference Bureau.

Easterlin, Richard A. 1987. *Birth and Fortune*. New York: Basic Books.

Edmonston, Barry, and Jeffrey Passel. 1994. "The Future Immigrant Population of the United States." Pp. 317–353 in *Immigration and Ethnicity: The Integration of America's Newest Arrivals*, edited by Barry Edmonston and Jeffrey Passel. Washington, DC: The Urban Institute Press.

Foner, Nancy. 1997. "The immigrant Family: Cultural Legacies and Cultural Changes." *International Migration Review* 31:961–974.

Fong, Rowena. 1995. "Families." Pp. 401–411 in *The Asian American Encyclopedia*, Vol. 2, edited by Franklin Ng. New York: Marshall Cavendish.

Goldscheider, Francis K., and Linda J. Waite. (1986). "Sex Differences in Entry into Marriage." *American Journal of Sociology* 92:91–109.

Gonzalez de La Rocha, Mercedes. 1994. *The Resources of Poverty: Women and Survival in a Mexican City*. Oxford: Blackwell.

Jasso, Guillermina. 1997. "Migration and the Dynamics of Family Phenomena." Pp. 63–78 in *Immigration and the Family: Research and Policy on U.S. Immigrants*, edited by Alan Booth, Ann C. Crouter, and Nancy Landale. Mahwah, NJ: Laurance Erlbaum.

Kibria, Nazli. 1993. *Family Tightrope: The Changing Lives of Vietnamese Americans*. Princeton, NJ: Princeton University Press.

Lessinger, Johanna. 1995. *From the Ganges to the Hudson: Indian Immigrants in New York City*. Boston: Allyn and Bacon.

Lesthaeghe, R. 1995. "The Second Demographic Transition in Western Countries: An Interpretation." Pp. 17–62 in *Gender and Family in Change in Industrialized Countries*, edited by Karen Oppenheim Mason and An-Magritt Jensen. Oxford: Clarendon Press.

Nash, Amy. 1995. "Korean Americans." Pp. 837–856 in *Gayle Encyclopedia of Multicultural America*, Vol. 2, edited by Rudolph J. Vecoli, Judy Galens, Anna Sheets, and Robyn V. Young. New York: Gale Research Inc.

Oppenheimer, Valerie Kincade. 1994. "Women's Rising Employment and the Future of the Family in Industrial Societies." *Population and Development Review* 20:293–294.

Oppenheimer, Valerie Kincade, and Lisa Lewin. 1999. "Career Development and Marriage Formation in a Period of Rising Inequality: Who Is at Risk? What Are Their Prospects." Pp. 189–225 in *Transitions to Adulthood in a Changing Economy*, edited by Alan Booth, Anne C. Crouter, and Michael J. Shanahan. Westport, CT: Praeger.

Oropesa, R.S. 1996. "Normative Beliefs about Marriage and Cohabitation: A Comparison of Non Latino Whites, Mexican Americans, and Puerto Ricans." *Journal of Marriage and the Family* 58:49–62.

Oropesa, R.S., Daniel T. Lichter, and Robert N. Anderson. 1994. "Marriage Markets and the Paradox of Mexican American Nuptiality." *Journal of Marriage and the Family* 56:889–907.

Portes, Alejandro, and Robert Bach. 1985. *Latin Journey: Cuban and Mexican Immigrants in the United States*. Berkeley, CA: University of California Press.

Portes, Alejandro, and Ruben G. Rumbaut. 1996. *Immigrant America: A Portrait*, 2nd ed. Berkeley, CA: University of California Press.

Rumbaut, Ruben G. 1997. "Ties That Bind: Immigration and Immigrant Families in the United States." Pp. 3–46 in *Immigration and the Family: Research and Policy on U.S. Immigrants*, edited by Alan Booth, Ann C. Crouter, and Nancy Landale. Mahwah, NJ: Lawrence Erlbaum.

Schafer, J.L. 1997. *Analysis of Incomplete Multivariate Data*. London: Chapman and Hall.

Thornton, Arland. 1989. "Changing Attitudes Toward Family Issues in the United States." *Journal of Marriage and the Family* 51:873–893.

Tiano, Susan. 1994. *Patriarchy on the Line: Labor, Gender, and Ideology in the Mexican Maquila Industry*. Philadelphia, PA: Temple University Press.

Trent, Katherine, and Scott J. South. 1992. "Sociodemographic Status, Parental Background, Childhood Family Structure, and Attitudes Toward Family Formation." *Journal of Marriage and the Family* 54:427–439.

Triandis, Harry C. 1994. *Culture and Behavior*. New York: McGraw-Hill.

Waite, Linda, and Glenna D. Spitze. 1981. "Young Women's Transition to Marriage." *Demography* 18:681–694.

Waters, Mary. 1994. "Ethnic and Racial Identities of Second Generation Black Immigrants in New York City." *International Migration Review* 28:795–820.

Williams, Norma. 1990. *The Mexican American Family: Tradition and Change*. New York: General Hall.

Wilson, William Julius. 1987. *The Truly Disadvantaged*. Chicago, IL: University of Chicago Press.

11

Values and Living Arrangements: A Recursive Relationship

GUY MOORS

INTRODUCTION

One of the salient characteristics of demographic changes since the 1960s is the emerging diversity in living arrangements of young adults. The incidence of sharing residence, living independently, or cohabiting has increased both as intermediate states as well as alternatives to marriage. In explaining these demographic changes economic rational choice theories seem to have dominated the debate. However, a number of scholars have argued that the significance of ideational changes cannot be ignored. In this chapter the significance of values is discussed. The key question of this research refers to the classical discussion about causality, i.e., *"do values influence choices regarding living arrangements in an autonomous way, and to what extent is the relationship reversed?"* This research presents the findings from a German panel study including a random sample of young women. In what follows I will first discuss the theoretical propositions before turning to the data and empirical findings.

VALUES AND BEHAVIOR: THEORETICAL CONSIDERATIONS

To some of us it may seem commonplace to suggest that ideational factors influence choices people make, hence, why not the choice regarding living arrangement? However, within social science the issue is not taken as being so obvious. Rational choice theories, for instance, are notorious for neglecting ideational factors (Lesthaeghe and Surkyn, 1988; Devine, 1998), whereas sociological approaches focusing on social structure argue that values are merely spuriously related to behavior, taking an explicit structuralist position in the culture versus structure debate (Thompson et al., 1990). Neither of these two arguments, however, should lead to the conclusion that ideational factors need to be dropped from analysis—on the contrary.

Of those approaches that explicitly give credit to the cultural argument, several also question the usefulness of the concept of values in causal explanations (Adler, 1956; Blake and Davis, 1968; Cancian, 1975; Fishbein and Ajzen, 1975; Laudon, 1986). Instead, they refer to other aspects of culture, such as norms, attitudes, or intentions, as being more distinctive and indispensable concepts in social research. Since theoretical perspectives are entwined with their key concepts, at least some considerations regarding the difference between values and other ideational factors are in order. Unfortunately, there is little agreement on the subject. Since reviewing the discussion is beyond the scope of this chapter, I will present only my own point of view, which I developed (Moors, 1997) in reference to the work of Rokeach (1968, 1973).

In my view, the major differences between values, norms, attitudes, and intentions relate to two issues. First, are these concepts object and situation specific or rather from a more general nature? Second, to what extent are they defined as individual characteristics? As far as the former issue is concerned, attitudes and intentions are more object-related and situation-specific ideational factors than values that are of a more general nature. Norms, on the other hand, refer to prescriptions of how to behave. They constitute sets of (normative) rules and, by consequence, prevail at the society or macrolevel. Of course, these modes of conduct may be internalized and, consequently, define values orientations. Values bridge the gap between attitudes and norms because values are individual predispositions as well as characteristics of depersonalized entities, as in, for instance, "the values of the working class." From this perspective I have argued (1997) that theoretically values can be described as *ideational organizations of attitudes* focusing on different objects and situations. Consequently, at the empirical level, values can be inferred from the response pattern on several sets of attitudinal questions. In this chapter, for instance, the latent dimension "traditional family values" includes attitudinal scales such as "traditional opinion about marriage," "the importance of children," "gender-specific attitudes regarding domestic work," etc. Each of these attitudes is measured by summing the scores on several attitudinal questions. As such, the measurement procedure is consistent with the conceptual frame of reference.

Values researchers within demography found inspiration in one particular theory on values, i.e., Inglehart's thesis (1977) regarding a generational pattern of values change (Lesthaeghe and Surkyn, 1988; Lesthaeghe and Moors, 1996; Inglehart, 1990). What Inglehart did was little more than expanding Norman Ryder's (1965) concept of social metabolism—in which social change is induced by a process of succession of generations—to the field of political sociology and values. Basically, Inglehart argues that an individual's values reflect his or her socioeconomic environment: one attaches relatively more importance to relatively scarce objects. However, these values do not reflect the current conditions of life, but rather the historical circumstances in which one is raised, i.e., the so-called formative years. After all, Inglehart argues, values tend to crystallize in personality as people reach (young) adulthood. The latter argument constitutes the heart of Inglehart's thesis since it allows culture change to be predicted, i.e., younger less "materialist" cohorts gradually replace older more "materialist" cohorts. The attractiveness of Inglehart's theory is that it allows us to hypothesize dividuals. By the same token, it also focuses on one particular direction of causality, i.e., values influencing behavior.

That values may reflect temporal conditions of life and, consequently, are susceptible to change is exactly the heart of Kohn's theory on values (Kohn, 1977; Kohn and Slomczynski, 1993). Kohn primarily focuses on occupational conditions, but paraphrasing Kohn by generalizing his argument to other spheres of life as well we could argue that "people learn to value characteristics that are appropriate to their conditions of life." It is exactly this idea of values *adapting to* changes in conditions that Oppenheimer (1994) explicitly raised as a critical issue for those who argue that values influence demographic behavior.

Need we now conclude that these two values theories yield mutually exclusive propositions and that empirical results should focus on pointing out a winner (cf. Lesthaeghe, 1998)? Not necessarily. As Rokeach' research has demonstrated (Ball-Rokeach et al., 1984), the notion of relatively enduring values orientations after the formative years is not incompatible with the idea that values may change due to "strong" incentives (Moors, 1997). Dramatic or intense experiences may function as such. Furthermore, changes in the life course may reaffirm values rather than altering them. Young people valuing a traditional family life, for instance, may be attracted toward marriage, decide to marry, and then find affirmation of their opinion regarding traditional family life. What has become clear is that even stability in values orientation may form part of a dynamic process.

Within demography reconciling the different perspectives on values is important since few researchers would doubt that changes in family life are intense experiences. The consequences of this line of reasoning to our research are the following. First, from a theoretical point of view there is as much reason to believe that values (autonomously) influence choices regarding living arrangements, as there is to expect that values will adapt to the consequences of these choices. The relative significance of both directions within the recursive relation, however, remains an open-ended question. Second, we should be aware of the fact that the adaptation of values can be twofold: values may be affirmed as well as denied. Third, irrespective of their research focus[1] Inglehart and Kohn seem to agree on the types of values that are important. On the one hand, they refer to autonomy, self-directedness, and independence; on the other hand, they list conformity, materialism, and security. It is a small step to link the former values with more "modern" patterns of living arrangements such as cohabitation or living independently, and the latter orientations with a more "traditional" pattern of marriage.

DATA AND METHODOLOGY

Given the propositions presented in the previous section it is obvious that only panel data allow us to explore the recursive relationship between values and choices regarding living arrangements. After all, the research question requires a design in which values are measured both before and after major choices are made or events occur. To the best of our knowledge, such data are rare. This is particularly true in the case of social demography. Panel data that allow measuring values as I have described are (virtually) nonexistent. Of course, the work that has been done on the Detroit Metropolitan Area panel study (Axinn and Thornton, 1992a,b, 1993; Goldscheider et al., 1993; Thornton, 1992; Thornton et al., 1983, 1992, 1993; Thornton and Camburn, 1987; Thornton and Freedman, 1979; Weinstein and Thornton, 1989) or the National Longitudinal Survey of the High School Class of, 1972 (Goldscheider and DaVanzo, 1989; Clarkberg et al., 1993) is impressive. However, these data are limited in two ways. First, they allow us to focus only on a limited set of attitudes. Second, and perhaps more importantly, the samples are not drawn randomly, but refer to a homogeneous category of educated people. Whether their findings expand to other categories as well has remained an open question. The German panel study on "Familienentwicklung in Nordrhein-Westfalen" used in this chapter, by contrast, consists of a random sample of young women aged 18 to 30 in 1982, and reinterviewed 2 years later. Furthermore, over 50 attitudinal questions were asked in the first and second interview round. Unarguably, these two characteristics are the trumps of this dataset. As such our analyses complement the findings from the aforementioned U.S. studies.

However, our dataset also has some limitations. First, the dropout rate between waves is considerable: only 56% of the original sample participated in the second round. However, a large part of this dropout can be explained by the fact that the researchers had to ask the respondents at the end of the interview (due to the privacy protection law) to sign a declaration in which they agreed to participate in following waves, allowing the researchers to store the address of the respondent. Discussing the implications of this dropout rate in detail goes beyond the topic of this chapter. The most important finding from a series of analyses regarding the effect of dropout on the principal relations I present in this chapter is that they revealed that the interpretations of the relationships are reasonably immune to selection biases (Moors, 1997). Second, the questionnaire was not developed according to an event-history approach. Only *current* status at the time of the interview was ascertained. Consequently it is impossible to study the different pathways out of the parental home. For the women who were married it was possible to distinguish between those who cohabited with their husband prior to the marriage versus those that had not. Although important, this classification captures only part of the heterogeneity of the class of married women. We do not know whether they experienced a period of cohabitation with another partner, nor is there information regarding other intermediate living arrangements such as living independently. The major consequence of this lack of information is that the analyses underestimate the differences in values. After all, it can be expected that among the married women, those who left the parental home through marriage will be more "traditional" as far as their values are concerned than those married women who went through intermediate stages of cohabitation or living alone. By the same token, it is obvious that if significant associations between living arrangements and values emerge from the analyses, this pattern of associations would be more strongly observed with improvement of the data.

In discussing the concept of values I argued that values could be measured inferentially from different sets of attitudinal questions. This is done in two stages, similar to the procedure suggested by Middendorp (1978, 1993). In the first stage attitudinal scales are constructed by summing the scores on attitudinal questions (items) that refer to a particular aspect of life. Items that proved to reduce the reliability of the summed rating scales were excluded. In the second stage, the attitudinal scales were submitted to a principal component analysis, revealing two values dimensions.

Table 11.1 reports the correlations between the two latent dimensions and the nine attitudinal scales. The items defining the nine attitudinal scales are listed below them. The latent values dimensions are standardized factor scores operationalized as the weighted sum of scores on the attitudinal scales. Latent variables in the second interview are measured in exactly the same way.

The six scales that correlate substantially with the first dimension indicate different aspects of "traditional family values," whereas the three remaining scales correlating with the second dimension refer to "personal and economic independence or autonomy." Despite the fact that Midden-

Table 11.1. Correlations between the Summed Attitudinal Scales and the Latent Values Dimensions[a]

	Principal Component 1	Principal Component 2
Principal Component 1: Traditional family values		
Summed attitudinal scales and items		
a. Children as giving meaning to life ($\alpha = .80$)	.78	−.04
Due to children one really becomes a woman.		
Having children is the most important thing in a woman's life.		
Children give meaning to one's life.		
Without children one cannot be really happy.		
Children imply life fulfillment.		
b. Responsibility as a parent ($\alpha = .74$)	.73	−.05
Raising children means taking responsibilities for something that is worthwhile.		
It is important to teach one's children one's own experiences.		
Sometimes children give a feeling of being used.		
Nothing is so beautiful as seeing children grow up.		
I cannot imagine a life without children.		
It is only natural that a woman wants children.		
c. Traditional opinion about marriage ($\alpha = .79$)	.73	.04
If one wants to start a family, one should get married.		
Through marriage the partnership becomes more solid and profound.		
Through marriage partners become more closely related.		
It is self-evident that one marries once one has found a partner with whom one wishes to stay together.		
Marriage gives a sense of security.		
d. Importance of family life ($\alpha = 0.77$)	.72	−.20
Important in life: being a good mother.		
Important in life: having children.		
Important in life: enjoying a good family life.		
Important in life: being married.		
Important in life: managing the household.		
e. Household as a priority and duty of the wife ($\alpha = .69$)	.70	−.16
It is my duty to be engaged in the household.		
Her family will come first in the life of a woman.		
Even when a woman is employed, doing the housekeeping is her job.		
A woman should refrain from her interests, if it concerns her family.		
I am of more use to my family when taking care of the household than being employed.		
f. Subordination to the man ($\alpha = .044$)	.65	−.02
When a man has to achieve something in his work, a wife should take that into account.		

(Continued)

Table 11.1. Correlations between the Summed Attitudinal Scales and the Latent Values Dimensions[a]

	Principal Component 1	*Principal Component 2*
In difficult situations a wife should follow the advice of her husband.		
Principal Components 2: Autonomy and independence through work		
Summed attitudinal scales		
g. Importance of paid work (α = 0.54)	−.05	.80
Important in life: having my own old age pension when I am retired.		
Important in life: getting ahead in my job.		
Important in life: having a paid job.		
Important in life: having pleasure in my daily job.		
h. Importance of money (α = .47)	.06	.73
Important in life: that I can buying more things in the future than now.		
Important in life: saving money for myself.		
i. Importance of personal freedom and independence (α = .70)	−.35	.68
Important in life: finding new challenges in life.		
Important in life: to travel, exploring the world.		
Important in life: personal freedom.		
Important in life: to continue to develop myself.		
Important in life: to be engaged in politics.		
Important in life: going out, undertaking things.		
Important in life: being independent.		
Important in life: having friends.		
%variance	37.60	17.20

[a]Principal component analysis with varimax rotation.
Source: The Familienentwicklung in Nordrhein-Westfalen panel study: 1982–1984.

dorp (1978, 1993) demonstrated that this two-stage procedure produces fairly stable dimensions, I researched the robustness of the dimensional structure by means of a more "modern" structural equation technique, i.e., confirmatory common factor analysis. Several models were tested, but the model that corresponds with the aforementioned solution (Table 11.1) produced one of the better fits ($\chi2$ = 360.295, *df* = 19, rmr = .004, AGFI = .920). Only omitting the paths from scales to dimensions when their standardized regression weights dropped below .10 slightly improved the model ($\chi2$ = 366.020, *df* = 23, rmr = .004, AGFI = .933). Also imposing orthogonality in the initial solution presented in Table 11.1 did not bias the results since only a negligible correlation of .01 was found when allowing the latent dimensions to correlate. Consequently, it is reasonably safe to conclude that the operationalization of the values dimensions is quite robust and that both dimensions are virtually independent of one another.

The choice of methodology is somewhat troublesome. In an analysis focusing on the impact of values (measured at first interview) on the transitions to alternative living arrangements (second interview) the dependent variable is multinomial, whereas in the analysis focusing on the reverse relation, i.e., the impact of transitions on values (measured at second interview) the dependent variable is at the interval level. The consequence of choosing two different types of analysis, although appropriate, would be, however, that it becomes difficult to judge the relative importance of the two directions of the recursive relationship. After all, both methods produce a different set of parameters. Furthermore, the question of whether transitions reaffirm rather than alter values is also difficult to answer. For this reason I adopted a research strategy that resembles a quasi-experimental design. First, I constructed a typology of transitions in living arrangements by cross-tabulating the living arrangement measured at both interviews (Table 11.2) distinguishing among "living in the parental home," "living independently" (single), "cohabiting," and "marriage." For those women who were married at the time of the first interview the information regarding the period of cohabitation with the husband allowed me to distinguish between two subcategories, i.e., married women who have and who have not cohabited with their husband. This information is disregarded if marriage took place after the first wave because of small numbers. The limited number of cases also "forced" me to collapse the categories "single" and "cohabitation" except for the category of women living in the parental home at the time of the first interview. This collapsing of categories, however, did not bias the analyses since no significant differences in values were found among the four original categories

Table 11.2. Typology of Living Arrangements: Cross-Tabulation of Current Status at First and Second Interview

Living Arrangement at Second Wave	*Living Arrangement at First Wave (Number of Cases)*		
	Parental Home	*Single or Cohabiting*	*Married*
Parental home	250	(<20)	
Single	59		(<20)
		157	
Cohabiting	38		
Married	38	41	
No prior Cohabitation			374
Prior Cohabitation			152

Source: The Familienentwicklung in Nordrhein-Westfalen panel study: 1982–1984.

of the larger cross-tabulation in which "single" and "cohabiting" were defined as separate categories. I also omitted categories with less than 20 observations. A small number of women ($N = 28$) experienced a divorce between interviews. No significant difference in values with the category of married women was observed. Given the number of observations I preferred dropping the divorced category rather than "overemphasizing" the latter finding.

Second, for each values dimension and on each occasion, i.e., the first and second interview, mean scores are calculated for the different categories of living arrangements.

The figures reported in Table 11.3 are controlled for age, education level, employment, and occupational status. These variables capture the core of factors that could identify the spuriousness of the relationship between values and living arrangements—at least to a large extent.

To calculate the mean scores and the significance levels multiple classification analysis is used. Significance levels are calculated relative to the grand mean of the column category. For instance, the significance levels within the first column of women living in the parental home at the time of the first interview should be interpreted as "significantly different from the grand mean" of that particular category. Each cell entry contains three mean scores on the values dimensions with their corresponding significance levels, the mean score at the time of the first interview, the second interview, and the difference between the two, respectively.

My approach resembles a quasi-experimental design because I compare the different categories within the "natural experiment," i.e., the transition to alternative living arrangements, with respect to their values before and after these changes. As far as living arrangements are concerned each column refers to a homogeneous category at first interview that becomes heterogeneous between two waves. Comparing the values scores of the first interview within each column then indicates to what extent the diversity in living arrangements at the second interview is already reflected in the values these women held prior to the transition. In this case values are "predictive" of transitions. Differences in mean scores on the values dimension measured in the second interview, on the other hand, indicate the "change" in values due to changes in living arrangements. The third cell entry indicates the direction of the change in values. Taken together these figures allow me to broach the key questions of this research.

ANALYSES AND DISCUSSION

One obvious finding is that the two values dimensions tell a different story. The impact of values (first interview) on choices regarding living arrangements is more pronounced in the case of "traditional family values" than in the case of "autonomy."

The differences in "traditional family values" (Table 11.3a) for the category of women who were living in the parental home (first column of cell entries) are modest: there is little difference between those who married and those who cohabited between the two interviews. Only women who moved to a single-person household were significantly less traditional at first interview. However, we should be aware of the fact that the women who left the parental home and moved to a single or a nonmarital double household are quite heterogeneous. These alternative living arrangements may merely function as transitionary situations before marriage. The second column provides evidence for this argument. A clear and significant difference is observed between the categories that decided to marry versus that decided not to marry, indicating that women who decided to marry were already more oriented toward traditional family values in the first interview than women who did not experience such a transition. This pattern of findings suggests that if values influence the choices regarding living arrangements it does so in terms of desired end-states and that the significance of values may not be fully reflected at the onset of the process of family formation. Consequently, singlehood and cohabitation have different meanings depending on whether they function as transitionary states or as alternatives to marriage.

As far as adaptation of traditional family values is concerned, the change may be interpreted as a reaffirmation of initial differences. Irrespective of the type of living arrangement at the time of the first interview, marriage increases the level of traditional family orientation to the level of those women who married prior to the first interview. An opposite trend is observed for those women who entered or remained in a consensual union or single household. The "power" of marriage in directing the values of women is also reflected in the comparison of the two categories of women who were married at the time of the first interview (third column of cell entries). Women who have experienced a period of cohabitation prior to their marriage were less traditional than those who have not. By the time of the second interview, this difference has vanished. The main reason married women with cohabitation experience became more traditional family oriented between waves is that they were more likely to experience another demographic transition, i.e., motherhood. No significant difference between the two categories of married women was found when controlling for the latter transition.[3] Again, this finding indicates that values influence the choice regarding the desired end-state of family formation. At the same time the sociological meaning of "marriage" is emphasized, i.e., it extends to the value of children.

In general, the pattern of associations between traditional family values

Table 11.3. Mean Values Scores by Living Arrangement Typology, Controlling for Age, Education, Employment, and Occupational Status[a]

Living Arrangement at Second Wave	Living Arrangement at First Wave								
	Parental Home			Single or Cohabiting			Married		
	T1	T2	T2–T1	T1	T2	T2–T1	T1	T2	T2–T1
a. Traditional Family Values[b]									
Parental home	1.42	−1.80	−3.22		—[c]			—[c]	
Single	−22.77*	−31.37***	−8.60						
				−47.04***	−51.29***	−4.25*			
Cohabiting	−2.33	−3.24	−0.92						
Married	7.79	45.29***	37.50**	−5.58**	32.74***	38.32**			
No prior Cohabitation							41.10**	32.57	−8.53**
Prior Cohabitation							18.63***	31.04	12.40**
b. Autonomy Values[b]									
Parental home	32.80	39.61**	6.81		—[c]			—[c]	
Single	38.18	42.17	3.99						
				19.36	36.60**	17.23**			
Cohabiting	18.55	13.36	−5.19						
Married	27.21	−22.76***	−49.96***	28.29	8.62**	−19.68**			
No prior Cohabitation							−36.15	−50.83	−14.68
Prior Cohabitation							−44.29	−50.88	−6.59

Source: The Familienentwicklung in Nordrhein-Westfalen panel study: 1982–1984.

[a]All figures controlled for age, education, and occupational status. T1, mean score on values dimension at T1 first interview and significance level (deviation method); T2, mean score on values dimension at T2 second interview and significance level (deviation method); T2–T1, difference in mean score between two interviews and significance level of difference between T1 and T2.

[b]Scale mean = 0; scale standard deviation = 100.

[c]—, Omitted category, $N < 20$.

Significance levels (F-test): * $<.10$;** $<.05$; *** $<.01$.

and living arrangements that emerges from the analysis is consistent with our theoretical perspective. The two directions of association, i.e., values influencing behavior and vice versa have about equal importance. Furthermore, the "change" in values never contradicts the pattern development in living arrangement initiated by values measured prior to the transitions. On the contrary, initial differences are reaffirmed and reinforced.

By contrast, the "autonomy" dimension is more prone to change than the "traditional family values" dimension. Furthermore, there is little evidence that autonomy values function as selection in choosing between alternative living arrangements. The change in values is the more remarkable. Whereas changes in "traditional family values" reflect affirmation of prior differences, most changes in "autonomy values" should be interpreted as denial. Marriage in particular implies a denial of initial levels of "autonomy values." In the first interview, women who marry afterward value "autonomy" to a slightly higher degree, although not significantly, than women who entered cohabitation (first column of cell entries) or than women deciding not to marry while being single or cohabiting at the time of the first interview (second column of cell entries). A woman's urge for "autonomy," however, drops considerably after gaining security in and through marriage.

This pattern of findings regarding autonomy values appears to be more consistent with Kohn's basic argument than with Inglehart's perspective. Kohn argues that people learn to value characteristics that are appropriate to their conditions of life. As long as one is not married it seems "appropriate" to appreciate, at least, a certain level of autonomy and independence. Marriage itself is even today a tie that binds, hence, making "autonomy" and "independence" less appropriate values. However, we should be prudent to argue that Inglehart's argument regarding the significance of "stable values after the formative years" does not hold in the case of autonomy values. The data only focus on one particular age group and change is observed only in a relatively short time span of 2 years. We cannot exclude the possibility that autonomy values become stable characteristics after family formation. What is significant, nonetheless, is that Inglehart should at least accept that the "formative years" may go well beyond the life-stage in which young adults constitute families.

A final remark has to be made since the analyses merely indicate adaptation processes at the categorical but not at the individual level. If the relative position of a category on a values dimension has not changed over time, this does not necessarily imply that the respondents in this category hold stable values orientations. Aggregate stability is not incompatible with individual change since the former may be the outcome of individual changes in opposite directions. For this reason we operationalized the absolute difference in scores for the values dimensions measured at the first and second interview. Of course, this is a very crude measure of individual stability that ignores the problem of measurement error reducing stability. Nevertheless, even adopting more appropriate measures (Inglehart, 1990) would not change the major conclusion of our exploratory analysis. We found that none of the independent variables was significantly related to the indices of absolute differences in values over time (Moors, 1997). Hence, the *level of change* in values does not depend on the transitions we studied. Transitions in living arrangements structure *the way* values change, and not the absolute level of change.

CONCLUSION

The purpose of this chapter was to demonstrate the dynamics of the relationship between values orientations and living arrangements. Values theory clearly "predicts" that values influence choices, but also that values adapt to the consequences of these choices, i.e., changes in conditions of life. The latter change may imply a continuing affirmation of the initial differences in values as well as a denial or reversal in orientation. The empirical findings seem to support these arguments, but at the same time they demonstrate the complexity of the subject. Traditional family values, on the one hand, proved significant in terms of structuring choices regarding desired end-states of family formation, i.e., marriage, whereas autonomy values, on the other hand, were much more the outcome of changes in living arrangements of young women than the other way around. These changes even implied a reversal of orientation (denial), whereas the changes in traditional family values were more congruent with an interpretation in terms of reaffirmation. The values–behavior relationship proved to be not only dynamic, but also differentiated.

Our research also raises some questions that could not be answered with the available data. Why is it, for instance, that "traditional family values" but not "autonomy values" influence choices regarding living arrangements? Why is it that differences in "autonomy values" manifest themselves only after demographic transitions occurred, whereas the differences in "traditional family values" are merely strongly articulated after these changes? Is it because different types of values are "socialized" in different stages of the life-course, or are particular values more susceptible to change in reference to current conditions of life, whereas other values are more grounded in historical circumstances? It is obvious that our research scratched only the surface of these issues. What we need is information about other age groups, as well as more detailed information regarding the current and historical life conditions of the respondents. At the attitudinal level Thornton (1992) demonstrated that historical circumstances defined by the parental home do seem to matter. As such, partial evidence is provided for one of the concluding open-ended questions of this chapter.

ACKNOWLEDGMENTS

I would like to express my gratitude to Professor F. X. Kaufman and Professor K. P. Strohmeier (Univeristät Bielefeld) and the Zentralarchiv für Empirische Sozialforschung (Köln) for allowing use of the data (ZA-N 1736-38). The Research Council of the Free University of Brussels partially financed the program. I also thank Ron Lesthaeghe and anonymous reviewers for their helpful comments. The content of this chapter, however, is fully my responsibility.

NOTES

1.   Inglehart discusses political values, whereas Kohn focuses on educational and work-related values.
2.   Multiple classification analysis produces results similar to dummy regression, except that it uses deviation coding (comparing to the grand mean) instead of dummy coding (comparing to a reference category) (Retherford and Coe, 1993).
3.   Analysis not reported; information available from the author on request.

REFERENCES

Adler, F. 1956. "The Value Concept in Sociology." *American Journal of Sociology* 65:272–279.
Axinn, W. G., and A. Thornton. 1992a. "The Relationship between Cohabitation and Divorce: Selectivity or Causal Influence?" *Demography* 29:357–374.
Axinn, W. G., and A. Thornton. 1992b. "The Influence of Parental Resources on the Timing of the Transition to Marriage." *Social Science Research* 21:261–285.
Axinn, W. G., and A. Thornton. 1993. "Mothers, Children and Cohabitation: The Intergenerational Effect of Attitudes and Behavior." *American Sociological Review* 58:233–246.
Ball-Rokeach, S. J., M. Rokeach, and J. W. Grube. 1984. *The Great American Values Test. Influencing Behavior and Belief through Television.* New York: Free Press.
Blake, J., and K. Davis. 1968. "Norms, Values and Sanctions." Pp. 456–484 in *Handbook of Modern Sociology,* edited by R.E.L. Faris. Chicago: Rand McNally.
Cancian, F. M. 1975. *What Are Norms? A Study of Beliefs and Action in a Maya Community.* Cambridge: Cambridge University Press.
Clarkberg, M., R. M. Stolzenberg, and L. J. Waite. 1993. "Attitudes, Values and the Entrance into Cohabitational Unions." *Research Report,* Population Research Center, NORC and the University of Chicago, Chicago IL.
Devine, F. 1998. "Class Analysis and the Stability of Class Relations." *Sociology* 32:23–42.
Fishbein, M., and I. Ajzen. 1975. *Belief, Attitude, Intention and Behavior. An Introduction to Theory and Research.* Reading, MA: Addison-Wesley.
Goldscheider, F. K., and J. DaVanzo. 1989. "Pathways to Independent Living in Early Adulthood: Marriage, Semiautonomy, and Premarital Residential Independence." *Demography* 26:597–614.
Goldscheider, F., A. Thornton, and L. Young-DeMarco. 1993. "A Portrait of the Nest-Leaving Process in Early Adulthood." *Demography* 30:683–699.
Inglehart, R. 1977. *The Silent Revolution.* Princeton, NJ: Princeton University Press.
Inglehart, R. 1990. *Culture Shift in Advanced Industrial Society.* Princeton, NJ: Princeton University Press.

Kohn, M. L. [1969] 1977. *Class and Conformity. A Study in Values*. Chicago: University of Chicago Press.

Kohn, M. L., and K. M. Slomczynski (eds.). 1993. *Social Structure and Self-Direction: A Comparative Analysis of the United States and Poland*. Oxford: Blackwell.

Lesthaeghe, R. 1998. "On Theory Development: Applications to the Study of Family Formation." *Population and Development Review* 24:1–14.

Lesthaeghe, R., and G. Moors. 1996. "Living Arrangements, Socio-Economic Position and Values among Young Adults: A Pattern Description for France, Germany, Belgium and The Netherlands 1990." Pp. 163–221 in *Europe's Population in the 1990's*, edited by D. Coleman. New York: Oxford University Press.

Lesthaeghe, R., and J. Surkyn. 1988. "Cultural Dynamics and Economic Theories of Fertility Change." *Population and Development Review* 14:1–46

Middendorp, C. P. 1978. *Progressiveness and Conservatism. The Fundamental Dimensions of Ideological Controversy and Their Relationship to Social Class*. The Hague: Mouton.

Middendorp, C. P. 1993. "Authoritarianism—Personality and Ideology—Their Political Relevance and Relationship to Left-Right Ideology in the Netherlands (1970–1985)." *European Journal of Political Research* 24:211–228.

Moors, G. 1997. "The Dynamics of Values-Based Selection and Values Adaptation. With an Application to the Process of Family Formation." Ph.D. dissertation, Centrum voor Sociologie, Vrije Universiteit Brussel, Brussels.

Oppenheimer, V. K. 1994. "Women's Rising Employment and the Future of the Family in Industrial Societies." *Population and Development Review* 20:293–342.

Retherford, R. D., and M. K. Choe. 1993. *Statistical Models for Causal Analysis*. New York: Wiley.

Rokeach, M. 1973. *The Nature of Human Values*. New York: Free Press.

Rokeach, M. [1968] 1976. *Beliefs, Attitudes and Values. A Theory of Organization and Change*. San Francisco: Jossey-Bass.

Ryder, N. B. 1965. "The Cohort as a Concept in the Study of Social Change." *American Sociological Review* 30:843–861.

Thompson, M., R. Ellis, and A. Wildavsky. 1990. *Cultural Theory*. Boulder, CO: Westview Press.

Thornton, A. 1992. "The Influence of the Parental Family on the Attitudes and Behavior of Children." Pp. 247–266 in *The Changing American Family: Sociological and Demographic Perspectives*, edited by S. J. South and S. E. Tolnay. Boulder, CO: Westview Press.

Thornton, A., and D. Freedman. 1979. "Changes in the Sex Role Attitudes of Women, 1962–1977: Evidence from a Panel Study." *American Sociological Review* 44:831–842.

Thornton, A., D. F. Alwin, and D. Camburn. 1983. "Causes and Consequences of Sex-Role Attitudes and Attitude Change." *American Sociological Review* 48:211–227.

Thornton, A., W. G. Axinn, and D. H. Hill. 1992. "Reciprocal Effects of Religiosity, Cohabitation, and Marriage." *American Journal of Sociology* 98:628–651.

Thornton, A., L. Young-DeMarco, and F. Goldscheider. 1993. "Leaving the Parental Nest: The Experience of a Young White Cohort in the 1980s." *Journal of Marriage and the Family* 55:216–229.

Weinstein, M., and A. Thornton. 1989. "Mother-Child Relations and Adolescent Sexual Attitudes and Behavior." *Demography* 26:563–577.

12

Religion as a Determinant of Entry into Cohabitation and Marriage

EVELYN L. LEHRER

INTRODUCTION

A growing body of research documents that religion plays an important role in the economic and demographic behavior of individuals and families, ranging from investments in human capital to patterns of female employment, fertility, and marital stability (see reviews of this literature in Lehrer, 1996a, 1999; Iannacconne, 1998). Religion has been identified as a trait that is complementary in the context of marriage and for which positive assortative mating is optimal (Becker 1991; Chiswick and Lehrer, 1991); empirically, it has been found to have an important effect on the choice of marital partner (Sander, 1993a; Waite and Sheps Friedman, 1997; Lehrer, 1998). Less attention has been paid to the influence of religion on other aspects of union formation: the timing of the first union and whether it takes the form of marriage or cohabitation. This chapter focuses on these two interrelated decisions, examining them from the perspective of women.

The religion in which an individual is brought up is expected to influence entry into marriage and cohabitation because of its impact on certain key economic and demographic variables that have a bearing on union formation. Specifically, previous research indicates that religion affects educational attainment, attitudes toward premarital sex, desired fertility, expectations regarding the intrafamily division of labor over the life cycle, and the perceived costs of divorce. Based on this evidence, this chapter develops hypotheses regarding patterns of entry into marriage and cohabitation for the five main religious groups in the United States: mainline Protestants, fundamentalist Protestants, Catholics, Mormons, and Jews. These hypotheses are tested using data from the 1987–1988 National Survey of Families and Households (NSFH). A special effort is made to identify changes over time in the effects of religion on the timing of entry into first union and on the form that such union takes.

This chapter is organized as follows. The first section presents a theoretical framework for understanding the role of religious affiliation in union formation. The data and methods used in the empirical analysis are described next, followed by a discussion of the findings. The final section summarizes the main results and suggests directions for further research.

ANALYTICAL FRAMEWORK

The faith in which a young woman is raised may affect age at first union and the type of union formed through various channels. These include effects operating via differences among religious groups in education, attitudes toward premarital sex, fertility, the intrafamily division of labor, and the costs of marital dissolution. Using mainline Protestants as the comparison group, each of these mechanisms is developed below.

Education

The connection between educational attainment and age at marriage is well established: women who pursue more advanced levels of schooling generally delay their entry to marriage (Michael and Tuma, 1985). On the other hand, the linkage between religion and education has become clear only recently. The early literature on this relationship focused primarily on two groups, Catholics and Protestants, generally finding small, often conflicting effects (Featherman, 1971; Greeley, 1976, 1981; Roof, 1979; Tomes, 1985). However, studies that have gone beyond the conventional Catholic–Protestant comparisons have begun to uncover a systematic pattern of education by religion, after controlling for a rich set of family background variables. In particular, this research finds that educational attainment is highest for Jews, lowest for fundamentalist Protestants, with mainline Protestants and Catholics at the center of the distribution (Chiswick, 1988, 1993; Sherkat and Darnell, 1997; Darnell and Sherkat, 1997; Lehrer, 1999). Less is known about the relative schooling levels of Mormons, but the available evidence suggests that their attainment is similar to that of Catholics and mainline Protestants (Keysar and Kosmin, 1995).[1] Education differentials by religion have been interpreted within a human capital framework: religious affiliation is viewed as reflecting distinctive features of the home environment that affect both the demand and supply of funds for investments in schooling (Chiswick, 1988; Lehrer, 1999).

Since it is difficult to combine the roles of student and spouse (Thornton et al., 1995), those religious groups that promote high levels of investment in secular human capital also encourage, indirectly, a late transition to marriage. However, they do not necessarily encourage a delayed entry into cohabitation: the more tentative nature of this arrangement may be more compatible than formal marriage with pursuing full-time schooling into the mid- and late twenties. Two other factors reinforce this influence. First, efficient search in the marriage market is hindered when there is a great deal of uncertainty regarding traits that are relevant to assortative mating—as would be the case for an individual who is a long way from the transition to a fairly stable career (Oppenheimer, 1988; Chiswick, 1998). Such an individual has incentives to postpone the strong commitment that marriage entails until enough information is available to prevent a serious mismatch. Second, the initial period of uncertainty that characterizes high level careers—regarding the nature of alternative career paths, the time demands involved, and location—makes it difficult for people to settle down, both literally and figuratively.

Given that the level of schooling is lowest for fundamentalist Protestants and highest for Jews, this mechanism operating through education leads to the hypothesis that, other background variables held constant, age at marriage should be relatively low for the former and relatively high for the latter. In addition, this effect predicts that Jews will be found disproportionately in cohabiting arrangements.

Attitudes Regarding Premarital Sex

Although most religions value marriage and family life, often with proscriptions against premarital sex, Mormons and fundamentalist Protestants tend to be the most conservative in this and other areas. Sweet and Bumpass (1990) report that for these two groups, the level of approval of cohabitation is lowest. At the same time, Jews are found to be at the other end of the spectrum, with relatively high levels of approval.[2] Estimates of the actual prevalence of cohabitation by religion among white women are consistent with these results (Heaton, 1992).

Based on these considerations, the probability that the first union takes the form of cohabitation is expected to be lowest for fundamentalist Protestants and Mormons and highest among Jews.

Fertility

The optimal timing of entry into marriage is intimately related to desired fertility: women who wish to form large families clearly have an incentive to marry earlier than those who plan to have only one or two children.

The Catholic theology is strongly pronatalist, and, historically, the large family size of this group has been the most salient fertility differential by religion in the United States. However, it is well known that the influence of the Catholic Church on its members has been declining, and several studies have documented a convergence of Catholic fertility toward the mainline Protestant pattern (Jones and Westoff, 1979; Mosher et al., 1992; Lehrer, 1996b). Contrary to the case of Catholics, the fertility of Mormons, another strongly pronatalist group, has remained at unusually high levels (Thornton, 1979; Heaton, 1986; Lehrer, 1996b). Some aspects of fundamentalist Protestant theologies are also pronatalist, and the fertility of this group exceeds that of mainline Protestants by a small margin (Marcum, 1981; Lehrer, 1996b). At the other end of the continuum, Jews in the United States have consistently displayed an unusually low level of fertility (Goldscheider, 1967; Della Pergolla, 1980).

These considerations related to family size imply that compared to mainline Protestants, age at marriage should be relatively high for Jews. An early entry into first marriage is expected for fundamentalist Protestants and even more so for Mormons. For Catholics, the prediction from this channel of causality is a relatively young age at marriage for the earlier cohorts and no significant difference from mainline Protestants for women born more recently.

Intrafamily Division of Labor

The optimal timing of entry into marriage also depends on women's expected allocation of time over the life cycle. Young women who intend to orient their future energy and efforts to paid work have incentives to delay marriage and make investments that are labor-market specific. The opposite is true for women whose plans for the future are centered around domestic activities: they have incentives to marry early and begin investing in home production at a young age.

Religions differ in their approach toward gender roles; generally, those that encourage high fertility also emphasize women's roles as mothers and homemakers. Consistent with this idea, fundamentalist Protestant and Mormon women are more likely than their mainline Protestant counterparts to orient their efforts to home activities (Heaton and Cornwall, 1989; Chadwick and Garrett, 1995; Lehrer, 1995). In the case of Catholics, several studies have documented a trend toward convergence to the mainline Protestant behavior in the areas of female time allocation and labor supply (Brinkerhoff and MacKie, 1984, 1988; Lehrer, 1995), mirroring the transformations that have taken place in the fertility domain. At the other end of the spectrum, although Jewish women are known to be very responsive in their labor supply to the presence of young children (Chiswick, 1986), their overall commitment to the labor market is stronger than that of their non-Jewish counterparts (Hartman and Hartman, 1996).

Ceteris paribus, this influence through differences by religion in the intrafamily division of labor suggests that age at marriage should be high for Jews and relatively low for fundamentalist Protestants and Mormons. For Catholics, the prediction is a young age at marriage for the earlier cohorts and no significant difference from mainline Protestants for the more recent generations.

Costs of Divorce

To the extent that religions are generally family oriented, affiliation with any faith would tend to increase the costs of marital dissolution. This effect has been particularly pronounced for Catholics, as the Catholic Church specifically prohibits divorce. The higher cost of making a mistake in the marriage market suggests that compared to members of other faiths, Catholics would tend to have a more prolonged period of marital search and a later age at marriage. As in other aspects of family life, however, this distinctive Catholic effect is expected to be weaker for the more recent cohorts. Indeed, although Catholic marriages used to be less likely to end in dissolution than other unions (Christensen and Barber, 1967; Michael, 1979), recent research finds that this difference no longer exists (Lehrer and Chiswick, 1993).

Summing Up

The various mechanisms outlined above suggest several hypotheses regarding differences by religion in patterns of entry into marriage and cohabitation. Women brought up as fundamentalist Protestants and as Mormons are expected to marry early, because their faith encourages high fertility and an orientation to home activities, for Mormons particularly. The relatively low schooling level of fundamentalist Protestants is another factor operating in the same direction. The conservative attitude of both groups regarding premarital sex predicts a low prevalence of cohabitation.

Jewish women are expected to delay entry into marriage for several interrelated reasons: their high educational attainment, their low desired level of fertility, and their strong commitment to the labor market. A disproportionate representation of Jewish women among those whose first union is informal is also anticipated, partly because of their high propensity to pursue advanced schooling and partly because of their liberal attitudes toward premarital sex.

For Catholics, effects operating in opposite directions have been discussed. On the one hand, the fact that the cost of divorce is high for this group implies a longer period of marital search and a low probability of a very early marriage. On the other hand, the pronatalist norms of the Catholic Church encourage marriage, suggesting a low likelihood of a very late union. Based on these countervailing influences, Michael and Tuma (1985) suggest that affiliation with the Catholic faith should have a nonlinear impact, promoting an intermediate timing of marriage as opposed to one that is very early or very late.[3] Both of these effects are expected to be weak for the more recent cohorts, implying no significant difference from the mainline Protestant pattern.

DATA AND METHODS

The empirical analysis is based on data from the 1987–1988 National Survey of Families and Households, an extensive questionnaire addressed to a main sample of 9643 male and female respondents, representative of the U.S. population aged 19 and above. An additional 3374 cases correspond to an oversampling of special groups of the population, including African-Americans, Hispanics, and families with stepchildren.[4] The analyses presented here are weighted, and restricted to non-Hispanic white female respondents.[5] The survey is rich in economic, demographic, and family background variables. For the purposes of the present research, one of its important features is that it documents not only the current religious affiliation of respondents but also the faith in which they were brought up. Another advantage of this data set, compared to those used in previous efforts in the literature, is the relatively large size of the sample.

The empirical analysis is based on reduced-form equations that provide estimates of the impact of religion on union formation, other family background variables held constant. No attempt is made to disentangle influences that operate through the effects of religion on the woman's educational attainment, her preferences regarding premarital sex, her expected fertility and employment, and her perceived costs of divorce.

The above discussion made reference to differences over time in the expected effects of religion on union formation. Preliminary runs confirmed these differences, and also uncovered very pronounced structural changes in the effects of other family background variables. Thus the empirical work was conducted separately for two birth cohorts.

The analysis focuses first on respondents born in the post–World War II decade (1945–1955) who were in the 32–43 age bracket at the time of the survey. The models for this cohort are based on women who had already experienced their first transition to union formation. Censoring is not a serious problem as 93% of the respondents born in this period had already entered their first marriage by the interview date ($n = 1254$) and fully 95% had completed their transition to either first marriage or cohabitation ($n = 1286$).

Using multinomial logit, age at first marriage is analyzed as a dependent variable with three categories: early (18 years or less), intermediate (19–26 years), and late (27 years or over). Although the cutoff at 18 years at the low end seems natural, there is more arbitrariness in the definition of the late category. Preliminary analyses were run with this category beginning at 26, 27, and 28 years of age; the middle figure was chosen based on McFadden's (1973) pseudo-R^2 as the goodness-of-fit criterion. The same categories are used for the analysis of entry into first union.

The multinomial logit specification provides a straightforward way to test for the types of nonlinearities that are anticipated. As noted earlier, affiliation with the Catholic religion is expected to encourage an intermediate timing of first union, as opposed to entry at an early or late age. In addition, work by Waite and Spitze (1981) suggests possible nonlinearities in the effects of other family background variables. The authors reason that although families with abundant resources may use them to give their children attractive alternatives to an early marriage (e.g., educational opportunities), they may also try to facilitate marriage for a daughter who is still single in her late 20s.[6]

The analysis then turns to a second sample, corresponding to women born after 1960 ($n = 765$). These respondents were all relatively young at the time of the interview, between the ages of 19 and 27. Following closely previous work by Thornton et al. (1992), four Cox proportional hazards models are estimated to study union formation for this group. These include the hazard of cohabitation treating marriage as a competing risk, the hazard of marriage treating cohabitation as a competing risk, the hazard of marriage ignoring cohabitation, and the hazard of total union formation (either marriage or cohabitation, whichever came first). The Cox technique takes into account the fact that a large number of respondents in this second sample had not yet experienced their first transition to union formation. Although the estimated equations do not allow for the types of nonlinearities suggested above, this is not a problem here: the women in this sample had not yet reached the later ages, at which such nonlinearities become relevant.[7]

The cases included in the analysis correspond to individuals whose religion of upbringing is one of the five major religious groups considered in this study: Catholic, mainline Protestant, fundamentalist Protestant, Jewish, and Mormon.[8] The classification of Protestants is based on the categories employed by Lehrer and Chiswick (1993:390) for these data. Episcopalians, Methodists, Presbyterians, Lutherans, Unitarians, and various other ecumenical bodies are classified as mainline Protestants. The fundamentalist group includes Baptists, Jehovah's Witnesses, Seventh-Day Adventists, Christian Scientists, and a large number of other exclusivist groups. The NSFH includes all Baptists in one category, so it is not possible to make finer distinctions within this group.[9] This limitation of the data implies that the respondents classified in this study as fundamentalist Protestant include a small number of nonfundamentalists, suggesting a bias toward zero in the coefficient on the fundamentalist Protestant dummy variable. Thus the positive effect of membership in fundamentalist denominations on the speed of entry into union formation documented in the next section is more pronounced than indicated by the estimates.

Previous research suggests that current religious affiliation is determined simultaneously with education, fertility, and other economic and demographic variables (Sander, 1995; Waters et al., 1995; Lehrer, 1998). The analyses presented here are thus based on the faith in which the individual was raised, a measure less affected by problems of endogeneity.

Table 12.1 presents descriptive statistics on age at union formation. Religious differentials in the proportion that had entered marriage by age 18 are very pronounced for the earlier cohort. The probability is lowest for Jews (.04) and highest for Mormons and fundamentalist Protestants (.35–.37); Catholics and mainline Protestants are at the center (.13–.17). For the later cohort, marriage by age 18 is generally less common and the prevalence of cohabitation much higher. The table also reveals that religious differentials in entry to first union tend to be less accentuated than the corresponding differentials in entry to marriage.

Table 12.2 provides definitions and means for the variables used as controls in the empirical analysis. These include the father's socioeconomic status as measured by the Stevens–Cho (1985) index and the mother's years of schooling.[10] A set of dummy variables controls for various categories of nonintact family background as of age 16: whether the respondent lived with her biological mother only, with her mother and a stepfather, or in a different type of household structure (e.g., with her biological father and stepmother). Additional variables indicate the number of siblings, whether the mother worked in the labor market for at least 12 months when the respondent was a preschooler and during the school years, and the region of residence at age 16. For the earlier birth cohort (which spans a 10-year interval), dummies for various date-of- birth categories allow for possible changes within the period.

EMPIRICAL RESULTS

The 1945–1955 Birth Cohort

Table 12.3 presents two multinomial logit models: for age at first marriage and age at first union, defined as either marriage or cohabitation (whichever occurred earlier). The estimates in this table show how each

Table 12.1. Descriptive Statistics on Age at First Union by Religion in Which Respondent Was Raised

	Proportion of Cases in Each Religious Group	Median Age at Marriage	Proportion That Entered Marriage by Age 18	Proportion That Entered Cohabitation by Age 18	Proportion That Entered Union by Age 18
Birth Cohort: 1945–1955 (n = 1286)					
Mainline Protestant	.38	20.9	.17	.02	.18
Fundamentalist Protestant	.24	19.0	.37	.04	.38
Mormon	.03	20.2	.35	.02	.36
Jewish	.04	23.5	.04	.05	.08
Catholic	.31	21.3	.13	.03	.16
	1.00				
Birth Cohort: Post-1960 (n = 765)					
Mainline Protestant	.32	—	.10	.10	.16
Fundamentalist Protestant	.31	—	.31	.17	.38
Mormon	.03	—	.39	.07	.42
Catholic	.34	—	.09	.09	.15
	1.00				

Table 12.2. Definitions and Means of Explanatory Variables

		Birth Cohort	
		1945–1955	Post-1960
Father's SES	Steven and Cho's (1985) index of socioeconomic status (SES) corresponding to the father's occupation (or the stepfather's if he lived with the respondent at age 16). The lowest value is assigned if neither was present or if the respondent (R) did not give a valid answer.[a]	33.7	34.4
Mother's education	1 if mother's years of regular schooling is in category indicated		
<12		.29	.23
12 (benchmark)		(.38)	(.43)
13–15		.13	.15
≥16		.15	.15
Missing		.05	.04
Nonintact family			
Mother only	1 if at age 16 R lived with biological mother and stepfather was not present	.07	.13
Mother and stepfather	1 if at age 16 R lived with biological mother and stepfather	.05	.11
Other	1 if at age 16 R lived in other type of nonintact family (e.g., with biological father and stepmother)	.07	.11
Both parents (benchmark)	1 if at age 16 R lived with both biological parents	(.81)	(.65)
Number of siblings	Total number of biological siblings and stepsiblings	3.1	3.1
Mother worked	1 if mother ever held a paid job for 12 months or more when R was in age category indicated		
0–5		.22	.43
6–17		.55	.74
Residence at age 16	1 if R lived in the location indicated at age 16		
Northcentral		.32	.33
Northeast		.23	.18
West		.15	.17
South (benchmark)		(.26)	(.30)
Foreign country		.04	.02
Date of birth	1 if R's date of birth is in category indicated		
1945–1948 (benchmark)		(.31)	—
1949–1951		.30	—
1952–1955		.39	—

[a]Preliminary analyses also included a dummy to indicate that the respondent did not give a valid answer for father's SES. This variable was always insignificant and was dropped.

variable affects the odds of early versus intermediate timing, and of late versus intermediate timing; the estimated coefficients and t-ratios provide information on the direction and significance of each effect. The magnitudes of the various influences may be assessed more easily from Table 12.4, which reports probabilities of early, intermediate, and late entry, calculated for selected values of the covariates. Table 12.5 presents a logit equation for the determinants of cohabitation: the dependent variable equals 1 if the respondent's first union took the form of a cohabiting arrangement, 0 otherwise. Together, Tables 12.3, 12.4, and 12.5 provide a fairly complete picture of patterns of union formation for the 1945–1955 cohort.[11]

Religion Effects. Focusing first on the effects of religious upbringing on age at first marriage, Table 12.3 indicates that fundamentalist Protestants are more likely to enter marriage at an early rather than an intermediate age ($t = 2.9$). They are also less likely to do so at a late rather than an intermediate age ($t = -2.0$). Thus affiliation with a fundamentalist Protestant denomination uniformly encourages an earlier transition to marriage, an effect that is large in magnitude as shown in Table 12.4. For the reference case, a mainline Protestant woman with typical values for the control variables, the probabilities of early, intermediate, and late age at first marriage are, respectively, .12, .76, and .12. For her fundamentalist Protestant counterpart, the corresponding estimates are quite different: .20, .74, and .06. These results are consistent with Sander's (1993b) finding of early entry into marriage among Baptists, the major fundamentalist Protestant denomination.

A Mormon upbringing also encourages early rather than intermediate age at first marriage ($t = 1.8$). For this group, the probabilities of an early, intermediate, and late transition are .23, .72, and .05, respectively, a pattern similar to that uncovered for fundamentalist Protestants.

Being raised in a Jewish home has the opposite effect: it encourages an intermediate rather than an early age at marriage. Although the number of Jews in the sample is small and statistical significance is marginal ($t = -1.5$), the estimated magnitude of the effect is large. The probability of a late transition for Jewish women is fully .20; at the same time, the probability of early entry is only .04, by far the lowest among all religious groups. These findings are consistent with the pattern of delayed marriage among Jews reported by Chiswick (1998).

The influence of a Catholic upbringing is nonlinear, discouraging both an early and a late age at first marriage ($t = -2.3; t = -1.8$). Table 12.4 shows this effect clearly: the probability of an intermediate timing for Catholics is .83, higher than for any of the other religious groups. At the same time, the probability of an early marriage is relatively low (.08), as is the probability of a late marriage (.09). This nonlinearity is precisely as hypothesized by

Table 12.3. The Effects of Religious Upbringing on Age at First Union: Multinomial Logit Estimates: Birth Cohort. 1945–1955[a]

	First Marriage		First Union (Marriage or Cohabitation)	
	Early vs. Intermediate	Late vs. Intermediate	Early vs. Intermediate	Late vs. Intermediate
Control variables				
Father's SES	−.019 (−3.4)**	−.002 (−.4)	−.022 (−4.1)**	−.007 (−1.2)
Mother's education				
<12 years	.406 (2.3)**	−.996 (−3.3)**	.434 (2.5)**	−.906 (−2.7)**
13–15 years	−.435 (−1.5)#	.329 (1.3)	−.178 (−0.7)	.439 (1.6)*
≥ 16 years	−.308 (−0.9)	.413 (1.4)#	−.497 (−1.4)#	.374 (1.1)
Missing	.545 (1.2)	−1.170 (−1.7)*	.748 (1.7)*	−1.034 (−1.3)
Nonintact family				
Mother only	.111 (0.4)	−.210 (−.5)	.025 (0.1)	−.414 (−.8)
Mother and stepfather	.889 (2.9)**	−.175 (−.3)	.826 (2.8)**	−.506 (−.7)
Other	.842 (3.1)**	.314 (.7)	.772 (2.9)**	−1.240 (−1.5)#
Number of siblings	.129 (4.0)**	.030 (.6)	.143 (4.5)**	.01 (.002)
Mother worked				
Age 0–5	.432 (2.3)**	−.199 (−.7)	.432 (2.4)**	−.219 (−.7)
Age 6–17	.348 (2.1)**	−.263 (−1.3)	.403 (2.5)**	−.213 (−.9)
Residence at age 16				
Northcentral	−.638 (−3.1)**	−.244 (−.9)	−.811 (−4.1)**	−.138 (−.5)
Northeast	−.097 (−.4)	−.176 (−.6)	−.298 (−1.3)	−.054 (−.2)
West	−.159 (−.6)	−.242 (−.7)	−.232 (−1.0)	−.255 (−.7)
Foreign	−.404 (−.8)	1.503 (3.7)**	−.562 (−1.1)	1.451 (3.4)**
Date of birth				
1949–1951	−.015 (−.1)	.154 (.6)	−.078 (−.4)	−.126 (−.4)
1952–1955	.211 (1.2)	.499 (2.1)**	.309 (1.7)*	.221 (.9)
Religion variables				
Fundamentalist Protestant	.557 (2.9)**	−.615 (−2.0)**	.501 (2.6)**	−.708 (−2.0)**
Mormon	.754 (1.8)*	−.911 (−1.2)	.691 (1.7)*	−.586 (−.8)
Jew	−1.196 (−1.5)#	.511 (1.2)	−.329 (−.6)	.156 (.3)
Catholic	−.490 (−2.3)**	−.429 (−1.8)*	−.339 (−1.7)*	−.535 (−2.0)**
Constant	−1.373 (−4.1)**	−1.498 (−3.9)**	−1.255 (−3.9)**	−1.331 (−3.2)**
χ^2(42 df)	253.9**		254.9**	
n	1254		1286	

[a]t-values are in parentheses.
**$p < .05$; *$p < .10$; #$p < .15$.

Michael and Tuma (1985). Empirical analyses covering a similar period have emphasized the Catholic pattern of avoiding an early marriage (Sander, 1993b; Mosher et al., 1992). The tendency for Catholics to avoid also a very late marriage has not been documented before, in part because the statistical models employed have not permitted the detection of such nonlinearity.

Table 12.4. Predicted Probabilities. 1945–1955 Birth Cohort

	First Marriage			First Union		
	Early (≤ 18 years)	Intermediate (19–26 years)	Late (≥ 27 years)	Early (≤ 18 years)	Intermediate (19–26 years)	Late (≥ 27 years)
Reference case[a]	.12	.76	.12	.11	.79	.10
Selected cases[b]						
Father's SES						
25th percentile	.14	.74	.12	.13	.76	.11
75th percentile	.09	.78	.12	.08	.82	.10
Mother's education						
< 12 years	.18	.78	.05	.16	.79	.04
13–15 years	.07	.75	.17	.09	.76	.15
≥ 16 years	.08	.74	.18	.06	.79	.15
Nonintact family						
Mother only	ns[c]	ns	ns	ns	ns	ns
Mother and stepfather	.25	.66	.09	.22	.72	.06
Other	.22	.63	.14	.22	.75	.03
Number of siblings						
2	.10	.78	.12	.09	.80	.10
4	.13	.75	.12	.12	.78	.10
Mother worked: 0–5	.17	.73	.10	.16	.76	.08
Mother did not work: 6–17	.08	.76	.16	.07	.80	.13
Residence at age 16						
Northeast	.18	.70	.12	.16	.73	.10
West	.18	.70	.12	.18	.74	.09
South	.19	.67	.14	.21	.69	.10
Foreign	.09	.47	.44	.10	.55	.35
Date of birth						
1945–1951	ns	ns	ns	ns	ns	ns
1952–1955	.13	.70	.16	.14	.72	.13
Religion						
Fundamentalist Protestant	.20	.74	.06	.17	.78	.05
Mormon	.23	.72	.05	.20	.75	.05
Jew	.04	.76	.20	.08	.80	.12
Catholic	.08	.83	.09	.08	.85	.06

[a]The reference case corresponds to a woman raised in a mainline Protestant denomination. Her other characteristics are set at the mean for the continuous variables and at the modal group for the categorical variables: her mother has 12 years of schooling, her family of origin is intact, her mother did not work when she was 0–5 but was employed when she was 6–17; the date of birth is 1949–1951 and the region of residence is Northcentral.

[b]The cases below differ from the reference woman in only one characteristic, as indicated in the stub.

[c]ns indicates that this case is not significantly different from the reference case at the .15 level.

Table 12.5. The Effects of Religious Upbringing on Likelihood That First Union Is Cohabitation: Logit Estimates. Birth Cohort: 1945–1955[a]

Control variables	
Father's SES	.001 (.4)
Mother's education	
< 12 years	−0.565 (−2.7)**
13–15 years	.519 (2.3)**
≥ 16 years	.743 (3.0)**
Missing	−1.558 (−3.2)**
Nonintact family	
Mother only	.698 (2.5)**
Mother and stepfather	−.130 (−.3)
Other	.944 (3.3)**
Number of siblings	.047 (1.4)#
Mother worked	
Age 0–5	.289 (1.5)#
Age 6–17	.073 (.4)
Residence at age 16	
Northcentral	.021 (.1)
Northeast	.114 (.5)
West	.171 (.7)
Foreign	.102 (.2)
Date of birth	
1949–1951	.811 (3.5)**
1952–1955	1.212 (5.8)**
Religion Variables	
Fundamentalist Protestant	−.219 (−1.0)
Mormon	−.971 (−1.6)*
Jew	.992 (2.6)**
Catholic	−.027 (−.1)
Constant	−2.756 (−8.0)**
χ^2 (21 df)	120.8**
n	1286
Mean of dependent variable	.20

[a]t-values are in parentheses.
**$p < .05$; *$p < .10$; #$p < .15$.

Overall, the results for the 1945–1955 cohort on the effects of religion on marriage are consistent with the hypotheses outlined earlier: Mormons and fundamentalist Protestants tend to marry at an early age, Jews tend to delay the transition to marriage, and the effect is nonlinear for Catholics.

Turning now to the second model in Table 12.3, for entry to first marriage or cohabitation, the main change is that the Jewish effect disappears. The Mormon effect decreases, although this change is small in magnitude and not significant. As Table 12.5 shows, these results are related to the fact that the probability that the first union takes the form of a cohabiting arrangement is highest for Jews ($t = 2.6$) and lowest for Mormons ($t = -1.6$). Thus, although a Jewish upbringing delays marriage, it does not delay the formation of a union broadly defined. Table 12.4 shows that the probability of early entry into a union is .08 for Jews, the same as for Catholics, and not too far from the estimate for mainline Protestants, .11. These results are consistent with the notion that the effects of a Jewish upbringing on union formation are due in part to the unusually high educational attainment of this group and to their liberal attitudes toward premarital sex.

Table 12.4 shows that although Mormon women are clear outliers in the distribution of age at first marriage, they do not stand out as much in the distribution of age at first union. This pattern follows from their low propensity to form their first union through cohabitation. The influence of a fundamentalist Protestant upbringing on the probability of cohabitation is also negative, as anticipated, but it is not statistically significant.

Effects of the Control Variables. Factors indicating greater resources and more attractive circumstances in the family of origin are expected to be associated with more educational opportunities and a lower probability of an early transition to marriage (Michael and Tuma, 1985; Axinn and Thornton, 1992). The results generally support this hypothesis. The father's socioeconomic status (SES) has a negative influence on the odds that the first marriage will be at an early rather than an intermediate stage ($t = -3.4$). The coefficient on late versus intermediate timing is insignificant, however, implying that the effect is nonlinear: although a high level of resources delays marriage initially, it does not continue to do so at the later ages. Maternal education below 12 years of schooling is associated with faster entry into marriage, and this influence persists throughout the entire range of the age variable ($t = 2.3$ and $t = -3.3$).

Although women who lived only with their mother at age 16 have the same rate of entry into marriage as their counterparts raised by both of their parents, the other two types of nonintact family structure are associated with a high probability of early entry ($t = 2.9$, $t = 3.1$). A larger family size is also linked with earlier marriage ($t = 4.0$), as is maternal employment during the preschool years and concurrent with school ($t = 2.3$, $t = 2.1$). All of these effects are nonlinear: they are limited to the comparison between early and intermediate timing, becoming insignificant afterward.

Residence in the Northcentral region at age 16 decreases the odds of early rather than intermediate timing ($t = -3.1$). Women who lived in a foreign country have higher odds of late rather than intermediate entry into marriage ($t = 3.7$), reflecting the difficulty in some cases of finding a suitable partner in an unfamiliar location with a different culture. Compared to 1945–1948, women born in 1952–1955 also have a greater likelihood of marrying at a late rather than an intermediate age ($t = 2.1$), consistent with the well-known increase in the average age at marriage over this period.

The results for age at first union broadly defined differ in some interesting ways from the patterns just described, and the cohabitation model in Table 12.5 sheds some light on these differences. This table shows that the probability that the first union takes the form of a cohabiting arrangement is positively associated with the level of schooling attained by the respondent's mother ($t = -2.7, 2.3, 3.0$). This result provides an explanation for the pattern in Table 12.4: for the daughters of college-educated women, the probability of late entry into first marriage is .18, compared to a probability of late entry into a first union of only .15.

Table 12.5 also shows that growing up in a disrupted home has significant implications. The odds that the first union takes the form of cohabitation are highest for respondents who lived in the "other" family structure at age 16, i.e., with the biological father and a stepmother, or some other unusual arrangement ($t = 3.3$). As Table 12.4 reveals, this influence is very pronounced: although the probability of a late marriage for such women is .14, the probability of a late union is only .03.

The likelihood of entering the first union through cohabitation increased markedly over the period, being highest for women born in the latest interval, 1952–1955 ($t = 5.8$). Consistent with this observation, Table 12.3 indicates that although being born in 1952–1955 increases the odds of a late rather than an intermediate entry into first marriage ($t = 2.1$), it also raises the odds of an early rather than an intermediate entry into first union ($t = 1.7$). The rising age at marriage over the period was clearly accompanied by an influence in the opposite direction in the cohabitation dimension, as documented in earlier work by Bumpass et al. (1991).

The effects of the control variables provide a way to assess the relative importance of religion as a determinant of union formation. Among the control factors, the mother's educational attainment and a nonintact family of origin have the largest influences. An increase in maternal education from under 12 years to 16 years or more lowers the probability that the first marriage will take place early from .18 to .08—a difference of 10 percentage points. Similarly, the probability of an early first marriage increases from .12 to .25 if the respondent lived with her biological mother and stepfather at age 16 rather than with both of her natural parents—a difference of 13 percentage points. By comparison, the corresponding difference between fundamentalist Protestants and Catholics is 12 percentage points, and the difference between Mormons and Jews is fully 19 percentage points. The religion effects clearly rival in magnitude those of the mother's education and family structure.

Zero-Order Effects. The models of Tables 12.3 and 12.5 were rerun excluding all of the control variables, to ascertain whether there are additional effects of religion on union formation that work through its influence on the other family background factors. The estimates are not reported here for the sake of brevity, but are included in an Appendix available from the author on request. Although all of the qualitative conclusions described above regarding the effects of religious affiliation continue to hold, the coefficients on the religion variables are both larger in magnitude and stronger in significance in this new specification. This result implies that the total impact of religion on union formation is in fact more pronounced than indicated by the estimates in Tables 12.3, 12.4, and 12.5.

The Post-1960 Cohort

The results for the younger respondents in the post-1960 cohort are displayed in Tables 12.6 and 12.7. The sample size, $n = 765$, is not as large as that available in the previous analysis, limiting what can be learned about Mormons ($n = 20$). Observations corresponding to Jews were excluded, as there were only 12 cases. The first two columns of Table 12.6 present Cox proportional hazards models of cohabitation and marriage, treating the other state as a competing risk. The Cox regression of marriage shown in the third column ignores cohabitation; in this model those who first cohabited and then went on to formal marriage are included in the ranks of the married. The last model considers the hazard of union formation defined as either marriage or cohabitation. In all of these analyses, exposure to the risk of union formation is assumed to begin at age 13.

Table 12.7 shows predicted probabilities of an early first marriage and an early first union (by age 18) based, respectively, on the models of columns 3 and 4 in Table 12.6. These estimates, obtained from the complement of the survival function evaluated at $t = 5$ years for selected values of the covariates, are directly comparable to those reported in Table 12.4, columns 1 and 4, for the earlier generation. They thus provide an easy way to assess changes over time in the effects of religion on union formation.

Religion Effects. Focusing first on the case of a fundamentalist Protestant upbringing, the model in column 1 of Table 12.6 shows that it has no significant impact on cohabitation. The next two models reveal a positive influence on marriage ($t = 3.3$ and $t = 2.9$), and the last model indicates a positive effect on total union formation ($t = 2.2$). Thus the pace of union formation for this cohort continues to be faster among fundamentalist Protestants, consistent with findings for Baptists reported by Sander (1993b). However, a comparison of Tables 12.4 and 12.7 reveals that the effect associated with fundamentalist Protestantism has become somewhat weaker. For the earlier cohort, the probability of marriage by age 18 was .20 for fundamentalist Protestants, compared to .12 for mainline

Evelyn L. Lehrer

Table 12.6. The Effects of Religious Upbringing on Union Formation: Cox Proportional Hazards Models. Birth Cohort: Post-1960[a]

	Cohabitation (Marriage as Competing Risk)	Marriage (Cohabitation as Competing Risk)	Marriage (Ignoring Cohabitation)	Total Union Formation
Control variables				
Father's SES	−.010 (−2.8)**	−.008 (−2.4)**	−.007 (−2.4)**	−.009 (−3.6)**
Mother's education				
< 12 years	.284 (1.9)*	.114 (.8)	−.110 (−.9)	.225 (2.1)**
13–15 years	−.186 (−1.0)	−.279 (−1.5)#	−.282 (−1.9)*	−.245 (−1.9)*
≥ 16 years	−.302 (−1.3)	−.665 (−2.6)**	−.618 (−3.1)**	−.440 (−2.6)**
Missing	.451 (1.2)	1.050 (2.8)**	.529 (1.7)*	.715 (2.8)**
Nonintact family				
Mother only	.446 (2.6)**	−.559 (−2.5)**	−.351 (−2.2)**	−.010 (−.07)
Mother and stepfather	.496 (2.6)**	−.144 (−.7)	−.041 (−.3)	.172 (1.2)
Other	.863 (5.0)**	.118 (.6)	.022 (.1)	.506 (3.8)**
Number of siblings	−.0043 (−.1)	−.054 (−1.9)*	−.027 (−1.3)	−.025 (−1.3)
Mother worked				
Age 0–5	.027 (.2)	.131 (1.0)	.163 (1.6)*	.078 (.8)
Age 6–17	.279 (1.8)*	−.130 (−.9)	−.055 (−.5)	.068 (.7)
Residence at age 16				
Northcentral	.061 (.4)	−.438 (−3.0)**	−.304 (−2.5)**	−.193 (−1.8)*
Northeast	.055 (.3)	−.699 (−3.4)**	−.535 (−3.5)**	−.316 (−2.3)**
West	.809 (4.6)**	−.278 (−1.4)	−.108 (−.7)	.323 (2.5)**
Foreign	.809 (2.4)**	−.339 (−.6)	−.379 (−.9)	.429 (1.5)#
Religion variables				
Fundamentalist Protestant	−.102 (−.6)	.519 (3.3)**	.359 (2.9)**	.241 (2.2)**
Mormon	−.745 (−1.4)#	1.245 (3.8)**	1.004 (3.6)**	.299 (1.1)
Catholic	−.148 (−1.1)	−.127 (−.8)	−.012 (−.1)	−.129 (−1.2)
χ^2 (18 df)	97.4**	110.2**	94.6**	121.3**
n	765	765	765	765

[a]t-values are in parentheses.
**$p < .05$; *$p < .10$; #$p < .15$.

Protestants. For the more recent cohort, the corresponding estimates are .13 and .09, respectively, indicating a narrower gap. A similar pattern of change over time is observed for the timing of first union.

In the case of Mormons, the estimates suggest two opposing influences. The first column of Table 12.6 shows a large negative effect on cohabitation; however, significance is only marginal ($t = -1.4$). The next two columns indicate a positive impact on formal marriage ($t = 3.8$; $t = 3.6$). Thus Mormons are less likely to cohabit, but they marry earlier. The last column reveals that these influences cancel each other out, and that the net

Table 12.7. Predicted Probabilities. Post-1960 Birth Cohort

	First Marriage	First Union
	Early (≤ 18 years)	Early (≤ 18 years)
Reference case[a]	.09	.15
Selected cases[b]		
Father' SES		
25th percentile	.10	.17
75th percentile	.08	.15
Mother's education		
<12 years	ns[c]	.18
13–15 years	.08	.12
≥16 years	.05	.10
Nonintact family		
Mother only	.06	ns
Mother and stepfather	ns	ns
Other	ns	.24
Number of siblings		
2	ns	ns
4	ns	ns
Mother worked: 0–5	.11	ns
Mother did not work: 6–17	ns	ns
Residence at age 16		
Northeast	.07	.13
West	ns	.24
South	.12	.18
Foreign	ns	.22
Religion		
Fundamentalist Protestant	.13	.19
Mormon	.23	ns
Catholic	ns	ns

[a]The reference case corresponds to a woman raised in a mainline Protestant denomination. Her other characteristics are set at the mean for the continuous variables and at the modal group for the categorical variables.
[b]The cases below differ from the reference woman in only one characteristic, as indicated in the stub.
[c]ns indicates that this case is not significantly different from the reference case at the .15 level.

impact of a Mormon upbringing on union formation is zero. A comparison of the estimates in Tables 12.4 and 12.7 indicates that the Mormon differential in the timing of first marriage increased by a small amount over time. Although the probability of entering marriage at an early age declined from .12 to .09 for mainline Protestants, the figure remained stable at the high level of .23 in the case of Mormons.

Interestingly, the Catholic variable is insignificant throughout. It should be noted that this is not a sample size issue, as Catholics are more numerous than fundamentalist Protestants. The lack of significance of the Catholic coefficient is consistent with other research showing that the effect of a Catholic upbringing on union formation has disappeared for more recent generations (Sander, 1993b).

Effects of the Control Variables. For the cohort born in the post–World War II decade, cohabitation was seen to be most common among women brought up by highly educated mothers. The opposite is true for the post-1960 cohort: the likelihood of cohabitation is highest among respondents whose mothers have less than a high school degree ($t = 1.9$); in addition, the father's SES has a significantly negative influence on cohabitation ($t = -2.8$). These data suggest a major shift over time in the socioeconomic determinants of cohabitation, consistent with patterns reported by Raley (1998).

The percentage of respondents growing up in broken families is much larger in the more recent generation (35% compared to 19%), and the way in which this factor influences union formation has also changed markedly over time. For the earlier cohort, where significant, the nonintact family-of-origin variables were associated with a higher probability of both cohabitation and early marriage. For the more recent generation, living with the mother only actually delays marriage ($t = -2.5$ and $t = -2.2$); the other two types of nonintact family structure have no significant effect on entry into formal marriage. However, a broken family background continues to have a strong, positive impact on the likelihood of cohabitation ($t = 2.6$; $t = 2.6$; $t = 5.0$). This pronounced change in the influence of growing up in a disrupted home is consistent with results of other research (Thornton, 1991; Kiernan and Hobcraft, 1997).

The prevalence of maternal employment also increased substantially from the first sample to the second and its influence declined in importance. Table 12.6 shows a marginally significant effect of employment during the preschool years on marriage, only in the model that ignores cohabitation ($t = 1.6$), and a positive influence of employment during the school years on the likelihood of cohabitation ($t = 1.8$).

The geographic patterns of marriage and cohabitation have also changed. For the more recent cohort, entry into formal marriage is slowest for respondents who at age 16 lived in the Northcentral ($t = -3.0$; $t = -2.5$) and Northeastern regions ($t = -3.4$ and $t = -3.5$). At the same time, cohabitation is most likely for those who grew up in the West ($t = 4.6$) or in a foreign country ($t = 2.4$).

Overall, as informal unions have become more common, the patterns of entry into cohabiting relationships have become an increasingly important part of the total union formation picture; at the same time, the socioeconomic determinants of cohabitation have undergone major structural changes.

Zero-Order Effects. A pattern similar to that uncovered for the earlier generation emerges when the background variables are excluded from the regressions: the coefficients on the religion variables generally become stronger, both in magnitude and in significance. The implication of these results, which are available from the author, is that the total effects associated with religion are larger than those suggested by the estimates in Tables 12.6 and 12.7.

CONCLUSIONS AND DIRECTIONS FOR FURTHER RESEARCH

Using data on white, non-Hispanic female respondents from the 1987–1988 National Survey of Families and Households, this study presents a comparative analysis of union formation by religious upbringing. For women born in the 1945–1955 period, the chapter documents important differentials by religion. Compared to mainline Protestants (the benchmark group), fundamentalist Protestants and Mormons have a pattern of earlier entry into marriage, and Jews tend to delay marriage. For Catholics, a nonlinear influence is found: a tendency to enter marriage at an intermediate age, avoiding both early and late entry. The likelihood that the first union is a cohabiting relationship is highest among Jews and lowest among Mormons. The results for union formation, broadly defined as either marriage or cohabitation, reveal that Mormons and fundamentalist Protestants have the earliest entry; the pattern for Catholics is nonlinear, similar to that uncovered for marriage. In the case of a Jewish upbringing, the tendencies to enter cohabiting arrangements and to delay formal marriage exert opposing influences of similar size, and the net effect on the timing of entry into some sort of union is zero.

Among women born in the post-1960 period, fundamentalist Protestants and Mormons continue to display a pattern of early marriage, consistent with the distinctive behaviors that they presently display in other domains of family life. In addition, Mormons continue to be the least likely to cohabit, although this effect is only marginally significant. In terms of total union formation, this influence cancels out the positive effect of a Mormon upbringing on the timing of formal marriage; the net effect is that Mormons do not differ from mainline Protestants in their rate of entry into a union, broadly defined. The only significant religious influence on total union formation is a fundamentalist Protestant affiliation, which remains linked with an unusually early entry. No conclusions can be drawn about the effects of a Jewish upbringing for this cohort because of the limited number of cases available.

It is also not possible with these data to determine whether the Catholic pattern of avoiding a very late entry into marriage has disappeared; the answer to this question will have to await more recent information. At the low end of the age distribution, however, there has been a clear pattern of convergence to the mainline Protestant pattern: the distinctive Catholic tendency to avoid an early first union no longer prevails. This result is consistent with the fact that Catholics have been losing their former distinctiveness in virtually all other areas of economic and demographic behavior.

The religion variables included in the 1987–1988 NSFH are considerably richer than those available in most other sources; however, they are not ideal. In particular, it would have been desirable to have information on the salience of religion in the family of origin and on the religious beliefs actually held by the various family members. Research by Thornton et al. (1992) suggests that religiosity is an important determinant of patterns of entry into union formation, and additional research on this relationship would be desirable.

Although the main focus of this study has been on the effects of religious affiliation, the results on the other family background variables reveal a striking transformation over time that merits further investigation. For the more recent cohort, cohabiting relationships are most prevalent among women coming from disadvantaged backgrounds—a clear departure from the pattern for the earlier generation, which may reflect the growth in transfer programs over the time period. In addition, while growing up in a disrupted family used to encourage both early marriage and the formation of cohabiting relationships, the first effect no longer prevails. At the same time, as cohabitation has become more common, its weight in patterns of total union formation has increased.

At the methodological level, the results in this chapter underscore the importance of nonlinearities in union formation, an issue that has received very little attention in the literature to date. The fact that the nature of most of the effects varies throughout the distribution of the age variable will be a key point to keep in mind in future analyses of entry into cohabitation and marriage.

ACKNOWLEDGMENTS

This chapter has benefited from many helpful comments by Barry Chiswick, Arland Thornton, anonymous referees, and participants in the NIH conference on

"The Ties That Bind: Perspectives on Marriage and Cohabitation," June 29–30, 1998, Bethesda, Maryland. I am indebted to Lei Han for her skillful research assistance in this project.

NOTES

1.   Data from the earlier period of the 1970s suggest that brides in Utah, who are predominantly Mormon, are more likely than their counterparts in other states to have education beyond a high school degree; however, they are also generally less likely to have completed 4 years of college (Smith, 1985).

2.   These findings are based on attitudinal questions in the same data set used in this study, the 1987–1988 NSFH. But while the present research uses a subsample of cases selected on the basis of birth cohort, gender, and race, as described in the section on Data and Methods, Sweet and Bumpass (1990) analyze all respondents age 25 and older.

3.   Michael and Tuma (1985) did not test for such nonlinearities, as their sample included only young people.

4.   This survey was designed at the Center for Demography and Ecology at the University of Wisconsin–Madison under the direction of Larry Bumpass and James Sweet. The Institute for Survey Research at Temple University did the fieldwork.

5.   It is well known that patterns of union formation vary markedly by race and ethnicity, making it inappropriate to pool all groups together. The sample sizes for Hispanics and African-Americans in the NSFH are too small to permit separate analyses.

6.   An alternative specification was also considered, namely, a discrete-time hazards model, including a variable for age at the beginning of the time interval to allow for nonlinearities. This approach has the advantage of more fully utilizing information on the timing of the union; however, since the effects of virtually all variables are in fact nonlinear (see Tables 12.3 and 12.4), it would require an unwieldy number of interaction terms (between age and each of the covariates). The multinomial logit approach used here does not have this shortcoming. As the next section shows, it provides a straightforward way to detect nonlinearities and evaluate their magnitudes.

7.   The Cox proportional hazards model handles censoring but does not allow for nonlinearities; the opposite holds for the multinomial logit procedure. Note that the first sample analyzed here consists of an older group of women for whom censoring is not a major problem; the second sample is a young group for whom the issue of nonlinearities does not arise. Predicted probabilities calculated from both models provide an easy way to compare the effects of the explanatory variables across the two samples.

8.   Individuals who report no religion are not studied here as this group is small and heterogeneous: the NSFH does not distinguish between atheists, agnostics, and respondents who were raised without an affiliation for other reasons (e.g., being a child from an interfaith marriage). The implications for age at first union are likely to differ across these various categories. The second sample also excludes observations corresponding to Jews, as there were only 12 cases.

9.   In his research on the classification of Protestant groups, Smith (1987) considers three main categories: fundamentalist, moderate, and liberal. He distinguishes between seven different Baptist denominations, classifying six of them as fundamentalist and one as moderate.

10. Preliminary analyses suggested that cases in which the respondent did not know the mother's education are associated systematically with unusually low levels of respondent's schooling. Thus no imputation is made and instead the set of dummy variables for maternal education includes a category for cases with missing information.

11. Although the hypotheses on the effects of religion suggest one-tailed tests, p-values for the more conservative two-tailed tests are reported in the tables.

REFERENCES

Axinn, William G., and Arland Thornton. 1992. "The Influence of Parental Resources on the Timing of Transition to Marriage." *Social Science Research* 21: 261–285.

Becker, Gary S. l991. *A Treatise on the Family*. Cambridge, MA: Harvard University Press.

Brinkerhoff, Merlin B., and Marlene M. MacKie. 1984. "Religious Denominations' Impact Upon Gender Attitudes: Some Methodological Implications." *Review of Religious Research* 25(4):365–378.

Brinkerhoff, Merlin B., and Marlene M. MacKie. 1988. "Religious Sources of Gender Traditionalism." Pp. 232–257 in *The Religion and Family Connection*, edited by D.Thomas. Salt Lake City: Religious Studies Center, Brigham Young University.

Bumpass, Larry L., James A. Sweet, and Andrew Cherlin. 1991. "The Role of Cohabitation in Declining Rates of Marriage." *Journal of Marriage and the Family* 53(November):913–927.

Chadwick, Bruce A., and H. Dean Garrett. 1995. "Women's Religiosity and Employment: The LDS Experience." *Review of Religious Research* 36(3):277–293.

Chiswick, Barry R. 1986. "Labor Supply and Investments in Child Quality: A Study of Jewish and Non-Jewish Women." *Review of Economics and Statistics* 68(4): 700–703.

Chiswick, Barry R. 1988. "Differences in Education and Earnings Across Racial and Ethnic Groups: Tastes, Discrimination, and Investments in Child Quality." *Quarterly Journal of Economics* 103(3):571–597.

Chiswick, Barry R. 1993. "The Skills and Economic Status of American Jewry: Trends Over the Last Half-Century." *Journal of Labor Economics* 11(1):229–242.

Chiswick, Carmel U. 1998. "The Economics of Contemporary American Jewish Family Life." Pp. 65–80 in *Coping with Life and Death: Jewish Families in the Twentieth Century, Studies in Contemporary Jewry*, Vol. 14, edited by Peter Y. Medding. Oxford: Oxford University Press.

Chiswick, Carmel, and Evelyn Lehrer. l991. "Religious Intermarriage: An Economic Perspective." *Contemporary Jewry* 12:21–34.

Christensen, Harold T., and Kenneth E. Barber. 1967. "Interfaith versus Intrafaith Marriage in Indiana." *Journal of Marriage and the Family* 29(3):461–469.

Darnell, Alfred, and Darren E. Sherkat. 1997. "The Impact of Protestant Fundamentalism on Educational Attainment." *American Sociological Review* 62(April): 306–315.

Della Pergolla, Sergio. 1980. "Patterns of American Jewish Fertility." *Demography* 17(3):261–273.

Featherman, David L. 1971. "The Socioeconomic Achievement of White Religio-Ethnic Subgroups: Social and Psychological Explanations." *American Sociological Review* 36(April):207–222.

Goldscheider, Calvin. 1967. "Fertility of the Jews," *Demography* 4:196–209.

Greeley, Andrew M. 1976. *Ethnicity, Denomination and Inequality*. Beverly Hills, CA: Sage.

Greeley, Andrew M. 1981. "Catholics and the Upper Middle Class: A Comment on Roof." *Social Forces* 59(3):824–830.

Hartman, Moshe, and Harriet Hartman 1996. *Gender Equality and American Jews*. Albany, NY: State University of New York Press.

Heaton, Tim B. 1986. "How does Religion Influence Fertility? The Case of Mormons." *Journal for the Scientific Study of Religion* 25(2):248–258.

Heaton, Tim B. 1992. "Demographics of the Contemporary Mormon Family." *Dialogue: A Journal of Mormon Thought* 25(3):19–34.

Heaton, Tim B., and Marie Cornwall. 1989. "Religious Group Variation in the Socioeconomic Status and Family Behavior of Women." *Journal for the Scientific Study of Religion* 28(3):283–299.

Iannaccone, Laurence R. 1998. "An Introduction to the Economics of Religion." *Journal of Economic Literature* 36(September):1465–1496.

Jones, Elise F., and Charles F. Westoff. 1979. "The End of 'Catholic' Fertility." *Demography* 16(2):209–218.

Keysar, Ariela, and Barry A. Kosmin. 1995. "The Impact of Religious Identification on Differences in Educational Attainment Among American Women in 1990." *Journal for the Scientific Study of Religion* 34(1):49–62.

Kiernan, Kathleen E., and John Hobcraft. 1997. "Parental Divorce during Childhood: Age at First Intercourse, Partnership and Parenthood." *Population Studies* 51:41–55.

Lehrer, Evelyn L. 1995. "The Effects of Religion on the Labor Supply of Married Women." *Social Science Research* 24:281–301.

Lehrer, Evelyn L. 1996a. "The Role of the Husband's Religion on the Economic and Demographic Behavior of Families." *Journal for the Scientific Study of Religion* 35(2):145–155.

Lehrer, Evelyn L. 1996b. "Religion as a Determinant of Fertility." *Journal of Population Economics* 9:173–196.

Lehrer, Evelyn L. 1998. "Religious Intermarriage in the United States: Determinants and Trends." *Social Science Research* 27:245–263.

Lehrer, Evelyn L. 1999. "Religion as a Determinant of Educational Attainment: An Economic Perspective." *Social Science Research* 28:358–379.

Lehrer, Evelyn L., and Carmel Chiswick. 1993. "Religion as a Determinant of Marital Stability." *Demography* 30(3):385–404.

Marcum, John P. 1981. "Explaining Fertility Differentials Among U.S. Protestants." *Social Forces* 60(2):532–543.

McFadden, Daniel. 1973. "Conditional Logit Analysis of Qualitative Choice Behavior." Pp. 105–142 in *Frontiers in Econometrics*, edited by Paul Zarembka. New York: Academic Press.

Michael, Robert T. 1979. "Determinants of Divorce." Pp. 223–268 in *Sociological Economics*, edited by in Louis Levy-Garboua. Beverly Hills, CA: Sage.

Michael, Robert T., and Nancy Tuma. 1985. "Entry into Marriage and Parenthood by Young Men and Women: The Influence of Family Background." *Demography* 22(4):515–544.

Mosher, William, Linda B. Williams, and David P. Johnson. 1992. "Religion and Fertility in the United States: New Patterns." *Demography* 29(2):199–214.

Oppenheimer, Valerie K. 1988. "A Theory of Marriage Timing." *American Journal of Sociology* 94:563–591.

Raley, Kelly. 1998. "Recent Trends in Marriage and Cohabitation." Presented at the NIH conference on "Ties that Bind: Perspectives on Marriage and Cohabitation," Bethesda, MD, June 29–30.

Roof, Wade C. 1979. "Socioeconomic Differentials Among White Socioreligious Groups in the United States." *Social Forces* 59(3):831–836.

Sander, William. 1993a. "Catholicism and Intermarriage in the United States." *Journal of Marriage and the Family* 55:1037–1041.

Sander, William. 1993b. "Catholicism and Marriage in the United States." *Demography* 30(3):373–384.

Sander, William. 1995. *The Catholic Family: Marriage, Children, and Human Capital.* Boulder, CO: Westview Press.

Sherkat, Darren E., and Alfred Darnell. 1997. "The Effects of Parents' Fundamentalism on Children's Educational Attainment." Unpublished manuscript.

Smith, James E. 1985. "A Familistic Religion in a Modern Society." Pp. 273–300 in *Contemporary Marriage: Comparative Perspectives on a Changing Institution,* edited by Kingsley Davis (in association with Shoshana Grossbard-Shechtman). New York: Russell Sage Foundation.

Smith, Tom W. 1987. "Classifying Protestant Denominations." General Social Survey Methodological Report No. 43.

Stevens, Gillian, and Joo Hyun Cho. 1985. "Socioeconomic Indexes and the New 1980 Census Occupational Classification Scheme." *Social Science Research* 14:142–168.

Sweet, James A., and Larry L. Bumpass. 1990. "Religious Differentials in Marriage Behavior and Attitudes." NSFH Working Paper No. 15, University of Wisconsin.

Thornton, Arland. 1979. "Religion and Fertility: The Case of Mormonism." *Journal of Marriage and the Family* 41(1):131–142.

Thornton, Arland. 1991. "Influence of the Marital History of Parents on the Marital and Cohabitational Experiences of Children." *American Journal of Sociology* 96(4):868–894.

Thornton, Arland, William G. Axinn, and Daniel H. Hill. 1992. "Reciprocal Effects of Religiosity, Cohabitation, and Marriage." *American Journal of Sociology* 98(3):628–651.

Thornton, Arland, William G. Axinn, and Jay D. Teachman. 1995. "The Influence of School Enrollment and Accumulation on Cohabitation and Marriage in Early Adulthood." *American Sociological Review* 60 (October):762–774.

Tomes, Nigel. 1985. "Religion and the Earnings Function." *AEA Papers and Proceedings* (May):245–250.

Waite, Linda J., and Judith Sheps Friedman. 1997. "The Impact of Religious Upbringing and Marriage Markets on Jewish Intermarriage." *Contemporary Jewry* 18:1–23.

Waite, Linda J., and Glenna D. Spitze. 1981. "Young Women's Transition to Marriage." *Demography* 18:681–694.

Waters, Melissa, Will C. Heath, and John K. Watson. 1995. "A Positive Model of the Determination of Religious Affiliation." *Social Science Quarterly* 76(1):105–123.

13

A Typology of Processes of Commitment to Marriage:

Why Do Partners Commit to Problematic Relationships?

CATHERINE A. SURRA and CHRISTINE R. GRAY

> "You've got to dance with who brung you.
> Swing with who swung you.
> Life ain't no 40-yard dash.
> Be in it for the long run.
> In the long-run you'll have more fun
> If you dance with who brung you to the bash."
> —Ray Benson, *Asleep at the Wheel*

INTRODUCTION

In this lyric from their popular song, the Texas swing band Asleep at the Wheel is cautioning their listeners about commitment. The band conveys the message that people should stick *by* their partners—even at a dance hall—and stick *with* their partners until the end. Their message is unusual, for most popular songs of any musical genre do not have to do with commitment, but with love—love found, love lost, and love betrayed. Their message is important because if individuals want to understand why their love relationships break up or why they last, they should be more concerned about commitment and its maintenance than they are about love. Likewise, professionals who want to understand why relationships do or do not end should focus on commitment, the construct that directly concerns the stability of relationships.

In previous research (Surra and Hughes, 1997), we have identified different processes by which premarital partners become more or less com-

mitted to marrying one another over time. The different processes constitute a typology of pathways of commitment to marriage. We call them
processes of commitment because the types are derived from information
about how and why commitment to marrying evolves over time. The
types are formed on the basis of three sources of information: information
about progressions and regressions in commitment, the amount of variability in commitment, and partners' own explanations for why their commitment changed over time. One purpose of the study reported here is to
determine whether the typology identified previously replicates with data
obtained from a more diverse, random sample. A second purpose is to
examine whether the types differ with respect to key factors that are
believed to foster commitment to heterosexual relationships. In particular,
we are trying to understand why in one type of process partners appear to
remain committed even though their relationships are problematic and
relatively unsatisfying.

A larger goal of this program of research is to understand what it is about
the early history of relationships that result in marriage that predicts later
marital success, where success is defined in terms of spouses' satisfaction
with and the permanence of their unions. Many scholars have attempted to
answer questions about why some marriages are successful and others are
not (e.g., Bradbury, 1998; Gottman, 1994; Huston and Vangelisti, 1991;
Matthews et al., 1996). The investigations designed to answer this question
usually study people who are already married, and follow the spouses over
time (see, for example, Bradbury, 1998). Such research implicitly assumes
that relationships sour after marriage, and ignores the possibility that the
roots of marital success are planted early while the partners are dating.
Some research on subsequent marital success has looked at the courtship
period; however, the data on courtship are usually retrospective, based on
already married partners' memories of their dating experiences (e.g., Huston and Houts, 1998; Kelly et al., 1985; Orbuch et al., 1993; Surra et al., 1988;
Veroff et al., 1993). The problem with studying the courtships of people
already married is that we do not know why some decide to wed and others do not. In addition, data derived from memories of courtship may not
yield a valid and reliable picture of what really occurs during dating. Still
other research on marital success has been done on partners who were not
yet married, but who were already engaged to wed or planning marriage
at the start of the study (e.g., Hahlweg et al., 1998; Lindahl et al., 1998; for
an exception, see Hill and Peplau, 1998). This method cannot reveal the way
partners utilize diagnostic information about the merits of their relationships from their beginnings. The research reported here is aimed at over-
coming some of these limitations.

Another goal of this program of research is to understand how people
go about choosing a mate. Although researchers have devoted consider-

able attention to factors that they think influence the selection of mates (see Surra, 1990, for a review), surprisingly few inquiries have been aimed at the factors that partners *themselves* consider when making mate selection decisions (for an exception, see Bolton, 1961). Decisions of whether and whom to wed are among the most consequential decisions individuals make over the course of their lives. It is particularly important to know what partners think about when they choose mates. Do some individuals, for example, carefully weigh the quality of their match and the characteristics of their partners whereas others ignore or minimize the significance of such information? Do individuals adjust their commitment accordingly when they have high levels of conflict in their relationships or after learning that their partner has a mean streak or is repeatedly unfaithful? Under what circumstances do partners persist with high commitment or terminate relationships in the face of negative information? People's own reasons for committing to marriage tell the story of what people know about their relationships and how they act on what they know. Reasons for commitment are valuable to study because they are accessible to education and intervention programs aimed at adolescents and young adults of dating and marriageable age.

Defining Commitment

Definitions of commitment have in common a concern with the continuation of relationships over time. (For a review, see Surra et al., 1999.) Definitions include decisions to continue a relationship (Johnson, 1991), the intention to remain in a relationship over the long run (Rusbult, 1983, 1991), the desire or motivation to continue a relationship (Sacher and Fine, 1996), and beliefs about whether the relationship will continue over the long run (Surra and Hughes, 1997).

Most definitions of commitment are global definitions, which means that they ignore the particular relational context (Surra et al., 1999). In the study of heterosexual relationships, for example, most definitions make no distinction between commitment to continuation of a dating relationship, commitment to getting or staying married, or commitment to a long-term cohabiting relationship. In other words, definitions do not allow for the variety of forms of relationships to which partners can be committed. This lack of specification is unfortunate because the relationship context is sure to bring into play different causes of commitment. Partners' commitment to a recreational dating relationship, for instance, is apt to be more affected by the rewards they derive from the relationship than it is by any moral obligation to continue it. Commitment to marriage, in contrast, is likely to bring to bear the full force of the moral, normative, economic, and legal considerations that constrain participation in this social institution.

Our research on commitment has focused on commitment to marriage among never-married premarital partners and married partners. We define marital commitment as partners' beliefs about the likelihood that they will form and maintain a marriage to a particular partner for the fore-seeable future (Surra and Hughes, 1997).

Outsiders' and Insiders' Views of the Causes of Commitment

Scholars generally agree that personal, moral, and structural factors combine to promote or interfere with commitment (see for example, Adams and Jones, 1997; Johnson, 1991; Kelley, 1983; Rusbult, 1980, 1983, 1991; Stanley and Markman, 1992; Surra et al., 1999). Personal factors include attractions to the relationship, dedication to the relationship, inter-personal attitudes such as love or trust, and satisfaction with the relation-ship. Moral influences on commitment include pledges or promises to maintain the relationship, feelings of obligation that stem from personal orientations or religious beliefs, and individuals' more general values regarding the importance of following through with lines of action once begun. Structural factors stem from the economic and social context of the relationship. Examples of structural factors are investments in the rela-tionship, the quality and attractiveness of alternatives to being in the rela-tionship (e.g., getting another partner or being alone), pressures from the social network to maintain or discontinue the relationship, and the like.

The personal, moral, and structural causes of commitment constitute social psychological conditions thought to influence commitment. These conditions are only one source of influence, however, the influences that researchers, or outsiders to the relationship, believe are important. Another set of influences is insiders' own reasons for becoming commit-ted, that is, the set of causes that partners themselves weigh when making commitment decisions. (See Surra et al., 1999, for more on this distinction.) Insiders' reasons include, for instance, partners' beliefs about whether marriage is a desirable or necessary state, whether their relationship is suited for marriage, their interpretations of interactions that take place within the relationship and with third parities, and their life circum-stances. Insiders' views of the causes of commitment may or may not over-lap with outsiders' views, depending on the extent to which partners themselves weigh the factors that researchers say are important to com-mitment. A full understanding requires attention to both insiders' and out-siders' assessments of the factors that influence commitment.

In this chapter, we use information from both insiders and outsiders' explanations of commitment. First, we identify different types of commit-ment based on the insiders' views of the causes of commitment and other information about commitment. Then we examine whether the types also differ with respect to social psychological conditions thought to affect commitment. In the next section, we summarize the research that led to the study reported here.

Processes of Commitment to Marriage

We have studied commitment to wed by having married individuals or dating partners graph how their estimates of the chance of marriage to their partners changed over the course of their relationships. The estimate is plotted on a graph with the chance of marriage, which ranges from 0 to 100%, along the Y-axis and time in months along the X-axis (cf. Huston et al., 1981). Each time respondents report a change in the chance of marriage they tell in their own words why it occurred. We code these explanations into different categories called *reasons for commitment*. The reasons represent insiders' views of the causes of commitment.

In our early studies, newlyweds reconstructed from memory the evolution of commitment to wed throughout their courtship. This research showed significant associations between the reasons newlyweds gave for changes in commitment and the way in which commitment changed on the graphs (Surra et al., 1988). Reasons that concern interaction with and beliefs about the social network, that is, the third parties with whom newlyweds were involved, were associated with declines in commitment. Some reasons were associated with upturns in commitment; for example, reasons that concern activities done together or time spent together, referred to as behavioral interdependence, and reasons that refer to positive beliefs about the partnership. Some reasons were associated with changes in commitment that occurred at a fast rate, such as those that referred to disclosure of information to the partner or reasons that involved the social network. Other reasons, such as those involving behavioral interdependence, were associated with slow rates of change in commitment. Some of the same reasons that were associated with declines in commitment and fast changes in commitment were also related to less satisfaction with the marriage 4 years later. The results of the newlywed studies suggested the hypothesis that different pathways to marital commitment can be identified and that the different pathways may lead to different relationship outcomes.

Surra and Hughes (1997) tested this hypothesis on a sample of 60 college-student dating couples, who first graphed the early stages of their relationships from memory and then reported concurrently on recent changes in commitment. The goal was to identify groups of partners based on differences in the reasons they reported for commitment and the characteristics of changes in the graphs. The groups were identified on the basis of two characteristics derived from the graphs, the rate of changes in commitment and declines in commitment, and seven types of reasons for commitment that previous research indicated had strong associations with the graphs (see Surra and Hughes, 1997, for details). We used cluster analysis to identify the groups of partners.

This method resulted in two groups of partners each of whom engaged in a different commitment process. We called the groups relationship-driven commitments and event-driven commitments. For relationship-driven partners, changes in commitment were mostly positive and occurred at a moderate rate. Relationship-driven partners more often gave reasons for changes in commitment that concerned activities and time spent together and positive beliefs about the relationship. Relationship-driven men also referred more to the couples' interaction with the social network and to positive beliefs about the social network. On an objectively derived measure of compatibility between partners on their preferences for leisure activities, relationship-driven women were more compatible than event-driven women. On standard questionnaire measures, relationship-driven partners reported less conflict, less ambivalence about getting seriously involved, more satisfaction at the start of the study, and greater increases in satisfaction over a 1-year period. Relationship-driven commitments parallel the depiction of compatibility testing in the literature on mate selection, in which commitment decisions are thought to be based on time spent together and positive views of the relationship that result from interaction.

Findings from the study of college students revealed a second commitment process, called event-driven. In this case, changes in commitment were more likely to be negative, and both positive and negative changes occurred at a relatively fast rate (Surra and Hughes, 1997). According to partners' accounts of why their commitment changed, the rockiness of commitment stemmed from negative occurrences punctuated by positive ones. The accounts showed a preponderance of references to conflict episodes, negative beliefs about the partnership, and negative beliefs involving the network. Explanations of network interaction focused on the partners' separate, rather than joint, networks, suggesting that separate network interaction may prevail and may interfere with the development of a joint social group. Women who had event-driven commitments were less compatible with their partners on preferences for leisure activities, and event-driven men and women reported more conflict. On standard indicators, event-driven partners had more ambivalence about involvement, and were less satisfied, both at the start of the study and 1 year later.

One limitation of the research on the commitment processes is that the data were obtained from a college student sample. The sample was homogeneous with respect to education, race, ethnicity, and social class. As a result, the generalizability of the processes to a more diverse population is uncertain. In the study reported here, we examine whether the typology of commitment processes replicates with a larger, more diverse, randomly selected sample of couples.

Partners in the event-driven group described their relationship in more negative, ambivalent terms, said it was more conflict ridden, and had less satisfaction than did those in the relationship-driven group. Despite these differences, the two groups did not differ on any measure of involvement, including length of relationship, stage of involvement (e.g., causal versus serious dating), level of commitment, or whether they broke up after 1 year (Surra and Hughes, 1997). One question remains: Why do event-driven partners stay in such problematic, unsatisfying relationships while they are dating? In the next section, we examine four sets of explanations for why partners might remain committed to unsatisfying relationships. These explanations are grounded in social psychological theories of the causes of commitment that were described in the previous section.

Commitment Processes and Social Psychological Conditions

Partners may stay in unrewarding, unsatisfying relationships because they feel they have to (Johnson, 1991), that is, they are constrained or feel constrained by the social structure in which the relationship is embedded (cf. Johnson, 1991; Levinger, 1991). One source of constraint is that individuals may perceive that they have few viable alternative options. They may believe that were they to end the relationship, other relationships would be equally unrewarding, their economic well-being would suffer, or their overall quality of life would deteriorate. Taken together, such beliefs constitute the perceived quality of alternative options. Other sources of constraint are pressures from the social network to continue the relationship and investments of resources in it. When social pressures and investments in the relationship are high, partners will feel constrained to remain in the relationship even though it is unrewarding. Thus, Hypothesis 1 is that event-driven partners will report more structural constraints than will relationship-driven partners.

Another possibility is that event-driven relationships have attractions that keep partners committed. These attractions may differ from those that keep relationship-driven partners committed. Previous work on event-driven commitments suggested that when the relationship is going badly partners perceive some positive event that jolts their commitment out of its decline (Surra and Hughes, 1997). The very drama of event-driven relationships may be attractive. This possibility led Surra and Hughes (1997) to propose that the commitments of event-driven and relationship-driven partners are rooted in different kinds of love. Passionate love is believed to be fueled by need for the other, feelings of uncontrollableness, sexual attraction, and obstacles (Hatfield and Sprecher, 1986; Kelley, 1983). The love experienced by partners in event-driven relationships may be flamed by the very drama of events and the instability of their commitment. The love felt by relationship-driven partners may be based more in friendship-based love. This type of love evolves out of enjoyment of interaction, compatibility, and mutual trust and involvement (Grote and Frieze, 1994; Kelley, 1983). Thus, Hypothesis 2a is that relationship-driven partners will report more friendship-based love than will event-driven partners. Hypothesis 2b is that event-driven partners will report more passionate love than will relationship-driven partners.

Partners in event-driven commitments reported that they were more ambivalent about getting involved than were partners in relationship-driven commitments (Surra and Hughes, 1997). This ambivalence may be a key reason why partners remain in relatively conflict-ridden, unhappy relationships. Over time, partners may give and receive mixed messages to one another about how involved they are or want to be. Under such persistent conditions of uncertainty, partners will become hypervigilant for information relevant to commitment, interpreting every event that comes along as commitment enhancing or commitment reducing (Surra, 1995a). A similar phenomenon might result under conditions of medium or uncertain trust (Holmes and Rempel, 1989). When partners do not trust their partners' attachment to them, all information is potentially diagnostic of how their partners' feel about them. Hypothesis 3 is that event-driven partners will be more ambivalent about involvement and will have less trust in their partners than will relationship-driven partners.

Hypothesis 4 is that event-driven partners will make more self-attributions for problems in the relationship than will relationship-driven partners. This hypothesis is derived from theories and findings on why women stay in abusive relationships. According to this hypothesis, which has received some limited support, women in abusive relationships blame themselves for the problem, either their character or their own behaviors, more than they blame their partners or other factors (Andrew and Brewin, 1990; Hilberman, 1980; Holtzworth-Monroe, 1988; Shields and Hanneke, 1983; Walker, 1979). In situations of self-blame, individuals may be more inclined to stay in negative relationships. We tested this hypothesis indirectly by examining attributions made to the self and partner for why commitment changes in relationships.

METHOD

This study was conducted in three phases that took place over a 9-month span. Phase 1 was a long interview that lasted from 1 to 3 hours.

Phase 2 was a series of seven short interviews (15 to 30 minutes) conducted about once per month. Phase 3 was another long interview that occurred about 1 month after the completion of Phase 2. All interviews were face to face, and coupled partners always were interviewed separately. Only data from and the procedure for Phase 1 are reported in this chapter.

Sample

Participants were recruited by means of random digit dialing of phone numbers in greater Austin, Texas. Eligible participants were single, had never been married, were between the ages of 19 and 35 years, were currently in a heterosexual dating relationship, and were available to be interviewed over a 9-month period. Approximately 36,000 phone calls generated the eligible persons who were invited to participate. Those who agreed to participate were asked to give the name and address of their dating partners, who were then contacted separately about participating. Out of 861 eligible people identified in the phone calls, 27% agreed to participate, their partners also agreed to participate, and both partners did participate. In all, 464 individuals, 232 couples, completed the initial interview.

The sample was diverse with respect to race, ethnicity, and social class, and participants were somewhat representative of the population from which they were drawn. When asked about their race, 70% of the respondents said they were Anglo, 16% said Hispanic, 8% said African-American, 6% said Asian or Pacific Islanders, and less than 1% said Native American. According to the demographics for 19 to 34 year olds living in the Austin standard metropolitan statistical area, 58% are Anglos, 19% are Hispanic, 9% are African-American, 4% are Asian or Pacific Islanders, and 0.30% are Native American. Thus, compared to the population of young adults in Austin, those who participated in the study were somewhat more likely to be Anglo, but slightly less likely to be Hispanic, African-American, or Asian. With respect to educational level, 76% had some college education or a college degree, and 9% went on to or completed graduate or professional school. One percent did not finish high school, and 14% had a high school diploma. Students comprised 33% of the sample. About half of the sample reported that the annual income that they themselves earned was between $5,000 and $20,000. Another 22% earned between $20,000 and $50,000, and 26% earned less than $5,000. A small percentage (2%) earned more than $50,000 per year.

Procedure

During the first interview, respondents answered questions about their personal and family backgrounds. Then they completed questionnaires that assessed personality characteristics, and they rated their individual preferences for doing selected leisure, domestic, and interpersonal activities. During the next part of the interview, respondents were asked to construct from memory a graph of changes in the chance of marriage to their partner over the course of their relationship. The graphing procedure incorporated techniques to minimize error due to faulty recall (Fitzgerald and Surra, 1981). The interviewer rechecked information obtained throughout the interview, gathered the data in chronological order, and provided contextual cues and a novel task (constructing the graph) to stimulate memory. Respondents were shown a blank graph that had "chance of marriage," which ranged from 0 to 100%, on the vertical axis, and "time" in months on the horizontal axis. The chance of marriage was defined this way:

> There may have been times when you have thought, with different degrees of certainty, about the possibility of marrying [the partner]. These thoughts have been based on *your* ideas about eventually marrying [the partner] and on what you think have been [the partner's] thoughts about marrying you. Taking both of these things into consideration, we will graph how the chance of marrying [the partner] has changed over the time you have had a relationship.

Participants were told that if they were certain they would never marry their partner or if they had never even thought about marriage even briefly, the chance of marriage would be 0%, but if they were certain they would eventually marry their partner the chance would be 100%. The definition asked respondents to consider their own and their partner's feelings about marriage because committing to wed cannot be done unilaterally. Participants were asked not to equate the chance of marriage with their degree of love for or desire to marry their partners, but to consider all factors.

The date when the relationship began and the date of the interview (*today*) and other key events were marked on the bottom of the graph. The chance of marriage today and the chance at the beginning of the relationship were marked. Respondents were asked when they were first aware that the chance of marriage had changed from its initial value. The new value was marked, and respondents were asked about the shape of the line that should connect the two points. The period of time covered by the line that connects the two points constitutes a *turning point*. After the line was drawn, the interviewer asked, "Tell me, in as specific terms as possible, what happened here from [date] to [date] that made the chance of marriage go [up/down] [____%]?" Participants were asked, "Is there anything else that happened . . ." until they said, "No." These two questions provided an account of the reasons for the change in commitment. Then they were asked when they were next aware that the chance of marriage had changed, and the structured questions were repeated for each turning point until the graph was completed to *today*. The graphing portion of the interview was audiotaped. Respondents were asked to indicate on the graph when any of these four stages of involvement had occurred: (1) casually dating, a time when the partners did not see themselves as a couple, and they may or may not have been dating others; (2) seriously dating, a time when each partner and other people saw them as a couple; (3) privately committed to marriage, which meant that the partners had arrived at a private understanding that they would get married; and (4) engaged, which meant that the couple had made an official commitment to marry and had announced their intentions to others.

Respondents who said they would never marry because they were philosophically opposed to marriage were given the option of graphing lifelong commitment instead of chance of marriage. Seven respondents chose this option at Phase 1.

After the graph was completed, respondents filled out questionnaires and provided other information about their relationships. In this chapter, we report data from one questionnaire that included items from three measures: a passionate love scale (Hatfield and Sprecher, 1986), a friendship-based love scale (Grote and Frieze, 1994), and a dyadic trust scale (Larzelere and Huston, 1980). Items on this questionnaire were rated on a seven-point Likert scale ranging from 1 (*strongly disagree*) to 7 (*strongly agree*). Participants also rated on nine-point scales items that measured four relationship dimensions: love, conflict and negativity, ambivalence about serious involvement, and relationship maintenance (Braiker and Kelley, 1979). Two questionnaires were administered to assess factors predictive of commitment (Stanley and Markman, 1992) and perceived alternatives to the relationship (Udry, 1981). Items for these questionnaires were rated on seven-point and four-point Likert scales, respectively. Satisfaction with the relationship was rated on a 10-item, seven-point semantic differential scale with bipolar adjectives (e.g., miserable/enjoyable, hopeful/discouraging) and a single-item rating of satisfaction with the relationship (Huston and Vangelisti, 1991). Respondents were paid $20 for completing the Phase 1 interview.

Measurement

Variability in Commitment to Marriage. We assessed the degree of variability of commitment to marriage by means of variables derived from the Phase 1 graphs. *Proportion of downturns*, a measure of regressions in commitment, is the number of downturns in the graph divided by the total number of turning points in the graph. The *mean absolute slope* is an aver-

age rate of change in commitment per month, regardless of whether commitment increased or decreased.[1] To obtain information about rate of
change separately for increases and decreases, we also calculated the *mean
slope of positive turning points and the mean slope of negative turning points.*

Reasons for Commitment.   Accounts of commitment were transcribed
from audiotapes, and were coded into separate reasons using a coding
scheme that was developed from qualitative analyses in earlier studies
(Surra, 1995b). Definitions and examples of the categories of reasons
reported in this chapter are shown in the Appendix. Cohen's κ averaged
81% between independent coders for the half of the Phase 1 transcripts
that was checked for reliability. The proportion of reasons in each category
was calculated by dividing the frequency of reasons in the category by the
total number of reasons reported in the graph.

Predictors of Commitment.   To assess the hypothesized social psychological predictors of commitment, we factor analyzed each scale. (For
details on the analyses and results, contact the first author.) Factor scores
are used in all analyses.

In this chapter, we report data on three structural constraints: alternatives to the relationship, investments, and positive social concern for the
relationship. We employed four different measures of alternatives to the
relationship; three of these were derived from a scale developed by Udry
(1981): *ease of partner replacement,* or the ease with which the partner could
be replaced with a better one; *prospects for a happy life* (e.g., If your relationship were to end, how likely is it that your life would be ruined), and
alternative economic well-being (e.g., If your relationship were to end, how
likely is it that you would be better off economically). The final measure of
alternatives, which was derived from Stanley and Markman's (1992)
measure of predictors of commitment, is the degree to which respondents
report a *desire for alternative partners* (e.g., I think a lot about what it would
be like to be dating someone other than my partner). For measures of
alternatives, higher scores indicate that the alternative is viewed as more
attractive. The two remaining measures of structural constraints were also
derived from Stanley and Markman's scale: *investments* (e.g., I have put a
number of tangible, valuable resources into this relationship) and *positive
social concern* (e.g., My family really wants this relationship to work).

Four subscales were derived from the one questionnaire used to assess
love and trust: *passionate love* (e.g., I sense my body responding when
[partner] touches me); *friendship-based love* (e.g., The companionship I
share with my partner is an important part of my love for him/her); *trust
in a partner's benevolence* (e.g., My partner treats me fairly and justly); and

trust in a partner's honesty (e.g., I feel that I can trust my partner completely). *Ambivalence* about serious involvement (e.g., To what extent do you feel "trapped" or pressured to continue in this relationship) was assessed using the results of the factor analysis of Braiker and Kelley's (1979) measure of relationship dimensions.

RESULTS

The first question is: Does the typology of commitment processes identified from the college student sample (Surra and Hughes, 1997) replicate with a randomly selected sample? In this study, we used the same variables from Phase 1 data and the same method (a cluster analysis) that were used originally to group partners into different types of commitment. The variables included two derived from the graphs, proportion of downturns and mean absolute slope of turning points, and seven of the reasons categories, which are defined in the Appendix: behavioral interdependence, conflict, positive and negative attributions about the relationship, separate network interaction, joint network interaction, and positive network attribution. Of the 464 participants, 24 were not included in identification of the typology. Of these 24, 13 reported no changes in the chance of marriage over the course of their relationship, and, as a result, reported no reasons; three were missing transcripts because of equipment failure during the interviews, seven chose to graph lifelong commitment instead of chance of marriage, and one was an outlier on mean absolute slope (i.e., a 100% change in the chance of marriage in a 1-day period) and could not be entered into the cluster analysis.

The results of the cluster analysis indicated two very distinct clusters.[2] All individuals included in the analysis fell clearly into one of the two groups.

We examined differences between the two groups on the variables used to create them. The results on these variables replicated those reported by Surra and Hughes (1997) almost exactly. Therefore, we named the groups relationship-driven and event-driven commitments. Compared to relationship-driven partners, event-driven partners had a higher average proportion of downturns (33.5 versus 10.9% for women and 32.0 versus 11.7% for men) and a greater average rate of change per turning point (23.0 versus 12.0% for men and 28.0 versus 13.0% for women). The differences between the groups on proportions of reasons for commitment are shown in Figure 13.1 for women and Figure 13.2 for men.[3] Relationship-driven men and women made relatively more references, on average, to positive dyadic attributions, behavioral interdependence, joint network interaction, and positive network attributions than did event-driven men and women. Event-driven men and women made relatively more references, on average, to conflict, negative dyadic attributions, and separate network interaction than did their relationship-driven counterparts.

It is possible that the major difference between relationship-driven and event-driven commitments on graph variables is due entirely to downturns in the graphs; that is, it could be that the rate differences between the two groups all stem from rates of change of downturns. Closer examination of other variables derived from the graphs indicates that this is not the case. Event-driven partners had faster rates of change than relationship-driven partners on both positive and negative turning points. For women, the average rate of change of positive turning points was 21.7% per month for event-driven partners and 11.8% for relationship-driven partners, t (147) = 2.47, $p < .05$, whereas the average rate for negative turning points was –5.6% for relationship-driven partners and –29.8% for event-driven partners, t (124) = –2.82, $p < .01$. For men, the average rate of change for positive turning points was 25.1% per month for event-driven partners and 11.6% for relationship-driven partners, t (125) = 3.01, $p < .01$, whereas the average rate for negative turning points was –12.5% for relationship-driven partners and -38.2% for event-driven partners, t (125) = –2.35, $p < .05$.

The number of people in each commitment process was close to equal; 221 respondents fell into the relationship-driven group and 219 into the event-driven group. In 32% of the couples (n = 67), both partners were event driven, and in 30% (n = 64), both were relationship driven. In 15% of the couples (n = 32), the male partner was event driven and the female partner was relationship driven. In the remaining 24% of the couples (n = 50), the male partner was relationship driven and the female partner was event driven. Thus, in most cases coupled partners fell into the same commitment process, although for a substantial minority this was not the case.[4]

Figure 13.3 shows a graph from one respondent in each type. Both of the respondents are women, but similar examples are easily found for men. Consistent with the findings in Figure 13.1 and Figure 13.2, the woman in the relationship-driven group made frequent references to spending time and doing activities together and to positive beliefs about the partner and the relationship, as seen in this quotation for the first increase of 50% over a 12-week period:

> I had moved from one place to another during that time and he was extremely helpful and very supportive and encouraging. . . . There's nothing really specific of what happened. It's the fact that I've been able to communicate with him whenever I've had a problem with this or that . . . to say right or wrong this is how I feel . . . and he reciprocates.

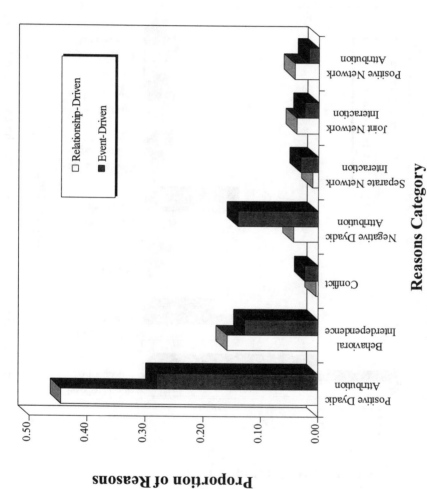

Figure 13.1. Cluster means on reasons for commitment for men.

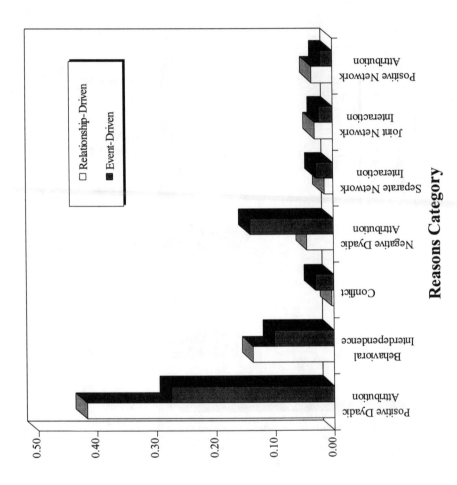

Figure 13.2.   Cluster means on reasons for commitment for women.

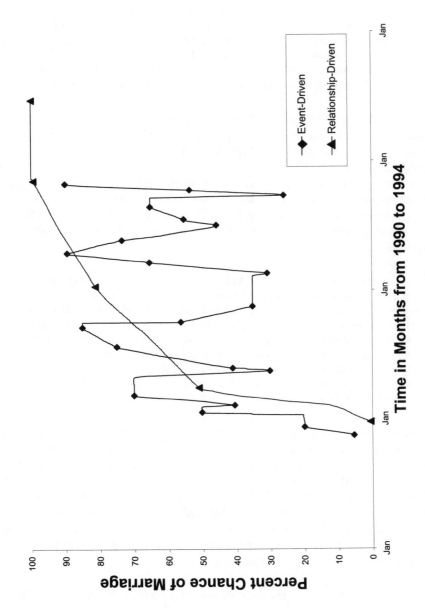

Figure 13.3. Sample graphs of relationship-driven and event-driven commitments.

She gave a similar account of the next increase of 30% over 37 weeks:

> When I moved in next door, he would come over and stay with me 2 or 3
> nights a week and working with his work schedule . . . I just finally said,
> "Why don't you move all your stuff over here because you're here more of
> the time than you're *not*. . . . And those nights I get off work we like to wake
> up and then we have coffee together before I go to bed and he goes up to
> work. . . . We just started spending more time together and we talked."

The defining characteristics of relationship-driven commitments are
evident here, with the moderately paced changes in commitment that are
attributed to interaction with the partner and to the positive reaction to the
quality of that interaction.

The partner with an event-driven commitment in Figure 13.3 had a different experience. The first large downturn in commitment, a 40%
decrease over 9 weeks (Turning Point 5), is attributed to her sole interaction with the network, then to negative beliefs about the relationship, then
to conflict:

> I got invited to my cousin's wedding, and before asking Thomas to go with
> me, I went ahead and asked my dad because it was my cousin's wedding on
> my mother's side of the family, and my dad is on somewhat shaky terms
> with my mother's side of the family. But my dad wanted to go. I spoke to my
> dad about having Thomas go, because first of all, we are a racially mixed
> couple and . . . my mother's side of the family is fairly prejudiced against
> anyone other than Mexicans so my dad didn't think it was a good idea that
> I took Thomas along. . . . So Thomas was mad at me because my family was
> somewhat prejudiced against him even though they hadn't met him.

Subsequently, she went to the wedding without him, and the partner
got even angrier because he had "expected her not to go." Her description
of the interaction with the separate network surrounding the wedding and
the conflict with her partner is characteristic of the way in which event-
driven partners take note of singular occurrences in accounting for commitment. The volatility of these relationships and the manner in which
such downturns get reversed is illustrated in the next upturn (Turning
Point 6), where there are references to the resolution of the conflict and to
positive beliefs about the relationship:

> When I came back from my cousin's wedding, finally after we started talk-
> ing again, we came to an understanding about the whole situation as to why
> I decided to go. . . . We came to an understanding that, even though my fam-
> ily hasn't met him and may not like him, that doesn't mean that I'm gonna
> turn away from my family just for him.

Another conflict ensued at the next downturn, a 30% decline over 2 weeks (Turning Point 9) over the fact that he quit his job to start his own company. She had no problem with his quitting, but they fought because he could no longer pay his share of their rent. The next two downturns were also attributed to arguments involving his business conflicting with the relationship. She attributed the resolution of the conflicts once again to incidents of positive self-disclosure, in which he apologized and they talked about the problems. She also reported: "He asked me if I would help [with his business] and I said, 'Yes,' and we actually started working together" (Turning Point 12). As the later downturns indicate, however, the resolution was followed by more conflicts and more short-lived resolutions. We turn now to tests of hypotheses regarding the social psychological conditions thought to affect commitment.

Commitment Processes and Social Psychological Conditions

The first hypothesis is that event-driven partners will score higher on structural constraints than will relationship-driven partners. The analyses showed no support for the hypotheses (see Table 13.1). In fact, the results were opposite of what was expected. With respect to alternatives, both men and women in event-driven commitments believed they would fare better without the present partner. Relationship-driven women reported that they desired alternative partners less than did event-driven women, although no such effect was found for men. Relationship-driven men reported more positive concern on the part of the network than did event-driven men. Compared to their relationship-driven counterparts, event-driven women thought that they would have an easier time replacing their partners, and event-driven men thought they would fare better economically without their partners. No differences were found for prospects for a happy life or for investments.

We also hypothesized that relationship-driven partners would report more friendship-based love than event-driven partners but that the reverse would be true for passionate love. We found no support for either hypothesis (see Table 13.1), and no differences at all on scores for passionate or friendship-based love.

Hypothesis 3 was confirmed for both men and women, although the findings were somewhat stronger for men (see Table 13.1). Compared to relationship-driven men, event-driven men were more ambivalent about serious involvement and had less trust in the benevolence of and the honesty of their partners. For women, the strongest difference between the two groups was for trust in a benevolent partner; for trust in an honest partner and for ambivalence, the significance of the group difference was borderline for women.

Table 13.1. Means for Structural Constraints, Love, Trust, and Ambivalence by Commitment Process and Gender[a]

Variable	Relationship Driven[b]	Event Driven[c]	t
Women			
Structural constraints			
Alternatives to relationship[d]			
Ease of partner replacement	−.292	.077	3.34**
Prospects for a happy life	−.039	.075	1.13
Economic well-being	.019	.023	0.11
Desire for alternative partner	−.434	−.092	−2.91**
Positive social concern	.072	−.091	−1.26
Investments	−.076	.092	1.45
Passionate love	.075	−.023	−0.75
Friendship-based love	.234	.052	−1.60
Trust in a partner's benevolence	.284	−.280	−4.97***
Trust in a partner's honesty	.093	−.122	−1.74†
Ambivalence	−.259	−.058	1.91†
Men			
Structural constraints			
Alternatives to relationship[d]			
Ease of partner replacement	−.066	.127	1.61
Prospects for a happy life	−.079	−.008	0.66
Economic well-being	−.133	.107	2.30*
Desire for alternative partner	.142	.313	1.50
Positive social concern	.168	−.088	−2.15*
Investments	.001	−.001	−0.01
Passionate love	.072	−.054	−1.06
Friendship-based love	−.032	−.195	−1.49
Trust in a partner's benevolence	.184	−.206	−3.58***
Trust in a partner's honesty	.168	−.096	−2.17*
Ambivalence	.001	.325	2.79**

[a]Means are factor scores.
[b]$n = 101$ for women and $n = 120$ for men.
[c]$n = 118$ for women and $n = 101$ for men.
[d]For alternatives, higher scores indicate higher quality alternatives.
†$p < .08$; *$p < .05$; **$p < .01$; ***$p < .001$.

The findings were fairly consistent with Hypothesis 4: event-driven partners made more self-attributions for problems in the relationship than did relationship-driven partners (see Table 13.2). We tested this hypothesis using the proportion of reasons for commitment that were coded as positive and negative self-attributions, as defined in the Appendix. Both men and women in event-driven commitments made more self-attributions than did partners in relationship-driven commitments. The difference for women was significant only for negative self-attributions whereas for

Table 13.2. Mean Proportion of Self-Attributions by Commitment Process and Gender[a]

Reason	Relationship Driven[b]	Event Driven[c]	t
Women			
Positive self-attribution	.003	.004	0.75
Negative self-attribution	.003	.009	3.41**
Men			
Positive self-attribution	.003	.007	2.13*
Negative self-attribution	.002	.004	0.72

[a]Mean proportions are arc sine transformations.
[b]$n = 101$ for women and $n = 120$ for men.
[c]$n = 118$ for women and $n = 101$ for men.
*$p < .05$; **$p < .01$.

men it was significant only for positive self-attributions. The following illustrates the way in which event-driven partners employ such self-attributions in their thinking about the relationship. The respondent reported that the partners were spending too much time together, he did not want to do the things she wanted to do, and they failed to communicate. In the next turning point, however, the partner wanted to get more serious about marriage because they were working things out. The respondent said, "I guess I've just tried to address more of my own *personal* problems as far as being patient and try not to be as pushy."

DISCUSSION

In this chapter, we examined both insiders' and outsiders' views of the pathways by which premarital partners become more or less committed to marrying one another over time. We replicated, with a randomly selected sample, a typology of commitment processes. We also tested hypotheses about how social psychological conditions that affect commitment operate in each process. The typology identified in previous research (Surra and Hughes, 1997) did replicate, and two commitment processes were identified: relationship driven and event driven.

Relationship-Driven Commitments

The pathway of commitment of relationship-driven partners is made up of mostly positive changes with relatively few declines, and partners perceive that the changes occur at a slow to moderate rate. Roughly 50%, on average, of the increases in commitment for these partners are slow, occurring at a rate between 0 and 5% per month. It appears that relationship-driven partners take their time about making judgments that their commitment to wed has increased appreciably. This pathway is consistent with the reasons partners give for why their commitment changes. For the most part, their reasons concern factors that, according to theories of mate selection, take time to assess. These factors include time spent with and activities done with the partner and positive beliefs about the partnership, such as evaluations of interaction as enjoyable or compatible and of partners as considerate or trustworthy. Of all of the reasons that relationship-driven partners report, positive beliefs about the partnership make up nearly 45% of them, on average. Relationship-driven partners also pay more attention to the role of the coupled partner's joint network in their reports of why commitment changed. A key task confronted by coupled partners who are seriously dating or considering marriage is the joining together of their individual networks. The picture that emerges is that relationship-driven partners test their compatibility and make commitment decisions based on assessments of compatibility.

Analysis of the social psychological conditions that are believed to affect commitment indicates that the commitments of relationship-driven partners are connected to partners' positive interpersonal attitudes and to their positive perceptions of the social and economic context of their relationships. Relationship-driven men score higher on trust in the honesty and benevolence of their partners and lower on ambivalence about involvement than do event-driven men. The findings for relationship-driven women on trust and ambivalence are similar to those for men, although they are a bit weaker. With respect to structural constraints, relationship-driven women report fewer fantasies and desires for another partner than do event-driven women, and they feel that their present partner would be hard to replace with another that is equally good. For relationship-driven men, the constraints involve economics and the social network. They are more apt to report that their family and friends would like the relationship to work and that their economic situation would not be better off without the relationship. The fact that social and economic concerns show up as more significant for men than for women is consistent with other findings (cf. Jacquet and Surra, 1999).

The findings on conditions that affect commitment suggest that constraints may be the wrong word to use to describe the way relationship-driven partners view the context of their relationship. Rather than social and economic forces acting as barriers to ending relationships, the impression conveyed is that relationship-driven partners perceive that their social and economic situation supports a relationship with a number of other positive qualities. Rather than constraint, partners may perceive that their relationship helps to create a social and economic situation that is a source of alternative rewards above and beyond those wrought from the partnership itself.

Event-Driven Commitments

The pathway of event-driven commitments is variable and volatile. Compared to relationship-driven commitments, event-driven commitments evolve with a relatively large number of reversals, and both positive and negative changes happen at a rapid rate. The mean rate of change for both positive and negative turning points averages greater than 20% per month for men and for women, and is 38% per month for negative turning points for men. When reversals in commitment do occur, it often quickly rebounds to former levels.

According to the accounts of commitment, the volatility of event-driven commitments frequently stems from conflicts, negative relationship beliefs, and partners' interactions with the separate network. In between problematic occurrences are positive ones, which often are perceived to resolve earlier difficulties. The resolution is short lived, however, as the same or new problems reappear. Despite the perception of relationship problems, past research showed no differences between event-driven and relationship-driven commitments on several measures of depth of involvement or break up (Surra and Hughes, 1997).

We tested several explanations for why event-driven partners seem to stick with their relationships. Contrary to our hypothesis, event-driven partners are not more structurally constrained than relationship-driven partners. In fact, the reverse is true. Compared to relationship-driven women, event-driven women are more desirous of alternative partners and report that they would be better off with another partner. Event-driven men report lower amounts of positive concern for the relationship from their networks and thought they would be better off economically without the partner. Neither were event-driven partners more passionately in love.

What does seems to matter to event-driven commitments is partners' trust and ambivalence, particularly for men. Trust has to do with confidence that the partner can be relied on and is concerned about one's welfare and beliefs that the partner is truthful and sincere. These beliefs are held less strongly by event-driven than relationship-driven partners. In addition, event-driven partners, particularly men, have greater ambivalence. The items that measured ambivalence in this study have to do with feelings of being trapped, of losing independence, of the partner's demanding too much time and attention, and being confused about feelings about the relationship.

Another explanation for why partners stay in event-driven relation-ships is that they blame themselves more for relationship problems. We tested this hypothesis indirectly by examining the extent to which these partners attributed changes in commitment to the self. Compared to their relationship-driven counterparts, event-driven women report a higher average proportion of reasons that concern negative self-attributions whereas event-driven men report a higher average proportion of reasons that concern positive self-attributions. Event-driven partners may be more likely to see themselves as sources of problems in relationships, and believe that changing the self would help to resolve the problems the cou-ple experiences. An alternative interpretation is that event-driven partners are more inclined to think about the self as an individual than as part of a couple. Partners with a less well-developed couple identity would also be apt to report more individual or self-attributions for changes in commitment.

The findings for the two processes suggest that degree of uncertainty about the relationship plays a key role in the way commitment develops. The degree of uncertainty may affect the nature of the events that partners pay attention to, how often partners perceive that events have meaning for commitment, and how much events are perceived to affect commitment. When confidence in the relationship is high, as seems to be the case with relationship-driven partners, partners may be more apt to focus on their everyday interaction and to make small, smooth increments in their com-mitment. Event-driven partners, in contrast, appear to be more uncertain about where they stand in the relationship and to have lower levels of con-fidence in their partners. Such uncertainty is apt to make these partners hypersensitive to acquiring diagnostic information about commitment (Holmes and Rempel, 1989; Surra, 1995a; Surra and Bohman, 1991). Uncer-tainty, then, helps to explain why event-driven partners are more apt to focus on singular, episodic occurrences when deciding about commitment.

Uncertainty about a romantic relationship may have different sources. On the one hand, it may stem primarily from characteristics of individu-als partners, such as an attachment style that gives rise to low generalized trust. On the other hand, it might also be caused by features of the rela-tionship itself, such as poor quality interaction between partners, high lev-els of conflict, or the pursuit of alternative partners. In addition, in a climate where cohabitation provides a viable alternative to marriage and marital breakdown is common, uncertainty about commitment to mar-riage is likely to be prevalent.

Our work in progress is concentrated on disentangling the causal con-nections among trust, ambivalence, the quality of interaction, insiders' reasons for commitment, and commitment to marriage over time. We are also assessing the progress toward marriage and long-term stability of relationship-driven and event-driven commitments. We are particularly interested in learning more about the mechanisms by which uncertain partners might become increasingly committed to wed, even though they perceive the negativity of their relationships. Finally, we are examining the dynamics of being coupled with a partner who reports the same, or a different, type of commitment process.

ACKNOWLEDGMENTS

Preparation of this chapter was supported by a grant to the first author from The National Institute of Mental Health (R01 MH47975). We would like to thank Karin Samii, Denise Bartell, Susan Jacquet, Jason Gray, and Nate Cottle for their help with this chapter and the others who so diligently coded the accounts contained in nearly 2000 transcripts.

NOTES

1. Mean absolute slope is the sum of the absolute slope of each turning point divided by the total number of turning points in the graph. Absolute slope is the absolute value of percentage change in chance of marriage for each turning point (percentage at the end of the turning point minus percentage at the beginning) divided by the number of months in the turning point.

2. The cluster analysis is done with the individual as the unit of analysis; that is, men and women were included in one analysis. Cluster analysis accommodates any nonindependence of reports from coupled partners. If the covariation between reports from coupled partners is strong, they will fall into the same cluster. If the covariation is weak, they will not. We selected the number of clusters using criteria outlined previously in Surra and Hughes (1997).

3. For the figures and in subsequent analyses, all proportions were transformed into arc sines.

4. In this chapter, we focus on the characteristics of individuals in each type of commitment process. In future research we will examine the characteristics of couples who fall into the same type and into mixed types.

REFERENCES

Adams, Jeffrey M., and Warren H. Jones. 1997. "The Conceptualization of Marital Commitment: An Integrative Analysis." *Journal of Personality and Social Psychology* 72:1177–1196.

Andrews, Bernice, and Chris R. Brewin. 1990. "Attributions of Blame for Marital Violence: A Study of Antecedents and Consequences." *Journal of Marriage and the Family* 52:757– 767.

Benson, Ray. 1992. "Dance with Who Brung You." On *Asleep at the Wheel* [CD]. Austin, TX: (1991).

Bolton, Charles D. 1961. "Mate Selection as the Development of a Relationship." *Marriage and Family Living* 23:234–240.

Bradbury, Thomas N. 1998. *The Developmental Course of Marital Dysfunction.* Cambridge, England: Cambridge University Press.

Braiker, Harriet B., and Harold H. Kelley. 1979. "Conflict in the Development of Close Relationships." Pp. 135–168 in *Social Exchange in Developing Relationships,* edited by R. L. Burgess and T. L. Huston. New York: Academic Press.

Fitzgerald, Nancy M., and Catherine A. Surra. 1981. *Studying the Development of Dyadic Relationships: Explorations into a Retrospective Interview Technique.* Paper presented at the National Council on Family Relationships Preconference Workshop on Theory Construction and Research Methodology, Milwaukee, WI, October.

Gottman, John M. 1994. *What Predicts Divorce? The Relationship Between Marital Processes and Marital Outcomes.* Hillsdale, NJ: Lawrence Erlbaum.

Grote, Nancy K., and Irene H. Frieze. 1994. "The Measurement of Friendship-Based Love in Intimate Relationships." *Personal Relationships* 1:275–300.

Hahlweg, Kurt, Howard J. Markman, Franz Thurmaier, Jochen Engl, and Volker Eckert. 1998. "Prevention of Marital Distress: Results of a German Prospective Longitudinal Study." *Journal of Family Psychology* 12:543–556.

Hatfield, Elaine, and Susan Sprecher. 1986. "Measuring Passionate Love in Intimate Relationships." *Journal of Adolescence* 9:383–410.

Hilberman, Elaine. 1980. "The 'Wife-beater's Wife' Reconsidered." *American Journal of Psychiatry* 137:1336–1347.

Hill, Charles T., and Letitia A. Peplau. 1998. "Premarital Predictors of Relationship Outcomes: A 15-year Follow up of the Boston Couples Study." Pp. 237–278 in *The Developmental Course of Marital Dysfunction,* edited by T. N. Bradbury. Cambridge, England: Cambridge University Press.

Holmes, John, and John K. Rempel. 1989. "Trust in Close Relationships." Pp. 187–220 in *Review of Personality and Social Psychology,* Vol. 10, edited by C. Hendrick. Newbury Park, CA: Sage.

Holtzworth-Monroe, Amy. 1988. "Causal Attributions in Marital Violence: Theoretical and Methodological Issues." *Clinical Psychology Review* 8:331–344.

Huston, Ted L., and Renate M. Houts. 1998. "The Psychological Infrastructure of Courtship and Marriage: The Role of Personality and Compatibility in Romantic Relationships." Pp. 114–151 in *The Developmental Course of Marital Dysfunction,* edited by T. N. Bradburry. Cambridge, England: Cambridge University Press.

Huston, Ted L., and Anita L. Vangelisti. 1991. "Socioemotional Behavior and Satisfaction in Marital Relationships: A Longitudinal Study." *Journal of Personality and Social Psychology* 61:721–733.

Huston, Ted L., Catherine A. Surra, Nancy M. Fitzgerald, and Rodney M. Cate. 1981. "From Courtship to Marriage: Mate Selection as an Interpersonal Process." Pp. 53–88 in *Personal Relationships 2: Developing Personal Relationships,* edited by S. Duck and R. Gilmour. New York: Academic Press.

Jacquet, Susan E., and Catherine A. Surra. 1999. "Parental Divorce and Premarital Couples: Commitment and Other Relationship Characteristics." Manuscript submitted for publication.

Johnson, Michael P. 1991. "Commitment to Personal Relationships." Pp. 117–143 in *Advances in Personal Relationships,* Vol. 3, edited by W. H. Jones and D. Perlman. London: Jessica Kingsley.

Kelley, Harold H. 1983. "Love and Commitment." Pp. 265–314 in *Close Relationships,* edited by H. H. Kelley, E. Berscheid, A. Christensen, J. H. Harvey, T. L. Huston, G. Levinger, E. McClintock, L. A. Peplau, and D. R. Petersen. New York: Freeman.

Kelly, Carol, Ted L. Huston, and Rodney M. Cate. 1985. "Premarital Relationship Correlates of the Erosion of Satisfaction in Marriage." *Journal of Social and Personal Relationships* 2:167–178.

Larzelere, Robert E., and Ted L. Huston. 1980. "The Dyadic Trust Scale: Toward Understanding Interpersonal Trust in Close Relationships." *Journal of Marriage and the Family* 42:595–604.

Levinger, George. 1991. "Commitment vs. Cohesiveness: Two Complementary Perspectives." Pp. 145–150 in *Advances in Personal Relationships*, Vol. 3, edited by W. H. Jones and D. Perlman. London: Jessica Kingsley.

Lindahl, K., Mari Clements, and Howard Markman. 1998. "The Development of Marriage: A 9-year Perspective." Pp. 205–236 in *The Developmental Course of Marital Dysfunction*, edited by T. N. Bradbury. Cambridge, England: Cambridge University Press.

Matthews, Lisa S., K. A. S. Wickrama, and Rand D. Conger. 1996. "Predicting Marital Instability from Spouse and Observer Reports of Marital Interaction." *Journal of Marriage and the Family* 58:641–655.

Orbuch, T. L., Joseph Veroff, and Diane Holmberg. 1993. "Becoming a Married Couple: The Emergence of Meaning in the First Years of Marriage." *Journal of Marriage and the Family* 55:815–826.

Rusbult, Caryl E. 1980. "Commitment and Satisfaction in Romantic Associations: A Test of the Investment Model." *Journal of Experimental Social Psychology* 16:172–186.

Rusbult, Caryl E. 1983. "A Longitudinal Test of the Investment Model: The Development (and Deterioration) of Satisfaction and Commitment in Heterosexual Involvements." *Journal of Personality and Social Psychology* 45:101–117.

Rusbult, Caryl E. 1991. "Commentary on Johnson's 'Commitment to Personal Relationships': What's Interesting, and What's New?" Pp. 151–169 in *Advances in Personal Relationships*, Vol. 3, edited by W. H. Jones and D. Perlman. London: Jessica Kingsley.

Sacher, Jennifer A., and Mark A. Fine. 1996. "Predicting Relationship Status and Satisfaction after Six Months among Dating Couples." *Journal of Marriage and the Family* 58:21–32.

Shields, N. M., and C. R. Hanneke. 1983. "Attribution Processes in Violent Relationships: Perceptions of Violent Husbands and Wives." *Journal of Applied Social Psychology* 13:515–527.

Stanley, Scott M., and Howard J. Markman. 1992. "Assessing Commitment in Personal Relationships." *Journal of Marriage and the Family* 54:595–608.

Surra, Catherine A. 1990. "Research and Theory on Mate Selection and Premarital Relationships in the 1980s." *Journal of Marriage and the Family* 52:844–865.

Sura, Catherine A. 1995a. "Knowledge Structures in Developing Relationships: Progress and Pitfalls." Pp. 397–413 in *Knowledge Structures in Close Relationships*, edited by G. J. O Fletcher and J. Fitness. Hillsdale, NJ: Lawrence Erlbaum.

Sura, Catherine A. 1995b. *Reasons Coding Manual IV*. Unpublished manuscript, The University of Texas at Austin.

Surra, Catherine A., and Thomas Bohman. 1991. "The Development of Close Relationships: A Cognitive Perspective." Pp. 281–305 in *Cognition in Close Relationships*, edited by G. J. O. Fletcher and F. D. Fincham. Hillsdale, NJ: Lawrence Erlbaum.

Surra, Catherine A., and Debra K. Hughes. 1997. "Commitment Processes Accounts of the Development of Premarital Relationships." *Journal of Marriage and the Family* 59:5–21.

Surra, Catherine A., Peggy Arizzi, and Linda A. Asmussen. 1988. "The Association

Between Reasons for Commitment and the Development and Outcome of Marital Relationships." *Journal of Social and Personal Relationships* 5:47–63.

Surra, Catherine A., Debra K. Hughes, and Susan Jacquet. 1999. "The Development of Commitment to Marriage: A Phenomenological Approach." Pp. 125–148 in *The Handbook of Interpersonal Commitment and Relationship Stability,* edited by W. H. Jones and J. Adams. New York: Kluwer Academic/Plenum Publishers.

Udry, Richard J. 1981. "Marital Alternatives and Marital Disruption." *Journal of Marriage and the Family* 43:889–898.

Veroff, Joseph, Lynne Sutherland, Letha Chadiha, and Robert M. Ortega. 1993. "Predicting Marital Quality with Narrative Assessments of Marital Experience." *Journal of Marriage and the Family* 55:326–337.

Walker, Lenore. 1979. *The Battered Woman.* New York: Harper & Row.

APPENDIX

Definitions and Examples of Codes for Reasons for Commitment Used in Analyses[a]

Reason Category	A Reference to	Example
Dyadic		
Behavioral interdependence	Interaction or activities between partners	"We spent a lot of time together."
Conflict	Tension or arguments between partners	"We were fighting a lot."
Positive dyadic attribution	Positive beliefs about the other or the relationship	"We had similar interests."
Negative dyadic attribution	Negative beliefs about the other or the relationship	"He was acting like a jerk."
Social network		
Separate network interaction	Interaction or activities between one partner and third parties	"My friends kept saying that Sue was bad for me."
Joint network interaction	Interaction or activities between both partners and third parties	"She met my whole family."
Positive network attribution	Positive beliefs involving third parties	"I fit right in with his family."
Self-attribution		
Positive self-attribution	A positive attribution about the self	"I just matured a lot during that time."
Negative self-attribution	A negative attribution about the self	"I went a little bit crazy."

[a]Definitions are taken from Surra (1995b).

IV

ECONOMICS, ROLE SPECIALIZATION, AND THE RETURNS TO MARRIAGE

14

The Continuing Importance of Men's Economic Position in Marriage Formation

VALERIE KINCADE OPPENHEIMER

SPECIALIZATION MODEL

This chapter presents the argument that from both a theoretical and empirical perspective, economic factors continue to have a substantial impact on union formation. Hence it is important to consider whether they have been playing a major role in the rapid changes in marriage behavior during the past 25 years. So far, those arguing for the significance of economic explanations of these changes have primarily done so by invoking an economic model of marriage that is based on gender-role specialization. This is most explicitly outlined in the theory of marriage by the economist Gary Becker (1981). Becker argues that the major gain to marriage lies in the mutual dependence of spouses, arising out of their specialized functions—the woman in domestic production (and reproduction) and the man in market work. Marriage then involves trading the fruits of these different skills. In response to economic growth and the rising wages it produces, however, women's market work also rises. The result is that women become less specialized and more economically independent, leading, in turn, to a decline in the desirability of marriage. The sociologically parallel theory—exchange theory—essentially makes similar arguments. In sum, this view of marriage concludes that the increasing economic independence of women has led to a "retreat" from marriage—increasing proportions never marrying, greater marital instability, and a growing tendency to substitute more ephemeral cohabiting relationships for formal marriages. As such, it is a theory that predicts the inevitable and continuing decline of marriage and the family in modern industrial societies.

Although the women's economic independence explanation of the changes in marriage behavior has enjoyed considerable popularity, it has also been increasingly criticized on both theoretical and empirical grounds.[1] For example, Becker's theory essentially addresses the question of *nonmarriage*, not *delayed* marriage. An unfortunate consequence of this is that much of the discussion of recent marriage trends has been couched in terms of the desirability of marriage per se rather than considering what factors might be leading to marriage postponements. Yet, for American whites, at least, the major change, so far, has been one of increasingly delayed marriages. Hence there is something of a theoretical mismatch between the theory and at least some of the phenomena it is attempting to explain. Moreover, much of the empirical work on the independence hypothesis has not supported it. Thus, microlevel multivariate analyses of the effect of a variety of indicators of women's labor-market position by myself and others have found that these either have little effect on marriage formation or, where they do have an impact, it is positive rather than negative (Cherlin, 1980; Clarkberg, 1999; Goldscheider and Waite, 1986; Bennett et al., 1989; Lichter et al., 1992; Mare and Winship, 1991; Oppenheimer and Lew, 1995; Oppenheimer et al., 1995; Oppenheimer and Lewin, 1999; Qian and Preston, 1993) . For example, for women as well as men, both full-time/full-year employment and earnings increase rather than decrease their likelihood of marrying, although the impact is far greater for men. In short, there is little evidence that the desirability of marriage is reduced by the extensive employment of women in the American economy, a view that is further supported by the high proportion of married women actually employed at any given time—around 70%, even among those in the childbearing years (Cancian et al., 1993; Oppenheimer and Lewin, 1999).

WHY ECONOMIC FACTORS CONTINUE TO BE IMPORTANT

If the specialization model of marriage has serious deficiencies, how else might we view the impact of economic factors on marriage formation? There are a number of reasons for arguing that they have played, and will continue to play, a major role in many areas of family behavior. A basic one is that causal explanations of large-scale changes or major subgroup differences in demographic behavior should typically exhibit certain properties. First, the proposed explanatory factors should have a significant impact on individual-level behavior—for example, on the probability an individual marries in any given year. However, even if there is such an impact, this will not necessarily produce a sizable aggregate response unless a relatively large number of people are affected by the factor in question. According to these criteria, provided economic factors influence marital decisions at the individual level, major changes in the structure and health of the economy are likely to have a significant aggregate impact on family behavior because they affect the opportunities and constraints faced by so many. Moreover, major economic changes usually do not affect people equally, as has been the case in recent years; hence they can potentially play a major role in socioeconomic differentials in demographic behavior.

Another reason why economic factors are important for understanding family behavior is that the family is itself an economic institution of sorts. As such, its fate is linked to that of the economy. Important aspects of the family's economic function are its ability to foster socioeconomic as well as biological reproduction. Thus, couples do not just want to produce children per se, they want to produce children that will socioeconomically resemble themselves or even be upwardly mobile. All this takes economic resources. Furthermore, the family has an important role in maintaining and/or improving living levels over the family's developmental cycle, despite internally as well as externally produced challenges to the family's economic stability (Oppenheimer, 1982, 1994). In short, a family's long-term success in promoting the welfare of its members is greatly affected by its economic viability, which, in industrial societies, is largely determined by the earnings of its members. If this perspective on the family is valid, then the specialization and trading model of marriage overlooks a number of important economic advantages to marriage and married women's employment. Because it is intrinsic to the theory that women's more extensive employment should reduce the gain to marriage, it fails to consider how wives' employment may actually improve the economic viability of the marriage and thereby strengthen it.[2] Let us consider these issues in greater detail because they have such a direct bearing on how economic factors may affect union formation.

First, both marriage and cohabitation involve considerable economies of scale. However, marriage, more than cohabitation, encourages the accumulation of pooled savings and capital investments that provide greater long-term economic security. Second, sex-role specialization is essentially a high risk and inflexible family strategy in an independent nuclear family system unless accompanied by supplementary support mechanisms (Oppenheimer, 1982, 1994). An inherent problem is that the temporary or permanent loss of one specialist in a nuclear family can mean that functions vital to the well-being of the complementary specialist and their children are not being performed. For example, husbands/fathers can die or become ill or disabled; they can lose their jobs and have difficulty finding another one; they could desert the family or become an alcoholic; and so one. The result is that the family is left without its major source of income when specialization is the modus operandi. Wives' employment is one type of insurance against these risks as well as raising the family's living level at other times.

An additional issue is that the economic needs of the family vary over its developmental cycle, depending in large part on the number and ages of its children. In the nineteenth and early twentieth centuries the employment of children was often used to offset the risks of specialization and the variability in needs over the family cycle as well as to raise the family's level of living (Goldin, 1981; Haines, 1979; Rowntree, 1922; see Oppenheimer, 1994, for a review). However, relying on children's economic contribution was always a costly family strategy. A sufficient number of children old enough to make an economic difference was generally not available until the middle or later stages of the family cycle. Families that temporarily or permanently lost the contribution of the father early in the family cycle were not greatly helped by such a strategy. And if the mother was lost when the children were young the family might break up with children being parceled out among relatives or even going to orphanages. In general, this economic reliance on one's offspring often led to a pattern of "life cycle poverty" in which periods of poverty and comparative plenty alternated over the life cycle of workers (Rowntree, 1920). Another well-known disadvantage to the extensive employment of children to supplement their family's income was that it tended to discourage schooling and hence had a negative effect on children's adult socioeconomic status. Even aside from the drawbacks of using children's work to maintain a family's economic equilibrium, the economic advantages of this strategy were eventually bound to decline during industrialization as the adult labor force became more skilled and hence the relative economic contribution unskilled children could make declined. Furthermore, the cost of producing children at a similar or higher socioeconomic level as their parents also rose because of the importance of keeping offspring in school much longer. From an historical perspective, then, wives' employment might be viewed as a functional substitute for the work of their children, facilitating the more extensive schooling of the next generation and thereby fostering upward intergenerational social mobility. In fact, the extensiveness of wives' employment in contemporary American society suggests that the life style afforded by the combined income of both spouses is now probably providing the social standard against which others measure their well-being. If true, then it becomes increasingly difficult for single earners and married couples with a more traditional division of labor to achieve the same level of living as the two-earner family (Oppenheimer, 1982).

If our preoccupation with the negative impact of women's rising employment on marriage has led us to overlook its positive effects, it has also encouraged us to neglect the way in which *men's* labor market position may be affecting marriage behavior. There are two aspects of men's economic position that are relevant here. One is changes in the relative job stability and earnings of men at different skill levels, as roughly measured by educational attainment. The question is whether less skilled workers are falling behind economically compared to the more skilled and the implications of this for family behavior. The second issue is whether there have been changes in the nature of the career development process that are likely to have had an important effect on marriage behavior. Young men straight out of school have typically been at a relative disadvantage compared to somewhat older workers in any given type of job. New workers generally lack the skills obtained through more extensive work experience and employer investment in on-the-job training. Hence, they are usually paid less than more experienced workers and are often the first to be fired during recessions. All this is well documented by the lower earnings of younger compared to older men and by the much greater sensitivity of young men's unemployment rates to business cycle conditions.[3] Hence, a second important question is whether the relative economic disadvantage of the young has intensified in recent years and, if so, whether this has been more characteristic of the less as compared to the more skilled. If the answer is yes, this should have important implications for marriage formation. Both of these issues are concerned with changes over time in economic inequality.

The demographic relevance of men's economic position is consistent with a long tradition in demographic theory and research going back to Malthus, which has shown that the marriage timing of both men and women is strongly affected by men's economic position and how this varies over time (Banks, 1954; Easterlin, 1987; Goldstone, 1986; Thomas, 1925; Watkins, 1984). One major example of this in the twentieth century was the sharp drop in U.S. annual marriage probabilities during the Great Depression of the 1930s followed by a rapid rise during the prosperous postwar period, reaching a high plateau that lasted until around 1970, after which marriage rates started their rapid fall, which has continued into the 1990s (Rodgers and Thornton, 1985; U.S. Bureau of the Census, 1998). At the same time, there has been a substantial increase in labor-market inequality that has adversely affected the less skilled, particularly young men—a change that has not only been characterized by a rise in the economic position of those at the top but an actual deterioration in the position of those lower down the scale (Bound and Freeman, 1992; Duncan et al., 1996; Juhn, 1992; Juhn et al., 1993; Levy, 1998; Murname and Levy, 1993; Welch, 1990; Wetzel, 1995). Moreover, this deterioration has affected not only the least educated (high school dropouts) but the moderately educated (high school graduates) as well. And it has been experienced by whites as well as blacks, although blacks have suffered the most. In short, the pervasiveness of this growing pattern of labor-market inequality and the fact that it developed about the same time age at marriage started to rise could provide a potentially key factor in helping explain recent marriage trends. This chapter discusses some of the findings from research inspired by these inequality trends and the insights they provide into current marriage patterns (Oppenheimer et al., 1997).

MEN'S CHANGING ECONOMIC POSITION

The data for this analysis come from a longitudinal survey of young men's labor-market experience—the 1979–1990 annual interviews of the National Longitudinal Survey, Youth Cohorts (NLSY). The sample consists of a cohort of youths who were aged 14–22 at the first interview in 1979 and 25–33 in 1990. Although I have also used the NLSY to study women's marriage timing, the discussion here focuses on men (Oppenheimer and Lew, 1995; Oppenheimer and Lewin, 1999). Because it is a large panel study limited to young people and includes very detailed annual data on both marriage and labor market behavior, the NLSY is extremely valuable for investigating the relationship between young men's transition to work and marriage timing. The discussion here will focus on two major questions: (1) What is the nature and severity of the labor-market inequality experienced by different race-schooling groups of young men in the NLSY? and (2) How has this affected their marriage timing?

Most of the studies dealing with the rise in inequality in American society have used annual time-series of cross-sectional data—usually the Current Population Survey. Essentially what these analyses have done is compare annual data on the economic position of men at different skill levels—for example, those with varying amounts of work experience (roughly measured as their estimated time out of school) and different numbers of school years completed. Such analyses have been quite effective in documenting the declining labor-market position of younger workers as a group, particularly those with a high-school education or less.[4] These findings strongly imply that young men's career entry processes have become increasingly more difficult over the years. However, they do not directly show this because cross-sectional data cannot follow and compare the actual career-entry paths of earlier and more recent cohorts. For that longitudinal data are needed. Hence such studies do not examine changes in one potentially important dimension of economic inequality— inequality in the *pace* of career development. If youthful labor-market difficulties impede marriage formation, then underemployment or very low earnings in any particular year is only part of the problem. The other part is the number of years it takes an individual and, in aggregate, the cohort as a whole to overcome these difficulties, if indeed they do. Thus the pace as well as the degree of difficulty of the career development process should have a correspondingly important impact on the pace of marriage formation. Hence what is really needed is a life course approach to the analysis of young men's career development. The NLSY longitudinal data set is ideally suited to carry out such an investigation because it follows the same 8-year birth cohorts over much of their young adulthood. The analysis is necessarily limited, however, because it will be able to document the career development process and its resulting impact on marriage timing only for these very recent late-marrying cohorts. Historical comparisons with much earlier cohorts who married at a younger age await another study.

I will not burden you with a lot of statistical analyses in this discussion but will mostly summarize the gist of our findings.[5] Nevertheless, to understand the potential impact of men's career-entry difficulties on aggregate measures of marriage timing, it is helpful to deal with a few concrete examples. These will be limited to two indicators of labor-market position—the first is the proportion of the cohort working full-time year-round as a measure of employment stability and the second is annual earnings. Furthermore, only selected illustrative statistics will be provided. These comparisons of labor-market behavior are made according to the number of years young men were out of school, taking year of school leaving as a rough marker of the presumed beginning of their adult work life. Our measure of the pace of the career-development process is the number of years out of school it took for a cohort to achieve certain proportions in stable employment or earnings above the poverty line. All these measures are based on the total male sample in each race-schooling group and hence will overstate the economic position of the single as marriage selects out those in a more favorable labor-market position.

Table 14.1 shows race–schooling differences in the number of years out of school it took for 50 and then 70% of each NLSY race–schooling subgroup to have worked full-time/year-round for 1 year (the left panel). The longer it took to reach these levels of employment stability, the slower the pace of career development. To provide a somewhat more stringent measure of employment stability, the right panel tells us how long it took the cohort to work this much for two consecutive years. Moreover, by comparing the 2-year with the 1-year measure, we have an indicator of the extent to which individuals experience career reversals. Thus if no reversals are occurring and it takes 5 years for 50% of the cohort to work year-round/full-time for 1 year, it should take only about 6 years for the same proportion to have worked 2 years consecutively. Any larger discrepancy is an indication of the extent to which employment reversals are common.

If employment instability actually does discourage marriage formation, then the longer it takes for a substantial proportion of a cohort to move from a pattern of employment instability to one of stability, the slower will

Table 14.1.   Years Out of School Taken to Reach 50 and 70% Working Full-Time
(FT) Full-Year (FY) for 1 and 2 Years Consecutively: NLSY Non-Hispanic
White and Black Males

| | FT/FY for 1 Year | | | | FT/FY for 2 Years | | | |
| | Education (Years) | | | | Education (Years) | | | |
Working FT/FY (%)	0–11	12	13–15	16+	0–11	12	13–15	16+
Whites								
50	4	1	<1	1	—[a]	4	2	2
70	—[a]	5	2	1	—[a]	10	4	2
Blacks								
50	—[a]	2	1	1	—[a]	10	4	2
70	—[a]	—[a]	6	1	—[a]	—[a]	—[a]	3

[a]This proportion not yet reached by 1990.

be the cohort's cumulative pace of marriage formation. As Table 14.1
shows, less than 50% of black high school dropouts had worked full-
time/full-year for even 1 year by 1990, at which time they had been out of
school roughly 8–15 years, depending on their age in 1979; for white
dropouts the situation was somewhat better but still very poor. And for
high school graduates, although it took only 1 year for half of the whites
to be working that extensively, it took 5 years for 70% to achieve this much
employment stability, not only indicating that the pace of the career development process was slow but there was also substantial within-group
variability in the speed of the transition. For black high school graduates,
although it took only 2 years for half of them to have worked full-
time/year-round, less than 70% had achieved this level of employment by
1990 and it even took 6 years out of school for those with some college to
do so.

Comparing the proportions working full-time/year-round for 2 years
consecutively, as opposed to 1 year, shows that career reversals must have
been quite common. In the case of whites, although it took 5 years out of
school for 70% of high school graduates to have worked full-time/year-
round for 1 year, it took *twice* that long to have worked so extensively for
2 years straight. And, although it took 2 years for only 50% of black high
school graduates to have worked this much for 1 year, it took 10 years for
the 50% level to be achieved for 2 years consecutively. Even blacks with
some college experienced considerable delays in their transition to stable
employment.

The fact that a fairly substantial proportion (50%) of almost all
race–schooling groups had achieved apparent career stability fairly soon
after school leaving but often were taking substantially longer to increase

that proportion to 70% or to move from stability for 1 to 2 years indicates that there was considerable inequality in the pace of career development *within* as well as *between* the subgroups. This would even be true for dropouts, if I had shown percentages lower than the 50% presented in this abridged table. Hence, within-group inequalities may play an important role in subgroup differences in marriage timing. Moreover, these findings are consistent with other research using Current Population Survey (CPS) data, which also indicate the growth of within-group inequality (Juhn et al., 1993; Levy, 1998)

Although employment stability is an important indicator of economic viability, an examination of earnings provides additional insights into the possible impact of economic inequality on marriage formation. And for those with 1 or more years of college, earnings may more accurately reveal labor-market difficulties than employment stability as their greater skill level apparently ensures them more regular employment but not necessarily at a high earnings level. Table 14.2 shows the ratios of the first two earnings quartiles to the poverty threshold for a couple with two children as an indicator of the extent to which a young man's earnings are barely adequate for supporting a small family. However, "*in*adequate" rather than "*barely* adequate" would probably best characterize the poverty line benchmark for the more educated whose economic standards for establishing a marital household are likely to be considerably higher. Hence our measure is a conservative one. Quartile 1 earnings, as well as the medians, are shown because the first quartile demarcates a significant minority (i.e., 25%) whose low marriageability may have a substantial impact on the cohort's pace of marriage formation. The ratios are presented for two different number of years out of school—4, and 7.

Table 14.2.   Quartile 1 and Median Annual Earnings as a Ratio of the Poverty Line for a Couple with Two Children, by Years Out of School and Education: NLSY Non-Hispanic White and Black Males

| | *Quartile 1 Earnings* | | | | *Median Earnings* | | | |
| | *Education (Years)* | | | | *Education (Years)* | | | |
Years Out of School	*0–11*	*12*	*13–15*	*16+*	*0–11*	*12*	*13–15*	*16+*
Whites								
4	.37	.89	1.19	1.83	0.85	1.26	1.65	2.39
7	.55	1.04	1.24	1.95	1.04	1.51	1.83	2.58
Blacks								
4	.21	.47	.93	1.52	.57	.90	1.27	2.08
7	.27	.75	.83	—[a]	.68	1.11	1.62	—[a]

[a]Not available; sample size too small for this time out of school.

Throughout this period, high school dropouts exhibited extremely low earnings, particularly blacks. For neither blacks nor whites did the first quartile earnings even closely approach the poverty threshold by 7 years out of school and white dropouts' *median* earnings only just exceeded it by the seventh year out. The ratios rise with schooling levels but first quartile earnings remained very close to the poverty line even for those with some college and, for blacks, even the median earnings of high school graduates only slightly exceeded the poverty line by 7 years out of school.[6] The wide prevalence of persistently low earnings of this nature suggests that whether a marriage took place might have depended on whether the wife would be working, which is consistent with previous analyses that show that women's earnings have a positive effect on their likelihood of marrying (Lichter et al., 1992; Oppenheimer and Lew, 1995; Oppenheimer and Lewin, 1999). And, in fact, married women from the NLSY sample had very high rates of employment, hovering around 70% for both whites and blacks throughout most of their twenties (Oppenheimer and Lewin, 1999).

In sum, we have seen evidence of substantial race–schooling inequalities in both the pace and difficulty of the transition to a stable employment or to employment that affords moderate earnings. Moreover, although there has been a long-term increase in the proportion of young people attending college, they were still not in the majority for the NLSY males. Only 43% of non-Hispanic white males and 29% of blacks had completed 1 or more years of college by 1990. Furthermore, there were not only substantial *between*-group but also sizable *within*-group inequalities as well, particularly for those with a high school education or less.

IMPACT OF CAREER-ENTRY DIFFICULTIES ON
MARRIAGE FORMATION

How big an impact on marriage formation was likely to have resulted from these differences in the pace and difficulty of the career-entry process? To tackle this problem, we first had to investigate how much career-entry difficulties affected the likelihood of marrying in any given year. For example, were underemployed men less likely to marry in a year and why might this be the case? Then, by applying our knowledge of how long such employment problems persisted, it was possible to estimate race–schooling differences in the cumulative marriage timing impact of the career-development process.

To provide some background to our discussion, however, let us take a brief look at the pace of marriage formation that was actually observed among black and white NLSY males at different schooling levels. These are presented in Figure 14.1. Not all of those with 1 or more years of college were out the full 10 years presented in the figure, especially for blacks whose sample size was smaller. For blacks, each increase in educational attainment greatly increased the likelihood of ever having married at any year out of school. In the case of whites, a bifurcated pattern was observed. Those with 1 or more years of college were more likely to be married for most years out of school compared to those with 12 years of schooling or less. However there was a convergence over time among the educational groups for whites. Finally, there are sharp black–white differences in the pace of marriage formation, with the greatest differences for the less educated.

Before discussing how the speed and difficulty of young men's career development might affect marriage timing, let us first briefly consider why this might be the case. The analysis is guided by the basic hypothesis that adult men are normatively expected to have a relatively stable work career and work stability is particularly important in fulfilling their core economic role in the family. Rather than thinking of it as a concrete step, however, it is more useful to view an individual's transition to work as a process that is typically characterized by increasing degrees of career "maturity" over time. Certainly the results we have just summarized seem to support that view. Hence, young men's career maturity, as well as their actual earnings, are important indicators of their marriageability. A lengthy and difficult career development process should therefore delay marriage. One major reason for this is that young men in the early stages of their careers usually have relatively low earnings, often below the poverty line, as we have seen, making it more difficult to set up an independent household—at least one that meets socially defined minimal standards. The fact that most married women now work—at least part of the time—is probably attenuating the negative effect of young men's weak earnings position. However, given long-standing assortative mating patterns in the United States, young women who themselves have only a high school education, or even less, are also in a weak labor-market position. Hence, for these educational groups, there is a limit to the potential ability of comparably educated wives to attenuate the negative impact of young men's weak economic position (Oppenheimer and Lewin, 1999).

There are also other reasons why career immaturity might inhibit marriage formation. An unstable work pattern leads to uncertainties—uncertainty about a young man's ability and willingness to take on adult responsibilities and uncertainty about his long-term socioeconomic characteristics, thereby impeding assortative mating (Oppenheimer, 1988). An additional income in the household cannot assuage uncertainties of this nature. Moreover, the growing prevalence of cohabitation provides a way of experiencing many of the advantages of marriage when the appropriateness of the match is still uncertain. Recent research is consistent with

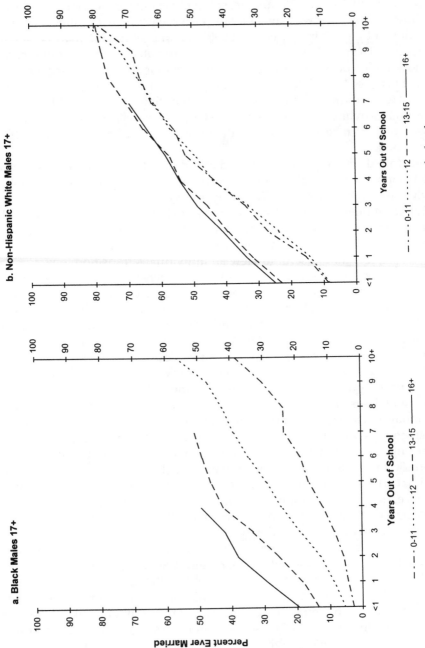

Figure 14.1. Percentage ever married by education and years out of school.

this possibility as it indicates that although economic position has a positive effect on the formation of both cohabiting and marital unions, it is more strongly related to marriage than to cohabitation and, moreover, both men and women who are economically unstable are more likely to cohabit (Clarkberg, 1999).

Using a multivariate regression technique called discrete time event-history analysis, we examined the effect of a variety of variables measuring young men's labor-market position on marriage formation in a year. We use a short period of time, such as a year, because young people's labor market characteristics are constantly changing and we want to detect the impact of these changes over time. Black and non-Hispanic white males were analyzed separately. I will not go into the details here but, in general, we found that for both blacks and whites, each of the economic variables studied had a substantial impact on the odds of marrying in any given year. For example, those who had worked less than full-time year-round in the previous year were much less likely to have married the following year. In addition, lower earnings in one year discouraged marrying in the next year. Moreover, earnings had a larger impact on black than white marriage formation (Oppenheimer et al., 1997:319).

Combining the information on the substantial effect of career-entry difficulties on marriage formation in any given year with our data on how many years these difficulties persisted, we estimated their combined impact on the pace of marriage formation. To estimate the effect of the considerable labor-market inequality observed *within* as well as *between* race–schooling groups, we first used the observed career-entry patterns within each group to construct two contrasting career-development models: a more difficult transition and an easier transition. Using these models plus our estimates of how the likelihood of marriage varied for each degree of difficulty in career transitions, we constructed two simulations of the transition to marriage for each of the race–schooling subgroups. In that way, we could compare, for example, how much more rapidly black high school graduates married if they were undergoing an easier transition than if they were experiencing a more difficult and protracted one—a within-group comparison. And we could compare the patterns between different educational groups for blacks, and for whites as well; comparisons of the pace of black as compared to white marriage transitions for the same schooling groups would also be possible. In this way we could obtain a much clearer picture of the effect on marriage timing of a variety of within- and between-group variations in economic inequality.

Table 14.3 presents a very abbreviated view of our results. For each race and schooling group it shows our simulations of what proportion would have ever married by 4 and then 7 years out of school to give an idea of the predicted pace of marriage formation. In general, our major findings are

Table 14.3.   Percentage Ever Married by Schooling, Difficulty of Career-Entry Transition, and Years Out of School: NLSY Non-Hispanic White and Black Males

	Out 4 Years				Out 7 Years			
	Education (Years)				Education (Years)			
Difficulty of Transition	0–11	12	13–15	16+	0–11	12	13–15	16+
Whites								
Difficult	30	31	47	48	48	50	71	67
Easier	50	46	58	59	73	67	78	75
Blacks								
Difficult	5	11	27	45	11	26	45	—[a]
Easier	24	30	46	58	39	48	63	—[a]

[a]Not available; sample size too small for this time out of school.

that substantially higher proportions of men undergoing an easier, as opposed to a more difficult, transition were ever married by both 4 and 7 years out of school. For example, for black high school dropouts, only 5% undergoing a difficult transition had ever married by 4 years out of school compared to 24% of those having an easier transition. The comparable proportions for white dropouts was 30 and 50%, respectively. Second, the higher the educational level, the higher the proportions ever married for each year out of school and each level of career-entry difficulty. This was consistently the case for blacks, whereas for whites, the major differences were between those with 1 or more years of college as compared to those with 12 years of schooling or less and was most apparent for those having a difficult transition. These findings largely reflect the fact that "difficult" transitions were even more difficult and more protracted for the less educated. Moreover, earnings were always lower for the less educated. Finally, for each schooling group and each degree of career-entry difficulty, much lower proportions of blacks were ever married than whites at both 4 and 7 years out of school. Thus for those out 7 years, only 26% of black high school graduates having a difficult career transition were ever married compared to 50% of whites. This too reflects the fact that whether easy or difficult by the standards of the *black* experience, transitions were almost always much more difficult and prolonged for blacks compared to whites at the same schooling level, as was graphically shown in Tables 14.1 and 14.2.

In sum, the simulations presented in Table 14.3 indicate that difficulties in the career development process have been making a substantial contribution to the delayed marriage of the NLSY cohorts and to the large differences in marriage timing between and within race–schooling subgroups.

However, just how much the *historical* increases in the age at marriage can be accounted for by the changing dynamics of men's career-entry process cannot be estimated from the NLSY data alone because they are limited to just a few recent birth cohorts. There are, of course, numerous studies using time series of cross-sectional data indicating that labor-market inequality has risen substantially during the past 25 years and that these changes have particularly affected younger less experienced workers with 12 years of schooling or less and blacks most of all. All this indicates that the career-entry process has become more difficult and more prolonged for young men. However, *directly* determining the impact on marriage postponement of this growth in inequality so that it also more accurately reflects inequalities in the *pace* of career development awaits a comparative cohort analysis.

CONCLUSION

This chapter presents the argument that economic factors are generally important to consider in the analysis of family behavior and are likely to have been particularly significant in recent trends in marriage timing. Does this mean that economic factors are the *only* ones affecting trends in marriage behavior? Not at all. For one thing, a rapid increase in the prevalence of cohabitation is likely to be delaying marriages. Although some reasons for cohabiting and postponing marriage for a while could, theoretically, be traced to uncertainties arising out of career-development difficulties, it is very unlikely that most of the upward trend in cohabitation can be explained by economic factors alone. A high proportion of those who cohabit appear to be doing so once they have already decided to marry— i.e., once they have become engaged. Nevertheless, cohabiting while engaged may still lead to some marriage postponements because, once living together, inertia may set in and there is also much less pressure to marry very soon. The marriage timing question may then turn into one of deciding when they can afford the expensive formal wedding that is grand enough to distinguish it from the informality of starting to cohabit. In addition, the timing of the wedding for cohabiting couples is more likely to be governed by things such as when it would be convenient to get all the relatives and friends together. Others now use cohabitation as a means of testing for compatibility.[7] In sum, the rising pattern of cohabiting preceding marriage is likely to be a continuing force for marriage postponement.

If young men's deteriorating economic position has had a significant role in the rising age at marriage, an important question is whether there might be some reversals in the trend if young men's economic situation improves. Here the argument is intrinsically different from other major explanations posited for the recent changes in marriage behavior. For example, as discussed earlier, the women's independence argument is essentially a theory that predicts the inevitable and continuing decline of marriage and the family in modern industrial societies. Similarly, those who argue that recent marriage trends represent a decrease in the importance of marriage as an institution and are a product of the rise of secular individualism as a necessary accompaniment to modernization are also positing a nonreversible trend (Lesthaeghe, 1995; van de Kaa, 1987). However, the argument regarding the role of men's economic position in marriage timing does not predict an irreversible decline. If young men's career-entry process becomes less difficult and drawn out, then age at marriage could decrease. Hence, in terms of the envisioned "fate" of the family in modern industrial societies, the position espoused in this chapter is much less apocalyptic than many other explanations of recent trends.

If age at marriage could go down again, as men's economic situation improves, the question is by how much? Is it likely to return to the young age at marriage observed in the postwar years up through the early 1970s? This is very unlikely for a large variety of reasons. One is that the rising importance of cohabitation as a prelude to marriage should continue to lead to some postponement of marriage, regardless of the economic ease or difficulty of the career entry process. Second, the demographic behavior of the postwar era was itself not typical of traditional marriage and family patterns in the United States. Annual fertility rose to levels higher than they had been for 50 years; marriage timing declined to levels well below those at the turn of the century when the age at marriage more closely resembled current patterns; even divorce became less frequent.[8] Hence, it is unlikely that American demographic behavior will return to the anomalous levels characteristic of the baby boom era.

From an economic standpoint, the 1950s through the 1960s were also highly unusual and it is doubtful that these conditions will be repeated any time soon in the United States.[9] It was a period when, almost alone among the survivors of World War II, the United States had its industrial infrastructure intact; it had a population characterized by a pent-up consumer demand from over 15 years of deprivation due to the Great Depression (when nobody had any money) and then the war (when there was nothing to buy). The result was a period of rapid economic expansion and prosperity with little competition from other actual or potential trading partners. What all this meant was a substantial increase in the number of good jobs for men right out of school—particularly for those with a high school degree or less whose economic position was also often subsequently protected by strong industrial unions. On the other hand, it is a very different world today. To name just a few of the changes, industrial restructuring and the growing importance of technology have primarily increased the demand for skilled educated workers at the expense of the *absolute* as well as the *relative* economic position of the moderately to less educated. And as the importance of unions has declined, there has been little to buffer the position of the semiskilled or unskilled workers. Moreover, for some years now that United States has been facing stiff foreign competition in manufacturing and trade, often from countries that pay their workers considerably less and that have been the recipients of the outsourcing of manufacturing processes from more industrialized nations. All this has also put a downward pressure on the wages of those who are facing the greatest competition from abroad—the less skilled. Hence, although it is *theoretically* possible that the economic position of the majority of young moderately to poorly educated men may improve considerably, thereby providing them with the career stability and earnings that support an earlier age at marriage, it is unclear whether this is likely to happen in the near term. Nevertheless, after a recession early in the 1990s, unemployment has decreased significantly in the United States in the last half of the 1990s, although earnings for mid- and lower-level workers have not been improving and long-term unemployment remains a serious problem (Levy, 1998; Goodman and Consedine, 1999). However, it is still too soon to determine whether these changes will lead to a reduction in the age at marriage, particularly for those with a high school education or less, as it is the length as well as the difficulty of career development that will affect the timing of marriage.

NOTES

1.   For a detailed critical review of the theoretical and empirical arguments concerning the independence hypothesis, see Oppenheimer (1994, 1997).

2.   For a more extensive discussion of this issue, see Oppenheimer (1994, 1995) and Cancian et al., (1993).

3.   For a detailed discussion of this based on 1960 and 1970 Census data, see Oppenheimer (1982, Ch. 3); also see Oppenheimer and Kalmijn (1995), which discusses some of these issues using 1970 and 1980 Census public use samples.

4.   Older men with a high school education or less have also been experiencing considerable labor market difficulties, raising serious doubts about any argument that young men's weak economic performance is *because* they are not interested in marrying (Levy, 1998).

5.   For the more detailed presentation and discussion of the findings, see Oppenheimer et al. (1997).

6.   Only those with some earnings are included in these calculations. Hence, the data greatly overstate the earnings position of these cohorts, particularly for the moderately to less educated, who are more likely not to have had any earnings in a year.

7.   Unfortunately, I have been unable to investigate the role of cohabitation (and its relationship to the career-development process) in marriage timing using the NLSY because its cohabitation data have some major deficiencies.

8.   For a more detailed discussion of the historically anomalous nature of American demographic behavior in the postwar era and for references to other related works, see Oppenheimer (1994).

9. For a detailed and excellent discussion of the changing economic position of American workers since the 1950s, see Levy (1998).

REFERENCES

Banks, J. A. 1954. *Prosperity and Parenthood*. London: Routledge and Kegan Paul.

Becker, G. S. 1981. *A Treatise on the Family*. Cambridge, MA: Harvard University Press.

Bennett, N. G., D. E. Bloom, and P.H. Craig. 1989. "The Divergence of Black and White Marriage Patterns." *American Journal of Sociology* 95:692–722.

Bound, J., and R.B. Freeman. 1992. "What Went Wrong? The Erosion of Relative Earnings and Employment Among Young Black Men in the 1980s." *The Quarterly Journal of Economics* 107:201–232.

Cancian, M., S. Danziger, and P. Gottschalk. 1993. "Working Wives and Family Income Inequality Among Married Couples." Pp. 195–221 in *Uneven Tides: Rising Inequality in America*, edited by S. Dansiger and P. Gottschalk. New York: Russell Sage Foundation.

Cherlin, A. J. 1980. "Postponing Marriage: The Influence of Young Women's Work Expectations." *Journal of Marriage and the Family* 42:355–365.

Clarkberg, M. 1999. "The Price of Partnering: The Role of Economic Well-Being in Young Adults' First Union Experiences." *Social Forces* 77:945—968.

Duncan, G. J., J. Boisjoly, and T. Smeeding. 1996. "Economic Mobility of Young Workers in the 1970s and 1980s." *Demography* 3:497–509.

Easterlin, R. A. 1987. *Birth and Fortune*. Chicago: University of Chicago Press.

Goldin, C. 1981. "Family Strategies and the Family Economy in the Late Nineteenth Century: The Role of Secondary Workers." In *Essays Toward an Interdisciplinary History of the City*, edited by T. Hershberg. New York: Oxford University Press.

Goldscheider, F. K., and L. J. Waite. 1986. "Sex Differences in the Entry into Marriage." *American Journal of Sociology* 92:91–109.

Goldstone, J. A. 1986. "The Demographic Revolution in England: A Re-examination." *Population Studies* 49:5–33.

Goodman, W. D., and T. D. Consedine. 1999. "Job Growth Slows During Crises Overseas." *Monthly Labor Review* 122:3–23.

Haines, M. M. 1979. "Industrial Work and the Family Life Cycle, 1889–1890." *Research in Economic History* 4:449–495.

Juhn, C. 1992. "Decline of Male Labor Market Participation: The Role of Declining Market Opportunities." *Quarterly Journal of Economics* 107:79–121.

Juhn, C., K. Murphy, and B. Pierce. 1993. "Wage Inequality and the Rise in Returns to Skill." *Journal of Political Economy* 101:410–442.

Lesthaeghe, R. 1995. "The Second Demographic Transition in Western Countries: An Interpretation." Chapter 1 in *Gender and Family Change in Industrialized Countries*, edited by K. O. Mason and A. Jensen. Oxford: Clarendon Press.

Levy, F. 1998. *The New Dollars and Dreams*. New York: Russell Sage Foundation.

Lichter, D. T., D. K. McLaughlin, George K., and D. J. Landry. 1992. "Race and the Retreat from Marriage: A Shortage of Marriageable Men?" *American Sociological Review* 57:781–799.

Mare, R.D., and C. Winship. 1991. "Socioeconomic Change and the Decline of Marriage for Blacks and Whites." Pp. 175–202 in *The Urban Underclass*, edited by C. Jencks and P. E. Peterson. Washington, DC: The Brookings Institute.

Murname, R. J., and F. Levy. 1993. "Why Today's High-School-Educated Males Earn Less than Their Fathers Did: The Problem and an Assessment of Responses." *Harvard Educational Review* 63:1–19.

Oppenheimer, V. K. 1982. *Work and the Family: A Study in Social Demography*. New York: Academic Press.

Oppenheimer, V. K. 1988. "A Theory of Marriage Timing." *American Journal of Sociology* 94:563–591.

Oppenheimer, V. K. 1994. "Women's Rising Employment and the Future of the Family in Industrialized Societies." *Population and Development Review* 20: 293–342.

Oppenheimer, V. K. 1995. "The Role of Women's Economic Independence in Marriage Formation: A Skeptic's Response to Annemette Sørensen's Remarks." Pp. 236–243 in *Family Formation in Modern Societies and the New Role of Women*, edited by H. Blossfeld. Boulder: Westview Press.

Oppenheimer, V. K. 1997. "Women's Employment and the Gain to Marriage: The Specialization and Trading Model." *Annual Review of Sociology* 23:431–453.

Oppenheimer, V. K., and M. Kalmijn. 1995. "Life-Cycle Jobs." *Research in Social Stratification and Mobility* 14:1–38.

Oppenheimer, V. K., and V. Lew. 1995. "Marriage Formation in the Eighties: How Important Was Women's Economic Independence?" Pp. 105–138 in *Gender and Family Change in Industrialized Countries*, edited by K. O. Mason and A. Jensen. Oxford: Clarendon Press.

Oppenheimer, V. K., and A. Lewin. 1999. "Career Development and Marriage Formation in a Period of Rising Inequality: Who Is at Risk? What Are Their Prospects?" In *Transitions to Adulthood in A Changing Economy: No Work, No Family, No Future?*, edited by A. Booth, A. C. Crouter, and M. J. Shanahan. Westport, CT: Greenwood Press.

Oppenheimer, V. K., H. Blossfeld, and A. Wackerow. 1995. "New Developments in Family Formation and Women's Improvement in Educational Attainment in the United States." Pp. 150–173 in *Family Formation in Modern Societies and the New Role of Women*, edited by H. Blossfeld. Boulder, CO: Westview Press.

Oppenheimer, V. K., M. Kalmijn, and N. Lim. 1997. "Men's Career Development and Marriage Timing During a Period of Rising Inequality." *Demography* 34:311–330.

Qian, Z., and S. H. Preston. 1993. "Changes in American Marriage, 1972–87: Availability Conditions and Forces of Attraction by Age and Education." *American Sociological Review* 58:482–495.

Rodgers, W. L, and A. Thornton. 1985. "Changing Patterns of First Marriage in the United States." *Demography* 22:265–279.

Rowntree, B. S. 1922. *Poverty: A Study of Town Life*. London: Longmans Green.

Thomas, D. S. 1925. *Social Aspects of the Business Cycle*. London: George Routledge and Sons.

U.S. Bureau of the Census. 1998. "Marital Status and Living Arrangements: March 1998 (Update)." *Current Population Reports*, P20-514.

van de Kaa, D. J. 1987. "Europe's Second Demographic Transition." *Population Bulletin* 42(March).

Watkins, S. C. 1984. "Spinsters." *Journal of Family History* 9:310–325.

Welch, F. R. 1990. "The Employment of Black Men." *Journal of Labor Economics* 9: S26–S74.

Wetzel, J. S. 1995. "Labor Force, Unemployment and Earnings." Chapter 2 in *State of the Nation*, Vol. 1, edited by R. Farley, New York: Russell Sage Foundation.

15

Female Wages, Male Wages, and the Economic Model of Marriage: The Basic Evidence

ROBERT A. MOFFITT

INTRODUCTION

The conventional economic model of marriage most often associated with the work of Gary Becker (1973, 1981) has been discussed by social scientists in several disciplines for at least two decades. The model has been examined empirically in dozens of studies and has been elaborated in many directions in an attempt to capture observed features of marriage more accurately. The model has also been attacked for its omission of many seemingly important factors influencing marriage. It is fair to say that the basic elements of the model, particularly those elements relating to the importance of women's connection to the labor market to marriage rates, have been widely incorporated into thinking about marriage even though it is often believed necessary to introduce other factors in order to gain a full understanding.

Despite the large amount of research on this topic, most has been conducted at a very detailed individual level, examining the relationship between economic variables and marriage rates while controlling for many other variables, usually in a single cross section of data or in a short panel data set. What has not been examined is whether the economic model has any prima facie validity at a more aggregate, macrolevel. This chapter examines the evidence at that level, but goes beyond an examination of pure aggregate marriage rates and wage rates and focuses instead on *differentials*. In particular, differential marriage rates by education, birth cohort, age, year, and race are made the focus of the analysis. Marriage rates are known from past research to differ by all these characteristics. The issue examined is whether these differentials are related to differentials in economic variables—female and male wage rates, in particular—in the way predicted by the simple economic model of marriage and therefore whether differences in wage rates can "explain" differences in marriage rates. The analysis compares marriage rates for different educational groups at a point in time to wage differences, as well as comparing trends in marriage rates and in wage rates over time for different education groups.

The analysis, which is entirely graphical, indicates that the economic model is roughly consistent with marriage differentials for white men and women but much less so for black men and women, at least for the period examined (1968 to the present). The analysis also leads to two important lessons for the study of marriage trends and economic influences. One is that male wage rates must be taken into account in assessing economic influences on marriage; an analysis that correlates marriage rates to female wages alone leads to incorrect conclusions and an erroneous interpretation of the data. The other is that the population must be disaggregated by education, for not only are marriage trends different by education but the economic reasons for the trends are different for different education groups. Any analysis that tries to assess the influence of economic factors on marriage across all education levels will lead to faulty conclusions.

The first section of the chapter discusses what will be meant by "the" economic model of marriage, for, in truth, there is no single such model. The simple version of the economic model used here will ignore many important extensions and elaborations of the model that have been examined in the literature, and will also ignore many of the other forces that are known to be important (e.g., cohabitation). The second section of the chapter shows the "facts"—the trends in marriage rates and wage rates by education, age, and birth cohort and by race, as all the analysis is so stratified, and considers whether these facts are consistent with the economic model.

THE ECONOMIC MODEL OF MARRIAGE

The most fundamental feature of the structure of the economic model is the framing of the marriage decision as a voluntary decision by two individuals to form a union for mutual emotional, social, and economic benefit. The decision in the simplest model is framed as a decision by each individual to remain single or to marry the other individual in question. The values put on marriage and on remaining single are assumed to be representable by "utility functions" familiar from economics, functions that in an abstract form denote the value put on marriage or being single and how they are influenced by the concrete circumstances of each situation—housing, other consumption goods, leisure time, children, and so on. Marriage is assumed to occur if both parties are made better off by the marriage, that is, if both have increases in utility from marriage compared to their utilities from being single.[1]

Even at this initial stage, the model is extremely stylized and ignores many obvious features of reality. The alternative to marriage is usually not permanent single status but rather a continued search for a different partner. Also, framing the decision as a search process, with attendant forms of uncertainty, would be more accurate than framing it as a static decision under complete certainty. The uncertainty of the quality of the "match" is ignored, for example, as is the uncertainty of how each individual's own situation—the future course of his or her labor market opportunities—will unfold. The implication is that these more "dynamic" decisions that involve transition rates into marriage and out of marriage (divorce) are ignored in favor of a simple one-time decision to marry or not each period. Also ignored in this simple model is the nature of the entire marriage market itself, and how equilibration (or nonequilibration) of that market would affect the gains to marriage, particularly if there are shortages of men or women.

The nature of the economic "gains" to marriage have been a subject of extensive discussion (we ignore the noneconomic gains, which we assume to be present, of course). Specialization and division of labor—also called increasing returns—are the most familiar, gains that arise because two individuals can divide up the work to be done in the household and can specialize in the performance of different duties. The gains to such specialization are generally thought to be greater, the farther apart the relative skill levels of the two individuals are (holding constant their average, let us say). The advantages of shared consumption of "public goods"—housing and children are the two major types—also constitute a gain to marriage, for these goods can be enjoyed by two people simultaneously. Other possible gains to marriage are those arising from imperfections in the credit market—each partner can "loan" the other one money and hence avoid going to a bank—and risk sharing through insurance—in the event of an adverse event such as losing a job or getting sick, the other partner can cover for them financially and otherwise on a temporary basis.[2]

The analysis in this chapter is exclusively focused on the role of male and female wage rates, the two key variables in most discussions of the economic model of marriage. In economics, the wage rate available to an individual in the labor market is the single best indicator of labor market skill, earning power, and labor market potential. Wage rate influences are most commonly discussed in the context of the specialization and division of labor form of marriage gains, for their influence on the magnitude of other types of gains (public goods, risk sharing, etc.) is less obvious. The most common presumption is that the gains to marriage from specialization are positively related to male wages and negatively related to female wages.[3] This presumption is based on the idea that the wider the gap between labor market skills for the two partners, the greater the gains from specialization, and the realization that, on average, male wages are greater than female wages. Consequently, an increase in the male wage widens the wage gap and an increase in the female wage narrows that gap, thereby leading to increases in gains from specialization in the first instance and reductions in gains from specialization in the second instance.

Left unspecified in the theory of specialization, however, is whether utility inside marriage is a function *only* of relative female–male wages, or whether it is, in addition, a function of their average level or, equivalently, their sum. Whether specialization gains are greater if, say, the wage gap is held constant but both male and female wages are higher is something that economic theory cannot strongly predict. However, it is likely that some of the other types of gains to marriage are greater, the higher the overall level of income. For example, couples with higher income will consume more housing and can afford to spend more on children, leading to greater gains from sharing the consumption of these items. Alternatively, it could be argued that the imperfect credit market type of gain—the fact that each spouse can support the other one, for example, in job search or education or other types of investment—is likely to be stronger at higher levels of income. None of these arguments is completely obvious, however, and some types of marriage gains (e.g., risk pooling) would be plausibly more important at low levels of income. But analytic work on income effects has received rather short shrift relative to the effects emphasized by relative wages. Here, it will be assumed that higher income leads to greater gains to marriage, but with the recognition that this prediction is not as well based on prior models as that predicting greater gains when wages are farther apart.[4]

The two predictions of the simple economic model are, therefore, that the magnitude of the gap between male and female wages increases marriage rates (the "price" effect) and that the magnitude of the sum of the female and male wages also increases marriage rates (the "income" effect).

As noted previously, this model ignores cohabitation and, in fact, a model of corresponding simplicity to the above model has not been worked out for cohabitation. At the simple level of the model outlined thus far, there is no distinction between marriage and cohabitation because no legal constraint or binding contract is part of the model. Cohabitation could be introduced in various ways, such as by supposing that there is a cost to marriage that could be avoided by a cohabiting union, for example; but in this case there would have to be a benefit of marriage as well to counter the cost, or else no one would marry. The benefit might be the protection against loss of income or past investments in the event of a dissolution. In any case, the Current Population Survey (CPS) data used below do not have information on cohabitation, so it will not be pursued further here. Nevertheless, it would be an interesting exercise to investigate, both theoretically and empirically, whether the two simple hypotheses developed above for marriage—that the gap between male and female wages increases marriage rates and that an increase in their sum also increases marriage rates—also holds for cohabitation rates.

This model ignores the influence of the sex ratio in the marriage market, which is a drawback. In addition, the model ignores many other economic factors. Perhaps those that have been discussed most often are those related to government policy, particularly on the tax side (marriage penalties, Earned Income Tax Credit) and on the transfer side (Aid to Families with Dependent Children, etc.), which provide their own sets of incentives for marriage and nonmarriage. Although these have changed over time and differ somewhat across individuals in cross section, it will nevertheless be presumed that the more basic wage rate forces are more important and it is those that are concentrated on below.

THE "FACTS" AND THE ECONOMIC "EXPLANATIONS": WHITE WOMEN AND MEN

The empirical analysis here employs data from the March CPS from 1968 to 1996. The CPS is a monthly, random survey of the U.S. population, and in March of every year information on earnings and weeks of work are obtained.[5] From each CPS we select all men and women 17–45 and we stratify the sample in each year by age, birth cohort, and education. For education, we use the highest grade completed and form three groups: less than high school, exactly high school, and more than high school. We also stratify the sample into two races, white and black, and do not examine other race groups. For each age, birth cohort, education, and race group, we calculate a marriage rate, a female wage rate, and a male wage rate. The marriage rate is the fraction of the group that is married, spouse present at the interview date; and the wage rate for each gender is the average weekly wage (annual earnings divided by annual weeks of work) in real 1992 dollars over the previous calendar year.[6,7] In accordance with our previous discussion, we also construct the ratio of the female wage to the male wage for each group. The analysis will be entirely graphical. We shall first consider the white and then the black population.

The first differential we examine is the cross-sectional variation by education. Figure 15.1 shows the cross-sectional relationship between education and cohort profiles of marriage and wages, illustrating it for women and men born 1950–1954. The upper panel shows that age–marriage profiles rise steeply at young ages and then flatten out over time, and start to decline in the mid-forties. The relationship between marriage and education changes with age, and thus demonstrates the importance of life course stage in examining educational differentials. The least- educated women (less than high school) have the most rapidly accelerating marriage rates at young ages and, from about age 20 to 24, have the highest marriage rates for any group. The findings in some past research suggesting that the relationship between age at first marriage and education is positive are consistent with this pattern. But the high school and greater-than-high-school groups catch up and eventually—after about age 30—have higher marriage rates than their less-educated counterparts. The higher marriage rates of the less-educated group at young ages are a matter of marriage timing; the proper characterization of the relationship is instead that higher education leads to higher marriage rates.

The relationship between the high-school-only and greater-than-high-school groups goes in the opposite direction, however. This may be the result of a reversal in the relative magnitudes of income and price effects in going first from the least-educated group to the middle-educated group, and then from the latter to the most-educated group—but some independent evidence for such an hypothesis is required. In any case, this is an interesting finding whose explanation is worthy of more detailed future investigation. Beyond age 35 or so the two are approximately the same, but prior to that age the greater-than-high-school group has lower marriage rates. This may again be a timing issue, but it is much more drawn out than for the less-educated women.

The middle lines in Figure 15.1 show wage rates for white women born 1950–1954 and reveal, as expected, that wages are greater for more-educated women than for less-educated women.[8] The higher female wage of more educated women might be taken to imply that marriage rates should be lower for more-educated women, whereas in fact marriage rates are higher (at least relative to less-than-high-school women). Thus the economic model, or at least the specialization theory, may seem to have little validity in cross section. However, this conclusion is premature because male wages have not yet been examined, and it is the value of female wages relative to male wages that determines marriage incentives. For example, male wages could also be higher for more-educated men—which we know must be true—but they may be even higher relative to female wages than among less-educated men and women, implying greater gains to specialization among the more-educated population.

The lower lines in Figure 15.1 show the female–male wage ratios by education.[9] Figure 15.1 indicates that the wage ratio is somewhat higher for more educated men and women, but only at some points. This differential mainly exists at the younger ages for the greater-than-high-school group, whose wage ratios are higher than either of those of the lesser edu-

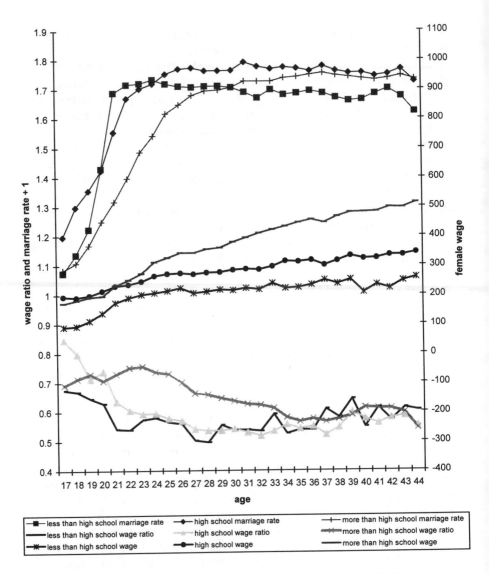

Figure 15.1. Marriage rates, female wage rates, and wage ratios of white women, 1950–1954 birth cohort, by education.

cated groups. However, after age 34 or so there is little difference, and at no age is there much difference between the wage ratios of the two less-educated groups. That there is not a large difference in the wage ratio at different education levels implies, in turn, that male and female wages rise by approximately the same proportion, generally, with education. But even though the wage ratios are about the same at different levels of education, the level of wages and income is not, and income will be much greater for the more educated. This implies that the income effects will dominate the price effects and, since income effects are presumed to positively affect marriage, we should expect marriage rates to be higher among more-educated groups. This is indeed what the data indicate, and therefore this is consistent with the economic model.

We turn next to differentials by birth cohort, considered separately by education. Figures 15.2 and 15.3 show marriage and wage profiles for less-educated and more-educated women, respectively, in three different birth cohorts (1930–1934, 1940–1944, and 1950–1954). Figures 15.2 and 15.3 show that marriage rates have been falling over time for both educational groups, on average—that is, at the same age, the more recently born cohorts have lower rates of marriage. Because rates vary with age, it is essential that age be held constant in this comparison; and given the time frame of the data (1968 to 1996), the cohorts can be compared only at particular ages. The profiles tend to converge as age increases, so the differentials appear at younger ages.

It can be seen from Figures 15.2 and 15.3, and confirmed by an examination of the actual numbers, that the declines in marriage rates have been greater for less-educated women. This is particularly apparent for marriage rates in the age range 25–35, but it is also true at older ages. Thus there are two "facts" revealed by Figures 15.2 and 15.3: (1) marriage rates have been declining for both more-educated women and less-educated women, and (2) the rates of decline are greater for less-educated women.

The middle and lower lines in Figures 15.2 and 15.3 show trends in female wages and wage ratios by cohort, allowing an assessment of their consistency with these two marriage facts. The middle lines in Figure 15.2 show that there has been essentially no change in the wage rates of less-educated white women over time, a phenomenon familiar from the literature on increasing earnings inequality in the United States and declining wages at the bottom of the skill distribution (Levy and Murnane, 1992; Mishel et al., 1997).[10] The middle lines in Figure 15.3 demonstrate, on the other hand, that wage rates for more skilled women have been rising over time, at least at many ages and for many educational differentials. Both of these patterns for less-educated and more-educated women are consistent with an increase in the dispersion of wage rates in the U.S. labor force that has been shown in other research to have occurred over this period.

Taken alone, these trends might be taken to imply that marriage rates for less-educated women should have risen—which they have not—and that marriage rates for more-educated women should have fallen—which they have. However, once again, this reasoning is incomplete because it is the female–male wage ratio that is the relevant determinant. The bottom lines in Figure 15.2 show that ratio for less-than-high-school men and women for the three birth cohorts, and demonstrate that the ratio has been

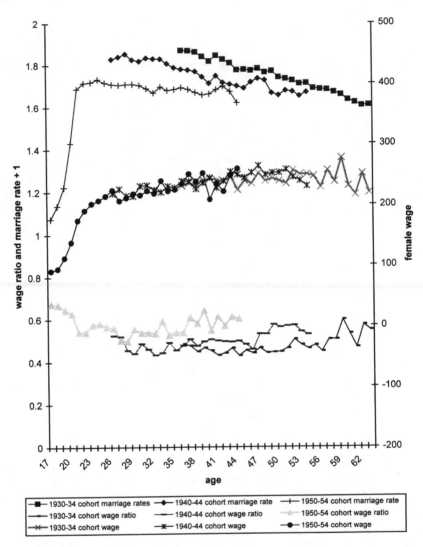

Figure 15.2. Marriage rates, female wage rates, and wage ratios of white women with less than high school education, by birth cohort.

rising over time, on average—not stable, as the case for the female wage alone. This implies that male wages of this group have been falling over time; this is indeed the case, although a figure showing male wages by cohort is not illustrated for brevity. In fact, this decline in the wage rates of less-educated men has also been extensively documented elsewhere, and has reflected a decline in the labor market situation of less-skilled workers

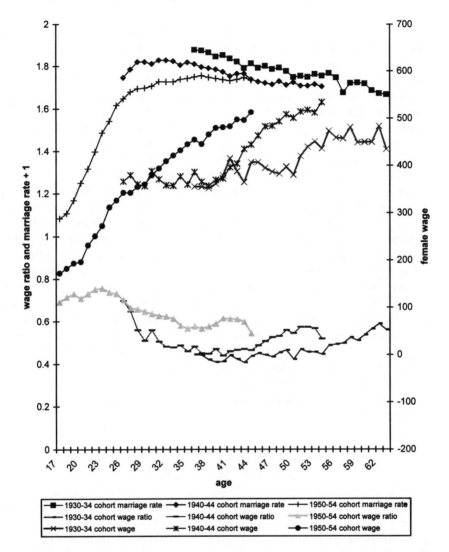

Figure 15.3. Marriage rates, female wage rates, wage ratios of white women with more than high school education, by birth cohort.

in the United States in general (Mishel et al., 1997:144). What this implies, however, is that incentives for specialization have fallen among the less-educated population, leading to falling marriage incentives—consistent therefore with the decline in marriage rates shown by the data.[11]

The wage ratio for more educated men and women has also been rising, as shown at the bottom of Figure 15.3, at least for ages past the late 20s or early 30s. However, unlike the less-educated group, in this group male wages have been rising over time (again, not shown graphically), as have female wages. But female wages have been rising even faster, leading to an increase in the wage ratio and therefore a decline in the gains to marriage from specialization. Thus at least the "price" effect arising from the wage ratio is, for the more-educated group, consistent with the observed decline in marriage for this group. On the other hand, that male wages have been rising (as have female wages) should have led to income effects that strengthen marriage; so consistency with the economic model in this case requires that the price effect dominate the income effect.

The other "fact"—that marriage rates have been declining faster among the less-educated population—follows from these same observations. Wage ratios have been rising for both more-educated and less-educated groups, which by itself would lead to comparable marriage trends, but the levels of average wages have gone in opposite directions. For the less-educated population, male wages have been falling and female wages have been level, leading to declines in income; but incomes have risen for the more-educated population as wages for both men and women have grown. Thus the income effects have reinforced the decline in marriage rates for the less-educated population but have retarded those declines for the more-educated population. This is consistent with a simple economic model, therefore, and illustrates directly both of the points mentioned in the Introduction—that the male wage is a necessary variable for explanation, and that more-educated and less-educated groups must be analyzed separately.

THE "FACTS" AND THE ECONOMIC "EXPLANATIONS": BLACK WOMEN AND MEN

Figures 15.4–15.6 show values for black men and women that correspond to Figures 15.1–15.3 for white men and women. Figure 15.4 shows age–marriage profiles by education group for the 1950–1954 birth cohort. The relative patterns by education are stronger for black women than for white women. More-educated black women have lower marriage rates at young ages but, by age 27, have higher marriage rates. After age 27, the three education groups are fully ordered by education, with more-educated women always having higher marriage rates—which was not the case for white women. Once again, however, the less-educated group is the farthest away from the other two groups, having significantly lower marriage rates.

The wage rate differentials by education shown in Figure 15.4 provide some support for the economic model. As expected, wages are higher for more-educated black women than for the less educated. Interestingly, the

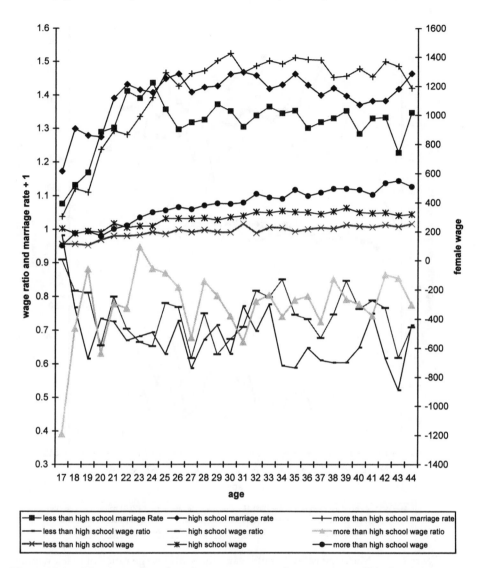

Figure 15.4. Marriage rates, female wage rates, and wage ratios of black women, 1950–1954 birth cohort, by education.

absolute magnitude of the wage gap is almost identical to that of white women, and thus the difference in marriage differentials is unlikely to be found here. However, female–male wage ratios by education for the black population are even less differentiated than those for the white population. The smaller wage ratio–education differential for the black population is a result of a wage–education differential among black males that is

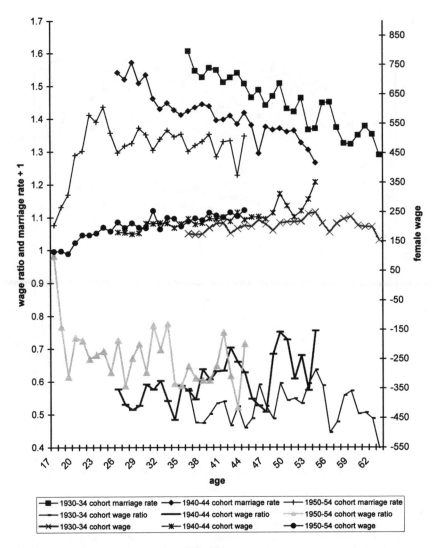

Figure 15.5. Marriage rates, female wage rates, and wage ratios of black women with less than high school education, by birth cohort.

considerably larger than that for white males, which may be interpreted either as relatively high wages for more-educated black men or relatively low wages for less-educated black men. Regardless of the source, this could help explain the stronger marriage–education differential among the black population, for the greater black male wage–education differential would, according to the economic model, push marriage rates down

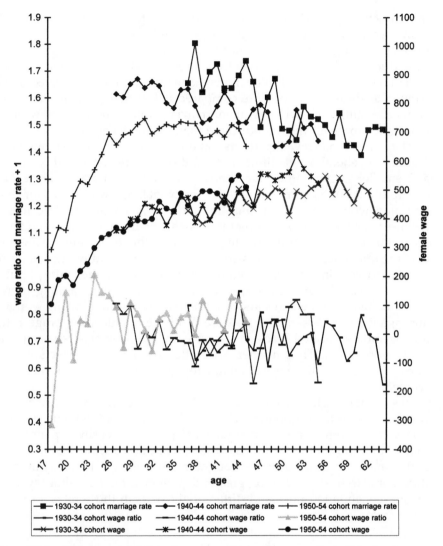

Figure 15.6. Marriage rates, female wage rates, and wage ratios of black women with more than high school education, by birth cohort.

among the less educated and up among the more educated in relative terms. In any case, the cross-sectional differentials among black men and women are somewhat consistent with the economic model but only from an entirely income-effect explanation.

Figures 15.5 and 15.6 show the trend evidence in marriage rates and wage rates by education for black women. Marriage rates are, as known from much other work, lower than those for white women (Cherlin, 1992). However, as for white women, marriage rates have declined over time for the black population. The magnitude of the decline is slightly greater for less-educated black women than for less-educated white women, but not by a great deal; and the decline in marriage rates for more-educated black women as different cohorts are compared is less marked than for white women.[12] Still, as for white women, marriage rates among black women have fallen more for the less educated than the more educated.

The wage trends reveal patterns somewhat different for the white population; in general, wage differentials and trends are considerably muted and smaller in magnitude than those for white men and women. For example, although Figure 15.5 shows somewhat larger wage gains for less-educated women over time than for white women (the middle lines), female–male wage ratios among the less-educated black population have risen much less than in the white population (the lower lines). Thus the decline of marriage among less-educated black men and women is more difficult to explain with wage trends than it was among the white population. Likewise, Figure 15.6 shows almost no wage gains among more-educated black women, in stark contrast to more-educated white women, and again shows essentially no growth in the female–male wage ratio among more-educated black men and women, in contrast again to the white population. Thus neither price effects nor income effects would appear to be a significant explanator for more-educated black men and women.

In summary, although cross-sectional wage differentials are reasonably consistent with the economic model, as they were for the white population, relative trends in marriage rates are much less easily explained by that model. Some other factors may therefore be at work among black men and women, which needs to be brought into the picture. This may involve differential trends in sex ratios, greater dependence on the welfare system, greater cohabitation rates and differential trends in those rates, or some other factor.

SUMMARY

This chapter has assessed the basic macrolevel evidence on white and black cross-sectional differentials and time-series trends in marriage rates and wage rates among men and women to assess whether those differentials and trends are roughly consistent with the basic economic model of marriage. The CPS data from 1968–1996 show a fairly high degree of consistency for the white population but a lesser degree for the black population. For the white population, the data on wages are consistent with the existence of a positive cross-sectional differential—higher marriage rates for higher-wage women—and with the time-series negative differential—declining marriage rates as female wage rates have risen. The reconciliation between these two differentials lies in the role of male wage rates, which in cross section are higher for more-educated men (which tends to make marriage rates higher among the more- educated population) but which have fallen relative to female wages over time.

The time-series analysis also goes beyond a simple overall examination of marriage rates and female wage rates, common in past work, to examine those trends separately for the more- educated and less-educated populations. Declines in marriage have occurred among both groups at the same time that female–male wage ratios have risen among both groups, but male wage rates have behaved very differently for the more educated and less educated. Although the wages of more-educated men have risen over time, those of less-educated men have fallen. The simple economic model of marriage predicts that this would force marriage rates down more among the less-educated than among the more-educated population, and this is indeed what has happened. Thus again the analysis has shown that the role of male wage trends must be included in a discussion of economic influences for a complete explanation.

The analysis also shows that it is seriously misleading to discuss the consistency of the economic model for marriage trends among men and women in general, without differentiation between high-wage and low-wage (i.e., more-educated and less-educated) strata of the population. The patterns are very different and it is not too far from the evidence to suggest that marriage declines among more-educated white men and women are a "story" of rising female wages, while those declines among less-educated white men and women are a "story" of declining male wages.

A significant puzzle identified in the analysis is the decreased ability of the economic model to explain marriage trends among the black population. Cross-sectional differentials show relatively weak effects of wage ratios, for example, suggesting less specialization and division of labor in black marriages, and time-series effects show that changes in those wage ratios have decreased explanatory power for changes in black marriage rates than for white women. These findings therefore suggest further work is needed for the black population.

Finally, the simplicity of the analysis here deserves repeated emphasis but it need also be noted that this simplicity does not have any necessary implications for the importance of economic influences relative to noneconomic influences in explaining differential marriage patterns. On the one hand, because noneconomic influences have been ignored, it is quite possible that those influences could provide an alternative explanation that is just as consistent with the data (for the white population, let us say) as for the economic model. No testing of alternative hypotheses has been performed. On the other hand, the economic model used here is of the simplest kind, and economic influences could be elaborated in many more directions, with a corresponding increase in the power of explanations of observed marriage patterns. Further work in both these directions would be fruitful.

ACKNOWLEDGMENTS

The author would like to thank Christine Bachrach and Linda Waite for comments and Xue Song for research assistance.

NOTES

1.   It is impossible to do justice to the enormous literature on the model by citation. The work of Becker (1973, 1981) is seminal, of course, and contains all the ideas noted in this section. But although the form of the model as given here is familiar, it cannot be found in exactly this form anywhere in Becker's work. The review paper of Weiss (1997) lays out many of the basic issues and provides additional citations.

2.   Becker (1973:305) did not initially assume any of these to represent the gains to marriage but rather assumed those gains to arise from simple complementarities in household production. However, later (Becker, 1981), he made specialization—through investment in either market or home skills—the central gain to marriage.

3.   This may be the best point to note that it is *potential* wage rates—the amount an individual could earn in the labor market, if he or she wished to work—that is the concept in the economic model. *Actual*, or *realized*, wages, or earnings—namely, labor market earnings that result from an individual's decision to enter the labor force and to work a certain number of weeks and hours—is as much the result of the marriage decision as its cause, and hence is not regarded in the economic model as an independent determinant of marriage gains. The modifier "potential" before "wages" is implicit throughout this chapter.

4.   But see Becker (1973:307) for an analysis of income effects that predicts a positive effect on gains to marriage.

5.   For more information on the CPS, see http://www.bls.census.gov/cps/.

6.   We ignore selectivity issues—wages are calculated for workers only—and leave an examination of this issue to future work. Put differently, we assume that the mean of observed wages is the same as the mean of potential wages—or at least that the education and birth cohort differentials in observed wages are the same as differentials in potential wages. This is no doubt an approximation at best, but the magnitude of the error is unlikely to affect the gross nature of the comparisons made here.

7.   The wage is calculated over all persons in the age–education-cohort–race cell, not just over married individuals. Note that this implies that the male and female wage in each cell is taken over never-married, divorced-separated, and widowed individuals as well as marrieds.

8. The wage profiles also rise over the life cycle and spread out from one another, patterns familiar from a large literature in labor economics. See Mincer (1974).

9. Males and females are matched up in the same age–education-cohort cells, thus ignoring the age and education gaps between husbands and wives that are known to exist. However, because our categories are broad relative to those gaps, this is unlikely to affect the relationships we are examining.

10. Some caution is needed in interpreting these trends for, as the general level of education has risen, an increasingly smaller fraction of women in each cohort has less than a high school education. Thus Figure 15.2 does not have necessary implications for trends in market wages for women of the same relative skill in the population. However, this issue does not affect the correlations of interest here because the marriage rates in Figure 15.3 to which these wage rates will be compared are for the same (size-decreasing) group.

11. Oppenheimer has also attributed much of recent declines in marriage to reductions in male earning power. See, e.g., Oppenheimer et al. (1997).

12. It should be emphasized that neither out-of-wedlock childbearing nor single motherhood in general is being examined here, which have increased at more differential rates for the two races. Nor is cohabitation included in these figures, which also differs between the races.

REFERENCES

Becker, Gary. 1973. "A Theory of Marriage." In *The Economics of the Family*, edited by Theodore W. Schultz. Chicago: University of Chicago Press.

Becker, Gary. 1981. *A Treatise on the Family*. Cambridge, MA: Harvard University Press.

Cherlin, Andrew. 1992. *Marriage, Divorce, and Remarriage*. Cambridge, MA: Harvard University Press.

Levy, Frank, and Richard Murnane. 1992. "U.S. Earnings Levels and Earnings Inequality: A Review of Recent Trends and Proposed Explanations." *Journal of Economic Literature* 30:1333–1381.

Mincer, Jacob. 1974. *Schooling, Experience, and Earnings*. New York: National Bureau of Economic Research.

Mishel, Lawrence, Jared Bernstein, and John Schmitt. 1997. *The State of Working America, 1996–1997*. Armonk, NY: M.E. Sharpe.

Oppenheimer, Valerie, Matthijs Kalmijn, and Nelson Lim. 1997. "Men's Career Development and Marriage Timing During a Period of Rising Inequality." *Demography* 34:311–330.

Weiss, Yoram. 1997. "The Formation and Dissolution of Families: Why Marry? Who Marries Whom? And What Happens Upon Divorce?" Pp. 81–123 in *Handbook of Population and Family Economics*, edited by Mark Rosenzweig and Oded Stark. Amsterdam: Elsevier North-Holland.

16

Marriage, the Costs of Children, and Gender Inequality

PAULA ENGLAND

The only thing worse than being dominated by a husband is not being dominated by a husband. (Paraphrase of Joan Robinson, who said "the only thing worse than being exploited by a capitalist is not being exploited by a capitalist.")[1]

It strikes me as a sad, revealing commentary on the benefits to women of the traditional . . . family that, even . . . when women and their children suffer substantial economic decline after divorce, so many regard divorce as the lesser of evils. (Stacey, 1993)

INTRODUCTION

Nothing generates a livelier debate than the question of whether marriage is good for women. In this chapter, I consider whether marriage (or cohabitation[2]) is good for women, and whether it is good for men. I also consider relative gains—whether marriage benefits one sex more than the other, or to put the same thing a different way, whether marriage is good for gender equality.

In a number of arenas of life there is substantial male advantage. This is, in a nutshell, the fundamental feminist claim. Looking at male advantage in marriage, feminists have often concluded that marriage is a sexist institution that must be bad for women. But some of the same factors producing male advantage in marriage also encourage male advantage among those who are single. These factors include sex discrimination in labor markets, women's disproportionate responsibility for children, and cultural meanings and scripts that encourage male power. If male advantage exists among singles and those who are married, then the fact of male dominance in marriage does not really tell us whether marriage is good or bad for women or for gender equality. The paraphrase of Robinson and the quote of Stacey with which I began both recognize this female disadvantage that extends across those who are married and single. Where they seem to disagree is on which is worse for women, being single in a male-dominated society or being married in a male-dominated society.

The oversimplified version of one feminist view is that since marriage is patriarchal, it must be bad for women. In Simone de Beauvoir's view ([1949] 1974), women's subjection to social roles that men invented in their own interest is epitomized in marriage and motherhood, both of which she recommended against, in favor of economic independence, political struggle, and intellectual endeavor. In general, liberal feminism has focused on attaining equality for women in the "public sphere" of politics and paid employment. There has been less emphasis on how the family might be changed. Thus, we might get the impression from this lack of emphasis on the private sphere that liberal feminists think that gender inequality in marriage is inevitable or unimportant.[3]

It is possible to argue against the view that marriage is bad for women by denying that there is typically male dominance in marriage. If there is no male dominance in marriage, then there is no reason to think that marriage is bad for women (or at least any worse for women than for men). This will not be my argument, since I think the evidence of male advantage in the typical marriage is quite clear.

It is possible to argue that marriage is typically good for women (as well as men) on empirical grounds without disputing the contention that men are typically advantaged in marriage. The best example of this line of argument is Linda Waite's (1995) presidential address to the Population Association of America and a recent book by Waite and Gallagher (2000). They present empirical evidence that, on average, for both men and women, those who are married have better physical and mental health, engage in less problem drinking and fewer risk-taking behaviors, have lower mortality, and have higher wealth and family income. And, contrary to stereotypes of the swinging sex life of singles, married people have sex more frequently and enjoy it more. This evidence casts doubt on the assertion that women are better off outside of marriage.

At first glance it looks like Waite (1995; Waite and Gallagher, 2000) and the feminists who argue that marriage is bad for women are asking the same question—is marriage good for women—and getting a different answer. However, on closer inspection it becomes clear that they are comparing women's well-being within marriage to two different alternatives. Waite is comparing married women to the average, empirically observed alternative. Included in her "single women" averages are childless women, divorced women with children, and never-married mothers who live in the contemporary real world. Feminist theorists often seem implicitly to be comparing women's situation in marriage to men's situation in marriage or to women's situation in some hypothetical less sexist alternative. What are the less sexist alternatives to marriage that feminists implicitly or explicitly envision when they argue that marriage is bad for women? Simone de Beauvoir ([1949] 1974) and most liberal feminists across the last two centuries have probably envisioned single career women without children. Some writers envision mutually satisfying, egalitarian lesbian partnerships, with or without children, as the alternative to marriage. How potentially desirable this option is for most women depends in part on the extent to which sexual orientation is socially constructed, a topic beyond my scope here. But, if we are willing to reject essentialism enough to treat sexual orientation as sufficiently plastic to be changed in adulthood, we might with no more controversy reject essentialism enough to posit that sexist social structures can be changed and men can be rehabilitated to the extent that egalitarian marriages, with or without children, are another possible alternative. Of course, uncoupled childlessness, lesbian partnerships with or without children, and egalitarian marriages with or without children might all be desirable alternatives to male dominance in marriage. It is possible to take the position that a good society would have all these alternatives available to women and men. Any of these alternatives entail less male dominance than the typical marriage.

However, it is important to remember what the current, usual *empirically observed* alternative to marriage (or cohabitation) is. For most women it is single motherhood. The United States and most industrial societies are in the midst of a dramatic retreat from marriage at all levels of the social class hierarchy, but particularly at the bottom. This trend is driven by divorce, later marriage, and later remarriage after divorce. Projections suggest that current trends will even lead to a nontrivial (though still small) proportion of people who never marry. Although most people still espouse a reverence for marriage, as a behavioral matter adults in modern societies are spending a lower proportion of their person-years in the married state than previously. Although some of this is explained by cohabitation emerging as a new premarriage union form, there appears to be some retreat from unions altogether.

Fertility has fallen along with marriage rates. But an equally important trend is a loosening of the tight link between childbearing and marriage. Many women are bearing children outside of marriage. In the main, this change results not from the fertility rate among unmarried women going up (it has gone up slightly among whites and down substantially among blacks); rather, the retreat from marriage has put women at risk of a nonmarital birth for more of their life span (Blank, 1997). Thus, the proportion of all births that are to unmarried women has surged, moving between 1960 and 1992 from about 2 to 17% among whites and from 25 to about 70% for African-Americans (Smith et al., 1996:142).

The prevalent emerging alternatives to marriage are characterized by much more male advantage than the hypothetical alternatives to marriage envisioned by feminists. In this brave new world, most men and women still practice heterosexuality, so any heterosexism and sexism encoded in the cultural meanings and scripts that guide sexuality are still operative. Most women still have children (though fewer than previously), and do most of the childrearing work when children are reared outside of marriage, as they do in traditional marriages. However, even very traditional marriages generally feature more child care by fathers than nonmarriage. Quasi-egalitarian marriages certainly have men doing more of the child care than in nonmarriage. Thus, women's disadvantage flowing from having responsibility for children is still very present. Women's disproportionate bearing of the work load of parenting affects their earning power when mothers are single, as it does when they are married (Waldfogel, 1997; Budig and England, 1999). In addition, because most unmarried parents do not live together[4] and most nonresident fathers pay little child support, women are providing a much higher proportion of the financial support of children than previously. Thus, in the new low-marriage regime, compared to the old regime, women are still providing most of the labor inputs to children and are providing much more of the financial support for children. To my mind, there is no contradiction between being a feminist and questioning whether this new regime of single motherhood is an improvement for women over traditional marriage. To do so is not necessarily to whitewash the male dominance of traditional marriage.

In sum, the problem with the view held by some feminists that women are better off without marriage is not its contention that men are advantaged in most marriages. They are right about that. The problem is rather that it is dangerous to romanticize the typical alternatives to marriage. The typical alternative of single motherhood features women bearing more of the costs of children than ever unless the state steps in to collectivize more of the costs of children, but trends in dismantling the welfare state run in the opposite direction. The limitation of Waite's (1995; Waite and Gallagher 2000) view is that it fails to notice, or at least to emphasize, the extent to which men are advantaged over women in marriage.

One feminist theorist who has recognized that both traditional marriage and the new gender regime featuring single motherhood preserve male dominance is British sociologist Sylvia Walby (1990, 1997). She describes recent changes this way:

> The domestic gender regime is based on household production as the main structure and site of women's work activity and the exploitation of her labour and sexuality and on the exclusion of women from the public. The

public gender regime is based, not on excluding women from the public, but on the segregation and subordination of women within the structures of paid employment and the state, as well as within culture, sexuality and violence. The household does not cease to be a relevant structure in the public form, but is no longer the chief one. In the domestic form the beneficiaries are primarily the individual husbands and fathers of the women in the household, while in the public form there is a more collective appropriation. In the domestic form the principal patriarchal strategy is exclusionary, excluding women from the public arena; in the public it is segregationist and subordinating. . . . Whether a move to a more public form of gender regime leads to a reduction of gender inequality is an empirical question rather than one to be determined in an a priori fashion. (Walby, 1997:6)

Walby argues that the extent of male advantage has been reduced to some extent by women's increased employment and the earnings it provides, but that there are many ways in which social structures still enhance male dominance. She ended her 1990 book on this pessimistic note: "Women are no longer restricted to the domestic hearth, but have the whole society in which to roam and be exploited" (Walby, 1990:201).

Another feminist writer who recognizes male advantage in both societies with high and low marriage rates is economist Nancy Folbre (1994a). Her book, *Who Pays for the Kids*, argues that the way in which rearing children contributes to the economy has been ignored in economics, as have the arrangements by which women bear most of the costs of children. She argues that social arrangements and public policies that shift costs of children between women and men are important determinants of gender equality. Marriage has the gender-equality-enhancing feature of getting men to contribute substantial cash to the rearing of children. However, it is not the only social mechanism that can do this. Another option is public funding of some of the costs of rearing children through mechanisms such as family allowances, universal health care, and child care, financed through progressive taxes on earnings and property. Stricter enforcement of individual fathers' child support requirements is another option. The thrust of Folbre's analysis is to shift our attention toward the allocation of the costs of children between men and women.

Folbre (1994a) argues that mothers have been progressively pauperized (relative to other adult men and women) and are bearing more of the costs of children today than in previous eras. What Folbre's argument does not make clear is how much this relative pauperization is because of the retreat from marriage and the increase in single motherhood. Women are disadvantaged in marriage by their bearing of the labor and opportunity costs (in earnings) of children. But when women bear children outside of marriage, they still bear the labor and opportunity costs of children, but lose much of their access to a share of the earnings of the fathers of their children.

The chapter will be organized as follows. I first discuss the way in which marriage, as typically organized, results in men having more power than women. I review the relevant theory about marital bargaining and then the available empirical evidence. I then argue that the typical situation of unmarried women and men also disadvantages women. I then consider the critical interaction effect, whether any benefits to marriage are greater for men than women, or, to put the same thing another way, whether marriage promotes or discourages gender inequality. I conclude that this depends on the arena examined, but that marriage probably benefits men more than women, and thus increases gender inequality in many domains except the provision of income. I note that the factors promoting gender inequality inside marriage overlap substantially with those promoting gender inequality outside marriage. These factors are labor market discrimination, responsibility for most of the labor of rearing children (with attendant opportunity costs), and cultural meanings and scripts that encourage male power. Thus, from a feminist perspective, whether women marry is less important than whether gender inequality is lessened inside and outside marriage. I end with a discussion of policies that would promote gender equality. Since I believe the question of who bears the costs of children has been ignored in most policy discussions, I focus on these issues.

CAUSES OF WOMEN'S DISADVANTAGE WITHIN MARRIAGE

Let us first look at arguments and evidence about male advantage in marriage. Social scientists generally see male power in marriage as flowing from some combination of male earnings and cultural meanings or beliefs. The greater theoretical energy has gone into discussing the effects of earnings on bargaining; I discuss these first.

Men's Higher Earnings as a Source of Bargaining Power

There is still a substantial sex gap in pay, with women who work full-time earning about 70% of what men do (Reskin and Padavic, 1999). Some of this is due to various types of sex discrimination by employers (Reskin and Padavic, 1999). Employers may be unwilling to hire women in better paying "male" jobs, they may pay women less than men for the same work, and they may take the sex composition of jobs into account when they set wages. Another portion of the sex gap comes from effects of motherhood. First, even though women's employment has increased dramatically among married mothers, when someone takes time out of employment for childrearing it is still generally the woman. During these times, married women have no earnings, or have much reduced earnings if they work part-time. But being a mother also leads to lower wages when returning to full-time employment. Mothers have lower wages, in part because they have lost experience and seniority (Waldfogel, 1997). In addition, there is an additional component of the "motherhood penalty" not well understood, but likely to be explained by some combination of employers' discrimination against mothers, motherhood lowering productivity, or women choosing "mother-friendly" jobs that trade off earnings for factors such as flexible hours. Despite the looser coupling of marriage and childbearing than previously, marriage still makes birth more likely. Thus, marriage may be indirectly responsible for women suffering the motherhood penalty. And, indeed, there is some evidence that married women suffer a slightly larger earnings penalty for motherhood than unmarried mothers (Budig and England, 1999). But both single and married women suffer a motherhood penalty.

The typical marriage features a husband with higher earnings than the wife. This can be because of employers' discrimination or because conventional gender norms make couples decide that the wife will focus on childrearing. Alternatively, it can be part of an efficient division of labor in which the couple decides that family utility is maximized if they follow each person's comparative advantage, and this dictates that he works in the market and she at home. The latter view is emphasized by Becker (1991) and the "new home economics." Becker's view ignored unequal bargaining power in marriage because it assumed that men would be sufficiently altruistic not to take advantage of any objective advantage in bargaining power they might have. But, contrary to this view there is substantial warrant in either economic or sociological theory for the view that a division of labor in which men specialize in market earning while women specialize in household labor will lead to greater male power.

Economists generally do not think that either party to a market exchange has power over imposing costs (prices) on the other because market competition prevents this. However, when there is no market with a large number of competitors (e.g., monopoly), neoclassical theory admits the relevance of power. Game theory, rather than supply and demand, is seen as the relevant theoretical tool. By this reasoning if we want to know if husbands have power over their wives (or vice versa), we have to ask whether, after marriage, partners are still facing competitive market forces of the marriage market. It is a bit like asking whether, after taking a job, either an employer or employee is still subject to the competitive pressures of the market.

From the perspective of economic theory, there is a very clear answer: the more either party has made investments that are specific to this relationship, the more both parties are in a situation of "bilateral monopoly." After relationship-specific investments in marriage, there is no other partner as "trained in" to one's particular needs. And of course no other partner would be the co-parent of whatever children the couple has had. Thus, there is no comparable partner on the external "marriage market" and so neither spouse is fully competing with other potential spouses their partner could leave them for. This makes both more likely to stay in the marriage, but also means that power will affect distribution of gains to marriage. The situation is now game theoretic, even by strict neoclassical reasoning.

Thus, it seems that there is ample warrant from an economic viewpoint to take a game-theoretic approach to marriage, and indeed some recent scholars have done so (Bergstrom, 1996; Katz, 1997; Sen, 1990; McElroy, 1990; McElroy and Horney, 1981). [See Lundberg and Pollak (1996) for an overview of such models.]

The theoretical reasoning of game theory is somewhat akin to Emerson's view of power-dependence theory within sociological exchange theory (see, e.g., Cook, 1987). An early sociological example of its application to marital power is found in Heer (1963). Later theorizing that attempts to integrate sociological and economic views is offered by England and Farkas (1986), England and Kilbourne (1990), and England and Budig (1998).[5]

In this bargaining view, couples bargain over how things (money, goods, leisure) will be distributed. Game theory (which assumes selfish actors) sees one's bargaining power affected by "threat points." The better one's alternatives for utility outside the relationship (relative to one's utility in the relationship), and the worse one's partner's alternatives outside versus inside the marriage, the harder one can afford to bargain. This is because the better the alternatives outside the relationship (relative to inside) the less one would lose if insisting on a better deal within the marriage drove the other person to divorce. And the worse one's alternatives outside the marriage, the more likely one is to "give in" to avoid a divorce. Even if we believe in some altruism in marriage, to whatever degree spouses are selfish, this model seems relevant.

Women are in a vulnerable situation, threat point-wise, in traditional marriages. Because they have been the ones at home with children, they have less job experience, which lowers what they could earn if they suddenly had to support themselves and their children. Employer discrimination and the absence of a generous social safety net for mothers also lower women's threat point situation in marriage. Men take their earning power with them in case of a divorce—so the very investments they have made during the marriage also help them if they leave. Because both spouses know that the homemaker has much to lose if the marriage breaks up, she gets less of what she wants when there is a disagreement than she would if she had better alternatives outside the marriage. In this theoretical view, it is the *portability* of earnings outside the marriage that make them generate more power than the domestic contributions women are making to the exchange. Put another way, it is the fact that the women typically do not withdraw the domestic contribution of rearing children in the event of divorce that makes this contribution generate less power than earnings.

Let us turn to empirical evidence on the effects of men's higher wages and its effects on gender equality in marriage. Does the theoretical view that men's greater earning power leads to more power in marriage fit empirical evidence? I would cautiously say yes, although I think this is an area that needs far more research.

One body of research relevant to this question is an older sociological research tradition, largely from the 1950s to 1970s, that attempted to directly measure marital power (conceptualized as being the person who got to make a decision or who got his or her way on some issue on which the couple disagreed). Probably the best exemplar of these early studies is one by David Heer (1958). In a Boston sample of 138 interviews, he interviewed both husbands and wives, asking them to identify some common disagreements and who usually got their way, or whether a mutual decision was generally reached.[6] He divided husbands into working and middle class, and showed that within each category male power was less extreme when women worked for pay at least 10 hours a week, and that this held net of a psychological measure of dominance. No other control variables were used.

Duncan and Duncan (1978:205) used 1971 data from Detroit. Their measure of power was simply the answer to a question on who usually makes the final decision about things such as what house or car to buy or whether the wife should work for pay. (A group of such items had been used in an earlier influential 1960 study by Blood and Wolfe; they were used in this study as well.) They showed that in couples with employed wives, women's power was higher. The effect was more a matter of women's employment lowering the likelihood that husbands make fewer final decisions and increasing decisions being made jointly (less a movement to wife's unilateral decision). Their analysis had no controls for husbands' or wives' education, earnings, or occupational status.

These early studies simply looked at the effects of women's employment versus nonemployment, rather than at effects of relative earnings. However, those who are employed have earnings and those who are not do not, and so one way to interpret the findings is to say they crudely support the notion that relative earning power affects marital power.

A more recent study, by Blumstein and Schwartz (1983), used data from a nonprobability sample with power measured by who the respondent said has more say about important decisions (measured on a nine-point scale). They found that the difference between the partners' annual incomes affected reported power (such that contributing more income leads to more power), and that this was true among married couples, cohabiting heterosexual couples, and cohabiting gay men, but not among cohabiting lesbians.

More recent studies having the advantages of using large national probability samples and multivariate analysis have the disadvantage of no attempt to measure power or advantage directly. A number of studies have purported to address issues of marital bargaining using the outcome of how much housework each spouse does, combined with the assumption that most people would prefer to do less. Thus, at least for employed adults (and women's employment is much more common during the period when these studies are being done), doing more of the housework is viewed as evidence that one has lost in the bargaining. The independent variable assumed to affect bargaining power is usually some measure of relative earnings of the spouses.[7] It makes sense from the threat-point logic discussed above that if earnings are resources portable out of the marriage, they will create bargaining power within the marriage.[8] Three studies have found that relative earnings affect household work such that the higher A's earnings relative to B, the less housework A does (Ross, 1987; Brines, 1994; Presser, 1994). However, neither Baxter and Bittman (1995) nor Shelton (1992) found such effects. Effects of relative earnings on hours of household work could also be predicted by Becker's notion that comparative advantage determines which kind of work (market or household) each spouse will spend the next hour of work in. However, his model does *not* predict that women's lower wages cause them to work more total hours (when household and market work are added together) than men and thus to have less leisure. Thus, I think a key distinction between the predictions of the theories is in whether the effect of relative earnings on (relative) housework holds, *net* of hours worked in the market. Unfortunately, none of the studies adequately controlled for hours of market work. Brines (1994) comes the closest, controlling for whether the woman's employment was full-time versus part-time, but did not distinguish hours among full-time workers. (Male full-time workers generally work more hours than female full-time workers.) Ross (1987) simply adds a dummy variable for whether the wife is employed.

Thus, overall, there is some, but not consistent, evidence that relative wages affect marital bargaining. (Evidence from third world settings is reviewed in Lundberg and Pollak, 1996.) In some cases, this bargaining leads women to do more housework than would seem equitable given their hours of paid employment, creating what Hochschild (1989) called the "second shift." But, if it affects housework, there is every reason to expect that it affects many other things that spouses disagree on, as the earlier research tradition suggested.

Cultural Meaning as a Source of Male Advantage

Another approach to male advantage in marriage is to focus on cultural meanings and beliefs. If there are norms that say that men should have power over their wives in marriage, this may give all men some power, regardless of earning power. Although the literature reviewed above showed some effect of relative earnings on advantage, it is also quite clear in the research on housework how limited this explanatory power is. Relative earnings explain much less than sex itself, with women doing far more than would be predicted on the basis of their relative wages. Some authors (Fenstermaker Berk, 1985; Shelton, this volume) take evidence like this to support a "gender display" or "doing gender" perspective. This perspective has roots in the interactionist and ethnomethodological position [Shelton (this volume)]. However, it also assumes certain cultural meanings that are carried across situations, but are open to much play and negotiation in specific situations. Also consistent with this "doing gender" interpretation is a nonlinearity that Brines (1994) found in her analysis. Although Brines' study shows a negative net relationship between one's relative wage and housework hours in most of the range, there is some nonlinearity in the relationship for men, such that when women's earnings become virtually the sole support of men, the curve reverses and men's housework declines. It is as if either the husband or wife thinks he needs to do less housework to shore up his sense of masculinity. This area in which the curve reverses is, of course, inconsistent with the threat-point logic that would see women's bargaining power as maximized when they are the sole support of couples. This suggests that cultural meanings, as they play out in interaction, also have a role.

Cultural meanings more generally define masculinity in terms of power and invulnerability, and women more in terms of nurturance and "niceness." Although relationships need mutual nurturance to survive, being nurturant in relation to someone who is emphasizing power cannot help but to create a power imbalance. Thus, it seems that such an imbalance is built into some of our most rudimentary ideas about gender.

MALE ADVANTAGE IN THE LOW-MARRIAGE REGIME

Even if we agree that women are disadvantaged by the traditional division of labor in marriage, in which women take most responsibility for children and the household, this does not necessarily mean that women are better off single. One of the things that clearly advantages men is the fact that women are doing most of the labor and thus bearing most of the opportunity costs (in foregone wages and then, when they return to employment, lower earnings and pensions) of children. However, male advantage may permeate the single state as well, particularly when single people have children. In marriage, at least, men generally contribute a large share of the money that is used to support their children.

How are men advantaged in a situation where marriage is less common? This is harder to see at first, because it is not obvious how to talk about a division of labor between men and women. Which men should we think of in relationship to which women? Since unmarried people increasingly have children, we need to think about the division of labor and exchange relations between mothers and fathers irrespective of whether they are married. It is also useful to compare the status of single men and single women in the aggregate.

The prevalence of unmarried parents comes from two trends, the increase in divorce up until about 1980 (Cherlin, 1996) and the increase in the proportion of births to unmarried parents (Smith et al., 1996; Blank, 1997). In only about a quarter to a third of nonmarital births are the parents cohabiting (Bumpass and Sweet, 1989; McLanahan et al., 1998). Indeed, one important difference between Europe and the United States is that in Europe more unmarried parents are cohabiting (McLanahan et al., 1998). As a result of the trends in divorce and nonmarital childbearing, more and more children are supported by their mothers with little or no help in labor or money from their fathers. In 1960 about 8% of children lived with a single parent; by 1991 the figure was 25% overall and over 50% for black children (Garfinkel et al., 1994, Chapter 1). Given that one parent usually earns less than two, and given women's relatively low earnings, the result is often poverty. Indeed, about half of children in households without adult men are in poverty (United States Bureau of the Census, 1993). All this would be very different if child support were always awarded and paid, but more than half of all children potentially eligible for child support receive nothing from their fathers (Garfinkel et al., 1994, Chapter 1). It would also be different if the United States had a system of public provision of health care, child care, or family allowances (Casper et al., 1994). Financing such programs through progressive taxation shifts some of the costs of children from women to men (as well as from parents to nonparents).

Thus, in a regime of childbearing but nonmarriage, fathers could in principle still provide financial support for children, but typically they do not, at least in the United States. Child support enforcement is not much better in Europe. The important difference between the United States and Europe (other than our higher divorce and nonmarital birth rates) is that European states provide more generous transfer payments to sole mothers, some of which are universal and available to married parents too. These in effect socialize some of the costs of childrearing.

Equally important, noncustodial fathers probably do less of the actual caretaking labor than even fathers in the traditional 1950s. Thus, using the criterion of who pays for the children, men pay for less of the labor and money costs of children in a nonmarriage regime.

Men still have higher earnings in a lower marriage regime, although the sex gap in pay is less among singles than among those who are married. All the cultural meanings, discussed above, that define maleness in terms of power and control while emphasizing nurturance and niceness in women are present as well, affecting male/female relationships in dating, neighboring, voluntary associations, and political activities. Sexist cultural meanings regarding sexuality, particularly the double standard in which women are harshly judged for being sexually active whereas men are praised for conquest, have an adverse effect on women in the single regime as great or greater than the effect on married women (Schwartz and Rutter, 1998).

IS GENDER EQUALITY BETTER REALIZED
BY MARRIAGE OR NONMARRIAGE:
THE CRITICAL INTERACTION EFFECT

I have discussed male advantage in marriage and male advantage in a low-marriage regime. The important point to notice is that the analysis has suggested commonalities to the two regimes, with women bearing more of the costs of children in each, having lower earnings in each, and being disadvantaged by cultural meanings encouraging male dominance.

But is male advantage is greater in marriage than nonmarriage? How would we assess this? If this was true then it would imply that the *returns* to marriage differ by sex. The two are really different ways of approaching the same interaction effect. Let us look at this in the abstract, statistically.

When we say that X and Z interact in their effect on Y, there are two ways to talk about it. We can say that the magnitude of the effect of X on Y changes as Z changes, or we can say that the magnitude of the effect of Z on Y changes as X changes. If one is true, both will be true, although we often choose one way to talk about it. Consider Y to be some outcome of interest on which there could be male or female advantage and that could possibly be a return to marriage and perhaps some sort of satisfaction. Let X be sex and Z be whether the individual is married. Then if there is an XZ interaction, we can say that the extent to which sex affects the outcome, that is, the extent of male advantage, varies by whether the individual is married or not. Alternatively, an XZ interaction means that the gains to marriage differ between men and women. These are two ways to say the same thing. Thus, if male advantage over women is greater in a nonmarriage regime than in marriage, then the gains from marriage are greater for women than men. If the male advantage over women is greater in marriage than outside marriage, then the gains from marriage are greater for men than women.

In the remainder of this section, I go through a number of arenas, and look at what past research says about whether the interaction effect discussed above is present. If male returns to marriage are higher (or costs of marriage lower) then that should also mean that male advantage is higher (or female advantage lower) in marriage than nonmarriage. The presence or absence of this interaction effect is the relevant question to assess the effects of marriage on gender equality. However, it is a separate issue from the existence of "main effects"—whether on average in either the married or nonmarried setting men are advantaged and whether marriage has advantages or disadvantages to either sex. I will, however, note these effects as well as the discussion proceeds.

Table 16.1 summarizes what I think the literature tells us. Let us look first at earnings. The higher earnings of men than women are well known. Men earn more among the married and the unmarried, but the sex gap in earnings is greater among the married (Waite, 1995). Putting it another way, although there is some evidence that women (particularly black women) actually reap some wage benefit from marriage, particularly if they do not have children, these "returns" to marriage are clearly higher for men than women (Waite, 1995; Budig and England, 1999).

If we do not distinguish between men's and women's personal earnings, but rather assume pooling of income within households, and look at household income or wealth, we get a very different picture. By definition, within every married couple, each partner has the same household income or wealth as the other. Thus, in the aggregate, average household income for married men must be equal to the average for married women. Overall, however, women live in poorer households than men (Spain and

Table 16.1.   Summary of Research on Gender Inequality Inside and Outside of Marriage with Attention to Interaction Effects

Arena	Gain from Marriage More (or Loss Less) for	Less Male (or More Female) Advantage in	Which Sex More Advantaged in Marriage	Which Sex More Advantaged among Singles
Earnings	Men	Unmarried	Men	Men
Household income	Women	Married	No difference	Men
Time with your children	Men	Unmarried	?	?
Access to another's unpaid labor to rear your children	Women	Married	Men	Men
Physical and mental health	Men	Unmarried	?	?
Satisfaction with sex	Men	Unmarried	Men	Men

Bianchi, 1996, Chapter 6), but the differential must (by definition) be coming entirely from differences between single men and women. Living in households with lower family income is particularly problematic for single women since they are much more likely to be living with and supporting children than single men. It is because of this that the increase in single motherhood in recent decades gave rise to a "feminization of poverty" (McLanahan and Kelly, 1999). Thus, women's "returns to marriage" in household income, as well as wealth, are greater than men's (Waite and Gallagher, 2000), and gender inequality in household income among the married is 0 by definition. This is just a technical way of telling us what the folk wisdom knows: in a world where women lose earning power to take care of children, and earn less because of discrimination and other social forces, many women are financially dependent on men, and the best way to get them to share their income on a consistent basis is to marry them (or live with them).

What are men dependent on women for? Given strong norms and practices that women live with and care for their children, most men are dependent on marriage to (or cohabitation with) their children's mother to get time with their children. I assume that most parents want some time with their children. We know that women spend much more time with children than men, and that in cases of divorce or nonmarital birth, women tend to have custody of children. Which sex is advantaged is unclear unless we know how much time men and women want with children; it is possible to have too much or too little, and how much time people want is affected by gendered social norms and past development of an attachment to the child. I offer some conjectures, but note question marks in Table 16.1 on which sex is advantaged. My guess is that married men spend closer to the amount of time they would prefer with children than do married women—who would probably prefer less. This is based on the idea that there are declining marginal gains to time with children, and women are more likely to be into the range where returns are negative. Among singles, women usually have custody of children and, although fathers generally have visitation rights, these may be limited and custodial mothers sometimes make geographical moves. That many single fathers see their children very little suggests that women may see their children closer to what they prefer in the single state than do men. Of course, men who have never had much of a link to their children, or who broke the link early, may sometimes not miss them. Still, presumably some single fathers genuinely miss their children. Whether one agrees with my conjectures about which sex is closer to what is for them seen as an optimal amount of time with their children, it seems uncontroversial that men are more dependent on marriage (or cohabitation) than women for time with their children, and thus the returns to marriage are higher for men on this dimension. Women generally live with their children whether they are married, divorced, or never married. Thus, there are few if any returns in time with their children to them from marriage.[9]

The other side of women's advantage in access to time with their children is that men have access to someone who will provide unpaid labor to rear their children. Men are advantaged on this in marriage and outside of marriage, but the male advantage is much greater in the unmarried state, since in most marriages men are contributing at least some (although the minority) of the labor that goes into rearing children. Thus, women actually have higher returns to marriage on this dimension.

If we look at physical and mental health, including health conditions that cause mortality, it is unclear who is advantaged overall. Men have higher mortality at every age, and yet there is evidence that women's mental and physical health is worse. This paradox is explained by the fact that men tend to have mental and physical problems, and engage in risky behaviors, that are more likely to kill them (Ross and Bird, 1994). So, on balance, perhaps women have more afflictions but men's are more serious, making it hard to say who we would consider advantaged. (There are also strong sex differences in typical types of health problems.)

What is clear is that men's health and mortality benefit more from marriage than do women's, as Waite and Gallagher (2000) clearly acknowledge. Women benefit on some dimensions, but lose on others, such as loss of a sense of control or autonomy (Ross et al., 1990; Ross, 1991). Marriage benefits physical and mental health, as well as how happy people report themselves to be (Waite and Gallagher, 2000). The general picture from this literature is that men benefit from women's physical and emotional caretaking, which they receive more regularly when they live with women, and living with women creates routines and responsibilities that make them less likely to engage in dangerous, risky, or unhealthy behaviors such as unhealthy eating, alcohol or drug abuse, crime, or suicide. Women receive some such gains from marriage, but are less likely to engage in risky behaviors with or without marriage than men. Women's health benefits from the increased income provided by access to male income in marriage. But women are also are exposed more directly to active forms of male interpersonal power when they live with men, and thus often lose a sense of control or autonomy to a greater extent than men (Ross et al., 1990).

What about sexuality? For men and women who have heterosexual partnered sex, evidence from the National Health and Social Life Survey presented by Waite (1995; see also Waite and Gallagher, 2000) shows that men report more physical and emotional satisfaction with partnered[10] sex than do women, and that this is true for married as well as single persons. (For a broader discussion of how male advantage in society affects sexuality, see Schwartz and Rutter, 1998.) They emphasize the finding in Waite's analysis that both sexes seem to find sex more satisfying when they are married. However, Waite's (1995) analysis shows something else that she does not discuss, that the difference between satisfaction in the single and married state is greater for men than women. This seems to imply that men benefit (in sexual satisfaction) more from marriage than women, and thus gender inequality favoring men is greater in the married than the single state.[11]

Overall, we see male advantage in many, though not all, arenas. The advantage on earnings and income is particularly important since money is a medium of exchange for so many other things, including, as we have seen, informal bargaining within the household. There is probably a tendency for marriage to be inequality inducing more than it is equality inducing (Table 16.1), but this depends heavily on how we weight the arenas. However, the fact that in many arenas marriage contains more gender inequality than nonmarriage does not necessarily imply that women are better off single. In some arenas, such as health, mortality, and frequency of and satisfaction with sex, marriage appears to have some returns for both sexes, but more returns for men than women.

Thus, although a division of labor in marriage in which women work in the household and men have earnings is not good for gender equality, the way nonmarriage generally plays out is quite inegalitarian as well, particularly for parents. In this regime, women do all the household and childrearing work associated with children as they did in the "high marriage" regime, but they do not have access to male income. Which is worse, I am not sure. What is more important for feminists is to focus on reducing the causes of gender inequality that are largely common to both the unmarried and married state.

POLICIES THAT WOULD REDUCE GENDER INEQUALITY

I have argued that the major factors promoting gender inequality are common to the married and unmarried state. Given that many of the same factors promote gender inequality outside as inside marriage, if gender equality is our concern, to marry or not to marry is *not* the feminist question. The important issue is how to change the factors that promote male advantage. These factors are sex discrimination in employment, cultural meanings and scripts that promote male dominance, and women's bearing of a disproportionate share of the costs of children. What policies would be helpful in reducing these sources of gender inequality?

How could public policy shape cultural meanings that contribute to gender inequality? Some possibilities are schools giving as much importance to teaching boys as girls to be parents. Other possibilities are public education campaigns directed at reducing coercive sexuality, giving men a sense of their obligation to participate in household work and childrearing, and working against defining masculinity in terms of power.

Policies directed at sex discrimination in employment have been much discussed and will only be reviewed briefly here. Legislation prohibiting sex discrimination in hiring, placement, promotion, and wages is contained in Title VII of the Civil Rights Act. Requirements that government contractors engage in affirmative action in hiring are relevant as well. Enforcement levels vary with administrations. We do not have policies that correct the sort of discrimination at issue in "comparable worth." This refers to a situation in which predominantly female jobs are assigned lower wages than male jobs that involve different tasks but are comparable in skill demands and onerousness, simply because of their sex composition (England, 1992). The courts have not interpreted existing legislation to require this.

We have had little policy discussion in this country about the equitable division of the costs of children, so I emphasize this factor here (see also England and Folbre, 1999). These costs come mostly in two forms. First there is money that is spent on feeding, housing, clothing, providing health care for, and educating children. This money can come from mothers, fathers, or the state. When it comes from the state, who is actually paying the bill is determined by what type of tax system finances the program. Second, there is the direct time spent with children. This has a pecuniary opportunity cost to the person providing the labor, if it is provided by a parent without pay, because spending time this way means foregoing the money that could have been earned in the same time. Women bear most of the opportunity costs of child care labor in both the marriage and non-marriage regimes. Increasingly they supply more of the money than previously. Yet proposals directed at issues such as child support seldom have gender equality as their focus. It is entirely appropriate to focus such policies on the well-being of children, but gender equality should not be forgotten.

What policies would reduce gender inequality in who pays more of the costs of children? First, since the way in which women "pay" opportunity costs is through taking time out of employment, anything that works toward equalizing the proportion of time taken out of employment (or in reduced hours) between men and women would help, since this affects future earnings trajectories and pensions.

Policies that do not allow employers to penalize part-time workers in wages or benefits (that is, that requires them to be proportional to hours) would reduce the effect of part-time work on present earnings. In this same vein, policies that required employers to allow workers to take time off for childrearing with their job held might help. This is a provision of the Family and Medical Leave Act, though it does not cover many workers, and extends for only a short time. (In Sweden, in contrast, the state pays some of the foregone earnings.)

Of course, higher awards and better enforcement of children support would benefit single mothers. However, a different approach that departs more from the notion that children are a private responsibility of their parents would have greater state support of the costs of children. Policies that would do this are public health care (which all industrialized nations except the United States have), publicly provided child care (much like public education, but from an earlier age), or allowances or tax breaks to families with children. Such program in effect redistribute some of the costs of children from women to men because women disproportionately live with and support children (so they would receive a disproportionate share of the benefits—either in improved services they cannot now purchase for their children or in not having to pay for things they are purchasing). If financed by progressive earnings or property- based taxes, the taxes would come disproportionately from men, since they earn more. Of course, in married couple households, both the benefits and costs would be shared between men and women, so the big redistribution would be among the single. Such programs also redistribute from nonparents to parents and from the affluent to the poor.

Such policies have not been persuasive to U.S. legislators because the family is seen as a private realm and children the private responsibility of their parents. Folbre (1994a,b) has argued that the labor parents (mostly mothers) put into rearing their children creates a public good. That is, the benefits of well-reared children accrue to their employers, spouses, friends, and others when the children are grown. These public benefits of children extend to men as much as to women. One might say, in this regard, that men "free ride" off women's labor. Public goods are well recognized by economists as an area in which we may need state support to have an optimal level of the good produced. The fact that economists typically have not applied this logic to supporting mothers probably says more about their gender biases and blinders than about lack of applicability of the concept. Thus, the fact that we all benefit when children are reared to be healthy, well-behaved workers, family members, and citizens is a rationale other than gender equality for public support of some of the costs of childrearing. State programs that provide services that ensure the healthy upbringing of children are an investment in human capital, broadly construed, that creates public goods for many. However, anything that shifts some of the costs of raising children from women to men is also a contribution to gender equality.

NOTES

1.   Robinson was referring to the plight of the unemployed, whereas I am referring to the plight of single mothers. In either case, it is the party often seen as oppressive who, nonetheless, provides sorely needed cash. Cited in a prepublication version of Bowles and Gintis (1993). In personal communication, Bowles reports that he was unable to find a citation for the quote, although many scholars of Robinson's work agreed they had seen the quote.

2.   Although there are differences between cohabitation and marriage that have been emphasized by Waite and Gallagher (2000), I will not distinguish between them here. I see the two as on a continuum of subjective commitment of the partners and extent of legal obligation. There is variation along this same continuum within both cohabitation and marriage as well.

3.   For an overview of liberal feminism and other strands of feminist writing, see Tong (1998).

4.   Bumpass and Sweet (1989) found about 25% of unwed parents cohabiting. McLanahan et al. (1998) found a higher proportion, about a third, of children born to unmarried women living with their fathers.

5.   The game-theoretic view of marital power also suggests that anything that affects how well women can fare outside marriages improves their "threat points" in marriage. How well single or divorced women fare varies importantly across nations, depending on how well child-support obligations are enforced, how generous the social safety net is (much more generous in Europe than the United States), whether women inherit land (crucial for third world peasant women), and the frequency of remarriage for women with children. Thus, it is not only women's access to earnings that this view suggests as relevant.

6.   Scanzoni (1970) uses a similar measure of power and data from a 1967 Indianapolis sample of about 900. He also reports that, holding men's education constant, employed women had more power than homemakers. However, an inspection of the relevant Table 16.(6-3) does not actually show this. The interest-

ing finding from his study, quite apart from wives' employment, is that although he expected men to have more power (relative to their wives) when their educational, occupational, and financial status was higher, he found the *opposite*, that working class men exerted more power than middle class men. However, wives found men's power less legitimate in the lower classes.

7.   There are a number of thorny measurement issues here. In the Beckerian model, labor supply to market and household work are both endogenous to wage rate a person could earn. Thus, we need a wage rate for both employed and nonemployed women, but nonemployed women have no current wage. In the threatpoint view, employment hours are seen as exogenous (or at least an exogenized measure of them is what we would want) and we might see actual earnings as relevant, where nonemployed women are counted as 0. Separate from this is how earnings or wages, however measured, are to be made into a measure that taps the *relative resources* of spouses. One possibility is a ratio, or a difference [used by Shelton (1992) and Ross (1987)]. An alternative is the gap in earnings over the total earnings of the couple [used by Brines (1994) and Baxter and Bittman (1995)]. Presser (1994) used the log of the ratio of the husbands earnings to wife's earnings.

8.   However, authors have not always explicitly recognized that it is the *portability* of earnings that, in theory, should lead them to provide power in the marriage. Some authors (e.g., Scanzoni, 1970) have written as if it were obvious that the party providing more money will have more power because they are providing a resource—as if a homemaker is providing nothing of value to the couple!

9.   Although most women live with their children whether married or not, it might be thought that marriage would allow women more hours with their children since it would provide the support that allows nonemployment or part-time employment. But, all the time spent with their children probably brings many nonemployed mothers into the range of declining marginal returns—where they would have preferred some respite from the caretaking.

10.   For married and cohabiting respondents, satisfaction is reported for the partner they live with. For others, analyses refer to satisfaction with primary partners if respondents expect to continue having sex with them. Respondents without regular partners are excluded. See Waite (1995, Appendix Table 16.A2).

11.   For sexual frequency, there is no interaction; men increase the frequency of sex by about the same amount through marriage or cohabitation as women do (Waite, 1995, Figure 9).

REFERENCES

Baxter, Jane, and Michael Bittman. 1995. "Measuring Time Spent on Housework: A Comparison of Two Approaches." *Australian Journal of Social Research* 1:21–46.

Becker, Gary S. 1991. *A Treatise on the Family*. Cambridge, MA: Harvard University Press.

Bergstrom, Theodore C. 1996. "Economics in a Family Way." *Journal of Economic Literature* 34:1903–1934.

Blank, Rebecca. 1997. *It Takes a Nation: A New Agenda for Fighting Poverty*. New York: Russell Sage Foundation.

Blood, R.O., Jr., and D.M. Wolfe. 1960. *Husbands and Wives: The Dynamics of Family Living*. New York: Free Press.

Blumstein, Philip, and Pepper Schwartz. 1983. *American Couples: Money, Work, Sex.* New York: William Morrow.

Bowles, Samuel, and Herbert Gintis. 1993. "The Revenge of Homo Economicus: Contested Exchange and the Revival of Political Economy." *Journal of Economic Perspectives* 7:83–102.

Brines, Julie. 1994. "Economic Dependency, Gender, and the Division of Labor at Home." *American Journal of Sociology* 100:652–688.

Budig, Michelle, and Paula England. 1999. "The Effect of Motherhood on Wages in Recent Cohorts: Findings from the NLSY." Presented at the 1999 American Economic Association meetings, New York.

Bumpass, Larry L., and James Sweet. 1989. "Children's Experience in Single-Parent Families: Implications of Cohabitation and Marital Transitions." *Family Planning Perspectives* 21:256–260.

Casper, Lynne M., Sara S. McLanahan, and Irwin Garfinkel. 1994. "The Gender-Poverty Gap: What We Can Learn from Other Countries." *American Sociological Review* 59:594–605.

Cherlin, Andrew J. 1996. *Public and Private Families.* New York: McGraw-Hill.

Cook, Karen, ed. 1987. *Social Exchange Theory.* Newbury Park, CA: Sage.

de Beauvoir, Simone. [1949] 1974. *The Second Sex,* translated and edited by H.M. Parshley. New York: Vintage.

Duncan, Beverly, and O.D. Duncan. 1978. *Sex Typing and Social Roles: A Research Report.* New York: Academic Press.

England, Paula. 1992. *Comparable Worth: Theories and Evidence.* New York: Aldine de Gruyter.

England, Paula, and Michelle J. Budig. 1998. "Gary Becker on the Family: His Genius, Impact, and Blind Spots." Pp. 95–112 in *Required Reading: Sociology's Most Influential Books,* edited by Dan Clawson. Amherst: University of Massachusetts.

England, Paula, and George Farkas. 1986. *Households, Employment, and Gender.* New York: Aldine de Gruyter.

England, Paula, and Nancy Folbre. 1999. "Who Should Pay for the Kids?" *Annals of the American Academy of Political and Social Science* 563:194–208.

England, Paula, and Barbara Kilbourne. 1990. "Markets, Marriages, and Other Mates: The Problem of Power." Pp. 163–189 in *Beyond the Marketplace: Rethinking Economy and Society,* edited by Roger Friedland and A.F. Robertson. Hawthorne, NY: Aldine de Gruyter.

Fenstermaker Berk, Sarah. 1985. *The Gender Factory: The Apportionment of Work in American Households.* New York: Plenum.

Folbre, Nancy. 1994a. *Who Pays for the Kids?* New York: Routledge.

Folbre, Nancy. 1994b. "Children as Public Goods." *American Economic Review* 84: 86–90.

Garfinkel, Irwin, Sara McLanahan, and Philip Robins (eds.). 1994. *Child Support and Child Well-Being.* Washington, DC: The Urban Institute Press.

Heer, David. 1958. "Dominance and the Working Wife." *Social Forces* 36:341–347.

Heer, David. 1963. "The Measurement and Bases of Family Power: An Overview." *Marriage and Family Living* 25:133-139.

Hochschild, Arlie. 1989. *The Second Shift.* New York: Viking Penguin.

Katz, Elizabeth. 1997. "The Intra-Household Economics of Voice and Exit." *Feminist Economics* 3:25–46.

Lundberg, Shelly, and Robert A. Pollak. 1996. "Bargaining and Distribution in Marriage." *Journal of Economic Perspectives* 10:139–158.

McElroy, Marjorie B. 1990. "The Empirical Content of Nash-Bargaining Household Behavior." *Journal of Human Resources* 25:559–583.

McElroy, Marjorie B., and Mary Jean Horney. 1981. "Nash Bargained Household Decisions." *International Economic Review* 22:333–349.

McLanahan, Sara, and Erin L. Kelly. 1999. "The Feminization of Poverty: Past and Future." Pp. 127–146 in *Handbook of the Sociology of Gender*, edited by Janet Chafetz. New York: Plenum.

McLanahan, Sara, Irwin Garfinkel, J. Brooks-Gunn, H. Zhao, Waldo Johnson, Lauren Rich, Mark Turner, Maureen Waller, and Melvin Wilson. 1998. "Unwed Fathers and Fragile Families." Unpublished manuscript, Department of Sociology, Princeton University.

Presser, Harriet B. 1994. "Employment Schedules, Gender, and Household Labor." *American Sociological Review* 54:348–364.

Reskin, Barbara, and Irene Padavic. 1999. "Sex, Race, and Ethnic Inequality in United States Workplaces." Pp. 343–374 in *Handbook of the Sociology of Gender*, edited by Janet Chafetz. New York: Plenum.

Ross, Catherine E. 1991. "Marriage and the Sense of Control." *Journal of Marriage and the Family* 53:831–838.

Ross, Catherine E., and Chloe E. Bird. 1994. "Sex Stratification and Health Lifestyles: Consequences for Men's and Women's Perceived Health." *Journal of Health and Social Behavior* 35:161–178.

Ross, Catherine E., John Mirowsky, and Karen Goldsteen. 1990. "The Impact of the Family on Health: The Decade in Review." *Journal of Marriage and Family* 52:1059–1078.

Scanzoni, John. 1970. *Opportunity and the Family*. New York: Macmillan.

Schwartz, Pepper, and Virginia Rutter. 1998. *The Gender of Sexuality*. Thousand Oaks, CA: Pine Forge.

Sen, Amartya. 1990. "Gender and Cooperative Conflicts." Pp. 123–149 in *Persistent Inequalities: Women and World Development*, edited by Irene Tinker. New York: Oxford University Press.

Shelton, Beth Anne. 1992. *Women, Men and Time: Gender Differences in Paid Work, Housework and Leisure*. New York: Greenwood Press.

Smith, Herbert L., S. Philip Morgan, and Tanya Koropeckyj-Cox. 1996. "A Decomposition of Trends in the Nonmarital Fertility Ratios of Blacks and Whites in the United States, 1960–1992." *Demography* 33:141–151.

Spain, Daphne, and Suzanne M Bianchi. 1996. *Balancing Act: Motherhood, Marriage, and Employment Among American Women*. New York: Russell Sage Foundation.

Stacey, Judith. 1993. "Good Riddance to 'the Family': A Response to David Popenoe." *Journal of Marriage and the Family* 55:545–547.

Tong, Rosemarie Putnam. 1998. *Feminist Thought*, 2nd ed. New York: Westview.

U.S. Bureau of the Census. 1993. *Poverty in the United States, 1992*. Current Population Reports, Series P-60, No. 185. Washington, DC: U.S. Government Printing Office.

Waite, Linda J. 1995. "Does Marriage Matter?" *Demography* 32:483–507.

Waite, Linda, and Maggie Gallagher. 2000. *The Case for Marriage*. New York: Doubleday.

Walby, Sylvia. 1990. *Theorizing Patriarchy*. Oxford: Basil Blackwood.

Walby, Sylvia. 1997. *Gender Transformations*. London: Routledge.

Waldfogel, Jane. 1997. "The Effect of Children on Women's Wages." *American Sociological Review* 62:209–217.

17

Understanding the Distribution of Housework between Husbands and Wives

BETH ANNE SHELTON

There is little dispute that the inequality in the division of household labor between husbands and wives has declined in recent years but still remains unequal (Brines, 1993; Robinson, 1988). In spite of agreement regarding the division of housework, significant disagreements over the implications and significance of recent changes in the division of housework as well as the reasons for continuing inequality remain. In this chapter I describe current patterns of the distribution of household labor between husbands and wives and assess attempts to account for its distribution. I begin the chapter with a discussion of the relationship between marital status and the distribution of housework.

Although few studies examine the relationship between marital status and women's and men's housework, those that do indicate that marital status is associated with housework time. In comparisons of married, single, and unmarried cohabiting women and men, researchers report that the gap between women's and men's housework time is greater for married couples than between either single or cohabiting women and men (McAllister, 1990; Shelton and John, 1993; South and Spitze, 1994; Stafford et al., 1977). This pattern indicates that marriage affects how women and men apportion their time on housework and, possibly, the meaning attached to housework. Thus, even if our interest is in understanding how husbands and wives distribute housework, data on how housework is distributed in a variety of other living situations will help us understand the dynamics of the division of household labor.

Unfortunately, most existing research focuses only on married women and men, possibly because issues of equity within marriage are tied to how family responsibilities are distributed. Without analysis of women's and men's investments in family work both inside and outside of marriage it is difficult to identify gender effects that are independent of marriage and those that interact with marriage. In this review, I summarize and assess attempts to understand the division of household labor between husbands and wives, but the lack of comparative research on married and unmarried women's and men's housework time is reflected in the review.

CONSEQUENCES OF THE UNEQUAL DIVISION OF HOUSEHOLD LABOR

Although it is not clear that women's housework time affects their paid work time, it does affect their earnings (Hersch, 1985, 1991; Hersch and Stratton, 1994; McAllister, 1990). In contrast, men's housework time has little or no effect on their paid work time or their earnings (Hersch, 1991). The lack of an association between men's housework time and their earnings may reflect either the types of activities on which they spend their time or their absolute housework time (Hersch, 1991). Men may be more likely to spend their time on housework that can be scheduled so as not to interfere with paid work time and, as a consequence, not to affect earnings. On the other hand, men's housework burden may simply not be heavy enough to interfere with their earnings.

Marital satisfaction is not related to the division of household labor per se, but does appear to be related to perceptions regarding whether household labor is fairly or unfairly divided. Most research indicates that women's marital satisfaction is enhanced when they feel their husbands do their "fair share" of housework (Blair, 1993; Perry-Jenkins and Folk, 1994; Robinson and Spitze, 1992). Consistent with this finding, Erickson (1993) reports that men's participation in emotion work is positively associated with women's reports of marital well-being (see also Broman, 1993; Ward, 1993).

The nature of the association between housework time and marital satisfaction for men is less clear. Some find that the less time men spend on housework the greater their marital happiness, but the effects are small (Robinson and Sptize, 1992) and there appears to be no association between men's proportional share of housework and their marital satisfaction.

Bird and Fremont (1991) report that household labor is negatively associated with both women's and men's health and conclude that women's greater household labor time is a significant factor negatively affecting their health. Similarly, others report that an unequal division of household labor is associated with women's depression (Glass and Fujimoto, 1994; Kurdek, 1993), although the effect may be indirect through the impact of housework on household strain. Once again, the nature of the association between the division of household labor and men's health is less clear. Some researchers find that men who share household labor report feeling more demoralized, anxious, and helpless than men who do less housework

(Rosenfeld, 1992), but a number of others find no association between men's housework time and their mental health (Golding, 1990; Orbuch and Custer, 1995).

Measuring Housework Time

Time diaries, completed for a 24-hour period, provide the highest quality estimates of housework time because they offer both detail and relatively accurate estimates of time use. These measures are, however, used only infrequently, primarily because they are expensive to administer, but also because other methods for gathering data on time use provide estimates that are not substantially inferior, although costing significantly less. In research comparing time use estimates from diary formats and direct questions about typical time use, there is evidence of some overestimation of time use when direct questions are used, but the overestimation is similar for women and men. Thus, in studies examining the gendered pattern of time use, direct questions provide data that are almost as useful as diary-produced data and significantly less expensive to collect. Direct questions that gather information regarding time spent in a variety of specific household activities provide higher quality estimates of time use than those with only general questions about typical amounts of time spent on housework (Baxter and Bittman, 1995; Marini and Shelton, 1993). Thus, most recent studies that use data generated from direct questions are based on information about time spent on a variety of specific housework tasks (see the 1997 and 1992 *National Survey of Families and Households*).

No matter how data are collected, they show that women continue to spend significantly more time on housework than do men and that this pattern persists whether women are employed or not (Berardo et al., 1987; Marini and Shelton, 1993; Presser, 1994). In the United States, the most recent estimates [from the second wave of the National Survey of Families and Households (NSFH)] are that women spend 32.7 hours per week on housework compared to 19.6 hours per week for men. These results are consistent with most other estimates (Greenstein, 1996) and support the view that the division of household labor, although somewhat less unequal than in the past, is not approaching equality. Although the size of the gap between women's and men's housework time is larger for some countries than for others, women's housework time is consistently greater than men's (Gershuny and Robinson, 1988).

EXPLANATIONS FOR THE DIVISION OF HOUSEHOLD LABOR

There are four general categories of explanations for the division of household labor that are most commonly evaluated in empirical studies.

These approaches focus on time constraints, sex role attitudes, resources, or the construction of gender in order to account for the gender gap in housework time, although there are conflicting explanations for some of the expected empirical associations. None of these approaches has been able to account fully for the observed gender inequality, although each receives some support in empirical assessments.

Time Constraints

One of the least conceptually developed of the approaches to explaining the division of household labor is the time constraints explanation. Within this perspective, women's greater housework time is depicted as resulting partly from their lower time investment in paid labor. In evaluations of how husbands and wives divide household labor, the fact that husbands typically spend more time in paid labor than their wives is used to account for part of the gap in their housework time (Greenstein, 1996). This approach to explaining the division of household labor is popular because most studies find a clear association between paid work time and housework time (Acock and Demo, 1994; Brines, 1993; Demo and Acock, 1993) as well as child care time (Coverman and Sheley, 1986; McHale and Huston, 1984).

One of the problems with explaining women's and men's housework time by reference to their paid labor time is that this pattern may reflect choices but not really "explain" the choices. That is, the time constraints approach does not help us account for decisions regarding how time will be allocated between paid work and housework, but identifies only the relationship between the two. That there is a relationship between time spent in one activity and time spent in another is not surprising, but it is not particularly helpful if we are trying to *understand* the distribution of time.

A second problem with the time constraints approach is that within this framework there is no reason to expect that the relationship between paid work time and housework time would vary by gender, but it does. Most studies report that the relationship between paid work time and housework time is stronger for women than for men and that even when women spend more time in paid labor than their husbands they continue to spend more time on housework than their husbands (Beckett and Smith, 1981; Kamo, 1988; Newell, 1993).

Some researchers also evaluate the impact of women's paid work time on their husbands' housework time, conceptualizing wives' paid work time as a constraint on husbands' time. Findings with respect to the association between women's paid work time and their husband's housework time are inconsistent. Some report that men's housework time is responsive to their wives' time spent in paid labor (Blair and Lichter, 1991; Brines, 1993), although other studies find a weak or nonexistent association (Levant et al., 1987). Efforts to synthesize the research on this relationship are made more problematic by studies that assess the impact of wives' paid labor time on men's relative share of housework (Coltrane and Ishii-Kuntz, 1992a; Ross, 1987). When relative share of housework is the dependent variable, it is impossible to determine the extent to which the effect reflects variation in women's time and/or variations in their husbands' housework time. Given the association between women's paid labor time and their housework time, some unknown portion of the variation in men's relative share reflects shifts in women's rather than men's housework time.

The association between women's paid work time and their housework time, coupled with the weak or nonexistent relationship between women's paid work time and their husbands' housework time, suggests that women's housework may be being replaced with market services (e.g., restaurant meals, cleaning services) rather than being redistributed between husbands and wives.

Although most studies of housework focus on time, some seek to account for how time is apportioned among a set of housework tasks (Blair and Lichter, 1991). These studies generally report that men's and women's time investments in paid labor affect how they allocate their housework time among specific tasks. The more time women spend in paid labor and the less time men spend in paid labor the less segregated the allocation of time among tasks. Given the wide variety of household tasks and the variation in the extent to which these tasks are discretionary (Shelton, 1992), the research on the allocation of time among specific tasks yields important information about gender differences in household work.

Finally, some researchers have evaluated the impact of work schedule on the division of household labor. In general these studies show that it is not only the amount of paid work time that affects the division of household labor but the amount of time that men, in particular, are home alone. The more time husbands spend at home when their wives are at work the more housework they do.

Another time constraint that affects housework time, but women's more than men's, is children (Gershuny and Robinson, 1988; Shelton, 1992). The presence of a child or children increases the total amount of time invested by a household in housework, but most of this increase is due to women's greater housework time (Brines, 1993; Presser, 1994). The gendered nature of the relationship between children and housework time also poses problems for the time constraints approach to understanding the division of household labor. In short, the logic of the time constraints approach is such that any time constraint (paid work time, children) should have the same effect on women's and men's housework time. Given the assumptions of the approach, there is no reason to expect that time constraints would be gendered. Even if the effects of time constraints were not different for women and men, the approach would be of limited utility because it fails to help us answer the question regarding what affects the allocation of time between paid labor and housework.

Sex Role Attitudes

Attitudes about who should do the housework also have been proposed as a possible explanation for the unequal division of household labor (Huber and Spitze, 1983; Spitze, 1986) with wives' and husbands' housework time conceptualized as the result of their attitudes regarding how it should be divided between them. Women with more egalitarian attitudes are expected to do less housework than those with more traditional attitudes and the reverse is expected for men. Of course, given the division of household labor, it would be expected that, in general, women and men feel that women should be responsible for more of the housework than should men.

For the most part, researchers have found that the association between women's and men's attitudes and their housework time is as expected (Coltrane and Ishii-Kuntz, 1992b), although there generally is a stronger association between men's attitudes and the division of household labor than between women's attitudes and the division of household labor (Blair and Lichter, 1991; Kamo, 1994; Presser, 1994; Ross, 1987; Shelton and John, 1993). In addition, men's attitudes typically have a stronger effect on women's housework time than on men's (Sanchez, 1994). These differential effects are not easily explained within the logic of the sex role attitude explanation and, consequently, are problematic.

Another problem with the sex role attitudes explanation is that variation in housework time, once again, is around a very unequal base. Even those couples with egalitarian attitudes have an unequal division of household labor, and it is only somewhat less unequal than the division for couples with traditional attitudes.

Resources

Two separate approaches to understanding the division of household labor examine resources. These two approaches, generally referred to as the relative resource (Brines, 1993) and neoclassical economic (Becker, 1985) approaches, offer different rationales for their expectation that individuals' education and earnings will be associated with their share of housework time. They differ in how they conceptualize the unit of analysis (individual or family) as well.

Blood and Wolfe's (1960) study of the relationship between spouses' relative resources and decision making serves as the foundation for what typically is referred to as the relative resources explanation for the division of household labor. This approach is premised on the idea that housework is something that individuals will try to avoid; thus, when one spouse has more resources (education, earnings, occupational prestige) than another, she or he will employ those resources to get out of housework (Brines, 1993).

A relationship between resources and housework time also may be explained within the neoclassical economic framework (Becker, 1985). If households, rather than individuals, make decisions about how most efficiently to allocate effort in order to maximize utilities, the individual with the highest wage rate or earnings potential would logically be expected to specialize in paid labor and the person with the lowest wage rate or earnings potential would be expected to specialize in housework. This type of allocation would produce the best outcomes for households.

The primary differences between the relative resource and neoclassical economic approaches are in the conceptualization of the unit that is maximizing utilities (the individual or the household, respectively) and in the extent to which the process is seen as involving the exercise of power. Within the relative resource perspective, the resources are a source of power that may then be used to get out of housework, whereas neoclassical economists see this as a more consensual process, mostly because the decision-making unit is conceptualized differently. It is not clear that any empirical pattern can definitively adjudicate between the relative resource and neoclassical economic explanations for any relationship between individual resources and the division of housework. Data may, however, fail to support either approach.

For the most part, the smaller the earnings gap between a husband and wife the more equal the division of labor (Blair and Lichter, 1991; Presser, 1994), although, as is the case with other effects, variation in the division of household labor occurs around a very unequal base and does not approach equality even for couples with similar earnings (Goldscheider and Waite, 1991). In addition, earnings account for only a small part of that gap between women's and men's housework time.

A second problem with the relative resource and neoclassical economic approach reflects the typical pattern of earnings within a household. In the majority of households, the husband earns more than the wife and most studies show that the smaller the gap in earnings the smaller the gap in housework time. However, Brines (1994) reports that in the minority of households in which the husband is economically dependent, husbands do not do more housework than their wives.

In addition to earnings, education often is conceptualized as a measure of resources, although its use as such is problematic given its strong correlation with gender role attitudes. In fact, the empirical studies of the relationship between education and housework time often are consistent with the sex role attitude explanation. Men's housework time typically is positively associated with education (Haddad, 1994; Presser, 1994; South and Spitze, 1994) rather than negatively as would be expected if education operates as a resource. Women's education, on the other hand, is negatively associated with their housework time (Bergen, 1991; Brines, 1993; South and Spitze, 1994), which is consistent with both the sex role attitude and relative resource/neoclassical economic explanations. Women with more education may be doing less housework because of their more egalitarian gender role attitudes or because their education is a resource that allows them to negotiate their way out of housework (Huber and Spitze, 1983). In summary, empirical assessments of the relative resource and neoclassical economic explanations for the division of household labor offer some support, but a number of observed patterns are inconsistent with either approach.

Construction of Gender

Although not always explicitly stated, the resource, time constraint, and gender ideology explanations for the division of household labor are premised on the assumption that housework is necessary to maintain a home, but does nothing else. Rather than accepting this assumption, a number of researchers have offered another way to conceptualize housework. They argue that housework may do more than produce a clean house; it may be used to construct (Berk, 1985; Potuchek, 1992; West and Zimmerman, 1987) or display (Brines, 1993, 1994) gender. This "construction of gender" approach to understanding the division of household labor has the potential to account for what appear to be anomalous empirical patterns.

With respect to gender differences in the relationship between the presence of children and housework time, the construction of gender approach offers a potential explanation. Women's housework time may be more strongly associated with the presence and/or number of children than is the case for men because in their responses to children, women and men attend not only to the needs of their children but also produce themselves appropriately as women or men. In other words, the gendered nature of parental expectations may reflect the fact that doing or not doing housework related to children may be a way that women and men establish their "appropriate" femininity and masculinity.

Moreover, the different relationship between women's and men's employment and their housework time may be accounted for in much the same way. Brines' (1994) finding that men who are economically dependent spend no more time on housework than men who are economic providers seems incongruous if we conceptualize housework as producing only a cleaner house. If, in contrast, we see housework (and employment) as resources women and men may use in order to construct themselves as women or men, the pattern can be explained. As Brines (1994) argues, economically dependent men are unable to establish their masculinity through their economic dominance and are therefore "unable" to participate in housework. Men's economic dominance, on the other hand, may free them to do housework, just as women's economic dominance may make their participation in housework "necessary" (see Silberstein, 1992). For women unable to display gender by their economic dependence, housework may be the resource that allows them to do so.

Lundberg and Pollak (1996) postulate a similar dynamic but do so in terms of preferences and social norms. They argue that social norms affect individuals' preferences and thus how women and men allocate time between employment and housework. They argue that a bargaining model of marriage can account for seemingly "irrational" outcomes by an emphasis on preferences (1996:155). In an earlier paper, Pollak and Wachter (1975:271) criticize the household production function model as it is applied to the allocation of time by arguing that housework represents joint production because it is a "source of satisfaction or dissatisfaction as well as an input into a production activity." We might add that there is joint production if housework produces both a clean house and one's gender identity. Thus, it may be possible to incorporate the insights of the construction of gender approach into economic models of behavior.

Empirical assessments of the gender display or construction of gender explanation for the division of household labor are few but there is some support for it. Brines (1994) finds that the relationship between economic dependency and housework time is consistent with the gender display model for men but not for women. She reports that men who are the most economically dependent on their wives do not do more housework than men who are the sole or primary support of their wives. It is among those couples where neither husband nor wife is extremely economically dependent that the division of household labor is most equal.

Although Brines (1994) reports no support for the gender display model for women, Greenstein (1998), in an unpublished manuscript, finds support for the gender display model for both women and men. His proportional measure may be superior in this instance because it more effectively controls for variations across households in the total amount of housework done. If, however, wives' earnings are used to purchase replacements for her household labor, men's greater proportional share when economically dependent may simply indicate that when women earn more than their spouses they are more likely to purchase replacements for their own housework. Using paid services to replace wives' household labor would raise men's proportional share even if their own housework time did not increase. Thus, although it may be important to control for the total amount of housework done, using a proportional measure to do so may introduce new problems.

In addition, if there is a relationship between economic dependence and housework time or share of housework that reflects a process of constructing gender, the reason for economic dependence may become more important. If, for example, a husband is economically dependent due to training or a temporary setback at work (e.g., lay-off) the implications for his housework time may be different than if he is more "permanently" economically dependent.

The gender display approach offers hope for better understanding the relationship between gender and housework time even though efforts to evaluate its usefulness are necessarily indirect. That is, there is no simple way to determine the extent to which unpaid work time is an expression of gender; we can determine only whether a particular pattern is consistent with the gender display model.

Nevertheless, the gender display approach has the potential to move research on housework in a direction that may allow us to understand it. Particularly since most women and men do not see the division of household labor as unfair, we need to begin to address more systematically what varied purposes housework may serve. If we take the insights offered by social constructionists and the gender display approach and reevaluate how we study household labor, and avoid using them to formulate just another variable or set of variables to add to existing models, we may yet achieve a better understanding of why the division of household labor is slow to change and also the meaning housework has for women and men.

ACKNOWLEDGMENTS

Robert Pollak provided helpful comments on a draft of this chapter. Research assistance was provided by Saedra Omas.

REFERENCES

Acock, Alan, and David Demo. 1994. *Family Diversity and Well Being*. Thousand Oaks, CA: Sage.

Baxter, Janeen, and Michael Bittman. 1995. "Measuring Time Spent on Housework: A Comparison of Two Aproaches." *Australian Journal of Social Research* 1(1):21–46.

Becker, Gary S. 1985. "Human Capital, Effort, and the Sexual Division of Labor." *Journal of Labor Economics* 3:S33–S58.

Beckett, Joyce O., and Audrey D. Smith. 1981. "Work and Family Roles: Egalitarian Marriage in Black and White Families." *Social Service Review* 55(2):314–326.

Berardo, Donna Hodgkins, Constance Shehanand, and Gerald R. Leslie. 1987. "A Residue of Tradition: Jobs, Careers, and Spouses' Time in Housework." *Journal of Marriage and the Family* 49:381–390.

Bergen, Elizabeth. 1991. "The Economic Context of Labor Allocation." *Journal of Family Issues* 12:140–157.

Berk, Sarah Fenstermaker. 1985. *The Gender Factory: The Apportionment of Work in American Households*. New York: Plenum.

Bird, Chloe E., and Allen M. Fremont. 1991. "Gender, Time Use and Health." *Journal of Health and Social Behavior* 32:114–129.

Blair, Sampson Lee. 1993. "Employment, Family, and Perceptions of Marital Quality among Husbands and Wives." *Journal of Family Issues* 14:189–212.

Blair, Sampton Lee, and Daniel Lichter. 1991. "Measuring the Division of Household Labor: Gender Segregation of Housework among American Couples." *Journal of Family Issues* 12:91–113.

Blood, Robert O., and Donald M. Wolfe. 1960. *Husbands and Wives*. Glencoe, IL: Free Press.

Brines, Julie. 1993. "The Exchange Value of Housework." *Rationality and Society* 5:302–340

Brines, Julie. 1994. "Economic Dependency, Gender, and the Division of Labor at Home." *American Journal of Sociology* 100:652–688.

Broman, Clifford L. 1993. "Race Differences in Marital Well-Being." *Journal of Marriage and the Family* 55:724–732.

Coltrane, Scott, and Masako Ishii-Kuntz. 1992a. "Predicting the Sharing of Household Labor: Are Parenting and Household Labor Distinct?" *Sociological Perspectives* 35:629–647.

Coltrane, Scott, and Masako Ishii-Kuntz. 1992b. "Men's Housework: A Lifecourse Perspective." *Journal of Marriage and the Family* 54:43–57.

Coverman, Shelly, and Joseph F. Sheley. 1986. "Change in Men's Housework and Child-Care Time, 1965–1975." *Journal of Marriage and the Family* 48:413–422.

Demo, David, and Alan Acock. 1993. "Family Diversity and the Division of Domestic Labor: How Much Have Things Really Changed?" *Family Relations* 423:323–331.

Erickson, Rebecca J. 1993. "Reconceptualizing Family Work: The Effect of Emotion Work on Perceptions of Marital Quality." *Journal of Marriage and the Family* 55:888–900.

Gershuny, Jonathan, and John P. Robinson. 1988. "Historical Changes in the Household Division of Labor." *Demography* 25:537–552.

Glass, Jennifer, and Takahiro Fujimoto. 1994. "Housework, Paid Work, and Depression among Husbands and Wives." *Journal of Health and Social Behavior* 35:179–191.

Golding, Jacqueline M. 1990. "Division of Household Labor, Strain, and Depressive Symptoms among Mexican Americans and Non-Hispanic Whites." *Psychology of Women Quarterly* 14:103–117.

Goldscheider, Frances, and Linda J. Waite. 1991. *New Families, No Families? The Transformation of the American Home*. Berkeley: University of California.

Greenstein, Theodore. 1996. "Husbands' Participation in Domestic Labor: Interactive Effects of Wives' and Husbands' Gender Ideologies." *Journal of Marriage and the Family* 58:585–595.

Greenstein, Theodore. 1998. "Economic Dependence, Gender, and the Division of Labor in the Home: A Replication and Extension." Unpublished manuscript.

Haddad, Tony. 1994. "Men's Contribution to Family Work: A Re-Examination of Time Availability." *International Journal of Sociology of the Family* 24:87–111.

Hersch, Joni. 1985. "Effect of Housework on Earnings of Husbands and Wives: Evidence from Fulltime Piece Rate Workers." *Social Science Quarterly* 66:210–217.

Hersch, Joni. 1991. "The Impact of Nonmarket Work on Market Wages." *Proceedings of the American Economic Association* 44:157–160.

Hersch, Joni, and Leslie Stratton. 1994. "Housework, Wages, and the Division of Housework Time for Employed Spouses." *American Economic Review* 84: 120–125.

Huber, Joan, and Glenna Spitze. 1983. *Sex Stratification: Children, Housework, and Jobs.* New York: Academic Press.

Kamo, Yoshinori. 1988. "Determinants of Household Division of Labor: Resources, Power, and Ideology." *Journal of Family Issues* 9:177–200.

Kamo, Yoshinori. 1994. "Division of Household Work in the United States and Japan." *Journal of Family Issues* 15:348–378.

Kurdek, Lawrence A. 1993. "The Allocation of Household Labor in Gay, Lesbian, and Heterosexual Married Couples." *Journal of Social Issues* 49:127–134.

Levant, Ronald F., Susan Slattery, and Jane Loiselle. 1987. "Father's Involvement in Housework and Child Care with School-Aged Daughters." *Family Relations* 36:152–157.

Lundberg, Shelly, and Robert A. Pollak. 1996. "Bargaining and Distribution in Marriage." *Journal of Economic Perspectives* 104:139–158.

Marini, Margaret Mooney, and Beth Anne Shelton. 1993. "Measuring Household Work: Recent Experience in the United States." *Social Science Research* 22:361–382.

McAllister, Ian. 1990. "Gender and the Division of Labor: Employment and Earnings Variation in Australia." *Work and Occupations* 17:79–99.

McHale, Susan, and Ted Huston. 1984. "Men and Women as Parents: Sex Role Orientations, Employment, and Parental Roles with Infants." *Child Development* 55:1349–1361.

Newell, Sue. 1993. "The Superwoman Syndrome: Gender Difference in Attitudes Towards Equal Opportunities at Work and Towards Domestic Responsibilities at Home." *Work Employment and Society* 7:275–289.

Orbuch, Terri L., and Lindsay Custer. 1995. "The Social Context of Married Women's Work and Its Impact on Black Husbands and White Husbands." *Journal of Marriage and the Family* 57:333–345.

Perry-Jenkins, Maureen, and Karen Folk. 1994. "Class, Couples, and Conflict: Effects of the Division of Labor on Assessments of Marriage in Dual-Earner Families." *Journal of Marriage and the Family* 56:165–180.

Pollak, Robert A., and Wachter, Michael L. 1975. "The Relevance of the Household Production Function and Its Implications for the Allocation of Time." *Journal of Political Economy* 832:255–277.

Potuchek, Jean L. 1992. "Employed Wives' Orientations to Breadwinning: A Gender Theory Analysis." *Journal of Marriage and the Family* 54:548–558.

Presser, Harriett B. 1994. "Employment Schedules among Dual-Earner Spouses and the Division of Household Labor by Gender." *American Sociological Review* 59:348–364.

Robinson, John P. 1988. "Who's Doing the Housework?" *American Demographics* 10:24–63.

Robinson, John, and Glenna Spitze. 1992. "Whistle While You Work?: The Effect of Household Task Performance on Women's and Men's Well-Being." *Social Science Quarterly* 73:844–861.

Rosenfeld, Sarah. 1992. "The Costs of Sharing: Wives' Employment and Husbands' Mental Health." *Journal of Health and Social Behavior* 33:213–225.

Ross, Catherine E. 1987. "The Division of Labor at Home." *Social Forces* 65:816–833.

Sanchez, Laura. 1994. "Gender, Labor Allocations, and the Psychology of Entitlement within the Home." *Social Forces* 732:533–553.

Shelton, Beth Anne. 1992. *Women, Men, and Time: Gender Differences in Paid Work, Housework, and Leisure.* Westport, CT: Greenwood

Shelton, Beth Anne, and Daphne John. 1993. "Does Marital Status Make a Difference? Housework among Married and Cohabiting Men and Women" *Journal of Family Issues* 14:401–420.

Silberstein, Lisa R. 1992. *Dual-Career Marriage: A System in Transition.* Hillsdale, NJ: Lawrence Erlbaum.

Spitze, Glenna. 1986. "The Division of Task Responsibility in U.S. Households: Longitudinal Adjustments to Change." *Social Forces* 64:689–701.

South, Scott J., and Glenna Spitze. 1994. "Housework in Marital and Nonmarital Households." *American Sociological Review.* 59:327–347.

Stafford, Rebecca, Elaine Backman, and Pamela Dibona. 1977. "The Division of Labor among Cohabiting and Married Couples." *Journal of Marriage and the Family* 50:595–618.

Ward, Russell A. 1993. "Marital Happiness and Household Equity in Later Life." *Journal of Marriage and the Family* 55:427–438.

West, Candace, and Don Zimmerman. 1987. "Doing Gender." *Gender & Society* 1:125–151.

18

On the Determination of Wages:
Does Marriage Matter?

JEFFREY S. GRAY and MICHEL J. VANDERHART

INTRODUCTION

One of the more robust findings of empirical investigations into the determinants of labor market wages is that married men earn substantially more than comparable single men do, a differential called the "marriage premium." Why married men consistently earn more than unmarried men is a question that is still debated. Employer discrimination in favor of married workers could explain the marriage wage premium. However, simple discrimination is inconsistent with the nature of the wage premium paid to married men as research has shown that married men experience faster wage growth than unmarried men (Duncan and Holmund, 1983; Bartlett and Callahan, 1984; Korenman and Neumark, 1991). The existence of compensating wage differentials—the idea that lower paying jobs are associated with greater nonpecuniary benefits, such as flex time or job safety—could explain the marriage wage premium. However, Hersch (1991) and Duncan and Holmund (1983) find little support for the theory that the willingness of married men to trade favorable job amenities for higher wages explains the marriage wage premium. Rather than compensating wage differentials or employer discrimination, the general consensus in the literature is that controlling for other observable characteristics, married men are simply more productive than unmarried men. The direction of the causality is, however, a question with which the literature continues to struggle. Does marriage make men more productive or are more productive men more likely to get married?

This chapter focuses on the first explanation. The willingness of a wife to invest in her husband should depend on the return expected for such an investment. Wives who face a high probability of divorce[1] are less likely to realize these returns, and therefore should be less likely to invest in their husbands. The probability of divorce, however, is in turn likely dependent on how much each partner invests in the marriage. In this chapter we develop and discuss the results of a two-stage estimation procedure that recognizes the simultaneous nature of divorce and the marriage wage premium. It is found that increasing divorce probabilities lower the marriage wage premium paid to men, supporting the theory that spouses reduce investments in their marriage as the likelihood of marital dissolution increases. We also find support for the idea that a higher marriage premium lowers the chance of divorce. Although these results are interesting, they rely on the proper identification of the divorce and wage effects. We present an alternative analysis by examining the effects of changes in the divorce law, which are arguably exogenous, on the marriage wage premium. Again, we find strong evidence that higher divorce probabilities result in lower marriage wage premiums. We conclude with summary remarks. Before we turn to a discussion of the methodology we first undertake a cursory examination of the relationship between the marriage wage premium and divorce.

THE MARRIAGE WAGE PREMIUM AND DIVORCE: A CURSORY EXAMINATION

According to standard economic theory the wages an individual can command in the marketplace are a function of the individual's stock of human capital. Throughout a lifetime this stock of human capital is constantly changing, either through investments made to augment the level of human capital or through the depreciation of capital over time. One of the more popular theories of the marriage wage premium views marriage as an alternative source of human capital investment. The union of two individuals through marriage allows for greater specialization, which can increase the accumulation of human capital for the working spouse. Daniel (1995) and Grossbard-Shechtman (1986) present theoretical arguments stressing the role of wives in the formation of their husband's human capital. How much human capital will be augmented through marriage depends on the willingness of both spouses to make the necessary investments. A married woman who faces a nonzero probability of divorce necessarily faces trade-offs in her decision to invest in the augmentation of her husband's human capital. Although investing in her husband increases her household's future earnings due to specialization effects, her realization of those future earnings depends on her future marital status.

A wife with a high probability of divorce is less likely to realize returns from current investments in her husband's human capital. This suggests that a married woman's investment in her husband—and therefore the marriage wage premium—should be a decreasing function of her perceived probability of divorce.

We perform a preliminary examination of the link between the wage premium paid to married men and marital dissolution using data from the National Longitudinal Survey of Youth (NLSY). The NLSY consists of a nationally representative sample of men and women who were 14 to 21 years old on January 1, 1979. The NLSY is an ongoing longitudinal survey as respondents are reinterviewed each year. Because the patterns of family formation and dissolution differ substantially between white and black Americans, separate analyses by race are warranted. Due to limited sample size we present results for whites only. The sample is restricted to employed men who were either never married or who divorced between 1979 and 1993. Information is extracted concerning the age, marital status, and wages of these men in each survey year. Thus, these data enable us to examine the change in men's marriage premium as they approach marital dissolution (see Figure 18.1).

Five years prior to their marital separation, married men earned 12% more than never-married men of the same age. In the year immediately preceding their divorce, the marriage wage premium declined to 8%. Thus it appears that either higher divorce probabilities contribute to a decline in men's wages or a fall in wages increases the likelihood that men's marriages will dissolve.

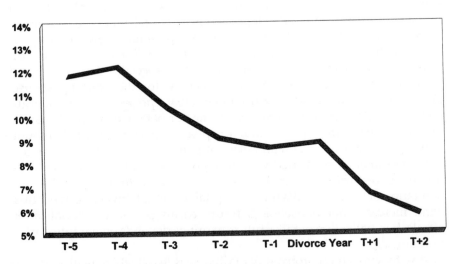

Figure 18.1.   Marriage wage premium and marital dissolution.

Although the likelihood of marital dissolution may affect a couple's specialization choices, these choices may in turn affect divorce probabilities. Becker (1981) has argued that the economic value of a marriage is an increasing function of a household's degree of specialization. To consistently estimate the effect of divorce probabilities on the marriage wage premium and the converse, a two-stage estimation procedure is undertaken. The next section describes this estimation procedure in greater detail and presents the results.

METHODOLOGY AND RESULTS

This section presents results from the estimation of a simultaneous system of divorce probabilities and the marriage wage premium. The 1990 cross section from the NLSY is used to estimate the simultaneous equations system. The sample is restricted to white men who were either currently married, spouse present, or never married in 1990. A variable for whether the man becomes divorced or separated over the next 3 years is constructed from subsequent waves of the NLSY.

Table 18.1 reports variable definitions and sample means for the sample of men who divorce, those who remain married, and for the entire sample. Of the 915 married men in the 1990 survey, 93 divorced or separated by 1993. Men in the sample who divorce have lower wages, less education, more previous labor market experience,[2] are more likely to have cohabitated before marriage, and are less likely to have grown up with two parents than men remaining married. This suggests that education, previous work experience, cohabitation before marriage, and the presence of both parents during childhood should be controlled for when estimating the impact of divorce probabilities on current wages.

Probability of Divorce and the Marriage Wage Premium

A two-stage procedure is used to estimate the simultaneous system of divorce probabilities and men's wages. In the first stage we estimate a reduced form probit equation for the probability of divorce and a reduced form wage equation. All exogenous variables in the system are used as regressors. The predicted probabilities from the reduced form probit equation provide an estimate of the likelihood that a man will divorce over the subsequent 3 years, based on all the direct and indirect measures in the model. The predicted wage has an analogous interpretation—it provides an estimate of a man's expected wage given all the factors in the model. The predicted variables from these regressions are then used as explana-

Table 18.1.   Variable Definitions and Mean Values of the Variables

Variable	Definition	All[a]	Divorce 1990–1993	Do Not Divorce[a]
Married	1 if married in 1990	.64	1	.61
Years married	Years of marriage	3.50	4.87	3.40
Divorce	1 if divorced or separated by 1993	.07	1	0
Wage	Logarithm of hourly wage	2.35	2.24	2.35
Two parents	1 if parents married in 1990	.73	.60	.74
Mother's education	Mother's years of schooling completed	11.66	11.22	11.69
Father's education	Father's years of schooling completed	11.98	10.89	12.05
Education	Years of schooling completed	13.51	12.54	13.58
Wife's education	Wife's years of schooling completed	13.19	12.08	13.32
Cohabitation	1 if cohabited before marriage	.24	.53	.22
Catholic	1 if Catholic	.33	.27	.34
Not religious	1 if not religious	.04	.09	.04
Church frequency	1 if attends church at least once a month in 1990	.43	.34	.43
Work experience	Years of work experience	9.59	9.78	9.57
South	1 if lives in South in 1990	.28	.38	.27
Urban	1 if resided in urban area in 1990	.72	.73	.71
Union	1 if member of union in 1990	.17	.14	.17
Age	Age of man in 1979	17.42	17.59	17.40
Wife's labor market hours	Wife's number of hours worked divided by 10	2.80	3.20	2.76
N		1429	93	1336

[a]Includes never married.

tory variables in the second stage (structural) estimation of how divorce probabilities affect men's wages and how men's wages affect their probability of divorce.

The theoretical model includes work experience, age, educational attainment, residence, and labor union status as variables affecting wages. Religion, church frequency, marital tenure, and whether the man lived with two parents from birth through age 18 do not affect labor market decisions, and therefore overidentify the wage equation. The man's labor union status and labor market experience, net of wages, is presumed not to affect divorce probabilities and therefore the divorce equation is also overidentified.

Table 18.2 presents results of the analysis of divorce probabilities. Column (1) reports reduced form estimates. Column (2) reports estimates

Table 18.2. Reduced Form and Structural Divorce Probit Equations[a]

Variable	(1) *Reduced Form*	(2) *Actual Wage*	(3) *Fitted Wage*
Age	.007	.003	.010
	(1.34)	(.65)	(1.70)
Years married	−.005	−.005	−.001
	(1.68)	(1.75)	(.27)
Two parents	−.052	−.052	−.032
	(2.34)	(2.32)	(1.36)
Mother's education	.003	.003	.004
	(1.05)	(1.01)	(1.26)
Father's education	−.001	−.001	−.001
	(.56)	(.56)	(.51)
Education	−.012	−.006	.008
	(2.09)	(1.14)	(.83)
Wife's education	−.011	−.012	−.008
	(2.76)	(2.91)	(1.73)
Cohabitation	.029	.031	.030
	(1.38)	(1.47)	(1.45)
Catholic	.000	.001	.036
	(.02)	(.05)	(1.22)
Not religious	.017	.026	.010
	(.40)	(.59)	(.25)
Church frequency	−.012	−.011	−.016
	(.58)	(.52)	(.80)
South	.026	.029	.018
	(1.20)	(1.34)	(.82)
Urban	.026	.025	.049
	(1.27)	(1.21)	(2.07)
Work experience	−.008		
	(1.13)		
Work experience sq	.000		
	(.13)		
Union	−.028		
	(1.21)		
Log wage		−.025	
		(1.24)	
Fitted wage			−.255
			(2.09)

[a]Absolute asymptotic *t* statistics are reported in parentheses.

from the structural model including current log wage as an explanatory variable. The estimated coefficients and standard errors are similar in these two equations. The likelihood of divorce decreases with the length of marriage. This finding is consistent with other studies of divorce (see, for example, Becker et al., 1977; Johnson and Skinner, 1986). A man is also less likely to divorce over the next 3 years if he, or his spouse, had more education, or if he lived with both parents throughout his childhood. Actual wages have a slightly negative, and insignificant effect on the probability of divorce. Coefficient estimates from the structural model that includes predicted log wages as a regressor are reported in the final column. Some of the estimates become less significant due to the simultaneous nature of divorce and labor force participation decisions. Urban residence remains positive and becomes statistically significant. The coefficient estimate of the impact of men's wages on the probability of divorce increases when using its fitted value and becomes significant at the usual confidence levels. A husband's wage is therefore found to have a negative effect on the probability he will divorce over the following 3 years.

Table 18.3 presents estimates of the test of how the probability of divorce affects the marriage wage premium. In addition to socioeconomic variables believed to affect labor market wages, the first equation includes whether the man divorces over the subsequent 3 years as an explanatory variable. The standard human capital variable estimates have their expected signs as wages are higher for men who live in urban areas, men with more education and experience, and men whose wages are covered by a collective bargaining agreement. The coefficient on the married dummy in column 1 suggests that men whose marriages remain intact earn 15% more than never married men do. On the other hand, the coefficient on the divorce dummy variable indicates that the marriage wage premium is only 6% for men who later divorce (.147 for being currently married less .089 for having a subsequent divorce). The difference between the marriage premium earned by men whose marriages remain intact and those whose marriages dissolve is significant at the 5% level using a one-sided test.

Column 2 reports results when the married men's predicted probability of divorce replaces the variable of whether they actually divorce. The coefficient on the fitted divorce variable, reported in column 2, has a different interpretation than the coefficient on the actual divorce variable in column 1. Whereas the coefficient on actual divorce implies the marriage wage premium is 9% less for men who go on to divorce, the estimate for the fitted divorce variable suggests that a 10% increase in a husband's probability of divorce lowers his marriage wage premium by 9%. A probability of divorce that exceeds 26% nullifies the wage premium of being married (approximately 4% of husbands have such an estimated divorce likeli-

Table 18.3. Impact of Divorce on the Marriage Wage Premium[a]

Variable	1	2	3	4
Married	.147	.230	.262	.309
	(5.11)	(6.01)	(6.88)	(7.50)
Education	.080	.070	.083	.073
	(13.57)	(10.69)	(14.00)	(11.10)
Work experience	.037	.030	.371	.031
	(5.00)	(3.97)	(5.07)	(4.14)
Work experience sq	−.0004	−.0003	−.0004	−.0003
	(3.57)	(3.08)	(3.53)	(3.12)
South	−.008	.006	.002	.012
	(.27)	(.19)	(.06)	(.40)
Urban	.100	.116	.104	.117
	(3.46)	(3.97)	(3.62)	(4.04)
Union	.141	.120	.140	.122
	(4.07)	(3.42)	(4.06)	(3.48)
Age	.018	.020	.015	.018
	(2.51)	(2.85)	(2.17)	(2.54)
Wife's labor market			−.041	−.032
Hours/10			(4.57)	(3.38)
Actual divorce	−.089		−.070	
	(1.67)		(1.33)	
Fitted divorce		−.881		−.767
		(3.56)		(3.17)
R^2	.18	.19	.20	.20
N	1429	1429	1429	1429

[a]Absolute t statistics are reported in parentheses.

hood). This is consistent with the hypothesis that wives in higher risk marriages invest less in their husband's human capital—whether or not the marriage actually ends in divorce.

If the marriage wage premium is due to specialization within marriage, then the wage premium should be particularly large for those men whose wives work less in the paid labor force. This is evidenced in the data, and reported in column 3, as the marriage wage differential is 4.1 percentage points lower for each additional 10 hours per week a wife works in the labor market. The marriage wage premium was nearly 26% for husbands who did not divorce and whose wives specialized in home production; the marriage wage premium was only 3% for husbands who subsequently divorce and whose wives worked 40 hours per week in the labor force. Column 4 shows that controlling for wives' labor market hours, a 10% increase in a husband's probability of divorce lowers his marriage wage premium by 8%.

DIVORCE LAWS AND THE MARRIAGE WAGE PREMIUM

The NLSY data suggest that increasing divorce probabilities lower the marriage premium paid to men. This supports the theory that spouses reduce investments in their marriage as the likelihood of divorce increases. Moreover, there is some evidence that the relationship is indeed circular. A higher marriage premium earned by men lowers the probability that they will divorce. However, the quality of the identification of divorce probabilities and wages is open to criticism.[3] Ideally we are interested in how an exogenous increase (or decrease) in divorce probabilities affects the observed marriage wage premium. Significant changes in divorce laws during the 1970s provide just such an opportunity.

Unilateral divorce laws allow either spouse to end a marriage simply by claiming that it has broken down.[4] Nearly half the states in the United States adopted a form of unilateral divorce by 1980. Friedberg (1998) shows that the adoption of unilateral divorce laws caused a 6% increase in the probability of divorce. Therefore, the adoption of these laws provides a natural experiment of how the marriage wage premium responds to an exogenous increase in the probability of divorce.

Table 18.4 presents results from the test of whether an increase in the probability of divorce influences the marriage wage premium. A sample of unmarried, married, and divorced men ages 24 to 55 is drawn from the 1970 and 1980 1/1000 Public Use Micro Sample of the United States Census of Population and Households (PUMS). No state had adopted unilateral divorce in 1970, whereas over half the states had implemented the statutes by 1980. Thus, men residing in states that did not adopt any changes to their divorce laws serve as a control group for examining the change in the marriage wage premium of men residing in states that did adopt unilateral divorce laws.

The first column in Table 18.4 examines whether the marriage premium in 1980 is different in unilateral-divorce states than in states that require mutual consent for divorce. The sample is restricted to a cross section from the 1980 PUMS. The data suggest that the wage premium is 3% lower in states that allow unilateral divorce. This difference is statistically significant at the 5% level on a one-sided test. This result is consistent with the theory that spouses invest less in their marriage in states where it is easier to dissolve a marriage.

However, it is possible that states in which men earn a low marriage wage premium tend to adopt unilateral divorce laws. If so, then an analysis that uses a single cross section could yield misleading results. Using data at two points in time enables the estimation of how unilateral divorce laws affect the *change* in the marriage wage premium. The second column presents regression estimates using data from both 1970 and 1980. State

Table 18.4. Impact of Divorce Law Changes on Marriage Wage Premium

Variable	1980 PUMS[a]	1970 and 1980 PUMS[b]
Married	.256	.259
	(20.78)[c]	(25.63)
Married × unilateral divorce	−.032	−.038
	(2.08)	(2.53)
Divorced/separated	.111	.123
	(7.86)	(10.97)
Unilateral divorce	.146	.044
	(1.01)	(3.02)
Married × year		.012
		(.90)
Year		−.033
		(2.60)
Education	.076	.073
	(66.14)	(92.79)
Potential experience	.037	.037
	(26.75)	(38.96)
Potential experience sq	−.0005	−.0006
	(16.97)	(27.20)
Urban	.146	.105
	(17.47)	(18.54)
N	28,236	52,293
R^2	.21	.23

[a]Regression using the 1980 PUMS includes three region dummies.
[b]Regression using the 1970 and 1980 PUMS includes 50 individual state dummies.
[c]Absolute *t* statistics are reported in parentheses.

dummy variables are added as regressors to control for state-specific effects contributing to men's wages. A year dummy variable is included to capture wage trends and aggregate business cycle effects. Blackburn and Korenman (1994) show that the marriage premium fell during the 1970s. The interaction term between the married and year dummy variables is included to capture the falling marriage premium over time. The unilateral divorce dummy variable measures the average change in men's wages in states that adopt unilateral divorce laws relative to the change in men's wages in other states. Therefore, the interaction between the unilateral divorce and the married dummy variables measures how the marriage wage premium changed after states adopted unilateral divorce relative to the change in the marriage wage premium in other states. These data suggest that the marriage wage premium decreased by three percentage points more in states that adopted unilateral divorce.

The PUMS data therefore provide estimates consistent with the simultaneous estimates found using the NLSY. The results suggest that an increase in the likelihood of divorce lowers the wage premium of married men.

CONCLUSION

Empirical investigations of the determinants of labor market wages reveal that married men are paid more than comparable unmarried men. Studies attempting to explain the existence of the marriage wage premium argue that the state of marriage is associated with higher levels of productivity. These higher levels of productivity are hypothesized to arise either from selection into marriage of more productive men or from productivity enhancing effects of marriage. Gray (1997) shows that the recent fall in the marriage premium is due largely to declining productivity effects of marriage. This chapter builds on that work and examines how the marriage premium responds to the increasing risk of marital dissolution.

Using data from the NLSY, we find that the marriage premium is a decreasing function of the probability of divorce. Conversely, we also find that the probability of divorce is a decreasing function of the marriage wage premium. The fact that men's wages decrease as they approach divorce supports the theory that wives decrease their investment in their husbands as the likelihood of eventual dissolution of the marriage increases.

Data from the PUMS suggest that the easing of divorce laws that permit either spouse to walk away from their marriage resulted in a relative decline in the marriage wage premium in those states. This is consistent with wives responding to the adoption of these statutes by investing less in their husbands' human capital.

Each of these data sources provides evidence of the self-reinforcing nature of the recent increase in divorce rates: as divorce rates increases, spouses are less inclined to invest in their marriages, and, as spouses invest less in their marriages, the economic value of marriages decreases and marital instability increases. This multiplier effect of factors that cause an exogenous increase in divorce rates should be considered carefully by policymakers as they legislate statutes governing the grounds for divorce.

NOTES

1. In this chapter we define marital dissolution to be either divorce or separation. These terms are used interchangeably throughout the chapter.
2. Labor market experience is constructed from respondents' answers to contemporaneous and retrospective questions concerning actual hours worked.

3. For example, one variable assumed to help identify the divorce equation, whether the man lived with two parents as a child, may also have a direct impact on his human capital development and therefore wages (see Krein and Beller, 1988).

4. Unilateral divorce laws are a subset of "no-fault" divorce laws where mutual consent or proof of fault is not required for granting a divorce. We follow the definition of unilateral divorce and mutual-consent divorce states described in Peters (1986) and Gray (1998). Mutual-consent divorce states are those jurisdictions with only fault grounds for divorce, those that explicitly require mutual consent, and states in which unilateral divorce is possible only after an extended period of separation. All states were mutual divorce states before 1970.

REFERENCES

Bartlett, Robin, and Charles Callahan. 1984. "Wage Determination and Marital Status: Another Look." *Industrial Relations* 23(1):90–96.

Becker, Gary. 1981. *A Treatise on the Family.* Cambridge, MA: Harvard University Press.

Becker, Gary, Elisabeth Landes, and Robert Michael. 1977. "An Economic Analysis of Marital Instability." *Journal of Political Economy* 85:1141–1187.

Blackburn, McKinley, and Sanders Korenman. 1994. "The Declining Marital-Status Earnings Differential." *Journal of Population Economics* 7(3):249–270.

Daniel, Kermit. 1995. "Does Marriage Make Workers More Productive?" *Mimeo*, The Wharton School of the University of Pennsylvania.

Duncan, Greg, and Bertil Holmund. 1983. "Was Adam Smith Right After All? Another Test of the Theory of Compensating Wage Differentials." *Journal of Labor Economics* 1(4):366–374.

Friedberg, Leora. 1988. "Did Unilateral Divorce Raise Divorce Rates? Evidence from Panel Data." *American Economic Review* 88:608–627.

Gray, Jeffrey S. 1997. "The Fall in Men's Return to Marriage: Declining Productivity Effects or Changing Selection?" *Journal of Human Resources* 32:481–504.

Gray, Jeffrey S. 1998. "Divorce Law Changes, Household Bargaining, and Married Women's Labor Supply." *American Economic Review* 88:628–642.

Grossbard-Shechtman, Amyra. 1986. "Marriage and Productivity: An Interdisciplinary Analysis." In *Handbook of Behavioral Economics*, Vol. 4, edited by B. Gilad and S. Kaish. Greenwich, CT: JAI Press

Hersch, Joni. 1991. "Male-Female Differences in Hourly Wages: The Role of Human Capital, Working Conditions, and Housework." *Industrial and Labor Relations Review* 44(4):746–759.

Johnson, William R., and Jonathan Skinner. 1986. "Labor Supply and Marital Separation." *American Economic Review* 76:455–469.

Korenman, Sanders, and David Neumark. 1991. "Does Marriage Really Make Men More Productive?" *Journal of Human Resources* 26:282–307.

Peters, Elizabeth H. 1986. "Marriage and Divorce: Informational Constraints and Private Contracting." *American Economic Review* 76:437–454.

19

Trends in Men's and Women's Well-Being in Marriage

LINDA J. WAITE

According to one popular view, the family is in trouble, and *marriage* is in really big trouble (Gallagher, 1996; Glenn, 1996; Popenoe, 1993). Declining marriage rates, high divorce rates, low rates of remarriage, increases in cohabitation, and increases in men and women not in any partnership all point to this conclusion. Changes in marriage have played a central role in increases in unmarried childbearing, which has reached historically unprecedented levels (Bachrach, 1998); in 1996 32.4% of all births and 44% of all first births occurred to women who were not married (Ventura et al., 1998). In 1970, unmarried people made up 28% of the adult population. In 1996, 40% of all adults were unmarried (U.S. Bureau of the Census, 1998).

Historically low rates of marriage and high rates of divorce indicate, some argue, that marriage is less beneficial than it was in the past. This argument appears in its clearest form for economic benefits: marriage has declined because women have become economically independent of it. As more women work for pay and as their earnings increase, according to this argument, the *economic* benefits of marriage fall and divorcing or remaining single becomes both a more feasible and a more attractive option (Becker, 1981; McLanahan and Casper, 1995). Declines in the earnings of young men, relative to young women, this reasoning goes, also reduce the economic attractiveness of marriage (Oppenheimer and Lew, 1995).

These arguments point to a decline in the benefits of marriage for women in particular, since they are the ones who have become more economically independent. Presumably the declines in the earnings of young men compared to young women have made marriage a *more* attractive proposition for young men, at least economically, since they would pay a lower share of the joint costs.

In 1972, when she published *The Future of Marriage*, Jessie Bernard convinced the scholarly community and the general public that marriage is good for men and bad for women. Bernard's image of "his" marriage, which brought him emotional well-being, career success, and health, and "her" marriage, which led to psychological distress and career stagnation, is widely used to describe contemporary marriage.

Is there evidence that the benefits of marriage have declined? Is there evidence that marriage is good for men and bad for women?

I address these questions by looking at changes in the well-being of men and women over the last quarter century. I compare married, never-married, and previously married men and women across a variety of indicators to address the following questions. What do men and women get from marriage? Have the benefits of marriage declined over the past 25 years? Have they declined for both sexes? And how does cohabitation compare to marriage or being single?

I present evidence on the benefits of marriage on the following dimensions: marital satisfaction, general happiness, physical health, satisfaction with family life, domestic violence, job satisfaction, and financial status. Because of data limitations, I present information on cohabitation versus marriage on only two of these dimensions—general happiness and domestic violence.

If we see declines in the benefits of marriage, then we can look to this change as a possible causal factor in the retreat from this institution. Of course, declines in the advantage shown by the married on these indicators of well-being could take place for other reasons, including a shift in the characteristics of married versus unmarried people. But if we see no declines in the benefits of marriage then this explanation for the retreat from marriage must be reconsidered. So we will look across dimensions for a substantial narrowing over time of any advantage shown by married people or even elimination of any of the advantages of marriage.

I use data from the General Social Survey (GSS), a repeated cross-sectional survey of about 1500 adults done in almost every year between 1972 and 1996 for a total sample of about 35,000 people. The GSS includes a particularly rich assortment of questions on satisfaction with life across a range of dimensions and I draw on these here. We will examine trends in each of the indicators of well-being looking particularly for gaps between married and unmarried adults when we take into account basic demographic characteristics such as age, race, income, education, and health. Since the dependent variables are all measured as scales of three to seven points, I estimate all models with ordinary least-squares regression. Each of these models is estimated separately for men and women, dividing marital status into currently married, never married, and previously married. Each model includes interactions between calendar year and marital status. I present the results from these models in Tables 19.1–19.8. I also estimate models that include measures of family structure that reflect both marital status and presence of children in the household. Note that the analytic methods used here, ordinary least-squares regression, combined with the measures of well-being, probably yield underestimates of the true relationship between marital status and well-being.

I focus primarily on the *evaluations* of individuals of their lives, which require that people filter the objective facts through the lens of their values, expectations, and perceptions. Some of the benefits of marriage can be measured only in this way; satisfaction with one's marriage is, by definition, an evaluation, for example. This is also the case for satisfation with the other dimensions of life that we examine here and with general happiness.

Several of our measures ask people to report on the objective situation directly; measures of self-rated physical health, relative financial status, and domestic violence fall into this category. I describe each measure in more detail when I present the results.

HAVE MARRIAGES BECOME HAPPIER?

Let us start by looking at marital satisfaction. Noval Glenn (1996) has pointed out that if high rates of divorce have systematically eliminated the most unsatisfactory marriages from the population, we should see an increase in satisfaction among those who remain married. However, other changes in marriage, the alternatives to it, and societal support for both may have affected marital satisfaction.

Figure 19.1 shows for 1972–1996 the percentage of men and women who say that their marriage is "very happy." The question that was asked is: "Taking all things together, how would you describe your marriage? Would you say that your marriage is very happy, pretty happy, or not too happy?" Glenn (1996) pointed out that if high rates of divorce have systematically eliminated the most unsatisfactory marriages from the population, we should see an increase in satisfaction among those who remain married.

We see, instead, a small decline in the proportion of married men and women who say that they are "very happy" with their marriage, from about 68% in 1972 to about 62% in 1996. So, decreases in marriage have not improved the quality of marriages that remain.

Table 19.1 shows results from a model of marital satisfaction for currently married men and women. Once we take age, race, education, income, health, and presence of children into account in a multivariate model, we see a small negative trend in marital happiness since 1972 for both men and women. This decrease in happiness that is reported for marriage is somewhat larger for women than for men, and small but signifi-

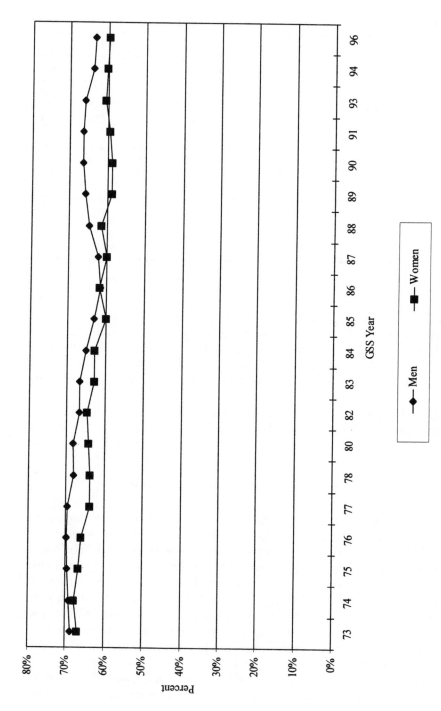

Figure 19.1. Marital satisfaction: percentage very happy men and women, 1972–1996.

Table 19.1.   Trends in Marital Satisfaction for Males and Females

| | Males | | | | Females | | | |
Variable	B	SE	Beta	Significance	B	SE	Beta	Significance
Constant	2.582	.115		.000	2.501	.116		.000
Age	.0031	.000	.091	.000	.0018	.000	.048	.000
Education	−.0002	.002	−.001	.922	.0051	.033	.025	.074
Race								
Black	−.130	.023	−.072	.000	−.212	.023	−.108	.000
Other	.0252	.042	.007	.548	−.0352	.042	−.010	.398
Health	.0856	.008	.138	.000	.108	.009	.156	.000
Ln income	.0056	.010	.008	.568	.0100	.010	.014	.297
Year	−.0039	.001	−.057	.000	−.0041	.001	−.056	.000
Children	−.0760	.019	−.051	.000	−.147	.019	−.091	.000
N		6,413				6,810		
R^2		.032				.054		

Source: General Social Survey, 1972–1996.

cant for both. So, apparently the married *are* less happy in their marriages than people like them were 25 years ago.

When we look explicitly for differences between husbands and wives in their satisfaction with their marriage (results not shown) we find that wives are significantly less satisfied than husbands, although the gap is quite small.

But how do the married compare to the unmarried? We can gauge the benefits of marriage by comparing only the well-being of married men and women to the well-being of those who are not married.

ARE MARRIED PEOPLE HAPPIER?

One simple measure of well-being comes just from asking people: "Taken altogether, how would you say things are these days—would you say that you are very happy, pretty happy, or not too happy?" The earliest studies of general happiness, done in the 1960s, showed very substantial advantages for married men and married women over the unmarried (Bradburn, 1969). Jessie Bernard (1972:51) also found that more married than unmarried women say they were happy; she attributed this to a sort of sickness on the part of married women: "to be happy in a relationship which imposes so many impediments on her, as traditional marriage does, a woman must be slightly ill mentally."

Most scholars, however, feel that marriage improves the emotional well-being of men and women by offering them social support and a confidant. Mirowsky and Ross (1989:91) argue that "A good marriage provides something very important: the sense of being cared for, loved, esteemed and valued as a person." Marriage also seems to provide individuals with a sense of meaning in their lives, a sense of purpose larger than themselves. Husbands and wives in good marriages realize that their partners' well-being depends on them. It gives them the incentive to take care of their health, so that they can meet their obligations to those who are counting on them. Meeting these obligations can provide a source of gratification (Umberson, 1987).

Marriage may provide less of these valued goods now than in the past, however. Glenn and Weaver (1988) found that the impact of marriage on reported happiness declined steadily from 1972 to at least 1986, primarily because an increasing proportion of never-married men reported being happy at the same time that a decreasing proportion of married women reported being happy. The authors speculate that married men and women act more in their individual interest and less in the interest of the marriage than they did in the past, reducing the benefits that marriage produces. Glenn (1996) argues that we have come to view marriage as a source of personal gratification; the successful marriage, then, provides happiness, satisfaction, and affirmation through the attraction and retention of a mate who meets one's emotional needs. Since unilateral divorce means that either partner can end the marriage for any reason at any time, personal gratification is a weak reed for supporting a lifetime bond. If, on average, the commitment of married men and women to *this* particular marriage has weakened, the emotional benefits of marriage may have declined and married men and women may not show the advantage in general happiness that early researchers observed.

Table 19.2 presents models of general happiness for men and women. The dependent variable is general happiness measured on a three-point scale from not too happy to very happy. This model includes measures of marital status (Previously Married and Never Married, with Currently Married the reference category), and interactions between each of the unmarried categories and year. The interactions allow us to see if any gap in general happiness that we find between married and unmarried people has been closing over time.

We see in Table 19.2 that men are about as happy in 1996 as they were earlier—the coefficient for Year is not significant—but women show small declines in their level of happiness since 1972. When we compare happiness of the married and unmarried, we see a significant disadvantage on this dimension for both the never married and previously married for both men and women. All four groups—never-married men, previously married men, never-married women, and previously-married women—say that they are less happy in general these days than married people of the

Table 19.2. Trends in General Happiness for Males and Females, Unmarried Individuals

Variable	Males				Females			
	B	SE	Beta	Significance	B	SE	Beta	Significance
Constant	.886	.104		.000	1.428	.097		.000
Age	.00542	.000	.144	.000	.00484	.000	.131	.000
Education	−.00149	.002	−.008	.442	.00524	.002	.024	.013
Race								
Black	−.106	.018	−.054	.000	−.154	.015	−.086	.000
Other	.05380	.036	.013	.139	−.04067	.034	−.010	.233
Health	.179	.007	.238	.000	.185	.007	.247	.000
Never married	−.438	.156	−.281	.005	−.373	.172	−.205	.030
Previously married	−.395	.180	−.221	.028	−.390	.131	−.279	.003
Never married × year	.00343	.002	.187	.064	.00282	.002	.133	.162
Previously married × year	.00123	.002	.059	.561	.00151	.002	.092	.330
Ln income	.04917	.008	.068	.000	.03310	.007	.051	.000
Year	.00169	.001	.021	.064	−.00313	.001	−.038	.001
N		10,914				13,214		
R^2		.118				.137		

Source: General Social Survey, 1972–1996.

same gender, once we take into account their other characteristics. The results show that both the happiness advantage of the married and the disadvantage of being unmarried are roughly similar in size for men and women. Married people report levels of happiness about .4 points higher than the unmarried.

We also see that the situation has not changed over the past 35 years. We see no significant shift in the "happiness gap" since 1972; neither of the interactions between year and marital status is significant for either men or women and both are trivially small.

One important change in family life over the past quarter century is the increasing separation of parenthood from marriage. We examine the consequences of this change for happiness by looking explicitly at married and unmarried parents and those with no children at home. These results (not reported here) show quite clearly that married people—both with and without children—report greater happiness than people who are not married, regardless of whether they have children at home. Married people with no children are *happier* than married parents, but unmarried people with or without children are similarly disadvantaged. Never-married people with no children show the smallest deficit in happiness compared to the married, but both previously married and never-married parents are substantially less happy than the married. So marriage improves happiness for parents and for those without children.

How does cohabitation fit into this picture? If marriage improves psychological well-being by providing people with a confidant, with someone who loves and esteems them, does cohabitation offer the same benefits? The evidence suggests not. Brown (1998) finds that cohabiting men and women report higher levels of depression and lower levels of life satisfaction than married men and women, primarily because they see their relationships as substantially less stable. These findings suggest that cohabitors will show lower levels of happiness than the married.

I mentioned earlier that data limitations restrict our ability to include cohabitors in most of these comparisons. In the early 1970s, *no* cohabitors appear in the GSS sample, even though the defintion of cohabitation is based on the composition of the household, and even in later years we see relatively few cohabitors compared to the number of married people. This makes it difficult to look at trends. Keeping that in mind, Figure 19.2 shows the percentage of people who say that they are very happy these days, for the married, cohabiting, never married, and previously married for men and women combined. This figure shows quite clearly that cohabitors resemble unmarried people—at least when it comes to their general satisfaction with life. But cohabitors differ in systematic ways from married people in characteristics that might affect their general happiness. So we look for a "married advantage" after taking the most important of these factors into account.

Table 19.3 shows results from a model of general happiness that distinguishes the currently unmarried into those who are cohabiting and those who are not. This table shows a sizable deficit in happiness for those who are unmarried and not cohabiting and a slightly smaller deficit in happiness for cohabitors than for those who are unmarried and not living with a partner. Although cohabitors show deficits in happiness that are just slightly smaller than the never married, the effect of cohabiting is not statistically significant for either men or women, probably because of the small number of cohabitors in the GSS. The happiness gap between cohabitors and the married did not close over the period, although the small number of cohabitors also interferes with our search for these changes.

HAS THE HEALTH ADVANTAGE OF MARRIAGE DECLINED?

Married people are healthier than unmarried people, as I have argued elsewhere and others have found (Hahn, 1993; Stack and Eshelman, 1998;

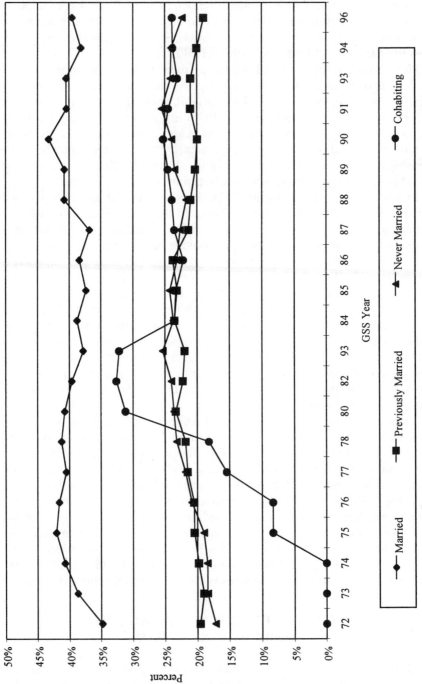

Figure 19.2.   General happiness: percentage very happy men and women.

Table 19.3. Trends in General Happiness for Males and Females, by Marital Status

Variable	Males				Females			
	B	SE	Beta	Significance	B	SE	Beta	Significance
Constant	.859	.104		.000	1.424	.097		.000
Age	.0055	.000	.147	.000	.0050	.000	.135	.000
Education	−.0015	.002	−.008	.449	.0055	.002	.025	.009
Race								
Black	−.105	.018	−.054	.000	−.156	.015	−.087	.000
Other	.0547	.036	.014	.133	−.0426	.034	−.010	.211
Health	.179	.007	.238	.000	.185	.007	.248	.000
Never married	−.362	.134	−.224	.007	−.361	.123	−.187	.003
Previously married	−.480	.137	−.259	.000	−.364	.119	−.254	.002
Cohabiting	−.337	.426	−.096	.428	−.335	.360	−.107	.351
Never married × year	.0026	.002	.140	.108	.0026	.001	.122	.074
Previously Married × year	.0021	.002	.100	.197	.0011	.001	.068	.430
Cohabiting × year	−.0003	.005	−.007	.953	.0006	.004	.016	.890
Ln income	.0494	.008	.068	.000	.0329	.007	.050	.000
Year	.0017	.001	.021	.065	−.0032	.001	−.038	.001
N		10,914				13,214		
R^2		.118				.137		

Source: General Social Survey, 1972–1996.

Waite, 1995). The mechanisms through which marriage affects health differ for men and women, but for both sexes marriage confers a health advantage. Married women have more economic resources than single women, and, as a result, better health (Hahn, 1993). Married women are more likely than unmarried women to have income in excess of their own, to own their own homes, and to have private health insurance; women with these economic advantages rate their health as substantially better than those without them. Interestingly, even when the economic advantages that often come with marriage are taken into account, married women *still* show better health than unmarried women (Hahn, 1993). For men, marriage seems to improve health habits such as diet, smoking, and drinking (Umberson, 1992). Marriage increases the likelihood of early detection of symptoms, encourages medical treatment, and aids in recovery from illness (Joung et al., 1997).

To the extent that the health benefits of marriage follow, for women, from economic advantages, as women become more economically independent, the health advantages of marriage may decline. And as more wives work outside the home, they have less time and attention to focus on their husbands and the health advantages of being married may decrease for men.

Table 19.4 shows models of self-rated health for men and women. Respondents were asked: "Would you say your own health, in general, is excellent, good, fair, or poor?" Table 19.4 shows a health deficit for never-married men but one that is marginally significant and probably shrinking slowly. Married and single women do not differ in their ratings of their health and we see no evidence of changes over the past 25 years in this picture.

This lack of an advantage in physical health for the married, particularly men, does not correspond to results from other studies using self-rate health (Hahn, 1993; Stack and Eshleman, 1998) and no obvious explanation presents itself. Clearly, this is a topic that deserves more attention.

HAVE MARRIED PEOPLE BECOME LESS SATISFIED WITH FAMILY LIFE?

When we think of family life, at least for adults, we think of parents and children, husbands and wives. As an adult, one's family life does not cen-

Table 19.4. Trends in Self-Rated Health by Gender

Variable	Males				Females			
	B	SE	Beta	Significance	B	SE	Beta	Significance
Constant	1.704	.133		.000	1.093	.126		.000
Age	−.01133	.000	−.227	.000	−.00951	.000	−.193	.000
Education	.04459	.002	.183	.000	.05423	.003	.187	.000
Race								
Black	−.07296	.023	−.028	.002	−.127	.020	−.053	.000
Other	−.03514	.047	−.007	.454	−.131	.044	−.024	.003
Never married	−.378	.201	−.183	.061	.01172	.224	.005	.958
Previously married	−.367	.232	−.155	.114	−.03632	.171	−.019	.832
Never married × year	.00423	.002	.174	.076	.00058	.003	.020	.825
Previously married × year	.00408	.003	.147	.135	.00034	.002	.016	.865
Ln income	.155	.010	.161	.000	.153	.009	.175	.000
Year	−.00285	.001	−.027	.016	.00204	.001	.019	.086
N	10,959				13,270			
R^2	.166				.177			

Source: General Social Survey, 1972–1996.

ter on relationships with parents but on relationships with the next generation and one's spouse. Single adults without children do not *have* a family life in this sense, although single parents certainly do.

Many scholars have argued that parenting alone is more difficult—more stressful, with fewer supports and fewer resources—than parenting with a spouse (Amato and Booth, 1997). More unmarried adults—both never married and previously married—are raising children than in the past. Single parents are much more likely to be poor than otherwise similar married parents. They have less time—either for paid employment or for parenting—than married parents. And they have no one to take over for them when they are tired or crabby (McLanahan and Sandefur, 1994).

Let us turn to a dimension of satisfaction with life that we would expect to show a large advantage of marriage—satisfaction with family life. Respondents were asked: "How much satisfaction do you get from your family?" Responses ranged from "none" to "a very great deal."

Table 19.5 shows that married men and women with and without children report the same high levels of satisfaction with family life, even when we take into account their other characteristics. All unmarried men and women get less satisfaction from family than the married with unmarried parents particularly disadvantaged. In fact, the small number of previously married fathers report levels of satisfaction from family life that are 1.8 points lower on a seven-point scale than married fathers. Previously married mothers and never-married mothers are also quite disadvantaged on this dimension, but less so than men in the same situation.

Table 19.5 also shows that satisfaction from family life has declined—but only modestly—since 1972 for both men and women.

IS THE MARRIAGE LICENSE REALLY A "HITTING LICENSE"?

We cannot discuss the well-being of men and women in marriage without addressing the issue of domestic violence, at least in part because there is substantial public concern with this problem. One widely cited article described "the marriage license as a hitting license" in response to the finding that the assault rate among married couples was much higher than the assault rate between strangers (Gelles and Straus, 1979). However, *domestic* violence is, by definition, restricted to couples, who may be married, cohabiting, or dating. In fact, couple violence does not appear only after the wedding, but is quite common in cohabiting and dating relationships. In a comparison of married, cohabiting, and dating couples, Stets and Straus (1989) found that in most violent couples, both partners initiate aggressive behavior. The rate of physical assault in their study was highest among

Table 19.5. Trends in Satisfaction from Family Life

	Males				Females			
Variable	B	SE	Beta	Significance	B	SE	Beta	Significance
Constant	4.094	.291		.000	4.262	.242		.000
Age of respondent	−.0014	.001	−.017	.187	−.0010	.001	−.014	.250
Education of respondent	−.0102	.005	−.025	.049	.0067	.005	.015	.211
Race								
Black	−.0458	.048	−.011	.338	−.192	.039	−.055	.000
Other	−.121	.109	−.012	.266	−.0616	.099	−.007	.532
Health	.152	.019	.092	.000	.214	.017	.146	.000
Family structure								
Married with children (omitted)								
Married no children	−.0724	.055	−.015	.185	−.0275	.050	−.006	.584
Never married with children	−1.161	.046	−.317	.000	−.632	.048	−.152	.000
Never married with no children	−.994	.127	−.088	.000	−.493	.087	−.063	.000
Previously married with children	−1.7660	.089	−.217	.000	−1.1400	.071	−.175	.000
Previously married with no children	−.1357	.052	−.295	.000	−.341	.037	−.116	.000
Ln income	.118	.020	.072	.000	.0549	.017	.042	.001
Year	.0092	.003	.040	.000	.0097	.002	.047	.000
N		6,854				8,468		
R^2		.212				.102		

Source: General Social Survey, 1972–1996.

cohabiting couples, for whom violence was also most severe. Stets (1991) argues that the social isolation of cohabiting couples provides them with few inhibitions against violence.

Brown and Booth (1996) argue that at least two types of cohabiting couples exist—those who are engaged and those who have no plans to marry. On a number of dimensions of the quality of the relationship, cohabitors as a group show worse outcomes than the married. But engaged cohabitors closely resemble the married on all dimensions of relationship quality. Apparently, cohabitors without plans to marry tend to be in relationships of poorer quality than either married people or cohabitors with plans to marry their partner. I extend this analysis to examine rates of domestic violence, comparing married respondents to engaged cohabitors and cohabitors without marriage plans.

Unfortunately, the GSS does not have information over time on domestic violence. So I turned to the National Survey of Families and Households (NSFH) (Sweet et al., 1988), which has information for the late 1980s. The NSFH1 asked questions about arguments between partners to married and cohabiting individuals. They asked: "During the past year, how many fights with your partner resulted in YOU hitting, shoving, or throwing things at him/her?" "During the past year, how many fights with your partner resulted in HIM/HER hitting, shoving, or throwing things at you?" Cohabitors report much higher levels of domestic violence than do married people, with 5% of the married and 15% of cohabitors saying that they or their spouse hit, shoved, or threw things.

But cohabitors differ from married people in many ways that may expose them to more violence; they tend to have less education and to be younger, for example. Table 19.6 shows results from a model of reports that arguments with the partner sometimes became physical, with either person hitting, shoving, or throwing things that takes into account several basic demographic variables. We compare married people, those who are cohabiting and say that they have definite plans to marry their partner, and cohabitors who say that they do not have marriage plans. Table 19.6 presents simple multivariate models of domestic violence for all married and cohabiting couples. These models show no significant gender differ-

Table 19.6. Probability of Domestic Violence in the Past Year in Married and Cohabiting Unions

Variable	Married			Cohabiting		
	Logit coefficient	*SE*	*Significance*	*Logit coefficient*	*SE*	*Significance*
Constant	1.250	.470	.008	1.214	.476	.011
Age	−.0722	.0063 4	.000	−.0635	.0060 9	.000
Education	−.0383	.0262	.144	−.0620	.0265	.019
	.635	.147	.000	.650	.148	.000
Cohabiting						
Engaged	.0617	.236	.794	.277	.229	.227
Not engaged	.885	.181	.000	1.01	.178	.000
N		6,163			6,146	
R^2		.101			.0969	

Source: National Survey of Families and Households, 1987–1988.

ence in violence—in most violent couples *both* partners hit, shove, or throw things. Note also that engaged cohabitors are no more likely to report violence than married couples, the omitted category. But cohabitors with no plans to marry are substantially and significantly more likely to report couple violence than either married or engaged couples.

I calculated predicted probabilities of reporting couple violence during the past year, using the results from the multivariate model. These are shown in Figure 19.3. Married couples face a probability of male-to-female violence of 3.6% and female-to-male violence of 3.2%. Engaged cohabitors are quite similar, with a probabilities of 4.7 and 3.4%. But cohabiting couples without definite plans to marry show a probability of male-to-female violence of 9.9% and a probability of female-to-male violence of 7.6%— each more than twice as high as the other two groups. Note that the male–female gap is greater for cohabiting than for married couples.

When we assess the benefits of marriage in reduced domestic violence, it is clear that the well-being of married *and engaged* cohabiting people is substantially higher on this dimension than less committed cohabiting couples. Some researchers suggest that commitment to the relationship and to the partner reduces couple violence and these differentials seem to support this view. We cannot say, however, whether marriage offers more or less protection against domestic violence now than in the past.

HAVE THE CAREER BENEFITS OF MARRIAGE DECLINED?

A sizable literature—almost all in economics—finds that married men earn more than unmarried men, primarily because marriage makes them more productive (Gray, 1997; Korenman and Neumark, 1991). At the same time, married women tend to work fewer hours and earn less than unmarried women, with most of the career costs of marriage for women coming from motherhood rather than marriage (Waldfogel, 1997). A recent study of research productivity by scientists found, however, that married male *and female* scientists showed higher productivity than unmarried scientists (Xie and Shauman, 1998). I assess a related measure of career rewards—job satisfaction. The question that was asked is: "On the whole, how satisfied are you with the work you do—would you say you are very satisfied, moderately satisfied, a little dissatisfied, or very dissatisfied?" Because parenthood and paid employment often exert competing demands, particularly on women, this analysis compares those with and without children at home.

Table 19.7 shows models of job satisfaction for employed men and women. These results show that job satisfaction is no different for unmar-

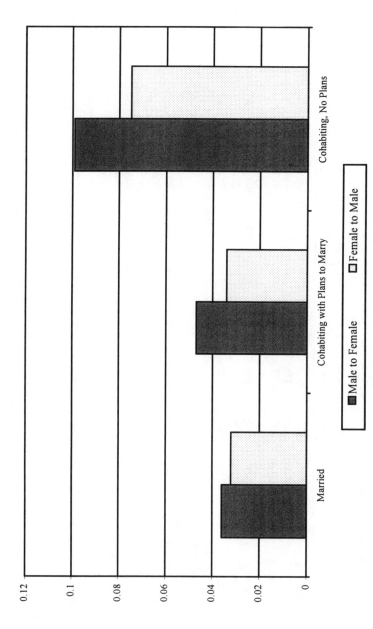

Figure 19.3. Physical aggression during arguments: NSFH 1987–1988.

Table 19.7.　Trends in Job Satisfaction by Gender

Variable	Males				Females			
	B	SE	Beta	Significance	B	SE	Beta	Significance
Constant	1.407	.200		.000	1.970	.181		.000
Age	.0110	.001	.178	.000	.0101	.001	.188	.000
Education	-.0026	.003	-.101	.451	.0058	.004	.019	.143
Race								
Black	-.107	.032	-.042	.001	-.0797	.028	-.035	.004
Other	.0106	.069	.002	.878	-.0687	.071	-.011	.331
Health	.131	.014	.121	.000	.150	.012	.152	.000
Family structure								
Married with children (omitted)								
Married no children	-.0204	.036	.000	.995	-.0580	.034	-.020	.084
Never married with no children	-.0426	.030	-.020	.155	-.091	.034	-.034	.006
Never married with children	.0393	.086	.006	.646	-.226	.063	-.043	.000
Previously married with no children	-.0166	.063	-.003	.792	-.0164	.054	-.003	.763
Previously married with children	-.0124	.037	-.004	.737	-.053	.026	-.027	.043
Ln income	.125	.014	.119	.000	.077	.013	.085	.000
Year	-.0269	.002	-.019	.123	-.0044	.002	-.030	.008
N	6418				7433			
R^2	0.07				0.071			

Source: General Social Survey, 1972–1996.

ried and married men, regardless of presence of children, and that there has been no change in men's job satisfaction over the 25 years we study.

Table 19.7 shows that married women with jobs—the sizable majority of married women in 1996—are more satisfied with their jobs than either single mothers or never-married women without children. Only previously married childless women are as satisfied with the work they do as married women are. I speculate that married mothers have more choice about when and whether and how much to work than single women, who must work to support themselves and, often, their children. So married women with unsatisfying jobs might be able to quit, but single women in the same situation cannot.

We have argued that men—but not women—get an earnings benefit from marriage. When we focus on satisfaction with work the picture changes. Men get no advantage from being married, but women do. Perhaps married men's focus on earnings comes partly at the cost of interesting and satisfying work. Married women's greater choice about whether and how much to work allows some whose paid jobs are unsatisfying to exit for work in the home. The result seems to be that married men are no more satisfied with their work than single men, but married women are more satisfied than (at least some) single women.

HAVE THE ECONOMIC BENEFITS OF MARRIAGE DECLINED?

Married couple families have substantially higher levels of income and assets than either single adults or single-parent families (Karoly, 1993). Married couple families with two earners are particularly advantaged on this dimension; in 1995, married couple families in which the wife was in the paid labor force had a median income of $55,823 compared to $32,375 among married couples in which the wife was not in the paid labor force. Family income for "female householder, no husband present" was $19,691. The comparable figure for "male household, no wife present" was $30,358 (U.S. Bureau of the Census, 1997, Table 703).

Given these very large differences in income, it would be expected that the married will report more satisfaction with their financial status than the unmarried. However, married couples share their income with each other and often with children.

As a final measure of the benefits of marriage, I examine satisfaction with financial status. Respondents were asked: "We are interested in how people are getting along financially these days. So far as you and your family are concerned, would you say that you are pretty well satisfied with your present financial situation, more or less satisfied, or not satisfied at all."

Table 19.8 presents results of models of satisfaction with financial status. Since children make large claims on financial resources of families, we compare married and unmarried people with and without children. This table shows that married men and women without children are more satisfied with their financial situation than married people with children. Interestingly, never-married men and women with children are also more satisfied than married parents. Since married parents have, on average, much higher family incomes than single parents, each group clearly compares itself with others like them, leaving all fairly satisfied in spite of the gap in resources. Table 19.8 also shows that previously married men— with or without children—are about as satisfied with their financial situation as married parents. The same is true of previously married mothers. But women who had been married and do not have children at home are *less* satisfied than married mothers.

Married couples have higher incomes than any other type of family. Even when we take into account the numbers of people sharing that income, married couples have more financial resources than single parents or childless singles. But they are not more satisfied with their financial situation.

CONCLUSIONS

What can we say from these results about trends in the well-being of men and women in marriage versus other union statuses? Married men and women generally do better than unmarried people on the dimensions we looked at and never do worse. We see little erosion of the long-term advantage of married men and women across a range of dimensions from happiness to health to satisfaction with job and family life, and financial well-being. In fact, we get an overall picture of much more stability than change. Cohabiting people fall between the single and the married on at least one dimension—happiness, and do much worse on another—domestic violence—unless they have plans to marry. This picture does not suggest a sizable decrease in the advantages of being married. So a decline in the benefits of marriage seems an unlikely candidate to account for delays in marriage and remarriage, increases in divorce, or the drop in the proportion of adults who are currently married. The substantial and stable advantages of the married over the unmarried suggest that we need to look elsewhere for an explanation of these trends.

We also see little evidence that marriage benefits men more than women, although wives characterize their marriages in slightly more neg-

Table 19.8. Trends in Satisfaction from Financial Situation

Variable	Males				Females			
	B	*SE*	*Beta*	*Significance*	*B*	*SE*	*Beta*	*Significance*
Constant	-.799	.111		.000	-.222	.098		.023
Age	0.01208	.000	.227	.000	.0132	.000	.308	.000
Education	-0.0016	.002	-.008	.473	-.0069	.002	-.027	.005
Race								
Black	-.137	.021	-.061	.000	-.095	.018	-.046	.000
Other	.0410	.042	.009	.327	.0149	.039	.003	.702
Health	.112	.008	.129	.000	.124	.008	.143	.000
Family structure								
Married with children (omitted)								
Married no children	.121	.024	.047	.000	.127	.023	.045	.000
Never married with children	.210	.020	.112	.000	.201	.021	.085	.000
Never married with no children	-.0342	.054	-.006	.524	.0372	.036	.009	.302
Previously married with children	.0458	.037	.011	.221	.0253	.032	.014	.100
Previously married with no children	-.0247	.022	-.011	.259	-.140	.016	-.082	.000
Ln income	.220	.009	.262	.000	.178	.008	.235	.000
Year	-.0032	.001	-.034	.000	-.0045	.001	-.047	.000
N	14,313				17,623			
R^2	.141				.154			

Source: General Social Survey, 1972–1996.

ative terms. Both men and women gain in happiness from marriage and by similar amounts. Neither gets substantial benefits in self-rated health (with the exception of never-married men). Wives and husbands both get more satisfaction from family life than unmarried women or men. Both see lower levels of domestic violence (although cohabiting women who are not engaged seem to face the biggest risks). Married women see an advantage in satisfaction from work, at least compared to never-married women, that men do not get. Neither men nor women benefit from marriage in *satisfaction* with their financial situation, although both do benefit from the situation itself.

But men and women *choose* to marry, to remain unmarried (at least for the time being), or to dissolve a union, and a great deal of evidence suggests that people with certain characteristics such as more education and higher incomes are more likely to marry and less likely to divorce (Goldscheider and Waite, 1986; Lillard and Waite, 1993). The selection of certain types of people into marriage and others into nonmarriage means that we have to be cautious in assigning responsibility for differences in current well-being to marriage itself. But recent research that tries to take selectivity into account has concluded that marriage *causes* at least some of the higher levels of well-being of the married (McLanahan and Sandefur, 1994; Marks and Lambert, 1998).

Marriage and family have followed increasingly divergent paths for blacks and whites in the United States over the past 40 or 50 years. In 1950 the proportion of all adults who were currently unmarried was only slightly higher for blacks than for whites. But by the mid-1990s the differences were dramatic; in 1993, 58% of all adult black men and 61% of adult black women were not married, compared with 38% of white men and 41% of white women. For blacks, much of the increase in this nonmarried occurred because of a sharp rise in the proportion that has never married. In 1993, 46% of all adult black men and 39% of all black women had never married, up from 28 and 22%, respectively, in 1950 (Waite, 1995). This rapid retreat from marriage did not happen for whites at anything like this scale. The divergence in the family-building behaviors of blacks and whites points to potential differences in well-being in marriage that we do not explore here but that deserve attention.

So why are fewer Americans married now than 30 or 40 years ago? A complex network of social changes underlies the shifts in marriage in particular and in intimate unions more generally.

Changes in divorce laws have made marriage less stable. Friedberg (1998) estimates that the shift to unilateral divorce by states between 1968 and 1972 *by itself* accounts for 17% of the increase in divorce rates that happened by 1988. Gray and Vanderhart (this volume) find that the wage premium that men get for being married falls significantly when state divorce laws shift to allow unilateral divorce. And as divorce rates rise and individuals see their marriages as more likely to end, they change their behavior as a result. Lillard and Waite (1993) show that wives who face a higher chance of divorce are less likely to have a birth in the future. Waite and Lillard (1991) find that the presence of young children reduces the likelihood that a couple will divorce. So increased chances of divorce reduce childbearing, which then increases the chances of divorce.

Increased marital instability and shifts in the legal treatment of divorcing couples lead rational people to invest less in their marriages. The rise of women's education and employment both reduced their dependence on marriage (McLanahan and Casper, 1995). Smaller family sizes mean reduced investments in marriage. The lower the investment in marriage, either *this* marriage or marriage in general, the higher the chances that a marriage will dissolve (Becker, 1981). So reduced investments in marriage, some of which result from increases in the chances of divorce, *cause* increases in the chances of divorce. Reduced investments in marriage also lead to lower returns from marriage (see Gray and Vanderhart, this volume).

At the same time, attitudes have changed in ways that are less supportive of marriage. Americans are much more accepting of divorce, even among couples with young children, than they were 30 years ago. They are more accepting of "premarital" sex, more accepting of childbearing by unmarried people, and more accepting of nonmarriage (Axinn and Thornton, this volume). These changes all reflect reduced social support for marriage as an institution and lower social costs of alternatives to marriage—singlehood, cohabitation, divorce, and unmarried childbearing.

These changes in attitudes have important consequences for the behavior of individuals. Amato and Rogers (1999) find that people who have more favorable attitudes toward divorce experience later declines in the quality of their marriage. Marital quality becomes *better* over time for those who see marriage as a lifetime commitment and divorce as an unattractive or unavailable option.

Finally, marriage may have become a less attainable goal—less affordable—for men and women with relatively low levels of education and potential earnings. Young men who have a difficult time finding stable work, becoming established in a career, and consistently earning enough to contribute to family income marry at much slower rates than others (Oppenheimer, this volume). Young women who hold a job and can help support a new family are more likely to marry (Goldscheider and Waite, 1986). As young men and women with little schooling fall economically behind both others with more education and their parents when they were the same age, government transfers that depend on marital status and household structure make marriage costly (Steuerle et al., 1998).

All these changes—attitudes, legal supports for marriage, women's and men's employment, and rational investment decisions of young people— affect choices to marry, to live with a partner, or to dissolve a relationship. These changes also, I suspect, affect the benefits and costs of each of these choices.

ACKNOWLEDGMENTS

This research was supported by a grant from the Center for Population Research, NICHD (Grant No. P50 HD-12639) to the RAND Corporation. I would like to thank Mark Nielsen and Yun-Suk Lee for research assistance and Tom Smith for advice on the General Social Survey

REFERENCES

Amato, Paul R., and Alan Booth. 1997. *A Generation at Risk: Growing Up in an Era of Family Upheaval.* Boston, MA: Harvard University Press.

Amato, Paul R., and Stacy J. Rogers. 1999. "Do Attitudes Toward Divorce Affect Marital Quality?" *Journal of Family Issues* 20:69–86.

Bachrach, Christine. 1998. "The Changing Circumstances of Marriage and Fertility in the United States." Pp. 9–32 in *Welfare, The Family, and Reproductive Behavior: Research Perspectives,* edited by R.A. Moffitt. Washington, DC: National Academy Press.

Becker, Gary S. 1981. *A Treatise on the Family.* Chicago, IL: University of Chicago Press.

Bernard, Jessie. 1972. *The Future of Marriage.* New York: Bantam.

Bradburn, Norman M. 1969. *The Structure of Psychological Well-Being.* Chicago: Aldine.

Brown, Susan L. 1998. "Cohabitation as Marriage Prelude versus Marriage Alternative: The Significance for Psychological Well-Being." Paper presented at the meetings of the American Sociological Association, August, San Francisco.

Brown, Susan L., and Alan Booth. 1996. "Cohabitation versus Marriage: A Comparison of Relationship Quality." *Journal of Marriage and the Family* 58:668–678.

Friedberg, Leora. 1998. "Did Unilateral Divorce Raise Divorce Rates? Evidence from Panel Data." *American Economic Review* 88:608–627.

Gallagher, Maggie. 1996. *The Abolition of Marriage: How We Destroy Lasting Love.* Washington, DC: Regnery.

Gelles, R. J., and M. A. Straus. 1979. "Determinants of Violence in the Family: Toward a Theoretical Integration." Pp. 549–581 in *Contemporary Theories About the Family,* edited by W.R. Burr et al., New York: Free Press.

Glenn, Norval D. 1996. "Values, Attitudes and American Marriage." Pp. 15–33 in *Promises to Keep: Decline and Renewal of Marriage in America,* edited by D. Popenoe, J. B. Elshtain, and D. Blankenhorn. Lanham, MD: Rowman and Littlefield.

Glenn, Norval D., and Charles N. Weaver. 1988. "The Changing Relationship of Marital Status to Reported Happiness." *Journal of Marriage and the Family* 50:317–324.

Goldscheider, Frances K., and Linda J. Waite. 1986. "Sex Differences in Entry into Marriage." *American Journal of Sociology* 92:91–109.

Gray, Jeffrey S. 1997. "The Fall in Men's Return to Marriage." *Journal of Human Resources* 32(3):481–503.

Hahn, Beth A. 1993. "Marital Status and Women's Health: The Effect of Economic Marital Acquisitions." *Journal of Marriage and the Family* 55:495–504.

Joung, I.M.A., K. Stronks, H. Van De Mheen, F.W.A. Van Poppel, J.B.W. van Der Meer, and J.P. Machenback. 1997. "The Contribution of Intermediate Factors to Marital Status Differences in Self-Reported Health." *Journal of Marriage and the Family* 59: 476–490.

Karoly, Lynn A. 1993. "The Trend in Inequality Among Families, Individuals, and Workers in the United States: A Twenty-five Year Perspective." Pp. 19–97 in *Uneven Tides: Rising Inequality in America*, edited by Sheldon Danziger and Peter Gottschalk. New York: Russell Sage.

Korenman, Sanders, and David Neumark. 1991. "Does Marriage Really Make Men More Productive?" *Journal of Human Resources* 26(2, Spring):282–307.

Lillard, Lee A., and Linda J. Waite. 1993. "A Joint Model of Marital Childbearing and Marital Disruption." *Demography* 30:653–682.

Marks, Nadine F., and James David Lambert. 1998. "Marital Status Continuity and Change Among Young and Midlife Adults: Longitudinal Effects on Psychological Well-Being." *Journal of Family Issues* 19:652–686.

McLanahan, Sara, and Lynne Casper. 1995. "Growing Diversity and Inequality in the American Family." Pp. 1–46 in *State of the Union: America in the 1990s. Vol. Two: Social Trends*, edited by Reynolds Farley. New York: Russell Sage.

McLanahan, Sara, and Gary Sandefur. 1994. *Growing Up with a Single Parent: What Hurts, What Helps*. Cambridge, MA: Harvard University Press.

Mirowsky, John, and Catherine E. Ross. 1989. *Social Causes of Psychological Distress*. New York: Aldine de Gruyter.

Oppenheimer, Valerie Kincade, and Vivian Lew. 1995. "American Marriage Formation in the 1980s: How Important Was Women's Economic Independence?" Pp. 105–138 in *Gender and Family Change in Industrialized Countries*, edited by Karen Oppenheim Mason and An-Magritt Jensen. Oxford: Clarendon.

Popenoe, David. 1993. "American Family Decline, 1960–1990: A Review and Appraisal." *Journal of Marriage and the Family* 55:527–542.

Stack, Steven, and J. Ross Eshleman. 1998. "Marital Status and Happiness: A 17-Nation Study." *Journal of Marriage and the Family* 60:527–536.

Steuerle, C. Eugene, Edward M. Gramlich, Hugh Heclo, and Demetra Nightingale. 1998. *The Government We Deserve*. Washington, DC: Urban Institute Press.

Stets, Jan E. 1991. "Cohabiting and Marital Aggression: The Role of Social Isolation." *Journal of Marriage and the Family* 53:669–680.

Stets, Jan E., and Murray A. Straus. 1989. "The Marriage License as a Hitting License: A Comparison of Assaults in Dating, Cohabiting, and Married Couples." Pp. 227–244 in *Physical Violence in American Families: Risk Factors and Adaptations to Violence in 8,145 Families*, edited by Murray A. Straus and Edward J. Gelles with the assistance of Christine Smith. New Brunswick, NJ: Transaction Publishers.

Sweet, James A., Larry L. Bumpass, and Vaughn Call. 1988. "The Design and Content of the National Survey of Families and Households." NSFH Working

Paper No. 1. Madison, WI: University of Wisconsin–Madison, Center for Demography and Ecology.

Umberson, Debra. 1987. "Family Status and Health Behaviors: Social Control as a Dimension of Social Integration." *Journal of Health and Social Behavior* 28:306–319.

Umberson, Debra. 1992. "Gender, Marital Status and the Social Control of Health Behavior." *Social Science and Medicine* 34(8):907–917.

U.S. Bureau of the Census. 1997. *Statistical Abstract of the United States: 1997* (117th edition). Washington, DC.

U.S. Bureau of the Census. 1998. "Marital Status and Living Arrangements: March 1998 (Update)" (P20-514). Available at http://www.census.gov/prod/99pubs/p20-514u.pdf.

Ventura, Stephanie J., Joyce A. Martin, Sally C. Curtin, and T.J. Mathews. 1998. "Report of Final Natality Statistics, 1996." *Monthly Vital Statistics Report*, Vol. 46, No. 11, Supplement. Hyattsville, MD: National Center for Health Statistics.

Waite, Linda J. 1995. "Does Marriage Matter?" *Demography* 32:483–508.

Waite, Linda J., and Lee A. Lillard. 1991. "Children and Marital Disruption." *American Journal of Sociology* 96:930–953.

Waldfogel, Jane. 1997. "The Effect of Children on Women's Wages." *American Sociological Review* 62:209–217.

Xie, Yu, and Kimberlee A. Shauman. 1998. "Sex Differences in Research Productivity: New Evidence about an Old Puzzle." *American Sociological Review* 63:847–870.

Index

Abortion, 133–134
Abuse, spousal, 379–383
Adultery, 100
African-American population (*see also* Race differentials)
  age at marriage (1870–1998) and, 65–67, 82
  divorce and, 182–183
  economic constraints on marriages in, 170–171
  economic model of marriage and, 312–316
  group differences and, 12
  occupational differentials and, 74–82
  single, 176
  values and, marital, 180–184
Age at marriage
  among blacks (1870–1998), 65–67, 82
  among whites (1850–1998), 63–65, 82
  economic position of men in marriage formation and, 298
  education and, 228
  before 1850, 61–63, 82
  race differentials and, 63–67
  religion and, 237–238
Akerlof, George A., 10, 138
Alexander, Richard D., 99
Amato, Paul R., 389
Asian population, 188, 190–201, 206–209 (*see also* Race differentials)
Assimilation perspective, classic, 208
Assortative mating, 115
Australia, 42
Autonomy values, 223–224
Axinn, William G., 13

Bales, Robert F., 129
Bargaining models, 139–141

Bargaining power
  of men, 325–330
  of women, 131–134
Bargaining theory, 6
Barich, Rachel R., 167
Baxter, Jane, 329
Bayesian procedures, 194
Beauvoir, Simone de, 321
Becker, Gary S., 114, 116, 118–119, 122, 126, 128, 283–284, 302, 326, 329, 359
Beckmann, Martin, 116
Behrman, Jere R., 122
Beneficiaries of marriage, 137–138
Bernard, Jessie, 129, 368–369, 372
Betzig, Laura L., 99–100, 102–104
Beutel, Ann M., 133
Bielby, Denise D., 167
Bird, Chloe E., 344
Birth cohort
  1945–1955, 234–243
  post-1960, 243–247
Birth control pill, 133–134
"Birth Matrix-Mating Rule" (BMMR) model, 112–113
Bittman, Michael, 329
Black-and-white differences (*see* African-American population; Race differentials; White population)
Blackburn, McKinley, 365
Blea, Irene I., 192
Blood, R.O., Jr., 328
Blumstein, Philip, 329
BMMR model, 112–113
Booth, Alan, 380
Boster, James, 98
Boswell, James, 101–102

Bridewealth, 98
Brines, Julie, 329–330, 349–351
Britain, 57 (*see also* European mar-
    riages; Western European coun-
    tries)
Brockmann, C., 183
Brown, Murray, 116
Brown, Susan L., 375, 380
Budig, Michelle J., 327
Bumpass, Larry L., 20–21, 29, 135,
    173–174, 229

Career benefits of marriage, 382–385
Career-entry processes, 292–297
Carmichael, G., 54
"Casual" relationships, 34
Catholicism, 231–233, 237–238 (*see also*
    Religion)
Census 2000, 82
Cherlin, Andrew J., 9, 13
Chicago stress study (1977), 174
Childcare, 10
Child support enforcement, 332
Childbearing, 157–158, 161, 322
Children, 320–325, 347–348
Chiswick, Carmel, 233
Chronological time, 193, 203, 207–208
Civil Rights Act, 337
Civil Solidarity Pacts (PACS), 56
Clarkberg, Marin, 132
Classical stable population theory
    (CSPT), 112
Coase, Ronald, 121
Cohabitation (*see also* Marriage)
    attitudes toward, 156–157
    decision-making approach to union
        formation and, 134–135
    definition of, 4
    dissolution of union and, 161
    divorce and, 161
    domestic violence and, 381–382
    duration of, in Europe, 51–53
    European marriages and, 42–43
    increase in, 34, 160–161
    as long-term arrangement, 134–135
    marriage versus, 4, 134–135
    in Nordic countries, 42

nubile, 42
postmarital, 42
premarital, 3
religion and, 243–246
sexual relationships other than,
    32–36
transformation in meaning of mar-
    riage and, 156–157
trends in, 19–20, 23, 28, 127
women and, 131–133
Collectivism, 206
"College Admissions and Stability of
    Marriage" (Gale and Shapley), 114
Commitment to marriage
    causes of, 256–257
    definition of, 255–256
    event-driven, 258–260, 275–277
    measurement in studying, 263–265
    method of studying, 260–265
    overview, 253–255
    predictors of, 264–265
    procedure in studying, 261–263
    processes of, 257–260
    psychological conditions of,
        259–260, 271–273
    reasons for, 257–259, 264
    relationship-driven, 258–259, 270,
        272–275
    results from studying, 265–277
    sample in studying, 261
    social conditions of, 259–260,
        271–273
    trust and, 275
    variability in, 263–264
Conflict in marriage, 101–104
Contraception, 133–134
Cox proportional hazards models, 233,
    243
Cox regression of marriage, 243
CPS (1995), 20, 24
CPS (1999), 60, 82
CPS data, 288, 291, 305–306, 316
Crawford, Charles, 94
Cross-cultural variations in marriage,
    168
Cross-national variations in marriage,
    13

CSPT, 112
Cuban-American population, 193,
    204–206 (*see also* Race differentials)
Cultural change, 131
Current Population Survey (CPS)
    (1995), 20, 24
Current Population Survey (CPS)
    (1999), 60, 82
Current Population Survey (CPS) data,
    288, 291, 305–306, 316

Daly, Martin, 13, 94, 100
Daniel, Kermit, 357
Darity, William A., Jr., 182
Darwin, Charles, 92–93
"De Gustibus Non Est Disputandum"
    (Stigler and Becker), 118
Decision-making approach to union
    formation
  beneficiaries of marriage and,
    137–138
  cohabitation and, 134–135
  from specialization to symmetry,
    127–128, 139
  gains to trade model and, 127–134,
    139–140
  marriage and, 134–135
  new paradigm for, 138–141
  overview, 126–127
  reasons for marriage and, 136–137
Delayed marriage, 161–162
Demographic indicators, 173
Denmark, 40, 42, 56 (*see also* European
    marriages; Nordic countries)
Dickemann, Mildred, 98
Differentials, 302–303 (*see also* Gender
    differentials; Race differentials)
  occupational, 72–82
  socioeconomic, 28–32
Dissolution of marriage (*see* Divorce)
Distribution of first marriage, 67–71
Distribution of housework between
    husbands and wives (*see* Division
    of labor, intrafamily)
Division of labor, intrafamily
  consequences of unequal, 344–345
  construction of gender and, 350–352

economic model of marriage and,
    304
  explanations for, 345–352
  gender differentials and, 185–159
  gender inequality in marriage and,
    158–159, 344–345
  measuring, 345
  overview, 343–344
  religion and, 230–231
  resources and, 348–350
  satisfaction and, marital, 344
  sex role attitudes and, 348
  time constraints and, 346–348
Divorce
  African-American population and,
    182–183
  attitudes toward, 150–151, 153–154
  cohabitation and, 161
  costs of, 231
  duration of marriage before dissolu-
    tion and, 103
  increase in rates of, 11, 160
  laws, 364–366, 388–389
  religion and, 231
  single people and, 182
  transformation in meaning of mar-
    riage and, 153–154
  wage determination and, 357–359
  wage premium and, 359–363
Dixon, Ruth, 168
Domestic violence, 379–383
Duncan, Beverly, 328
Duncan, Greg, 356
Duncan, O.D., 328

Eastern European countries, 42, 45–46,
    49–52, 54–55 (*see also* European
    marriages)
Economic benefits of marriage, 189,
    385–387
Economic model of marriage
  African-American population and,
    312–316
  conclusions from studying, 316–318
  description of, 303–306
  division of labor and, 304
  overview, 302–303

Economic model of marriage (*continued*)
    predictions of, 305
    race differentials and, 306–316
    specialization and, 305
    white population and, 306–312
Economic opportunities
    African-American marriages and,
        170–171
    economic need and, 189
    for men, 7–8
    Mexican-American marriages and,
        170
    for women, 8–9
Economic position of men in marriage
        formation
    age at marriage and, 298
    Becker and, 283–284
    career-entry process and, 292–297
    changes in, 288–292
    conclusions from studying, 297–299
    difficulties and, impact of, 292–297
    importance of, 284–288
    specialization model and, 283–284
Economic theory, 327
Education
    age at marriage and, 228
    marriage and, 12, 28, 307
    religion and, 228–229
Effective polygyny, 95–97
Efficiency, 111–112, 120–123
Empirical problem, 169–170
England, Paula, 6, 9, 133, 136, 327
Equilibrium, 111, 121
Erickson, Rebecca J., 344
Ethnicity (*see also* Race differentials)
    as independent variable, 194–195
    normative beliefs and, 192–193,
        196–203
Eurobarometer Surveys, 43
European marriages
    cohabitation and, 42–43
    duration of cohabitating unions and,
        51–53
    Fertility and Family Surveys and, 43,
        45–47, 55
    first unions and, 50–51
    in past, recent, 40

policy responses and, 56–57
    single people and, 46–50
    status distributions of, 43–45
    subgroup differences in, 53–56
    trends in, 40–42, 57
Event-driven commitment, 258–260,
    275–277
Evolutionary history, 5
Evolutionary psychology
    conflict in marriage and, 101–104
    described, 91–93
    gender differentials and, 93–97
    implications of, 104–106
    marriage and
    men and, 93–97
    negotiated exchange and, marriage
        as, 97–99
    reproductive union and, marriage
        as, 99–101
    women and, 93–97
Externalities, 121–122

Familism, 195–196
Family (*see also* Division of labor,
        intrafamily)
    attitudes, 9–11
    childcare and, 10
    equilibrium and, 121
    expectations, formation of, 172–173
    externalities and, 121–122
    gender differentials and, 9
    marriage and satisfaction with,
        378–379
    norms, 9–11
    perceptions, formation of, 172–173
    social organization of, 148–150
    symmetrical, 128
    transformation of, 19
    values, 9–11, 123, 172–173, 221–223
Farkas, George, 136, 327
Feedback loops within marriage sys-
        tem, 159–162
Fertility, 130–131, 229–230, 322
Fertility and Family Surveys (FFS), 40,
        43, 45–47, 55
FFS, 40, 43, 45–47, 55
First unions

European marriages and, 50–51
race differentials and, 24
in Sweden, 3
trends in, 19–23, 26
Fisher, Helen, 103
Fitch, Catherine, 13
Folbre, Nancy, 324–325
France, 56 (*see also* European marriages; Western European countries)
Franklin, Ben, 62–63
Fremont, Allen M., 344
Friedberg, Leora, 364, 388
Furstenberg, Frank F., Jr., 134
Future of Marriage, The (Bernard), 368

Gains to trade model
bargaining models and, 139–140
beyond, 129–134
decision-making approach to union formation and, 127–129, 139–140
Gale, David, 114
Gallagher, Maggie, 11, 321, 335–336
Game theory, 326–327
Game-theoretic literature, 140
Gaulin, Steven J.C., 98
Gender, construction of, 350–352
Gender differentials (*see also* Men; Women)
division of labor, 158–159
evolutionary psychology and, 93–97
expectations about marriage, 7, 11
family and, 9
happiness gap and, 373–374
job satisfaction, 382, 384–385
marital status and, 202
values and, marital, 174–177
Gender display model, 351–352
Gender inequality in marriage
child support enforcement and, 332
children and, costs of, 320–325
consequences of, 104
division of labor, 158–159, 344–345
economic theory and, 327
game theory and, 326–327
interaction effect and, 332–337
men's advantages, 9, 330–332
overview, 320–325
policies reducing, 337–339
women's disadvantages, 9, 325–331
General Social Survey (GSS), 150–151, 154–155, 159, 369, 375, 381
Generational time, 193, 203, 207
Germany, 57 (*see also* European marriages; Western European countries)
Glenn, Norval D., 370, 373
Gorman, Bridget K., 14
Governments, 13
Gray, Christine R., 14
Gray, Jeffrey S., 14, 366, 388–389
Greece, 45
Green Paper on the Family (1998), 57
Greenstein, Theodore, 351–352
Grossbard-Shechtman, Amyra, 357
Group differences, 11–13
GSS, 150–151, 154–155, 159, 369, 375, 381

Haig, David, 94
Haines, Michael R., 59
Hajnal, John, 61–63, 72
Happiness, 370–375
Happiness gap, 373–374
Hatchett, Shirley, 183
Health, 375–378
Heckman, ?, 121
Hedges, Larry V., 121
Heer, David, 328
Hispanic populations (*see* Race differentials; *specific types*)
Historical trends in marriage
age of marriage, 61–67, 82
data used in study, 59–61
distribution of first marriage, 67–71
method of study, 59–61
occupational differentials and, 72–82
single people and, 72
Hochschild, Arlie, 330
Holmund, Bertil, 356
"Home economics," 127
Homosexuality, 56, 113
Horney, Mary J., 116
Household production model, 117–118

Housework labor (*see* Division of labor, intrafamily)
Huber-White covariance matrices, 177
Hughes, Debra K., 257–259, 265

Ideational organizations of attitudes, 213 (*see also* Values, marital)
Immigration (*see* Race differentials; *specific populations*)
Index of Filial Obligations, 196, 202
Index of Parental Obligations, 195, 202
Inglehart, R., 213
Integrated Public Use Microdata Series (IPUMS), 60, 72
Interaction effect, 332–337
Intergenerational Panel Study of Parents and Children (IPS), 150–153, 156, 159
IPS, 150–153, 156, 159
IPUMS, 60, 72
Irons, William, 94

Job satisfaction, 382, 384–385
Johnson, Joyce S., 174
Johnson, Samuel, 101–102
Judaism, 231, 237 (*see also* Religion)

Kahneman, Daniel, 121
Kenrick, Douglas T., 102
Kibria, Nazli, 192
Kiernan, Kathleen, 13
Kilbourne, Barbara Stanek, 133, 327
Kohn, M.L., 214–215, 223
Koopman, Tjalling C., 116
Koopman-Beckmann assignment model, 116
Korenman, Sanders, 365
Ku, L., 155, 158

Latino population, 188–201, 204, 206–209 (*see also* Race differentials)
Latino-white gap, 207
LATS, 49
Lehrer, Evelyn L., 14, 233
Lessinger, Johanna, 192
Lesthaeghe, Ron, 119
Life cycle poverty, 286

Lillard, Lee A., 389
Liska, Allen E., 169
Living apart together (LATS), 49
Living arrangements
    conclusions from studying, 224
    data in studying, 215–220
    method of studying, 215–220
    results of studying, 220–224
    theoretical considerations and, 212–215
    values and, marital, 212, 220–224
Lu, Hsien-Hen, 135
Lundberg, Shelly, 116–117, 122, 330, 351

McElroy, Marjorie B., 116
McLanahan, Sara, 122–123
Manser, Marilyn, 116
Marini, Margaret Mooney, 133
Market, marriage, 6
Marriage (*see also* Age at marriage; Economic model of marriage; European marriages; Gender inequality in marriage; Historical trends in marriage; Theorizing marriage; Transformation in meaning of marriage; Values, marital)
    attitudes toward, 147–148, 150–151
    beneficiaries of, 137–138
    bridewealth and, 98
    career benefits of, 382–385
    career-entry processes and, 292–297
    changes in, reasons for, 7–11
    childbearing and, 157–158, 161, 322
    cohabitation versus, 4, 134–135
    conflict in, 101–104
    contexts, social and cultural, 6–7
    Cox regression of, 243
    cross-cultural variations in, 168
    cross-national differences and, 13
    decision-making approach to union formation and, 134–135
    definition of, 4
    delayed, 161–162
    distribution of first, 67–71
    division of labor and, 158–159

domestic violence and, 379–383
economic benefits of, 189, 385–387
education and, 12, 28, 307
expectations in, gendered, 7, 11
family satisfaction and, 378–379
feedback loops within system of,
    159–162
future of, 9
governments and, 13
group differences and, 11–13
happiness and, 370–375
health and, 375–378
interaction effect and, 332–337
job satisfaction and, 382, 384–385
men's advantages in, 9, 330–332
as negotiated exchange, 97–99
paradigm for, new, 138–141
purpose of, 4–7
race differentials and behavior
    toward, 12, 23–28, 388
rational choice and, 6
reasons for, 136–137
religion and behavior toward,
    12–13
as reproductive union, 99–101
same-sex, 113
sexual relationships other than,
    32–36
single people versus, 151–153
social organization of, 148–150
social status and, 137
socioeconomic differentials and,
    28–32
trends in, 3–4, 19–23, 28, 36, 147
trust and, 136–137
universalities in, 4–5
value differentiation and, 167–168
variation in, 5–6
women's disadvantages in, 9,
    325–331
women's predicament and, 133–134
Marriage premium, 14
Marriage-market models, 6, 111–113,
    116, 121, 123
Matching models, 6, 113–115, 123
Mate value, 100, 102
Material aspirations, 131

Mating rules, 111
Meaning of marriage (*see* Transforma-
    tion in meaning of marriage)
Men (*see also* Economic position of
    men in marriage formation; Gen-
    der differentials); Well-being in
    marriage, men's and women's
    advantages of, in marriage, 9,
        330–332
    bargaining power of, 325–330
    division of labor and, 158–159,
        230–231
    earnings declines and, 129–130
    economic opportunities for, 7–8
    economic responsibility and, 135
    evolutionary psychology and,
        93–97
    sexual proprietariness and, 102
    wages of, 305
Merton, Robert K., 135
Mexican-American population, 170,
    180–181, 204–205 (*see also* Race dif-
    ferentials)
Michael, Robert T., 232, 237–238
Middendorp, C. P., 216, 218
Mirowsky, John, 373
Moffitt, Robert A., 12, 14
Monitoring the Future (MTF) surveys
    (1977–1991), 133, 150–153, 157, 159
Monogamy, 98–99, 103
Moors, Guy, 10, 14
Mormonism, 231, 237, 240–241,
    244–245 (*see also* Religion)
Mortensen, Dale T., 114
MTF surveys (1977–1991), 133,
    150–153, 157, 159
"Murphy Brown" (TV show), 123
Murphy, Kevin M., 122
Myers, Samuel, Jr., 182

Nash, Amy, 192
National Center for Health Statistics,
    60
National Health and Social Life Sur-
    vey, 32, 336
National Longitudinal Survey of the
    High School Class of 1972, 132

National Longitudinal Survey, Youth
Cohorts (NLSY), 288–292, 296–297,
358, 365–366
National Opinion Research Center of
the University of Chicago, 150–151
National Survey of Black Americans,
174
National Survey of Families and
Households (NSFH) (1987–1988),
34, 129, 151, 153, 155–156, 159,
193–194, 204, 207, 227–228,
233–234, 247–248, 381
National Survey of Families and
Households (NSFH) (1988–1989),
20, 28–32
National Survey of Family Growth
(NSFG) (1995), 20–21
National Survey of Young Men (1988
and 1995), 154–155, 158
National Surveys of Adolescent Males,
154–155, 158
Nativity (*see also* Race differentials)
as independent variable, 194–195
normative beliefs and, 192–193,
196–203
Natural selection concept, 92
Negotiated exchange, marriage as,
97–98
Neoclassical economic approach,
348–350
Netherlands, 56 (*see also* European
marriages; Nordic countries)
Never-partnered (*see* Single people)
"New home economics", 127 (*see also*
Decision-making approach to
studying union formation)
New Zealand, 42
NLSY, 288–292, 296–297, 358, 365–366
Noncoresidential sexual relationships,
32–36
Nordic countries, 42, 43, 45–47, 56–57,
135 (*see also* European marriages)
Normative beliefs about marriage,
189–190, 192–193
ethnicity and, 192–193, 196–203
exposure to American society and,
193, 203–204

nativity and, 192–193, 196–203
panethnic designations and,
204–206, 208
underpinnings of, economical and
ideological, 189–190
Norms, 9–11, 213
Northern European countries, 40–41,
47, 55 (*see also* European marriages)
Norway, 51 (*see also* European marriages; Nordic countries)
NSFG (1995), 20–21
NSFH (1987–1988), 34, 129, 151, 153,
155–156, 159, 193–194, 204, 207,
227–228, 233–234, 247–248, 381
NSFH (1988–1989), 20, 28–32
Nuptiality (*see* Marriage)

Occupational differentials, 72–82
One-to-one matching, 114–115
Oppenheimer, Valerie Kincade, 14, 28,
130–131, 171, 183, 214
Opportunities, changes in, 117–120
Oropesa, R. S., 13–14, 180, 193, 196

PACS, 56
Pagnini, D.L., 158
Paige, Jeffrey M., 99
Paige, Karen E., 99
Paley, William, 92
Panethnic designations, 189, 204–206,
208
Paradigm for marriage, new, 138–141
Parental investment, 95
Parsons, Talcott, 126, 129
Pearlin, Leonard I., 174
Philipson, Tomas, 121
Policy
European marriages and, 56–57
gender inequality in marriage and,
reducing, 337–339
Pollak, Robert A., 112, 115–117, 119,
122, 136, 330, 351
Polygamy, 114
Polygyny, 95–97, 106, 114
Population and Households (PUMS),
364–366

Preferences, changes in, 117–120
Premarital sex, 154–156, 160, 229
Preston, Samuel H., 119
Protestantism, 231, 237 (*see also* Religion)
Puerto-Rican population, 193, 204–205 (*see also* Race differentials)
PUMS, 364–366

Quayle, Dan, 123

Race differentials (*see also* Normative beliefs; *specific populations*)
  age at marriage and, 63–67
  attitudes and, 195–196
  conclusions from studying, 206–209
  data in studying, 193–194
  demographic characteristics in studying, 195
  dependent variables in studying, 194
  economic characteristics in studying, 195
  economic model of marriage and, 306–316
  ethnicity terminology and, 196
  first unions and, 24
  group differences and, 12
  ideologies and, 195–196
  independent variables in studying, 194–195
  marriage behavior and, 12, 23–28, 388
  method of studying, 193–194
  occupational differentials and, 75–82
  overview, 188–189
  research issues, 192–196
  results of studying, 196–206
  theoretical background, 189–192
  values and, marital, 170–171, 175–177, 180–184
Raley, R. Kelly, 13, 183
Rasmussen, Dennis R., 105
Rational actor models, 111, 117–120
Rational choice, 6, 10, 212
Reasoned action theory, 169
Reduced-form demographic models, 112–113

Relationship-driven commitment, 258–259, 270, 272–275
Relative resource approach, 348–350
Religion
  age at marriage and, 237–238
  analytical framework, 228–232
  birth cohorts and, 234–247
  cohabitation and, 243–246
  conclusions from studying, 247–248
  control variables in studying, 241–242, 246–47
  data in studying, 232–234
  division of labor and, 230–231
  divorce and, 231
  education and, 228–229
  fertility and, 229–230
  future research and, 248
  group differences and, 12–13
  marriage behavior and, 12–13
  method of studying, 232–234
  overview, 227–228
  results of studying, 234–247
  sex and, premarital, 229
  socioeconomic status and, 241
  zero-order effects and, 242–243, 247
Reproductive union, marriage as, 99–101
Reservation wage, 115–116
Resources, personal, 173–174, 348–350
Rindfuss, R.R., 158
Rodgers, Willard L., 59
Rogers, Stacy J., 389
Rokeach, M., 214
Ross, Catherine E., 330, 373
Roth, Alvin E., 114
Ruggles, Steven, 13, 63, 168
Ryder, Norman, 213–214

Same-sex marriage, 113 (*see also* Homosexuality)
Sandefur, Gary, 122–123
Sander, William, 243
Scandinavia (*see* Nordic countries)
Schwartz, Pepper, 329
Search models, 6, 113, 115–117, 123
Seigal, Jacob S., 60
Self-blame, 260, 276

Serial mating, 103
SES, 137, 241
Sex, premarital, 154–156, 160, 229
Sex role attitudes, 348
Sexual proprietariness, male, 102
Sexual relationships other than marriage, 32–36
Shapley, Lloyd, 114
Shelton, Beth Anne, 6, 329
Shyrock, Henry S., 60
Single people
    African-American, 176
    attitudes toward, 150–151
    divorce and, 182
    in Europe, 46–50
    happiness and, 373–375
    historical trends in marriage and, 72
    marriage versus, 151–153
    transformation in meaning of marriage and, 151–153
Social metabolism concept, 213–214
Social organization of family and marriage, 148–150
Socioeconomic differentials, 28–32
Socioeconomic status (SES), 137, 241
Sotomayor, Marilda A. Oliverira, 114
South, Scott J., 188, 193, 196
Southern California study, 180
Southern European countries, 41, 43, 45–47, 51, 55 (see also European marriages)
Specialization, 127–128, 139, 304–305
Specialization model, 283–284
Spitze, Glenna D., 233
Spousal abuse, 379–383
Stable matching, 114–115
Status distribution of European marriages, 43–45
"Steady" relationships, 34
Stets, Jan E., 379–380
Stevens-Cho index, 234
Stigler, George J., 118–119
Straus, Murray A., 379–380
Subgroup differences in European marriages, 53–56
Surkyn, Johan, 119
Surra, Catherine A., 14, 257–259, 265

Survey Research Center of the University of Michigan's Institute for Social Research, 150, 171
Survival of the fittest concept, 93
Sweden, 3, 40, 42, 51 (see also European marriages; Nordic countries)
Sweet, James, 20–21, 173–174, 229
Symmetry, 127–128, 139
Symons, Donald, 95

Taylor, Pamela L., 183
"Technology shock," 133
Theorizing marriage
    efficiency and, 111–112, 120–123
    marriage-market models, 111–113, 116, 121, 123
    matching models, 113–115, 123
    opportunities and, 117–120
    preferences and, 117–120
    rational actor models, 111, 117–120
    reduced form demographic models, 112–113
    search models, 113, 115–117, 123
Thomas, Duncan, 122
Thornton, Arland, 13, 59, 167, 233, 248
Time constraints, 346–348
Title VII of the Civil Rights Act, 337
Transferable utility concept, 116
Transformation in meaning of marriage
    attitudes toward marriage and, 147–148, 150–151
    changes in, 159–162
    childbearing and, 157–158, 161
    cohabitation and, 156–157
    division of labor and, 158–159
    divorce and, 153–154
    feedback loops within marriage and, 159–162
    overview, 147–148
    sex and, premarital, 154–156, 160
    single people and, 151–153
    social organization of family and, 148–150
Treatise on the Family (Becker), 114
Trent, Katherine, 188, 193, 196
Trust, 136–137, 275

Tucker, M. Belinda, 12–13
Tuma, Nancy, 232, 237–238
Two-sex demographic models, 111–113

Uncertainty about relationship, 276
Union formation (*see* Decision-making
    approach to union formation;
    Marriage)
Utility functions, 303

Value differentiation, 167–168
Values, family, 9–11, 123, 172–173,
    221–223
Values, marital (*see also* Living arrange-
    ments)
  African-American population and,
    180–184
  autonomy and, 223–224
  conclusions from studying, 180–184
  contextual measures and, 174, 182
  cross-cultural variations and, 168
  demographic indicators and, 173
  economic constraints on African-
    American marriage and, 170–171
  empirical problem and, 169–170
  family formation expectations, val-
    ues, and perceptions and,
    172–173
  gap between behavior and, 167–170
  gender differentials and, 174–177
  Inglehart's theory of, 213
  Kohn's theory on, 214, 223
  marital expectancy and, predicting,
    177–180
  measures of studying, 172–174
  method of studying, 171–174
  Oppenheimer and, 214
  overview, 166–167
  procedures in studying, 171–172
  race differentials and, 170–171,
    175–177, 180–184
  reasoned action theory and, 169
  resources and, personal, 173–174
  results of studying, 174–180
  Rokeach's research on, 214
  Ryder and, 213–214
  sample in studying, 171–172

theoretical considerations and,
    212–215
  traditiona, 221–223
  value differentiation and, 167–168
Values, norms versus, 213
Vanderhart, Michael J., 14, 388–389

Wachter, Michael L., 351
Wage determination
  divorce and, 357–359
  divorce laws and, 364–366
  method of studying, 359
  overview, 356–357
  results from studying, 359–363
  wage premium and, 364–366
Wage premium, 359–366, 388–389
Waite, Linda J., 11, 14, 120–121, 123,
    233, 321, 335–336, 389
Walby, Sylvia, 323–324
Wallace, Alfred Russel, 92
Watkins, Susan Cotts, 119
Weaver, Charles N., 373
Weiss, Yoram, 114, 117
Well-being in marriage, men's and
    women's
  career benefits and, 382–385
  conclusions about studying, 386–390
  domestic violence and, 379–382
  economic benefits and, 385–386
  family life satisfaction and, 378–379
  happiness and, 370–375
  health and, 375–378
  overview, 368–370
Western European countries, 40–43, 45,
    47, 49–52, 54–57, 135 (*see also* Euro-
    pean marriages)
White population
  age at marriage (1850–1998) and,
    63–65, 82
  economic model of marriage and,
    306–312
  occupational differences and, 73,
    75–82
Whitehead, Barbara Dafoe, 123
Who Pays for the Kids (Folbre), 324
Williams, Norma, 192
Willmott, Peter, 128, 131

Wilson, Margo, 13, 94
Wilson, William Julius, 28, 170, 182
Wolfe, D. M., 328
Women (*see also* Gender differentials;
    Gender inequality in marriage;
    Well-being in marriage, men's and
    women's)
  abortion and, 133–134
  bargaining power of, 131–134
  cohabitation and, 131–133
  contraception and, 133–134
  disadvantages of, in marriage, 9,
    325–331

division of labor and, 158–159,
  230–231
economic opportunities for, 8–9
evolutionary psychology and, 93–97
marriage and situation of, 133–134
occupational differences and, 79, 82
wages of, 305
in workplace, 106
World War II, 41, 67, 75

Young, Michael, 128, 131

Zero-order effects, 242–243, 247